This book offers a detailed examination of warfare in the Latin East from the end of the Third Crusade to the demise of the Latin Kingdom in 1291. It considers not only the crusades, but also the long periods of truce during which warfare was restricted to raiding expeditions, and the many conflicts which took place among the Christians themselves.

A study of the organisation of the Latin armies is followed by an examination of the structures and functions of the strongpoints. There follows a consideration of the different types of armed conflict: battles, raids and sieges. Marshall depicts raiding expeditions as a vital factor in the Muslims' efforts to remove Latins from the East, and emphasises that in every aspect of military activity, the Latins' shortage of manpower is shown to have had major consequences. The book ends with a brief study of the work of scouts, spies and traitors in the Muslim and Latin armies.

Dr Marshall's book provides a fitting companion to *Crusading Warfare 1097–1193* by R. C. Smail. Like its distinguished predecessor, this new work will appeal to a wide range of medievalists and to all those interested in the conflict engendered by the crusades and in medieval warfare generally.

D1346742

*Cambridge studies in medieval life and thought*
*Fourth series*

General Editor:

D. E. LUSCOMBE

*Professor of Medieval History, University of Sheffield*

Advisory Editors:

R. B. DOBSON

*Professor of Medieval History, University of Cambridge, and Fellow of Christ's College*

ROSAMOND MCKITTERICK

*Reader in Early Medieval European History, University of Cambridge, and Fellow of Newnham College*

The series Cambridge Studies in Medieval Life and Thought was inaugurated by G. G. Coulton in 1921. Professor D. E. Luscombe now acts as General Editor of the Fourth series, with Professor R. B. Dobson and Dr Rosamond McKitterick as Advisory Editors. The series brings together outstanding work by medieval scholars over a wide range of human endeavour extending from political economy to the history of ideas.

For a list of titles in the series, see end of book.

# WARFARE IN THE
# LATIN EAST, 1192–1291

CHRISTOPHER MARSHALL

CAMBRIDGE
UNIVERSITY PRESS

CAMBRIDGE UNIVERSITY PRESS
Cambridge, New York, Melbourne, Madrid, Cape Town, Singapore, São Paulo

Cambridge University Press
The Edinburgh Building, Cambridge CB2 2RU, UK

Published in the United States of America by Cambridge University Press, New York

www.cambridge.org
Information on this title: www.cambridge.org/9780521394284

First published 1992
First paperback edition 1994
Reprinted 1996

*A catalogue record for this publication is available from the British Library*

*Library of Congress Cataloguing in Publication Data*
Marshall, Christopher.
Warfare in the Latin East, 1192–1291 / Christopher Marshall.
p.     cm. – (Cambridge studies in medieval life and thought:
4th ser.)
Includes bibliographical references.
ISBN 0-521-39428-7
1. Jerusalem – History – Latin Kingdom, 1192–1291. 2. Jerusalem – History, Military.
3. Crusades. I. Title. II. Series.
D183.M37   1991
956.94'4203–dc20   90–24162 CIP

ISBN-13 978-0-521-39428-4 hardback
ISBN-10 0-521-39428-7 hardback

ISBN-13 978-0-521-47742-0 paperback
ISBN-10 0-521-47742-5 paperback

Transferred to digital printing 2005

FOR MY PARENTS

# CONTENTS

# ILLUSTRATIONS

# ACKNOWLEDGEMENTS

It is a great pleasure to be able to thank those whose advice, guidance and friendship have helped me to complete this project. They include Dr P. W. Edbury and Dr J. Gillingham (the examiners of the University of London Ph.D thesis which was the basis of this study), Dr Steve Tibble, Mr Bill and Mrs Sally Hearn, Miss Sandra Pragnell, Mrs Joan Smail, the late Professor J. Prawer, Professor J. H. Pryor, Dr Denys Pringle, Professor R. B. C. Huygens, Dr Sylvia Schein, the Reverend and Mrs Michael West, Mr N. K. Alston and Mr A. N. C. MacDonald. There are, of course, many others; I am sorry not to have mentioned them.

Much of my research was carried out in the British Library, the Institute of Historical Research (University of London), the University of London Library and the London Library. The staff of these, and other institutions, were always helpful with queries or requests and I am grateful to them all. I must also mention the academic and administrative staff at Royal Holloway and Bedford New College (University of London), where I undertook both my undergraduate and postgraduate work. I was made very welcome at the British School of Archaeology in Jerusalem in the summer of 1984 and was particularly fortunate that my stay coincided with Dr Pringle's period as assistant director.

Mr Edwin Tatum helped with the preparation of the maps and plans. The sections in the book which deal with the French regiment and with the use of the charge in battles in the Latin East appeared, in a different form, in the *Journal of Medieval History* and *Historical Research*.

My greatest debts are, first, to the late Dr R. C. ('Otto') Smail. His book, *Crusading Warfare (1097–1193)* was the inspiration for much of my research; and I was fortunate to be able to discuss some of his ideas with him during the last years of his life. My wife, Louise, had to put up with a great deal during the final stages of my work. My mother and father typed the original thesis, and helped to proof-read both the thesis and the book more times than I care to remember. Their support has been unstinting and I dedicate the book to them, with my gratitude and love. Finally, I come to Professor Jonathan Riley-Smith. He introduced me to the crusades in 1978 and supervised both my MA and Ph.D. Without him, I would probably never have even thought about warfare in the Latin East, let alone written a book on the subject.

# ABBREVIATIONS

| | |
|---|---|
| *MGH* | *Monumenta Germaniae historica inde ab anno Christi quingentesimo usque ad annum millesimum et quingentesimum auspiciis societatis aperiendis fontibus rerum Germanicarum medii aevi*, ed. G. H. Pertz et al. (Hanover, Weimar, Berlin, Stuttgart, Cologne, 1826–) |
| *MGHS* | *MGH Scriptores in Folio et Quarto*, 32 vols., 1826–1934 |
| *MGHS rer. Germ.* | *MGH Scriptores rerum Germanicarum in usum scholarum separatim editi*, 61 vols., 1840–1937 |
| *MGHS rer. Germ. NS* | *MGH Scriptores rerum Germanicarum, Nova Series*, 12 vols., 1922–59 |
| *PL* | *Patrologiae cursus completus. Series Latina*, publ. J. P. Migne, 217 vols. and 4 vols. of indexes (Paris, 1844–64) |
| *QBSSM* | *Quinti belli sacri scriptores minores*, ed. R. Röhricht (Geneva, 1879) |
| *RHC* | *Recueil des historiens des croisades*, ed. Académie des Inscriptions et Belles-Lettres (Paris, 1841–1906) |
| *RHC Arm.* | *RHC Documents arméniens*, 2 vols. (Paris, 1869–1906) |
| *RHC Lois* | *RHC Lois. Les Assises de Jérusalem*, 2 vols. (Paris, 1841–3) |
| *RHC Oc.* | *RHC Historiens occidentaux*, 5 vols. (Paris, 1844–95) |
| *RHC Or.* | *RHC Historiens orientaux*, 5 vols. (Paris, 1872–1906) |
| *RHF* | *Recueil des historiens des Gaules et de la France*, ed. M. Bouquet et al., 24 vols. (Paris, 1737–1904) |
| *RIS* | *Rerum Italicarum scriptores*, ed. L. A. Muratori, 25 vols. (Milan, 1723–51) |
| *RISNS* | *Rerum Italicarum scriptores. Nova series*, ed. G. Carducci et al. (Città di Castello, Bologna, 1900–) |

xi

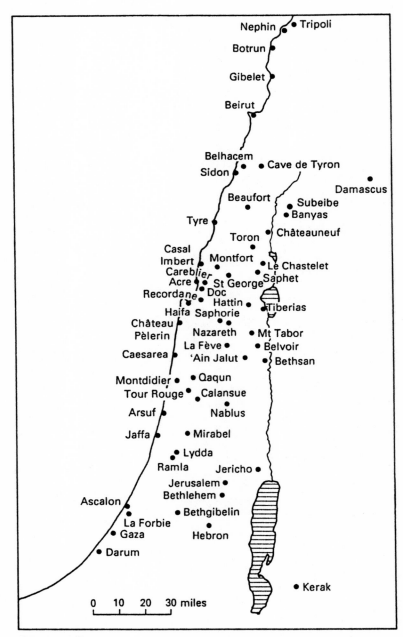

Figure 1. Palestine

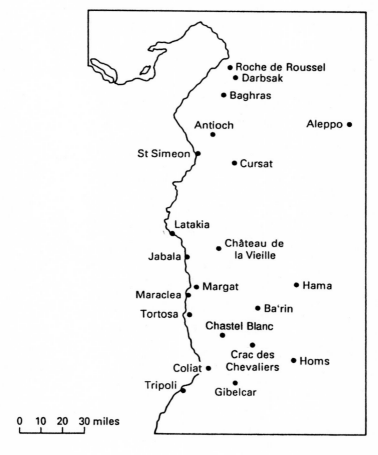

Figure 2. Syria

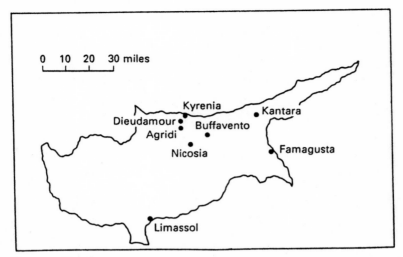

Figure 3. Cyprus

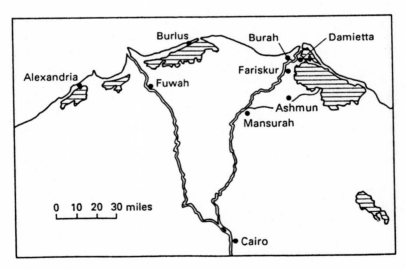

Figure 4. Egypt

# INTRODUCTION: THE STUDY OF WARFARE IN THE LATIN EAST

In May 1291 Muslim troops commanded by the Mamluk sultan al-Ashraf Khalil captured and destroyed the city of Acre. Although it was not the last Latin-held site to be surrendered, contemporaries regarded the fall of Acre as symbolic of the temporary end of Latin rule in the area.[1] Similarly, in July 1191, the capture of Acre by forces of the Third Crusade had been a decisive point in the campaign, even though the treaty of Jaffa, which acknowledged the re-establishment of the Latin Kingdom, was not signed until September 1192.[2] The Kingdom of Jerusalem, which had been virtually eliminated by Saladin after the battle of Hattin in 1187, was to survive, in a rather reduced form, for nearly a century. Until the defeat of St Louis's first crusade in 1250, the kingdom was maintained largely as a result of Muslim divisions, rather than Latin strength. After this, the Mamluks' usurpation of power in Egypt and their subsequent unification of the Muslim states in the area lead to the Christian losses of the 1260s. Only a few, mainly coastal, sites were able to hold out until 1291.

It would be quite unreasonable, however, to regard the 'Second Kingdom' as a mere appendix of the First. Recent work on the constitutional and social history of the Latin Kingdom has shown that there was much positive achievement in the later period – even allowing for a fragmentation of authority, implications of innate strength are apparent in, for example, the baronial resistance to the demands of Frederick II and the constitutional debates and internecine conflicts which raged throughout much of the thirteenth century.

---

[1] For an analysis of contemporary reaction see S. Schein, 'The West and the Crusade. Attitudes and Attempts, 1291–1312' (unpublished Ph.D thesis, Cambridge, 1979), pp. 27, and 79–113, *passim*.

[2] J. Prawer, *Histoire du royaume latin de Jérusalem* (2 vols., Paris, 1969–70), vol. II, pp. 67–8, 99.

# Introduction

## MILITARY HISTORIANS AND THE MILITARY HISTORY OF THE LATIN EAST

In 1956 R. C. Smail published his book on the military history of the Latin states from the period of their establishment to the end of the Third Crusade. By analysing a detailed body of evidence, Smail was able to place the military history of the period in its social and political context, and thus demonstrate the importance of warfare to the Latin East. He showed that this was in sharp contrast to the work of most military historians, who had been content to describe and sometimes analyse a quite arbitrary selection of battles, apparently chosen for their tactical significance.[3] Except for the study of castles, which will be considered later, the thirteenth century has had less attention from scholars concentrating on military affairs. John of Joinville's narrative of the battle of Mansurah seems to be the only contemporary account which has received widespread consideration.

Several scholars, however, have considered certain aspects of the subject. Delpech dealt with the battles at Agridi in 1232, near Gaza in 1239 and at Mansurah in 1250. But his work was coloured by a preconception that medieval armies not only knew precisely what they wanted to do (often based on the theories of classical authors such as Vegetius) but also had the ability to carry out complex manoeuvres in battle.[4] This, coupled with an uncritical use of source material, rendered questionable many of his conclusions regarding the tactics of the thirteenth century.[5] In the case of Gaza in 1239, Delpech was exceptional amongst general historians of medieval military history in making use of a very detailed account of this conflict.[6] His analysis of this battle suggested that he wished it to conform to three predetermined ideas, none of which can really be justified from an objective reading of the sources. First, he noted the exploitation of the terrain by Rukn-ad-Din al-Hijawi, although it was clearly the crusaders' own decision to camp in a valley surrounded by low hills: this position was in no way forced on them by the Muslim

---

[3] R. C. Smail, *Crusading Warfare (1097–1193)* (Cambridge, 1956), pp. 1–17.
[4] H. Delpech, *La Tactique au XIIIème siècle* (2 vols., Paris, 1886), vol. I, pp. 265, 331–54; vol. II, pp. 67–81, 130–46.
[5] See the summary dismissal of his work by J. F. Verbruggen, *The Art of Warfare in Western Europe during the Middle Ages* (Amsterdam, 1977), pp. 1–2.
[6] In 'Continuation de Guillaume de Tyr de 1229 à 1261, dite du manuscrit de Rothelin', *RHC Oc.*, vol. II (hereafter 'Rothelin'), pp. 541–6.

commander.[7] Secondly, following the account of Albert of Trois Fontaines, he emphasised the imbalance amongst the crusader forces caused by a lack of footsoldiers; in this he appears to have overlooked the assertion (in the 'Rothelin' account) that the mounted troops were reluctant to abandon their footsoldiers, even though this would have allowed the former, at least, to escape from the Muslims.[8] Thirdly, he criticised the crusader knights for charging the Muslims, and thus breaking formation. He ignored the statement that this charge was necessary because the crusaders' crossbowmen had run out of arrows.[9] These examples illustrate Delpech's tendency to manipulate the sources in order to justify certain preconceived ideas, thereby seriously diminishing the value of his study of battle tactics in the thirteenth century.

Oman incorporated a long account of the crusades and the Latin states into his study of medieval warfare. However, he dismissed the Second Kingdom as 'a mere survival without strength to recover itself', and he had little to say about its military history. He preferred to concentrate on the crusaders' invasions of Egypt which he regarded as 'wholly independent of the defence of Palestine', and his only use of material from the thirteenth century was that concerning the battle of Mansurah, for which he produced a composite account from some narrative sources. Oman also referred occasionally to evidence from the Latin East in his chapters on fortification and siegecraft.[10]

Lot dealt with the Latin East during the thirteenth century in a work which, like Smail's, attempted to place military history in its social and political context.[11] The results, however, are of limited value: Lot relied largely on secondary materials (which was understandable, given that his intention was to write a general survey of medieval warfare for French-speaking students) and he produced little more than a short political history with military overtones.

In more recent years two studies have added in different ways to the general understanding of medieval warfare. The first was

---

[7] 'Rothelin', pp. 541–2; Delpech, *La Tactique*, vol. II, pp. 68–9.

[8] Albert of Trois Fontaines, 'Chronicon', *MGHS*, vol. XXIII, p. 946; 'Rothelin', p. 543; Delpech, *La Tactique*, vol. II, p. 67.

[9] 'Rothelin', p. 544; Delpech, *La Tactique*, vol. II, p. 69 and note 2.

[10] C. Oman, *A History of the Art of War in the Middle Ages* (2 vols., London, 1924), vol. I, pp. 231–352, especially pp. 263, 266, 340–52; vol. II, pp. 37–9, 49, 51–3.

[11] F. Lot, *L'Art militaire et les armées au moyen âge*, vol. I (Paris, 1946), pp. 169–210.

Verbruggen's *Art of Warfare in Western Europe*. Apart from a section on strategy, the author was primarily concerned with the roles of knights, footsoldiers, archers and crossbowmen, and the tactics which were employed by combatants when they were in a battle situation.[12] Verbruggen was prepared to use material from battles which took place in the east, but for the thirteenth century he limited himself to occasional references to the battle of Mansurah. In a section on discipline he made extensive use of the Templars' *Rule*, which includes detailed regulations on how members of the Order should conduct themselves on campaign. Finally, in his chapter on strategy Verbruggen relied heavily on the plans to recover the Holy Land (the *De recuperatione Terrae Sanctae* texts) which were written in the west after the fall of Acre. Verbruggen's book provides many important insights into medieval warfare. However, his conclusion – that 'the weaker of the contestants took refuge behind the defence of his many fortresses ... [which] created a balance between the various countries which was not easily upset'[13] – cannot be applied to the situation in the Latin states during the thirteenth century. The Latins were sometimes able to use their strongpoints as places of refuge. But the balance, if there ever had been one, between Muslims and Christians was upset by the marked superiority of the former in most types of military encounter, and by the inability of the latter to deal with Muslim methods which were geared towards the progressive reduction of Christian territory in the area, primarily by the use of the siege. Contemporaries attested to the growing sense of panic and bewilderment amongst Christians as a result of this Muslim strategy.

Contamine, in *War in the Middle Ages*, illustrated how the schemes of the Franciscan Fidenzio of Padua, in his 'Liber recuperationis Terre Sancte', reflected the improved administrative techniques of the period as employed by Edward I of England, Philip IV of France and Charles I of Anjou. This is characteristic of Contamine's wide vision of warfare. He concentrated on the period c. 1100–1400, dealing not only with battlefield tactics but also such diverse aspects of warfare as armaments, siege techniques, the social impact of military affairs and the motivation of troops. His work, therefore, treated tactics

---

[12] This allowed him to consider some aspects of battlefield psychology; see Verbruggen, *Art of Warfare*, pp. 39–64, including (pp. 44–6) material from John of Joinville.

[13] *Ibid.*, pp. 66, 80, 82, 194, 76–9, 87–8, 92–3, 254–73, 300.

as one of many facets of warfare, whereas Verbruggen had considered tactics largely in isolation. Contamine's study of the period 1150–1300 examined most of the military resources which were available to the state. Beginning with manpower, he dealt with knights, other mounted troops (including crossbowmen), archers and various types of infantry, besides briefly considering the Military Orders as a separate element. Then he examined the methods by which the state could bring into existence a fighting force appropriate to its requirements and limited resources. These varied from the *arrière-ban* and the *servitium debitum* to services for money and ultimately the employment of mercenaries; during this period a shift occurred to 'an economy of paid feudal warfare', in which the fief, however, remained a central feature. Fortified sites were another major military resource dealt with by Contamine. The main development was the use of stone rather than wood for fortifications, whilst in suggesting the possible nature of a garrison force he made use of the text describing the rebuilding of Saphet, a Templar castle in Palestine, in the 1240s. Contamine also examined the likely course of a siege campaign. He showed that the assault improved in technique during this period, rather than in terms of the materials that were available to the attackers. He was able to create a general impression of how military institutions and activity were a product of their social context and he therefore concluded that warfare's increasing sophistication (at least on an organisational level) by the end of this period reflected developments within society as a whole. The military institutions of the Latin East were dealt with only briefly, however, and mostly from the researches of Smail. Contamine also had little to say about the thirteenth century in this respect, since his work was mainly concerned with north-western Europe.[14]

The achievements of military historians are impressive – not least because most have dealt with an enormous range of subject matter. It is not surprising that their analysis of the military history of the Latin East in the thirteenth century has been limited in scope. They have adopted two perspectives. First, historians of tactics, such as Delpech, Oman and Verbruggen, have concerned themselves with what happened when two armies met on the battlefield. Even on this level there is much material available, but

---

[14] P. Contamine, *War in the Middle Ages* (Oxford, 1984), pp. 59–118, *passim*, and 209.

these writers were largely content to examine, at most, three battles which were removed from their appropriate context and used in quite arbitrary fashion, either as a reflection of the 'crusaders' warfare' of the thirteenth century, or to illustrate points about western European warfare simply because (as in the case of Mansurah) the accounts contained what scholars saw as detailed, and therefore important, information about tactics and strategy. Most historians who have concentrated on battles have placed their accounts in an artificial setting which is unrelated to the actual historical context of the event.

Secondly, scholars such as Lot and Contamine have made some attempt to examine the social and institutional aspects of war. They did not divorce warfare from other aspects of history, but their treatment of the Latin East was restricted, in the case of Lot by the nature of his method, which largely produced a political narrative, and in the case of Contamine by his acknowledged bias towards material from north-western Europe. Smail's work on the twelfth century was unique in offering a study of warfare in the Latin East which combined the better features of these two perspectives: there was no lack of detail concerning the performance of armies in the area (and this was not restricted to the battle) and military history was shown to be an important aspect of the general history of the Latin states.

Most military historians have concentrated on the fighting man as the principal military resource at the disposal of a commander and the battle is therefore the subject of greatest interest to them. At a time when the number of soldiers was often restricted, however, other assets, particularly strongpoints, could have a crucial role to play in the survival of territory against an aggressor. Smail pointed out that the capture and maintenance of such sites was perhaps the key to the entire military history of the Latin East in the twelfth century,[15] and the same is true of the period to 1291. The study of the Latin East's castles has been intensive over the last century, but two features limit the value of much of the work. First, the approach of most scholars has been primarily architectural. Like most military historians who have studied battles, such authors prefer to examine their subject in isolation from its context, considering its form rather than the role that it may have played in the military establishment of the Latin

---

[15] Smail, *Crusading Warfare*, pp. 24–5.

# Introduction

East. One exception to this was Smail, though his work was concerned with the twelfth century.[16] The importance of architectural studies of this kind cannot be denied, but the value of such investigations is further restricted by a second feature: the visible materials available to facilitate such work are themselves far from adequate. There has not been enough archaeological investigation and an example of the difference that such an examination can make may be seen in the case of the castle of Belvoir, by comparing the very basic plan that Smail was able to produce with that of Prawer, when the site had been cleared and excavated. In the details of the inner defences, in particular, Prawer's plan is far more substantial.[17]

One of the first modern historians to examine the monuments of the Latin East was Rey.[18] His study, although over a hundred years old, remains useful as many sites have disintegrated since he visited them. Some of his work was consequently incorporated into Deschamps's *Les Châteaux des croisés en Terre-Sainte*.[19] The studies of Rey and Deschamps are the standard works on castles in the Latin East, and the authors did try to place this aspect of warfare in an overall context, but they made little attempt to analyse the information at their disposal. For most castles a description of the remains was complemented by a history which was dependent on the survival of narrative accounts. Deschamps went beyond this to consider the location of the site and its theoretical ability to control an area. His views will be discussed below when the functions of castles in the thirteenth century are examined.[20] Other studies, both of individual sites and of groups of them, will be noted later. But only detailed archaeological and architectural work and careful analysis of texts will produce advances in the present state of knowledge, after which more informed generalisations may be made. Dr Pringle has shown what can be achieved. In 1983 he directed a survey of the Frankish

---

[16] R. C. Smail, 'Crusaders' Castles of the Twelfth Century', *Cambridge Historical Journal*, 10 (1951), pp.133–49, and *Crusading Warfare*, pp. 60–2, 204–15.

[17] Smail, *Crusading Warfare*, p. 249; J. Prawer, *The Latin Kingdom of Jerusalem. European Colonialism in the Middle Ages* (London, 1972), p. 302.

[18] E. G. Rey, *Etude sur les monuments de l'architecture militaire des croisés en Syrie et dans l'île de Chypre* (Paris, 1871).

[19] P. Deschamps, *Les Châteaux des croisés en Terre-Sainte*, vol. I: *Le Crac des Chevaliers* (Paris, 1934), vol. II: *La Défense du royaume de Jérusalem* (Paris, 1939), and vol. III: *La Défense du comté de Tripoli et de la Principauté d'Antioche* (Paris, 1973).

[20] For example, in *Le Crac*, pp. 16–42. See below, pp. 129–31.

settlements (including a number of castles) in the Sharon Plain and an excavation of Tour Rouge. He has now published a study which analyses the archaeological, architectural, geographical and historical materials relating to the various sites. This has produced a detailed picture of the nature of Frankish settlement in the countryside; it emphasises the importance of castles at a local level, both in a military and an administrative context.[21]

The Military Orders are another element of the military establishment which has received attention. They became increasingly significant for the survival of the Latin states in the thirteenth century, but many studies of them are merely narrative accounts which fail to analyse the specific role which they played in the area's military structure. An example of this is the work by Melville, still the best general account of the Templars in the Latin East. She described some of the institutions of the Order, from the Templars' *Rule*, and considered the political history of the Latin Kingdom, but she was unable to bring the two elements together, except when the Templars played a clearly defined role, as in the final siege of Acre. Much of what she had to say about the thirteenth century is, therefore, just a political history with occasional references to the Templars.[22]

Another detailed study of a Military Order, this time the Hospitallers, was undertaken by Professor Riley-Smith. Like Melville, he gave a separate narrative account of the Latin settlement in the thirteenth century, but he was then able to place the Hospitallers within this political framework. The Hospitallers' role in the military history of the period received careful examination in his study, but his general analysis of warfare in the thirteenth century was somewhat tentative. An extensive account of the Hospitallers' activities in the Latin East thus remained rather isolated. Riley-Smith noted their provision of soldiers for raids, advice on military affairs, acceptance of responsibility for the defence of various sites and the strategies which were adopted

[21] R. D. Pringle, *The Red Tower* (London, 1986), pp. 12–15 and *passim*.
[22] M. Melville, *La Vie des Templiers* (Paris, 1951), pp. 239–44, and *passim*. Recently two scholars have dealt with public opinion regarding the Military Orders and their role in the politics of the Latin East, before and after 1291: see J. Prawer, 'Military Orders and Crusader Politics in the Second Half of the Thirteenth Century', in *Die geistlichen Ritterorden Europas*, ed. J. Fleckenstein and M. Hellmann (Sigmaringen, 1980), pp. 217–29, and A. J. Forey, 'The Military Orders in the Crusading Proposals of the Late-Thirteenth and Early-Fourteenth Centuries', *Traditio*, 36 (1980), pp. 317–45.

against their Muslim neighbours. By examining the extensive documentation of the Hospitallers, he established the overall structure of the Order. He then dealt specifically with the military side of the Order's operations, drawing conclusions about the role of the soldier which, if used carefully, have implications for the study of military life within the Latin East as a whole.[23] Riley-Smith's work was not primarily concerned with the military history of the Latin East, but it revealed much about a significant aspect of that history. He tried to describe the Order as an element that should not be divorced from its surroundings.

## HISTORIANS OF THE LATIN EAST AND MILITARY HISTORY

It has long been possible to write a reasonable narrative account of the Latin East's history during this period and, in all such works, military activity inevitably assumes great significance. Runciman's account of the period c. 1260–77, for example, reads as little more than a narrative of military events.[24] By the use of materials such as the kingdom's law books and charters and the papal registers it is possible both to produce a more complete narrative history and at the same time to examine the constitutional and social history of the kingdom in far greater depth. This can also yield a detailed picture of aspects of the military history of the kingdom.

In the early 1950s Prawer and Richard were able to redefine the constitution of the Latin Kingdom. The first narrative history to acknowledge this was Richard's *Royaume Latin de Jérusalem*, which appeared in 1953. The author used a wide range of sources besides the chronicles to produce a detailed impression of the Latin Kingdom's society. This extended to the field of military history, where he showed, for example, how important was assistance from Europe (with both money and men) to the survival of the kingdom in the thirteenth century, and demonstrated the significance of the patriarch in military affairs.[25]

[23] J. S. C. Riley-Smith, *The Knights of St John in Jerusalem and Cyprus, c. 1050–1310* (London, 1967), pp. 85–197, 236–40, 304–28 and *passim*.

[24] S. Runciman, *A History of the Crusades* (3 vols., Cambridge, 1951–4), vol. III, pp. 315–48.

[25] J. Richard, *The Latin Kingdom of Jerusalem* (2 vols., Amsterdam, 1979), vol. II, pp. 376–83. His ideas concerning the patriarch were developed by S. Schein, in 'The Patriarchs of Jerusalem in the Late Thirteenth Century – *Seignors Espiritueles et*

# Introduction

Prawer's *Histoire du Royaume Latin de Jérusalem* remains one of the best narrative accounts of the Latin Kingdom's history ever produced. His examination of military history was made outstanding by an intimate knowledge of the area's geography. He was thus able to discuss in theory and practice the significance of the treaties which were agreed between the Christians and Muslims in 1229 and 1240–1. The limited expeditions which took place when the troops of the Fifth Crusade gathered at Acre in the autumn of 1217 were similarly scrutinised, and information relating to a battle was shown to have additional interest if it could be placed in a geographical context. The value of the sources describing the battle near Gaza of 1239 has already been noted; Prawer was able, through his acquaintance with the region, to suggest the likely route taken by the crusaders from Jaffa, leading to their final defeat near the village of Beit-Hanun.[26]

One of the most influential historians of the Latin Kingdom's constitution is Riley-Smith. His major study of the kingdom's political ideas in theory and practice demonstrated again the significance of military affairs to almost any assessment of its history. Directly, he dealt, though not in great detail, with military service as a central element of feudalism in Palestine. Indirectly, the military situation often provided the background against which political, constitutional and economic developments took place. For example, the increasing poverty of the lords in the thirteenth century was due largely to expenses incurred in the defence of their fiefs; many of them were therefore obliged to alienate their properties to the Military Orders. Riley-Smith was particularly concerned with constitutional developments. The attempts by Frederick II to assert his authority, on Cyprus and on the mainland, led to a wide range of military engagements: Riley-Smith examined these as part of the Ibelin faction's efforts to secure their own position by use of the *Assise sur la ligece*. Similarly, during the War of St Sabas John of Jaffa and John II of Beirut manipulated the complex regency laws in order to switch

*Temporeles?*', in *Outremer*, ed. B. Z. Kedar, H. E. Mayer and R. C. Smail (Jerusalem, 1982), pp. 297–305.
[26] Prawer, *Histoire du royaume*, vol. II, pp. 137–43, 198–204, 272–4, 286–7. Knowledge of terrain has recently been used in a study which compared the tactics of 'Ain Jalut in 1260 with those employed at Tagliacozzo in 1268: see P. Herde, 'Taktiken muslimischer Heere vom ersten Kreuzzug bis 'Ayn Djalut (1260) und ihre Einwirkung auf die Schlacht bei Tagliacozzo (1268)', in *Das Heilige Land im Mittelalter: Begegnungsraum zwischen Orient und Okzident* (Würzburg, 1981).

the feudatories' support to the Venetians. Riley-Smith, however, did not always establish conclusively the link between military affairs and constitutional developments. He recognised the need, for example, for strong government in the 1260s, but his subsequent analysis of the period's regency debates paid little attention to the military context, about which contemporaries were clearly aware.[27]

## THE AIM AND SCOPE OF THIS STUDY

In this book, I have created a general picture of military life in the Latin East from the end of the Third Crusade to the fall of Acre in 1291. Many of Smail's conclusions for the twelfth century are equally true of the thirteenth, but it will become clear that not everything he wrote is valid for the later period, where the circumstances were radically changed by such factors as the increasing threat of the Muslims and a large-scale division of authority within the Latin states.

The range of materials available can be used to consider most of the elements which make up the sum total of military events in the area: previously, these materials have only been used piecemeal or as a part of a narrative account with little attempt at analysis. The reports of sieges, raids and the functions of castles have scarcely been scrutinised, yet all are significant components of the whole military picture which will be examined here.

The narrative accounts from the Latin Kingdom in this period do not compare with that of the twelfth-century chronicler William of Tyre, but the various Old French continuations of his work[28] and the collection known as the *Gestes des Chiprois*[29] provide useful details of military activity. The Arabic sources, too, are often full of information, one of the most important being the biographical account of the reign (1260–77) of an-Nasir

---

[27] J. S. C. Riley-Smith, *The Feudal Nobility and the Kingdom of Jerusalem, 1174–1277* (London, 1973), pp. 8–13, 28–32, 159–84 *passim*, 215–17, 198, 217–24. See also below, pp. 40–2.

[28] 'L'Estoire de Eracles empereur et la conqueste de la terre d'Outremer', *RHC Oc.*, vols. I–II (hereafter 'Eracles'), *passim*; 'Rothelin', *passim*. For the problems associated with these texts, see M. R. Morgan, *The Chronicle of Ernoul and the Continuations of William of Tyre* (Oxford, 1973) and 'The Rothelin Continuation of William of Tyre', in *Outremer*, ed. Kedar, Mayer and Smail, pp. 244–57. As Dr M. R. Morgan pointed out, the various versions of 'Eracles' have to be regarded as a collection of sources, rather than a single source. Their value is not consistent (*Chronicle of Ernoul*, pp. 177–9).

[29] *Les Gestes des Chiprois*, ed. G. Raynaud (Geneva, 1887).

Rukn-ad-Din Baybars by his secretary, Ibn 'Abd al-Zahir.[30] This was incorporated *en masse* into later works by writers such as al-Makrizi and Ibn al-Furat. These two main groups of narratives may be complemented by accounts from western sources. An event such as the fall of Acre in 1291 was written about by many contemporaries but, from a military standpoint, such accounts are often of limited value. Alternatively, some western narrative accounts may be wholly devoted to events in the east and most obviously to the process of a crusade. Oliver, the scholastic of Cologne and later bishop of Paderborn, not only preached the Fifth Crusade but also joined the army and wrote an account of his experiences.[31] John of Joinville also went on crusade – on the first of St Louis's expeditions – and his case for the king's canonisation involved him reporting extensively on Louis's crusading exploits.[32] Both these authors therefore provided interesting material concerning military events in the east. Other worthwhile information can be gleaned from letters, some of which are contained in western chronicles. There are many, for example, in the work of Matthew Paris, the Benedictine monk of St Albans.[33]

Legal texts can provide information on the structure of military society. Two of the most important were written by men who themselves made important contributions to events in the Latin East. We have already seen that John of Jaffa influenced the course of the War of St Sabas; later we shall examine his efforts to maintain the castle of Jaffa during the middle years of the thirteenth century. He also produced a great lawbook, the 'Livre des Assises de la Haute Cour'.[34] Philip of Novara was a Lombard who had travelled to the east by 1218. He held a fief from the Ibelins on Cyprus and was a committed supporter of their cause until his death, possibly in the late 1260s. He was best known as a lawyer, and he produced a work, the 'Livre de forme de plait',

---

[30] A. A. Khowayter, 'A Critical Edition of an Unknown Arabic Source for the Life of al-Malik al-Zahir Baybars' (unpublished Ph.D thesis, 3 vols., London, 1960), vol. II (hereafter Ibn 'Abd al-Zahir, 'Life of Baybars').

[31] Oliver of Paderborn, 'Historia Damiatina', ed. H. Hoogeweg, *Bibliothek des Litterarischen Vereins in Stuttgart*, 202 (1894); L. and J. S. C. Riley-Smith, *The Crusades. Idea and Reality, 1095–1274* (London, 1981), p. 135.

[32] See John of Joinville, *Histoire de Saint Louis*, ed. N. de Wailly (Paris, 1874).

[33] Matthew Paris, *Chronica maiora*, ed. H. R. Luard (Rolls Series, 57) (7 vols., London, 1872–83).

[34] John of Jaffa, 'Livre des Assises de la Haute Cour', *RHC Lois*, vol. I; see also J. S. C. Riley-Smith, *Feudal Nobility*, pp. 125–6, and above, p. 10, and below, pp. 139–44.

Plate 1. Miniature depicting the siege of Acre, 1291

which influenced John of Jaffa. He also wrote a (biased and, in places, egotistical) account of the civil conflicts on Cyprus and the mainland during the 1220s and 30s; this was inserted into the *Gestes des Chiprois*.[35]

Evidence from charters, the papal registers and materials relating to the Military Orders is valuable, and sometimes the author of an itinerary, such as Burchard of Mt Sion, gave an impression of the military situation as he travelled through a

---

[35] Philip of Novara, 'Livre de forme de plait', *RHC Lois*, vol. 1; see also J. S. C. Riley-Smith, *Feudal Nobility*, pp. 126–7; *Gestes des Chiprois*, pp. 25–138, and below, pp. 37–9 and *passim*.

region.[36] Finally, there are many miscellaneous texts to be examined: some, such as the anonymous eye-witness account *De constructione castri Saphet*[37] and the Franciscan Fidenzio of Padua's suggestions for the recovery of the Holy Land,[38] are primarily concerned with military matters, and therefore of considerable value.

Ideas about aspects of warfare can also be obtained from the arts of the period. There are many problems with the interpretation of contemporary illustrations, but some tentative suggestions are possible, particularly when they can be related to textual evidence. Examples of the artists' interest in military life include illustrations from manuscripts, seals and coins, effigies and sculptures. These have not been studied in any depth here, but they occasionally prove to be valuable, particularly in the fields of arms and armour (where the survival of thirteenth-century equipment is very rare) and siege techniques. It is a matter of coping with an artist's imagination and artistic licence: where this can be done, such materials will be used as additional evidence for an otherwise documented event. An example is a miniature from an Old French translation of 'De excidio urbis Acconis', probably produced around 1300 in Paris. It is regarded as one of the first illustrations of the fall of Acre and, at the very least, constitutes a near-contemporary visual impression of the loss of the Holy Land.[39] (See plate 1.)

Finally, material for the military history of a fairly compact area may be gathered by undertaking fieldwork. It is often possible to relate written sources to the remains of castles, towns and battle sites, whilst also considering the problems of terrain and climate which may have proved particularly awkward for crusaders from western Europe. In common with evidence from art, that produced by fieldwork will be analysed largely in connection with written sources, which it either confirms or raises

---

[36] Burchard of Mt Sion, 'Descriptio Terrae Sanctae', in *Peregrinatores medii aevi quatuor*, ed. J. C. M. Laurent (Leipzig, 1864).

[37] *De constructione castri Saphet*, ed. R. B. C. Huygens (Amsterdam, 1981), pp. 10–11 and *passim*. See also the important review article by R. D. Pringle, 'Reconstructing the Castle of Safad', *Palestine Exploration Quarterly*, 117 (1985), pp. 139–49.

[38] Fidenzio of Padua, 'Liber recuperationis Terre Sancte', ed. P. G. Golubovich, *Biblioteca bio-bibliografica della Terra Santa e dell'Oriente Francescano*, vol. II (Quaracchi, 1913).

[39] J. Folda, *Crusader Manuscript Illumination at Saint-Jean d'Acre, 1275–1291* (Princeton, 1976) pp. 158, 213.

doubts about. This will give a fairly complete impression of military history in the period from c. 1192 to 1291.

Consideration will be given to all the principal areas of Latin settlement in the thirteenth century: the Kingdom of Jerusalem, the Principality of Antioch and County of Tripoli, the Kingdom of Armenia and the Kingdom of Cyprus. Evidence from the two crusades which invaded Egypt will be examined, since conflicts between Christians and Muslims were quite uniform whether in Egypt, Palestine or Syria. Encounters between Christian forces will also be analysed: they provide additional and contrasting evidence to augment that provided by the Muslim–Christian struggle in the region.

We shall examine the Latin armies in the context of the military, political and economic circumstances of the Latin settlement. But analysis of the Muslim forces and military organisation will be restricted to areas where they came into direct contact with the Latins. In the second half of the thirteenth century, however, the Muslim threat became increasingly significant as the Latins' presence in the region was first reduced and eventually ended, as a consequence of the loss of their strongpoints. The Latins' problems were exacerbated by inter-Christian rivalry and conflict.

The treatment of this history will be thematic, not chronological. By adopting this approach it is possible to make far more sense of materials which, if used on their own, can be both limited in value and ambiguous. In the case of battles, for example, any effort to make sense of a single conflict in isolation is fraught with difficulties. There are inevitably gaps in accounts of individual engagements, so that even such detail as Joinville provided in his description of the battle of Mansurah is best regarded as referring to a series of isolated incidents.[40] The distortions of the source material combine with the rationalising tendencies of the historian to create a wholly artificial impression; to proceed from this to generalisations is unsatisfactory. Given the nature of the sources which will be looked at – diverse but often of restricted value – an attempt will be made to establish the tactics which appear to have been generally appropriate for use in the circumstances of the Latin East. It should then be possible to understand individual accounts more clearly.

[40] Joinville, *Histoire de Saint Louis*, pp. 118–34; on the problems of analysing accounts of battles in the twelfth century, see Smail, *Crusading Warfare*, pp. 165–8.

# Introduction

After some general remarks on the military situation in the Latin East during this period and its importance for the status of the Latin settlement, two principal elements of military history will be dealt with: the organisation of the resources which were available, and their application to a range of military activities. With regard to the former, the manpower (obtained from both inside and outside the Latin states) which produced the Latin armies will be discussed. There was a considerable diversity, both in terms of the source and the quality of troops, something to be examined further in an appraisal of the Latin army in action. The impact of the crusades on the ability of the Latin forces to deal adequately with the Muslim threat will also be considered. Besides their manpower, the principal assets of the Latins were their strongpoints. There were simple towers, examples of which dotted the coastal plain of the Kingdom of Jerusalem, great castles such as Crac des Chevaliers and Saphet and a number of fortified coastal towns and cities which were increasingly the main focal point of the Latin settlement in the area. The maintenance of such sites was fundamental to the survival of the Latin East; an examination will be made of their forms and functions.

The performance of the Latin armies will then be considered. Three types of military operation will be studied: the raid, the battle and the siege. In each instance, a wide range of evidence from the period will be used to suggest the Latin armies' abilities. As already noted, the discussion will not be confined to engagements with Muslim opponents. Much of the available evidence relates to conflicts with fellow-Christians in circumstances which had little to do with the external Muslim threat. It is not simply the survival of such material which makes it worth studying here. Many soldiers operating in the Latin East had to be able to deal with both Muslim and Christian enemies.

## Chapter 1

# WARFARE AND THE HISTORY OF THE LATIN EAST, 1192–1291

## INTRODUCTION

The aim of most warfare in this period was the capture or defence of territory, through the acquisition and retention of strongpoints. Commanders had to employ troops in the most efficient way in order to achieve this objective, subject to the restrictions imposed by the nature of medieval warfare, such as the problems of maintaining an army in the field for any great length of time. Three different types of engagement – the raid, the battle and the siege – were used to affect the territorial status of an enemy. The Latin armies, for various reasons, suffered from inadequacies in all three forms of warfare and these resulted in the gradual loss of their territories. Raids, battles and sieges will be examined in more detail later: in this chapter, after a brief review of the geography and politics of the Latin East and the surrounding area, the major outbreaks of war during this period will be considered in their historical context. This will establish a framework within which it will be possible to analyse the resources at the disposal of the combatants and the nature of warfare at this time.

## THE GEOGRAPHICAL AND POLITICAL BACKGROUND TO WARFARE

The habitable areas of Syria and Palestine consisted of a narrow strip of land between the eastern shores of the Mediterranean and the desert. The Latins did not, however, extend their territories to these natural limits; they were restricted, for the most part, to the coastal plain. This plain was relatively fertile and both agriculture and trade were profitable, though less so than they had been in the centuries before the arrival of the crusaders. Rainfall was almost entirely limited to the period from November to March, but moisture was retained in the higher ground to the east, to be released gradually to the coastal plain during the dry season. Retention of water was generally greater in the middle ages than now, because of the large areas of woodland.[1]

To the east of the coastal plain were mountain ranges, running parallel to the coastline for almost its entire length. These mountain ranges were divided, from north to south, by the valleys of the Orontes and Jordan rivers. The Jordan valley, as the river moved southwards, gradually dropped below the level of the sea, so that by the time it reached the Dead Sea, it was 1,290 feet below sea level. The mountain range to the east of the Jordan valley was more continuous than that to the west, whilst further to the east and south the mountains merged into the desert.[2]

The Latins, and even more the crusaders, must have been struck by the variations in climate in the region. On the coast, the winters were mild but the summers were hot and often oppressively humid. Further inland temperatures might be a few degrees lower, but in the Jordan valley the temperature could, again, become extremely hot. Temperatures as high as 43 °C have been recorded at Tiberias, for example.[3]

Three forms of warfare were critical to the continuing Latin presence in the area: the crusades, the resistance to the Muslim incursions, especially those organised by the Mamluk sultan Baybars and his successors, and the civil disruptions exemplified by the conflicts between Frederick II and the Ibelins. But these outbursts of intense military activity were uncharacteristic. Warfare in the Latin East during the thirteenth century was endemic, but often low-level. It was probably more recurrent than the available evidence suggests. The nature of the Latin settlement meant that even periods which appear to have been fairly calm may have witnessed numerous minor incidents which chroniclers did not bother to record. Some indication of this type of relatively minor conflict comes from evidence relating to the

---

[1] In 1265, the sultan Baybars went hunting in the forest of Arsuf. According to his biographer, Ibn ʿAbd al-Zahir, the area contained large numbers of wild animals and the sultan 'looked forward to ridding the forest of all such ferocious beasts' (Ibn ʿAbd al-Zahir, 'Life of Baybars', vol. II, p. 554).

[2] G. A. Smith, *The Historical Geography of the Holy Land* (London, 1931) pp. 45–50; Guides Bleus, *Syrie-Palestine* (Paris, 1932), pp. xvii–xxvii; M. Benvenisti, *The Crusaders in the Holy Land* (Jerusalem, 1970), p. 213; J. S. C. Riley-Smith, *The Crusades: A Short History* (London, 1987), p. 61.

[3] Guides Bleus, *Syrie-Palestine*, pp. xxvii–xxviii. See also below, pp. 86–92, *passim*.

first decade of the thirteenth century, when Muslims and Christians frequently clashed, though without any large-scale engagement taking place. In 1203–4, for example, a truce was repudiated and King Aimery led troops on a number of successful raids into Muslim territory. The sultan al-'Adil then moved a Muslim army to Mt Tabor and this led to a resumption of the truce.[4] The pattern of raid and counter-raid, mingled with periods of truce, was repeated throughout the century.

Restricted warfare in the form of raiding expeditions thus alternated with periods when concentrated efforts were made to achieve the primary aim of war – the acquisition of territory. Warfare, however, was not the only means of gaining land. The possible threat of a large, albeit temporary, influx of troops (most obviously a crusade) or the weakness of a Muslim state, or the desire for an alliance, could lead to some territory being offered to the Latins in return for peace. The second quarter of the thirteenth century was dominated in this respect by treaties which were a product of such circumstances. The major territorial gains in the Latin East during the thirteenth century were achieved through diplomacy, rather than aggression.

## The Principality of Antioch and the County of Tripoli

In the first half of the thirteenth century, the Principality of Antioch and the County of Tripoli were much more stable territorially than the southern Latin states, but conflict was far from rare. A war of succession at Antioch involved the Armenians and the Military Orders. It was concluded by the mid-1220s, but civil strife broke out again in the second half of the century with a succession of rebellions by the Genoese lords of Gibelet. Muslim control of Latakia increased the isolation of Antioch: the former was in fact captured by the Latins, with Mongol assistance, in 1261 but by this time the period of great Muslim successes had begun with the accession of the Mamluk sultan Baybars, and Antioch itself fell to the Muslims in 1268. Tripoli survived until 1289. Before the emergence of Baybars, however, and particularly in the first half of the thirteenth century, Muslims in the area had

---

[4] Ibn al-Athir, 'Kamel-Altevarykh', *RHC Or.*, vol. II, pp. 95–6, and 'Eracles', vol. II, pp. 258–63. According to the author of the 'Eracles' account (pp. 261–3), the two sides fought a battle near Doc, on the Plain of Acre. Details of the conflict are sketchy.

been much more threatened than a threat. Their own differences, combined with the strength of the Military Orders (centred on such strongpoints as Crac des Chevaliers, Margat, Chastel Blanc and Tortosa), enabled the latter frequently to assault the Muslim centres of Homs, Ba'rin and Hama. An aspect of the military history of this region was the use of raids by the Military Orders to maintain their predominance.[5] The Hospitallers at Margat continued with an aggressive policy even after the Muslims had captured most of the Christian territory in the area. Margat resisted a number of Muslim attacks, but finally capitulated after a siege in 1285. The Templars did not abandon Tortosa until 1291.[6]

### The Latin Kingdom of Jerusalem

In the Latin Kingdom the picture, superficially, was clear enough. Gains of lands by the Christians, particularly through the treaties of 1229 and 1240–1, were wiped out and then the kingdom was reduced by Baybars to a few isolated coastal sites which were all lost by 1291. Two factors made it more complex. First, the process of Muslim advance was by no means so clear-cut. Gains and losses of territory were a constant feature of the period's history, with sites such as Caesarea and Ascalon changing hands several times. Secondly, Latin worries about manpower and financial resources meant that there was no guarantee that sites which had been acquired would be subsequently fortified and garrisoned. In 1241, for example, the sultan of Egypt, as–Salih Aiyub, returned Bethgibelin and Belvoir to the Christians.[7]

---

[5] See below, pp. 187–8, 201.

[6] The most detailed account of the history of Antioch during this period is C. Cahen, *La Syrie du Nord à l'époque des croisades et la principauté franque d'Antioche* (Paris, 1940), pp. 579–721; see also J. Richard, 'Les Comtes de Tripoli et leurs vassaux sous la dynastie antiochénienne', in *Crusade and Settlement*, ed. P. W. Edbury (Cardiff, 1985), pp. 213–24. For the role of the Military Orders, see J. S. C. Riley-Smith, *Knights of St John*, pp. 136–41 and *passim*; J. S. C. Riley-Smith, 'The Templars and the Teutonic Knights in Cilician Armenia', in *The Cilician Kingdom of Armenia*, ed. T. S. R. Boase (Edinburgh, 1978), pp. 92–117. For information on the castles, see Deschamps, *La Défense du comté de Tripoli*. For the intrigues of the Aiyubids, see R. S. Humphreys, *From Saladin to the Mongols* (Albany, 1977), and H. A. R. Gibb, 'The Aiyubids', in *A History of the Crusades*, gen. ed. K. M. Setton (6 vols., Madison, 1969–89), vol. II, pp. 693–714.

[7] Matthew Paris, *Chronica maiora*, vol. IV, p. 142; *History of the Patriarchs of the Egyptian Church*, ed. and trans. A. Khater and O. H. E. Khs-Burmester (4 vols., Cairo, 1943–74), vol. IV, p. 221. On the significance of this treaty, see below, pp. 23–4.

Prawer suggested that the former secured a line of communication between Ascalon and Jerusalem, whilst Riley-Smith argued that it came back to the Hospitallers and may well have had a functioning burgess court.[8] There is no positive evidence that Bethgibelin was re-occupied during this period. Riley-Smith noted with regard to Belvoir that the Christians lost the castle in 1247,[9] presumably having refortified and garrisoned it after 1241. Again there is nothing to support this statement and archaeological evidence suggests a homogeneous twelfth-century structure, with no indication of Frankish re-occupation in the later period.[10]

Evidence from treaties and other documents is, nonetheless, important for establishing the state of the Latin Kingdom, provided it is used cautiously. The treaty of Jaffa of September 1192 reflected the limited recovery of land made by the Third Crusade. The re-established kingdom consisted, for the most part, of towns on the coast, whilst the walls of Ascalon (which had been destroyed by Saladin in 1191, then rebuilt by Richard I) were to be demolished again. Ramla and Lydda were to be divided between Muslims and Christians.[11] Five years later the Latins captured Beirut, but at the same time Jaffa was lost.[12] A period of relative calm ensued until the commencement of the Fifth Crusade, which Innocent III argued was needed partly because of the Muslim fortification of Mt Tabor: this fortress could not only

---

[8] Prawer, *Histoire du royaume*, vol. II, p. 287; J. S. C. Riley-Smith, *Knights of St John*, pp. 436–7.  [9] J. S. C. Riley-Smith, *Knights of St John*, p. 415.

[10] See Benvenisti, *Crusaders*, pp. 299–300.

[11] *La Continuation de Guillaume de Tyr (1184–1197)*, ed. M. R. Morgan (Paris, 1982), p. 153; Baha'-al-Din, *The Life of Saladin*, trans. C. W. Wilson (Palestine Pilgrims Text Society; London, 1897), pp. 380–7; R. D. Pringle, 'King Richard I and the Walls of Ascalon', *Palestine Exploration Quarterly*, 116 (1984), pp. 136–8; see Prawer, *Histoire du royaume*, vol. II, p. 99.

[12] 'Eracles', vol. II, pp. 218–19, 221, 224–5; Ibn al-Athir, 'Kamel-Altevarykh', vol. II, pp. 85–6. The capture of Beirut was particularly important. It not only re-established the coastal link of the mainland Latin states; it also meant that, in future, Muslim ships would be denied access to an important area of the Christian shipping lanes. Most Christian vessels travelling to the Holy Land made landfall around Tripoli or Beirut. Moreover, because of sailing conditions, they tended to arrive during two short periods of time: in late April or early May, or late September or early October. They were therefore, in theory, extremely vulnerable to attack by Muslim raiders. The extent of their vulnerability had been demonstrated by the activities of the pirate emir Usamah, who had been operating out of Beirut in the period leading up to its capture. Throughout the thirteenth century, however, the Egyptian fleet, based at Alexandria and Damietta, was probably unable to threaten the Christian shipping lanes for anything more than a few days at a time; there were no suitable sites available for it to take on supplies and particularly water. See J. H. Pryor, *Geography, Technology and War* (Cambridge, 1988), pp. 95, 116–19, 126, 130–1. See also below, p. 190.

threaten Acre but also the security of the rest of the kingdom.[13] Though the status of the Latin Kingdom itself was largely unaffected by this crusade (apart from the temporary loss and destruction of Caesarea and the construction of Château Pèlerin) it did lead to the Muslims' demolition of a number of sites which would have proved invaluable to an expanded Latin presence, including Toron, Saphet and Banyas.[14] The defences of Jerusalem were also dismantled.[15]

This scorched-earth policy meant that Muslim territorial concessions, particularly those of 1229 and 1240–1, were not quite as beneficial to the Latins as they initially appear to have been. Moreover, the Christians' manpower problems would have hampered any efforts to refortify and garrison the sites. From the military point of view the first of these treaties, between the sultan al-Kamil and Frederick II, was of little importance: it either acknowledged *faits accomplis* or granted territory such as Jerusalem, which in purely strategic terms was an unwanted drain on already stretched resources.[16] Three areas inland were now theoretically under Christian control: from Jaffa to Jerusalem and south to Bethlehem; the area around Nazareth; and the area to the north-west of the sea of Galilee, including Toron, although this was not to be fortified, and Montfort. Sidon, where an uncertain condominium had previously existed, was granted to the Christians, though they had already occupied and fortified it. The treaty seems to have accepted much of the rebuilding which had been a feature of the years since the arrival in the east of the Fifth Crusade. Frederick II mentioned that permission had been given to rebuild Jaffa, Caesarea, Sidon, 'and the castle of the House of

---

[13] Innocent III, 'Opera Omnia', *PL*, vol. CCXVI, col. 818.

[14] 'Eracles', vol. II, p. 339; Oliver of Paderborn, 'Historia', pp. 169, 244–5; Abu Shama, 'Le Livre des deux jardins', *RHC Or.*, vol. V, p. 171. The precise details are rather confused.

[15] Abu Shama, 'Livre des deux jardins', vol. V, pp. 173–5; al-Makrizi, *Histoire d'Egypte*, trans. E. Blochet (Paris, 1908), p. 330; Abu'l-Fida, 'Annales', *RHC Or.*, vol. I, p. 91.

[16] Little effort was subsequently made to protect Jerusalem; see 'Rothelin', pp. 529–30; 'Annales prioratus de Dunstaplia', ed. H. R. Luard, in *Annales monastici*, vol. III (Rolls Series, 36; London, 1886), p. 150. Dr Jackson has shown that the territory which al-Kamil ceded to Frederick was not, in fact, his to give, since it was in the possession of an-Nasir Da'ud, then prince of Damascus. Moreover, when Frederick left the Latin East, al-Kamil recognised an-Nasir's authority in the regions neighbouring the territory which had been surrendered, thereby absolving himself from responsibility for the observance of the truce; see P. Jackson, 'The Crusades of 1239–41 and their Aftermath', *Bulletin of the School of Oriental and African Studies*, 50 (1987), p. 36.

Saint Mary of the Germans' (Montfort);[17] all these sites had already been fortified.

The Muslims still retained considerable tracts of land, however, and this made the treaties of 1240 and 1241 rather more significant. They can be considered alongside a document written between 1236 and 1240, which suggests the extent of Muslim possessions in the area just before the agreement was reached. Again the possibility that many sites were abandoned must be allowed for, whilst some had been destroyed in the preceding years. But the list is an impressive one, indicating the potential threat which the Muslims constituted even to the west of the River Jordan. In the south they held Darum, Gaza and Ascalon on the coast; holding Jericho and Hebron, and to the north Nablus and Sabastiya in the area of Samaria, they were also well placed to strike at Jerusalem. But their possessions in the Galilee region, and beyond, must have been of particular concern to the Latins. These included Belvoir, La Fève, Mt Tabor, Saphorie, Tiberias, Saphet, Le Chastelet, Banyas, Châteauneuf, Toron and Beaufort.[18] Even though most of these sites were unoccupied at this time, it is clear that Christian repossession of areas around Nazareth and Toron would have been far from secure before the treaties of 1240–1.

The complex diplomatic manoeuvrings during the crusades of Theobald of Champagne and Richard of Cornwall reflected Muslim willingness to regard the Franks as potential allies, rather than as merely the objects of the *jihad*. Agreement was initially reached in the summer of 1240 between Theobald and as-Salih Isma'il of Damascus, who was in conflict with as-Salih Aiyub, the sultan of Egypt. The territories which the Muslims conceded included the area around Sidon, together with Toron, Châteauneuf, Tiberias, Saphet and, most importantly, Beaufort.[19] The garrison of Beaufort had to be prized out, indicating that this castle, at least, was functioning. The Latins were also able to buy arms and siege engines at Damascus, which scandalised many

[17] The full text of the treaty has not survived. See *Historia diplomatica Friderici secundi*, ed. J. L. de Huillard-Bréholles (6 vols., Paris, 1852–61), vol. III, pp. 91–2, 96–7, 105 (letters of Hermann of Salza, Frederick II and Gerald, Patriarch of Jerusalem); *Histoire de l'île de Chypre sous le règne des princes de la maison de Lusignan*, vol. III, ed. L. de Mas Latrie (Paris, 1855), pp. 626–9; *History of the Patriarchs*, vol. IV, p. 109.

[18] 'Etude sur un texte Latin énumérant les possessions Musulmanes dans le royaume de Jérusalem vers l'année 1239', ed. P. Deschamps, *Syria*, 23 (1942–3), pp. 87–90. As noted above, the Christians had been given possession of Toron, though without the right to fortify it, in 1229. It was granted to them again in 1240.

[19] Jackson, 'The Crusades of 1239–41', pp. 41–2 and note 65.

Muslims.[20] Alliances shifted, and in the spring of 1241 Richard of Cornwall came to an agreement with as-Salih Aiyub. This treaty, however, did little more than confirm the terms previously agreed with Isma'il. Moreover, Aiyub's concessions were largely theoretical, given that most of the territory which he granted to the Latins actually belonged to his enemies, Isma'il himself and an-Nasir Da'ud, prince of Kerak.[21] Nonetheless, taken together, the two truces gave the Christians the opportunity to re-establish control over substantial amounts of territory. In the Galilee region especially, where the Muslims had retained many sites, the Christians could have taken possession of Saphet, Belvoir, Tiberias, Beaufort, Mt Tabor, Toron and Châteauneuf, besides, further north, the areas around Sidon and Beirut. They may also have been given the Cave de Tyron, which was believed to have been Christian in 1250.[22] Further south, Ascalon, which was already being refortified, Mirabel and Bethgibelin became Christian, besides the territory around Gaza, though not the city itself.[23]

These gains, moreover, were not theoretical but real. Some sites may not have been re-occupied, but in the Galilee region a number were rebuilt, the best-documented example being Saphet. Richard of Cornwall's work at Ascalon could have had important implications for the military situation in southern Palestine and the relationship of that area with Egypt, but the site did not remain in Christian hands long enough to have much impact. In 1247 both Ascalon and Tiberias were lost.[24] The capture of Ascalon meant that Jaffa, thirty miles up the coast, had an important role in the military history of the next two decades; the fall of Tiberias, seemingly with no attempt made to relieve it, emphasised that despite the recent gains in the Galilee region, individual sites were extremely isolated and vulnerable.

---

[20] 'Eracles', vol. II, pp. 417–18; 'Rothelin', pp. 552–3; al-Makrizi, *Histoire d'Egypte*, p. 469.     [21] Jackson, 'The Crusades of 1239–41', pp. 45–7.

[22] For evidence on the Cave de Tyron see Matthew Paris, *Chronica maiora*, vol. VI, p. 196, and Ibn al-Furat, *Ayyubids, Mamlukes and Crusaders*, ed. and part trans. U. and M. C. Lyons, with historical introduction and notes by J. S. C. Riley-Smith (2 vols., Cambridge, 1971; hereafter Ibn al-Furat, *Ayyubids*), vol. II, p. 66 and p. 204, note 4, where Riley-Smith argues that it probably returned to the Muslims in 1253. It was rebuilt by them in 1264. See also *Tabulae ordinis Theutonici*, ed. E. Strehlke (Berlin, 1869), no. 110.

[23] *History of the Patriarchs*, vol. IV, pp. 221–2; Matthew Paris, *Chronica maiora*, vol. IV, pp. 141–3. See Prawer, *Histoire du royaume*, vol. II, pp. 286–7.

[24] 'Eracles', vol. II, pp. 432–4.

The first crusade of St Louis ended, in 1250, in a defeat which nearly cost the king his life, but in the Latin Kingdom, where he remained until 1254, his contribution was precisely what was required, though inadequate on its own. He established a contingent of French troops which played a significant part in many military actions of the following decades and he strengthened the kingdom's fortifications with work at Montmusard (the suburb of Acre), Caesarea, Jaffa and Sidon.[25] Within ten years, however, much of this work was being laid to waste with the campaigns of Baybars. By 1271 the Latin Kingdom, which had looked quite secure thirty years before, consisted of just a few coastal positions, notably Château Pèlerin, Acre, Beirut, Tyre and Sidon, each of which tended to function independently of the others. After the crusade of the Lord Edward (the future Edward I of England) in 1271, the final twenty years of the kingdom's history lacked any positive achievement in the military sphere, though its position was at least sustained by external support, such as that provided by Charles of Anjou.[26] The territorial stability of the Latin Kingdom prior to its final demise can be demonstrated by the fact that there was little change between a treaty which was agreed between Baybars and King Hugh in April 1272, the full text of which does not survive,[27] and one between Kalavun and the authorities of Acre in July 1283. In the latter, the Franks were to hold Acre, Sidon, Château Pèlerin and Haifa along with its castle. Haifa had presumably been re-occupied by the Christians after Baybars's attack of 1265, with the fortified position referred to perhaps being on Mt Carmel.[28] But, clearly, stability was in no way a reflection of strength. After St Louis's crusade, even limited Christian aggression in the area was

---

[25] Joinville, *Histoire de Saint Louis*, pp. 256–8, 282–4, 306–8, 336; Matthew Paris, *Chronica maiora*, vol. v, p. 257; William of St Pathus, *Vie de Saint Louis*, ed. H. F. Delaborde (Paris, 1899), p. 110. For the French regiment, see below, pp. 77–83.

[26] J. H. Pryor, '*In subsidium Terrae Sanctae*: Exports of Foodstuffs and War Materials from the Kingdom of Sicily to the Kingdom of Jerusalem, 1265–84', in *The Medieval Levant. Studies in Memory of Eliyahu Ashtor*, ed. B. Z. Kedar and A. L. Udovitch (Haifa, 1988), pp. 127–46, *passim*.

[27] Ibn 'Abd al-Zahir, 'Life of Baybars', vol. II, pp. 772–4; al-'Ayni, 'Le Collier de perles', *RHC Or.*, vol. II, p. 247; 'Eracles', vol. II, p. 462.

[28] D. Barag, 'A New Source concerning the Ultimate Borders of the Latin Kingdom of Jerusalem', *Israel Exploration Journal*, 29 (1979), pp. 199–200, 202, 207–8, 214–16, and P. M. Holt, 'Qalawun's Treaty with Acre in 1283', *English Historical Review*, 91 (1976), pp. 805–12.

only possible when there was a short-term injection of power provided by a crusading expedition.

### THE CRUSADES AND THE LATIN EAST, 1192–1291

We now turn to the impact of the crusades on the Latin East and the surrounding area. Later it will be seen that strictly temporary increases in Latin military power had many disadvantages, which were in some respects acknowledged but never rectified in the course of the century. Here it is necessary only to outline the crusades, although over and above the major and minor expeditions it is clear that people who were fulfilling a vow to crusade were a constant feature of the military establishment. In 1244, for example, a letter to Innocent IV complained that there were only a hundred pilgrim knights or footsoldiers in the Holy Land, to help to protect it against the Khorezmian threat.[29]

The first two crusades after the Third had relatively little impact on the Latin states, though for different reasons. The German crusade of 1197, which had succeeded in taking possession of Beirut, ground to a halt at the siege of Toron, following news of the death of Emperor Henry VI.[30] Only a few contingents from the Fourth Crusade journeyed to the Holy Land and some of these participated in raiding expeditions against the Muslims and in the war of succession in Antioch.[31] By contrast the Fifth Crusade (1217–21) made the greatest and most wide-ranging impact on the region of any crusade during this period. As already noted, its effects on the Latin Kingdom itself were relatively minor. However, the crusaders conducted raids into Muslim territory; they besieged, but did not capture, the recently built castle of Mt Tabor (one of the reasons for the preaching of a crusade); and they undertook building work at Caesarea and Château Pèlerin. The crusade then progressed into Egypt and captured Damietta in November 1219, after an eighteen-month siege. Subsequent efforts to advance towards Cairo in July 1221 were calamitous and resulted in a total collapse of the expedition. Whilst the crusade was in Egypt, the Muslims made peace offers

---

[29] *Chronica de Mailros*, ed. J. Stevenson (Bannatyne Club; Edinburgh, 1835), p. 158.
[30] Arnold of Lübeck, 'Chronica Slavorum', *MGHS*, vol. XXI, pp. 205–10; 'Eracles', vol. II, pp. 224–7; Ibn al-Athir, 'Kamel-Altevarykh', vol. II, pp. 85–9; E. N. Johnson, 'The Crusades of Frederick Barbarossa and Henry VI', in *A History of the Crusades*, gen. ed. K. M. Setton, vol. II (Madison, 1969), pp. 120–1.
[31] 'Eracles', vol. II, pp. 256–7, 260, 263.

which would have nearly reconstituted the Latin Kingdom in its pre-1187 state, apart from the Transjordan area. But these were rejected and the only other significant results of this campaign were the Muslims' dismantling of many strongpoints in Palestine which might have come within the new boundaries of the kingdom, and their capture of Caesarea. The garrison of Château Pèlerin managed to repulse an attack.[32]

It is an irony of Frederick II's crusade (1227–9) that an excommunicate was able to recover the Holy City and to make other territorial gains – although many of these gains, through diplomatic means, were theoretical rather than actual. Not surprisingly, his achievements were regarded with horror by many contemporary commentators. However, of greater benefit to the Latin states than the treaty with the sultan al-Kamil was a fair amount of work on fortifications. Before Frederick arrived at Acre in September 1228, work had already been carried out on the sea castle at Sidon, on Montfort and, after Easter 1228, on Caesarea.[33] In the winter of 1228–9, Frederick was involved in rebuilding at Jaffa.[34]

The next two significant crusading expeditions nearly overlapped. Between them, Theobald of Champagne and Richard of Cornwall managed to obtain treaties from the divided Muslims which gave hope for the long-term survival of the Latins in the east. Their other major achievement was the rebuilding of Ascalon, in which they both had some part. Theobald's crusade had been handicapped by the defeat of a large contingent of his force near Gaza. However, the Muslims' willingness to involve the Franks in their own squabbles did enable him to recover from this setback and engage in other military operations, including raids on Nablus and into the Jordan valley and an attack on Gaza, in the summer of 1240.[35]

---

[32] For the narrative history of the Fifth Crusade see J. M. Powell, *Anatomy of a Crusade, 1213–1221* (Philadelphia, 1986), pp. 123–93; Prawer, *Histoire du royaume*, vol. II, pp. 134–69; T. C. Van Cleve, 'The Fifth Crusade', in *A History of the Crusades*, gen. ed. K. M. Setton, vol. II (Madison, 1969), pp. 389–428; J. P. Donovan, *Pelagius and the Fifth Crusade* (Philadelphia, 1950), pp. 33–97. The Muslims also captured the Templars' fortified mill at Doc, near Acre (*History of the Patriarchs*, vol. IV, p. 45).

[33] *Chronique d'Ernoul et de Bernard le Trésorier*, ed. L. de Mas Latrie (Paris, 1871), pp. 458–9; 'Eracles', vol. II, p. 365; T. C. Van Cleve, 'The Crusade of Frederick II', in *A History of the Crusades*, gen. ed. K. M. Setton, vol. II (Madison, 1969), pp. 429–62.

[34] 'Eracles', vol. II, pp. 372–3; *History of the Patriarchs*, vol. IV, pp. 107, 109.

[35] 'Rothelin', pp. 526–56; Matthew Paris, *Chronica maiora*, vol. IV, pp. 138–45 (including a letter of Richard of Cornwall); *Gestes des Chiprois*, pp. 118–24; *History of the*

The first crusade of St Louis, like Theobald of Champagne's expedition, suffered a major reverse as a result of a battle. At Mansurah in February 1250, the crusaders were victorious but their heavy casualties, including the death of Louis's brother, Robert of Artois, gave the advantage to the Muslims, who finally defeated St Louis as he marched his force back from Mansurah in April. Despite the massive organisational achievements of the French monarchy in its preparations, it had again proved impossible, as on the Fifth Crusade, to project this degree of efficiency into the practicalities of a military campaign in Egypt. As already noted, St Louis returned to the Latin East following his release from captivity and remained there until 1254.[36]

St Louis's crusade was the final major expedition to the Holy Land. It is interesting to speculate about the possible impact of a successful crusade in Egypt on the Latin settlement: during the very last years of the kingdom's history, interest was still being expressed in Egypt as a target to ensure the security of the Latin Kingdom,[37] a theme also to be found in many of the *De recuperatione* texts. The final crusades before the fall of the Holy Land had little impact. The arrival in Acre in December 1269 of two bastard sons of the king of Aragon was greeted with a Muslim attack on the city which resulted in heavy Christian losses.[38] In 1271 the crusade of the Lord Edward organised two raiding expeditions, although one of these may also have tried to capture the important Muslim fortress of Qaqun. Edward nearly lost his life at the hands of a member of the Assassin sect and he had no part in the truce which was subsequently agreed with the Muslims in April 1272.[39] Despite Pope Gregory X's plans for another crusade which were mooted before and after the Council

---

*Patriarchs*, vol. IV, p. 217; Jackson, 'The Crusades of 1239–41', pp. 41–2; S. Painter, 'The Crusade of Theobald of Champagne and Richard of Cornwall, 1239–1241', in *A History of the Crusades*, gen. ed. K. M. Setton, vol. II (Madison, 1969), pp. 463–85.

[36] W. C. Jordan, *Louis IX and the Challenge of the Crusade* (Princeton, 1979), pp. 3–127, *passim*; J. R. Strayer, 'The Crusades of Louis IX', in *A History of the Crusades*, gen. ed. K. M. Setton, vol. II (Madison, 1969), pp. 490–508.

[37] See 'La Devise des Chemins de Babiloine', *Itinéraires à Jérusalem et Descriptions de la Terre Sainte*, ed. H. Michelant and G. Raynaud (Geneva, 1882), pp. 239–52. It is dated c. 1289–91 (p. xxxii).

[38] *Gestes des Chiprois*, pp. 183–5 (dated, wrongly, 1267); Ibn 'Abd al-Zahir, 'Life of Baybars', vol. II, pp. 726–9; 'Eracles', vol. II, pp. 457–8.

[39] 'Eracles', vol. II, pp. 461–2; Ibn 'Abd al-Zahir, 'Life of Baybars', vol. II, pp. 753, 762, 770–1, 776–7; *Gestes des Chiprois*, pp. 199–201; Walter of Guisborough, 'Chronica', ed. H. Rothwell, *Camden Third Series*, 89 (1957), pp. 207–10; see B. Beebe, 'Edward I and the Crusades' (unpublished Ph.D thesis, St Andrews, 1969), pp. 48–85.

of Lyons in 1274, the papacy and the European rulers became increasingly sidetracked by such issues as the conflict between Philip III of France and Alfonso of Castile, and a campaign against Peter of Aragon. Pope Martin IV, for example, is said to have shown 'almost pathological determination' in espousing the French cause against the Aragonese.[40] Major crusading projects concerned with the east would only be seriously contemplated again when the Latins had lost their grip on their possessions in the area.

### THE MUSLIM THREAT TO THE LATIN EAST

Warfare is an activity in which two sides oppose one another in a range of military operations, so its study requires an understanding of both groups' organisation, aims and performance. When we examine the Latin armies in greater detail it will also be necessary to deal with the Muslims, who were their principal adversaries. But before this the political and military background in Islam will briefly be considered and some suggestions made regarding the general tactics and strategy which the Muslims employed against their Christian opponents.

### *Aiyubid politics and the Latin states, 1193–1250*

Saladin, the sultan of Egypt and Syria from 1174 until 1193, was able to ensure that his family inherited his lands on his death. However, this inheritance did not go to a single ruler. Rather, the Aiyubid empire became a confederacy of local principalities, in which each ruler owed no more than formal allegiance to the sultan. This structure persisted under both al-'Adil (Saladin's brother) and his son al-Kamil, each of whom was able, after a time, to impose his authority on most of his relations and to provide the empire with a certain degree of unity. It was only under al-'Adil's grandson, as-Salih Aiyub, who ruled in Cairo and Damascus until 1249, that some of the features of a more centralised monarchy began to appear.[41]

The federal structure of the Aiyubid empire meant that

---

[40] M. Purcell, *Papal Crusading Policy, 1244–1291* (Leiden, 1975), p. 174; P. A. Throop, *Criticism of the Crusade* (Amsterdam, 1940), pp. 262–82.

[41] Humphreys, *From Saladin to the Mongols*, pp. 10, 41–66, 75, 97–125, 239–40, 299–301; Gibb, 'The Aiyubids', pp. 693–4.

throughout the period 1193–1249, its princes were often at odds with one another. Indeed, the history of the Aiyubids often appears to be little more than a sequence of shifting alliances and family feuds. This had some benefits for their Latin neighbours. Christian successes in northern Syria reflected the disunity of the Muslim rulers in that area. And, as already noted, the territorial concessions made by al-Kamil and, in particular, as-Salih Isma'il and as-Salih Aiyub were products of the search which each made for Christian support in the face of opposition from his co-religionists. On the other hand, the Aiyubids were able to overcome the two crusades into Egypt and this was no mean achievement, given that on each occasion their problems were exacerbated by the death of their sultan. In 1218–19, the demise of al-'Adil caused a temporary crisis amongst his sons, but al-Kamil combined with his brother al-Mu'azzam, operating in Egypt and Palestine respectively, to defeat the Franks.[42] A similar problem had to be faced in November 1249, when as-Salih Aiyub died. His former concubine and queen, Shajar ad-Durr, joined with other advisors and generals of the dead sultan to oppose St Louis's crusade. Early in the following year as-Salih Aiyub's son Turanshah responded to the summons of Shajar ad-Durr and the rest of the junta and hurried to Egypt to take command of the Muslim army; but by the time final terms had been agreed with the defeated crusaders, Turanshah himself had been murdered and power had passed from the hands of the Aiyubids into those of the Mamluks.[43]

## The Mamluks, the Mongols and the Latin states, 1250–1291

The Mamluks' seizure of power in Egypt, following the murder of Turanshah in May 1250, appears to have been a relatively easy process. Shajar ad-Durr became sultanah for a month; she then married Aybeg, a middle-ranking Turkish Mamluk emir, and abdicated in his favour.[44] However, subsequent events showed that the foundations of the *Bahri* Mamluk sultanate were by no

---

[42] Humphreys, *From Saladin to the Mongols*, pp. 161–70; Gibb, 'The Aiyubids', pp. 698–700.

[43] R. Irwin, *The Middle East in the Middle Ages: The Early Mamluk Sultanate 1250–1382* (London, 1986), pp. 19–23; M. M. Ziada, 'The Mamluk Sultans to 1293', in *A History of the Crusades*, gen. ed. K. M. Setton, vol. II (Madison, 1969), pp. 738–41.

[44] Al-Makrizi, *Histoire d'Egypte*, p. 547; Ibn 'Abd al-Zahir, 'Life of Baybars', vol. II, p. 321; Ziada, 'Mamluk Sultans', p. 741; Irwin, *Mamluk Sultanate*, p. 26.

means entirely solid at this stage. First, the *Bahris* themselves were not yet strong enough to overcome opposition in Egypt. Although it is customary to date the start of the *Bahri* Mamluk regime to 1250, none of the five rulers in the period 1250–60 was actually a *Bahri* and two were openly opposed to the *Bahri* faction.[45] Secondly, the Mamluks had to deal with the legitimist claims of the Aiyubids. By the autumn of 1250, the Aiyubid prince al-Nasir Yusuf had established himself as the ruler of an impressive empire in Syria which gave him access to an army of roughly 9,000 men. He marched into Egypt in February 1251 but was defeated by Aybeg at the battle of Kura. This did not mark the end of the Aiyubid challenge to the Mamluk regime, but the Aiyubids had failed to take what had been a great opportunity for them to regain control of their empire.[46]

Throughout the 1250s, however, it became increasingly apparent that the greatest threat to the Mamluks (and potentially, at this time, to the Latin East) came from the Mongols. In 1253 Hulegu, the brother of the Great Khan Mongke, left Mongolia with a huge army. The Assassins surrendered to him in 1256; he continued on to Baghdad, which was captured in 1258, and then Damascus, which fell in 1260.[47] Al-Nasir Yusuf had failed to respond positively to the Mongol invasion and it was now clear that the Mamluks, not the Aiyubids, had the responsibility for the defence of Islam. The Mamluk sultan Kutuz prepared to confront the Mongol army commanded by Kitbugha, which now numbered between 10,000 and 20,000 men.[48] The Mamluks defeated this contingent of the Mongol army at the battle of 'Ain Jalut in September 1260. The following month Kutuz was murdered and the *Bahri* Mamluk Baybars, who had been one of the chief conspirators against the former sultan, took his place.[49]

---

[45] Irwin, *Mamluk Sultanate*, pp. 23, 26. The *Bahris* were members of the *Bahriyah* regiment, which had been created by as-Salih Aiyub. See below, p. 33.

[46] Humphreys, *From Saladin to the Mongols*, pp. 305–33; Irwin, *Mamluk Sultanate*, pp. 27–8; Ziada, 'Mamluk Sultans', pp. 741–2; Gibb, 'The Aiyubids', pp. 712–14.

[47] D. Morgan, *The Mongols* (Oxford, 1986), pp. 147–55. According to the *Gestes des Chiprois* (p. 161), the Mongol army numbered 120,000 men. For the Mongol threat to the Latin East and the Latins' support for the Mamluks prior to the battle of 'Ain Jalut, see P. Jackson, 'The Crisis in the Holy Land in 1260', *English Historical Review*, 95 (1980), pp. 481–513.

[48] Irwin, *Mamluk Sultanate*, pp. 32–3; Jackson, 'The Crisis', p. 492. Hulegu had withdrawn the bulk of his army to north-western Persia following the death of Mongke (D. Morgan, *The Mongols*, p. 156).

[49] Ziada, 'Mamluk Sultans', pp. 745–6; Irwin, *Mamluk Sultanate*, pp. 33–4, 37.

Baybars was able to re-establish the unity between Egypt and Syria which had not really existed since the reign of Saladin. His attacks against the Latins substantially reduced the size of their territories.[50] In the spring of 1265, Caesarea, Haifa and Arsuf were captured. Saphet was taken in July 1266, after campaigns which had included the capture of some smaller fortresses around Tripoli. In the spring of 1268, Christian losses included Jaffa, Beaufort and Antioch; in early 1271 Baybars conquered Chastel Blanc, Crac des Chevaliers and Gibelcar, and later in the year Montfort was captured.[51]

Baybars died in June 1277, apparently after excessive consumption of fermented mare's milk; it was rumoured that he had been poisoned. His sons were unable to sustain his dynasty and by December 1279 another *Bahri* Mamluk, Kalavun, had claimed the sultanate.[52] The gradual reduction of the Franks' possessions continued. In May 1285 Margat fell,[53] followed by Latakia in 1287[54] and Tripoli in 1289.[55] Kalavun was already preparing for the siege of Acre when he died in late 1290;[56] his son, al-Ashraf Khalil, took up the task and completed it in May 1291,[57] after which the remaining Frankish strongpoints were rapidly captured or abandoned.[58]

### The Aiyubid and Mamluk armies

Apart from times when crusades were assisting the Latin East, a perennial problem for the Christians was a lack of manpower. It is unlikely that they could ever raise more than about 2,000 mounted troops with the equipment of knights on a permanent basis.[59] The total strength of the armies of the Aiyubid

---

[50] Baybars's achievement is all the more remarkable since his interests were by no means confined to the Latin East; this was only one of a number of areas of his concern, as is reflected in his biography by Ibn 'Abd al-Zahir.

[51] Ibn 'Abd al-Zahir, 'Life of Baybars', vol. II, pp. 554–72, 582–600, 636–9, 641–6, 656–64, 742–5, 748–9, 756–7.

[52] Ziada, 'Mamluk Sultans', p. 750; Irwin, *Mamluk Sultanate*, pp. 57–8, 62–4.

[53] Ibn 'Abd al-Zahir, 'Vie de Kalavun', in J. F. Michaud, *Bibliothèque des Croisades*, vol. IV (Paris, 1829), pp. 548–50; *Gestes des Chiprois*, pp. 217–18 (wrongly dated to 1284).

[54] *Gestes des Chiprois*, p. 230; Ibn 'Abd al-Zahir, 'Vie de Kalavun', in Michaud, *Bibliothèque*, vol. IV, p. 561.

[55] *Gestes des Chiprois*, pp. 234–8 (dated 1288); al-Makrizi, *Histoire des Sultans Mamlouks de l'Egypte*, trans. M. E. Quatremère (2 vols., Paris, 1845), vol. II (a), pp. 102–3.

[56] Ziada, 'Mamluk Sultans', p. 753.

[57] *Gestes des Chiprois*, pp. 241–56 (one of the most detailed of numerous accounts).

[58] See Prawer, *Histoire du royaume*, vol. II, p. 557.   [59] See below, pp. 51–2.

confederation, by contrast, was approximately 22,000 men, with a standing army in Egypt of between 10,000 and 12,000 cavalry.[60] The army of Baybars was even larger; it may have numbered 40,000 men.[61]

The Mamluks who seized power in Egypt in 1250 were military slaves. However, the term 'slave' is not used here with its menial or degrading implications. The Mamluk's slavery was the first stage in a career which could, after a long period of training, enable him to occupy some of the highest offices of state. By the ninth and tenth centuries the employment of Mamluks (who were usually of Turkish origin) had become widespread throughout Muslim territories.[62] Turkish Mamluks played a prominent role in the destruction of Fatimid power in Egypt, but under Saladin they were of comparatively little importance, at least in terms of affairs of state, until the very end of the reign.[63] Their role under al-'Adil is not well documented. Under al-Kamil, their influence grew, but it was during the reign of as-Salih Aiyub that there was a most noticeable increase in the number of Mamluks engaged by the sultan. Even before he became ruler, Aiyub had started to buy large numbers of Turkish Kipchak slaves, who were available because of the upheavals which had been caused by the Mongol invasion of central Asia. He created a new, elite Mamluk regiment of between 800 and 1,000 men, the *Bahriyah*, which was made up largely of Kipchaks.[64] The regiment's first great success came at the battle of Mansurah in 1250, when it destroyed the force led by Robert of Artois.[65]

In return for their services the Mamluks received, for a limited period, the tax revenues, either in money or in kind, levied on a particular area of land or other source of income. These allocations

---

[60] R. S. Humphreys, 'The Emergence of the Mamluk Army', *Studia Islamica*, 45 (1977), pp. 74–6. Some Christian estimates are 7,000 mounted (Oliver of Paderborn, 'Historia', p. 260) and 4,000 mounted, besides infantry and, in reserve, the Egyptian army (Joinville, *Histoire de Saint Louis*, p. 146). Such estimates have to be treated with considerable caution.

[61] P. Thorau, 'The Battle of 'Ayn Jalut: A Re-examination', in *Crusade and Settlement*, ed. P. W. Edbury, p. 237; D. Ayalon, 'Studies on the Structure of the Mamluk Army', *Bulletin of the School of Oriental and African Studies*, 15 (1953), pp. 222–3. The figures available vary considerably.    [62] Irwin, *Mamluk Sultanate*, pp. 3–5.

[63] D. Ayalon, 'Aspects of the Mamluk Phenomenon: Ayyubids, Kurds and Turks', *Der Islam*, 54:1 (1977), pp. 1–8; Humphreys, *From Saladin to the Mongols*, p. 34.

[64] Ayalon, 'Ayyubids, Kurds and Turks', pp. 21–3; Humphreys, *From Saladin to the Mongols*, pp. 222, 268; Irwin, *Mamluk Sultanate*, pp. 12, 17–18.

[65] Al-Makrizi, *Histoire d'Egypte*, pp. 526–7; Abu'l-Fida, 'Annales', p. 128; Irwin, *Mamluk Sultanate*, p. 20.

of revenue were known as *iqta*. During Baybars's first campaign in Palestine, *iqtas* were distributed to his emirs around Nazareth and Mt Tabor.[66]

The other main element of the Aiyubid and early Mamluk armies was the *halqa* (literally, the 'ring') which consisted largely of free (that is, non-Mamluk) cavalry. It first appeared as an elite bodyguard during the reign of Saladin. Its development under al-'Adil and al-Kamil is not recorded. During the reign of as-Salih Aiyub, however, the *halqa* was built up as a large cavalry army which was dispersed throughout Egypt, to be mobilised only for specific expeditions.[67] It continued to play an important role in the Mamluk armies, at least until the end of the thirteenth century. In the second half of the thirteenth century, it was augmented by large numbers of soldiers from immigrant tribes (including Mongols); these were known as *wafidiya*.[68] Members of the *halqa* could become emirs and hold *iqtas*, but the highest levels of the army and administration were generally the preserve of the Mamluks. In addition to the Mamluks themselves and the *halqa*, the Mamluk army would also have included volunteers for the *jihad*, and Bedouin and Turcoman cavalry who were recruited for specific campaigns.[69]

Baybars introduced significant improvements in the equipment, clothing and pay of the army.[70] In mid-1264, he ordered emirs to provide themselves and their Mamluks with complete equipment, and a military review was ordered for August of that year; following this, the troops went on to target practice.[71] In 1267, a hippodrome was constructed in Cairo and this became the main centre for the army's training exercises. The training, which was known as *furusiyya*, included practice in the use of the bow, the lance and the mace, games of polo and wrestling, hunting and horse-racing. The exercises became so popular during Baybars's reign that the numbers taking part had to be restricted, in case

---

[66] Irwin, *Mamluk Sultanate*, p. 11; R. Irwin, '*Iqta*' and the End of the Crusader States', *The Eastern Mediterranean Lands in the Period of the Crusades*, ed. P. M. Holt (Warminster, 1977), pp. 65–7.

[67] Ayalon, 'Ayyubids, Kurds and Turks', pp. 15–16; Ayalon, 'Studies on the Mamluk Army' (1953), pp. 448–9; Irwin, *Mamluk Sultanate*, p. 18.

[68] Ayalon, 'Studies on the Mamluk Army' (1953), p. 451; D. Ayalon, 'The Wafidiya in the Mamluk Kingdom', *Islamic Culture*, 25 (1951), pp. 89–104. Some *wafidiya* were able to join Mamluk regiments, but the majority enlisted in the *halqa*.

[69] Irwin, *Mamluk Sultanate*, p. 50.

[70] Ayalon, 'Studies on the Mamluk Army' (1953), p. 223.

[71] Ibn 'Abd al-Zahir, 'Life of Baybars', vol. II, pp. 514–15, 529–33.

the hippodrome became overcrowded.[72] Baybars again showed concern for the training of the army in October 1268, when he urged the practice of spear-throwing and archery. He was also interested, in 1272, in the manufacture of arrows.[73] Baybars's concern with arrow production and target practice is not surprising, since the principal Muslim weapon, used by the mounted troops who were the backbone of the army, was the bow. Its potency was recognised from the end of the tenth century to the end of the twelfth[74] and was also apparent in the thirteenth century, for which there are many examples of the effect of a shower of arrows, 'which caused greater obscurity than either rain or hail'.[75]

In open battle, Muslim soldiers posed a number of problems which Christian troops had to overcome if they were to have any chance of success. The Muslims' battle tactics will be considered in more detail later,[76] but in summary they relied on mobility, discipline and an ability to fight at close quarters if necessary. The Muslim soldiers were lightly armed and rode fast horses. They were therefore mobile enough to operate comparatively close to their heavier Christian opponents. They waited until the Christians either had to commit themselves to a charge (at which point the Muslims would scatter and retreat before reforming) or had sustained so many injuries that they were able to close in with a reasonable amount of impunity. Their mobility often allowed them to outflank Christian troops to gain additional advantage. Discipline enabled them to use manoeuvres such as feigned retreats and ambushes and it was also apparent when, despite their preference for the bow, they fought in close combat with Christian forces.

In March 1264, Baybars ordered his subjects 'to remove all

---

[72] D. Ayalon, 'Notes on the *Furusiyya* Exercises and Games in the Mamluk Sultanate', *Scripta Hierosolymitana*, 9 (1961), pp. 37–9, 44, 46.

[73] Ibn 'Abd al-Zahir, 'Life of Baybars', vol. II, pp. 696–7, 777.

[74] D. Ayalon, 'Aspects of the Mamluk Phenomenon: The Importance of the Mamluk Institution', *Der Islam*, 53:2 (1976), pp. 218–23.

[75] '...que pluie ne gresil ne peust pas faire greigneur oscurté' ('Rothelin', p. 544). Muslim mounted archers probably used a slightly lighter bow than footsoldiers, because of the difficulty of firing from the saddle. Assuming that lightweight arrows were also used, then this would help to explain the apparent lack of penetration of the Muslim bow, particularly when the Muslims were kept at a distance by Christian archers and crossbowmen. See W. F. Paterson, 'The Archers of Islam', *Journal of the Economic and Social History of the Orient*, 9 (1966), pp. 82–5. See also below, p. 160.

[76] See below, chapter 4.

excuse for abstaining from the Holy War'.[77] When the occasion
demanded, large quantities of soldiers could be recruited into the
Muslim armies, though they were often of doubtful quality. On
the Fifth Crusade, for example, when the crusaders first arrived
opposite Damietta, great numbers of men volunteered for the
*jihad*. As the threat to Damietta increased, al-Kamil ordered half
the occupants of Cairo to join the Muslim army, either
voluntarily or by compulsion. Finally, when the crusaders set out
from Damietta towards Cairo, every capable Egyptian was
mobilised to deal with the threat; only women, old men and
children were left behind.[78] Joinville observed conscripts of this
type in action at the battle of Mansurah. The Muslims sent some
peasants against two of the king's sergeants; the peasants
bombarded the sergeants with clods of earth.[79] Not all Muslim
infantry were so poorly armed, however, and there were
occasions, such as the battle of Gaza in 1239, when they were used
to complement the mounted troops.[80]

   Muslim footsoldiers may have been allotted more specialised
tasks during the siege of a Christian strongpoint. Muslim methods
in such situations, as will be seen in more detail later,[81] relied on
three principal elements: the use of ballistic weapons, mining and
a frontal assault. It was the efficient combination of these forms of
attack that broke down Christian defenders even when the latter
were protected by the strongest of their fortresses.

   The other main form of Muslim military activity was the
raid.[82] This did not aim directly at the acquisition of territory, but
nonetheless inflicted considerable damage on Christian lands and
people. However, whereas the Christians generally used the raid
as little more than a method of destruction, the Muslims
employed such expeditions as part of their overall military
strategy, which aimed at the extinction of the Latin states.
Raids were used to distract attention from the intended target of
a campaign and to prevent assistance being offered to that target.
They could also weaken a strongpoint which at that time might
be considered too well defended to besiege, or which might not
fall without a protracted siege campaign. Acre, for example, was

[77] Ibn 'Abd al-Zahir, 'Life of Baybars', vol. II, p. 507.
[78] *History of the Patriarchs*, vol. IV, pp. 44, 58, 74–5.
[79] Joinville, *Histoire de Saint Louis*, p. 132. Another peasant threw Greek fire, which
   nearly set light to one of the sergeants.        [80] See below, pp. 179–80.
[81] See below, chapter 6.        [82] See below, chapter 5.

raided by the Muslims throughout the century, but particularly in the 1260s.[83]

The Muslims deployed their resources carefully as they sought to achieve a desired end – the elimination of a Latin presence in the area – which might not be achieved in their lifetime but which even a small act of aggression could bring nearer. In a thirty-year period the expulsion of the Latins was achieved by various methods which all ultimately intended the same result. The Latins' defence against this assault was by no means so coherent.

### CIVIL WAR AND CHRISTIAN RIVALRY

In 1225 Isabel, the daughter of John of Brienne and the heiress to the Kingdom of Jerusalem, married the Emperor Frederick II. She was then crowned queen of Jerusalem. Frederick immediately demanded from John all the rights of the crown and for the next sixty years, with the brief exception of Hugh of Antioch-Lusignan, control of the kingdom was exercised by a succession of regents and lieutenants. These circumstances helped to produce an unstable political situation which found expression in a stream of constitutional and juridical disputes concerning the *de jure* rights, and limitations, of those who attempted to govern.[84] They also contributed to two major outbreaks of civil war. As has already been pointed out, medieval warfare was generally a low-key affair, but in view of the Latins' persistent manpower problems, civil conflict inevitably lessened their ability to deal with their Muslim neighbours.

From 1228 to 1242 the Palestinian barons, led by the Ibelin family, fought with the troops of Frederick II and his allies for control of Cyprus and the Latin Kingdom. It was fortunate from the Christian point of view that this coincided with a period of Muslim disunity and, paradoxically, the Latins were able to increase their territories through diplomatic endeavours at the same time as they fought amongst themselves. Most of the military engagements in this conflict came in the period from 1229 to 1233 and the warfare was unusual in that battles played a significant part in its outcome. In July 1229 the Ibelin faction

---

[83] See below, pp. 204–5.
[84] See J. S. C. Riley-Smith, *Feudal Nobility*, pp. 159–228, *passim*.

fought for control of Cyprus with the five *baillis* Frederick II had left in charge of the island. The Ibelins' victory at Nicosia was the platform for their subsequent success in the sieges of Kyrenia, Kantara and Dieudamour. The Ibelins soon captured Kyrenia but the other two strongpoints held out for ten months. Dieudamour offered particularly stout resistance and the Ibelins struggled to maintain a viable blockade. Both sieges were eventually ended by starvation.

In July 1230, the treaty of San Germano brought about a temporary reconciliation between Pope Gregory IX and Frederick II and encouraged the latter to intervene once more in the Latin East. A force led by Frederick's marshal, Richard Filangieri, besieged Beirut in the autumn of 1231, whereas the Ibelins had anticipated an attack on Cyprus. Although the threat to the city was raised by an Ibelin relief force which was sent into the citadel, baronial prospects remained uncertain in the first half of 1232. On Cyprus, Aimery Barlais, one of the five imperial *baillis*, overran most of the island except for Dieudamour and Buffavento. The defeat of a poorly organised Ibelin force at Casal Imbert (ten miles north of Acre) was a further setback and a number of villages had to be sold to finance a new expedition to Cyprus.

At Agridi in June 1232, a battle again caused a reversal in the fortunes of the antagonists. The Ibelins, despite being heavily outnumbered, were victorious and Dieudamour was relieved. The imperial forces fled to Kyrenia. A frontal assault on the town by the Ibelins failed and the garrison only surrendered after a year-long siege. They were allowed to join their colleagues on the mainland at Tyre, which was still held by Frederick's forces.[85] The position remained largely unchanged for the next decade. The Ibelins controlled Cyprus and most of the Latin Kingdom, whilst Frederick's troops had possession of Tyre. Diplomatic efforts to resolve this deadlock and outbursts of violence, often involving members of the pro-Ibelin Commune of Acre, were frequent.[86] One of the worst incidents, in the autumn of 1241, led

[85] *Gestes des Chiprois*, pp. 58–68, 77–114, 116–17; 'Eracles', vol. II, pp. 376–7, 380, 385–402; *Chronique d'Amadi*, ed. R. de Mas Latrie (Paris, 1891), pp. 140–79, 182 (adding little to the account of the *Gestes des Chiprois*).

[86] J. S. C. Riley-Smith, 'The Assise sur la ligece and the Commune of Acre', *Traditio*, 27 (1971), pp. 194–204; J. S. C. Riley-Smith, *Feudal Nobility*, pp. 181–2, 199–209. The Commune of Acre developed out of the Confraternity of St Andrew, which had been founded before 1187. See below, p. 77.

to the Hospitallers' quarter in Acre being besieged for six months because its occupants were suspected of complicity in an attempt by Filangieri to seize control of the city.[87]

In 1242 the Ibelins attacked Tyre. The defence of Lothair Filangieri was effective until the Ibelins captured his brother Richard, who had been shipwrecked. Lothair was forced to capitulate and the Lombard presence in Palestine was thus terminated.[88] The cost of this success must have been great, however. The correspondence of Gregory IX reveals the pope's concerns about the conflict and the damage which was being done to the kingdom.[89] Moreover, the drain on resources was considerable. Philip of Novara believed that in 1231 Richard Filangieri had with him 600 knights, 100 mounted squires, 700 footsoldiers and 3,000 marines.[90] The forces available to the kingdom would have been hard-pressed to cope with such opposition. The Ibelins had frequent recourse to mercenaries and troops from Genoa and Venice; the Venetians, for example, played a leading role in the capture of Tyre in 1242, in return for commercial privileges in that city.[91]

From 1256 the Italian city republics were again involved in warfare in the eastern Mediterranean, but this time they were at the centre of a conflict which subsequently drew in many of the other factions in the Latin Kingdom. The initial dispute concerned land in Acre which was owned by the monastery of St Sabas and claimed by both Genoa and Venice. Genoa's early successes were reversed after its erstwhile ally, Pisa, agreed to a ten-year alliance

---

[87] *Gestes des Chiprois*, pp. 124–7; 'Annales de Terre Sainte', ed. R. Röhricht and G. Raynaud, *Archives de l'Orient Latin*, 2 (1884), p. 441; see J. S. C. Riley-Smith, *Knights of St John*, pp. 179–80. For the date of the Lombard attack on Acre, see P. Jackson, 'The End of Hohenstaufen Rule in Syria', *Historical Research*, 59 (1986), pp. 33–4.

[88] *Gestes des Chiprois*, pp. 127–35; 'Eracles', vol. II, pp. 422, 426–7; *Urkunden zur älteren Handels- und Staatsgeschichte der Republik Venedig mit besonderer Beziehung auf Byzanz und die Levante*, ed. G. Tafel and G. Thomas, vol. II (Vienna, 1856), pp. 356–7. Dr Jackson has argued convincingly for 1242, rather than 1243, as the date of the fall of Tyre. The later date has generally been accepted because, according to Philip of Novara (in *Gestes des Chiprois*, pp. 128–9), Conrad's coming of age (in 1243) terminated the regency of Frederick. This allowed the Ibelins to appoint a new regent and attack Tyre. However, as Jackson shows, Conrad's attainment of his majority would not necessarily have marked the end of Frederick's regency. Moreover, dates in both narrative and documentary sources suggest 1242 as the more likely date of the capture of Tyre by the Ibelins (P. Jackson, 'The End of Hohenstaufen Rule', pp. 20–36).

[89] Gregory IX, *Registre*, ed. L. Auvray (4 vols., Paris, 1896–1955), nos. 836–8, 840, 1841, 2041, 2702–8, 2771, 2782, 2968–76. [90] *Gestes des Chiprois*, p. 77.

[91] *Urkunden der Republik Venedig*, vol. II, pp. 355–6.

with the Venetians. A Venetian fleet under Lorenzo Tiepolo broke the harbour chain which protected Acre's port, burned a number of Genoese ships and captured and destroyed the fortified properties of St Sabas. The Genoese, however, were able to retain control of their quarter, although their opponents subjected them to a blockade. In 1258 constitutional and military developments forced them to flee to Tyre. John of Jaffa's skilful handling of the regency laws caused the feudatories to switch their support to the Venetians, leaving Philip of Montfort as one of the few Genoese allies. In June he led an army to Acre, where it was joined by Hospitaller troops: a Genoese fleet was to attack the city simultaneously. The plan went awry as a Venetian fleet overwhelmed the Genoese sea force. Philip and the Genoese retreated back to Tyre and the Genoese quarter was overrun.

By 1261, something approaching normality had returned to Acre, but the Genoese did not receive their quarter back until 1288 and fighting between the Italian fleets remained a constant threat to the security of the area, even though such conflicts had little to do with the Latin East. In 1267, for example, a Genoese force was able to capture the Tower of Flies (strategically placed at the harbour entrance) and blockade the port of Acre. It was at least twelve days before it was driven off by a Venetian fleet.[92] The Muslims were also involved in the conflict. In 1266, Baybars had an arrangement with the Genoese, whereby he provided troops to support a Genoese fleet in an attack on Acre. But the Genoese failed to arrive.[93]

Contemporaries recognised the damage that such outbreaks of violence were doing to the Holy Land, and both Alexander IV and Urban IV tried to achieve a peace. Urban considered the problem of internecine strife in the context of the threat from outside the kingdom: 'at one time with growing fear about the Mongols, at another with rising terror about the heathens...'.[94] Another writer rued the damage which the War of St Sabas had

---

[92] *Gestes des Chiprois*, pp. 149–56, 186–7; 'Rothelin', pp. 633–5; 'Annales de Terre Sainte', pp. 447–8; 'Annales Januenses', vol. IV, ed. C. Imperiale di St Angelo, in *Fonti per la storia d'Italia Scrittori*, vol. XIII (Rome, 1926), pp. 30–6; Andrew Dandolo, 'Chronica', *RISNS*, vol. XII, pt I, pp. 307–9; Prawer, *Histoire du royaume*, vol. II, pp. 365–71; D. Jacoby, 'Crusader Acre in the Thirteenth Century: Urban Layout and Topography', *Studi Medievali*, 3rd Series, 20 (1979), pp. 7, 9–10, 18–19, 26, 28–30, 34–5, 37–8. [93] Ibn 'Abd al-Zahir, 'Life of Baybars', vol. II, pp. 588–9. [94] '...nunc timore imminente de Tartaris, nunc excrescente formidine de paganis...' (Urban IV, *Registre*, ed. J. Guiraud *et al.* (5 vols., Paris, 1899–1958), no. 867).

caused in Acre, 'As a result of which nearly all the towers and the fortified houses of Acre were completely destroyed, with the exception of the religious houses, and there were killed in that war 20,000 men on one side or the other ...'.[95] This high casualty figure, if approximately correct, would have been worrying at any time, given the Latins' persistent manpower shortages. However, as we saw earlier,[96] in the 1250s the Mongols had become a potentially major threat to the Latin East. In 1260 the leaders of the Latin states, including Thomas Agni, the legate, and Thomas Berard, the Master of the Templars, sent letters to the west describing the Mongols' progress and appealing for support. It was stated that apart from Acre and Tyre a total of only ten castles were ready to oppose the Mongol army. These ten sites were three Templar castles in Antioch, two in Tripoli (possibly Tortosa and Chastel Blanc) and two in Jerusalem (presumably Château Pèlerin and Saphet), plus two Hospitaller castles in Tripoli (probably Crac des Chevaliers and Margat, though the latter was in Antioch) and one castle in Jerusalem held by the Teutonic Knights (presumably Montfort). Moreover, damage to the economy of Acre, caused by the absence from the city of Genoese merchants, seems to have added to the problems which the Orders encountered in finding sufficient mercenaries to garrison the strongpoints.[97] If the Mongol threat had materialised then the effects of the War of St Sabas would have contributed to a major crisis for the Latin East. This particular menace evaporated, but the Latin states still had to face the challenge of the Mamluks.

Conflict amongst Christians was not only a feature of the Kingdom of Jerusalem. In Antioch and Tripoli, feuding constantly produced military encounters. Throughout the first

---

[95] 'Dont il avint que prez que toutes les torz et les forz maissonz d'Acre furent toutes abatues forz que tant seulement les maissonz de relegion, et i ot bien morz de cele guerre .xx..m. homes que d'une part que d'autre...' ('Rothelin', p. 635).

[96] See above, p. 31, and note 47.

[97] Letter of Thomas Agni and others in 'Lettre des Chrétiens de Terre-Sainte à Charles d'Anjou', ed. H. F. Delaborde, *Revue de l'Orient Latin*, 2 (1894), p. 214; letter of Thomas Berard (dated 1261, presumably in error) in 'Annales monasterii Burtonensis', ed. H. R. Luard, in *Annales monastici*, vol. 1 (Rolls Series, 36; London, 1864), p. 493. However, as P. Jackson points out (in 'The Crisis', pp. 487, note 1, and 492, note 2), a better rendering of Thomas's letter is in the verbatim account given by Gui de Basainville, Visitor *in partibus cismarinis*, in *Monumenta Boica*, ed. Academia Scientiarum Boica, vol. xxix, pt 2 (Munich, 1831), pp. 200–1. This is the version which has been used here. See also 'Rothelin', p. 636.

twenty years of the thirteenth century, the dispute over the rights of succession to Antioch involved not only the Antiochenes but Armenians, Muslims and the Templars and Hospitallers.[98] When Bohemond III died in 1201, Raymond Roupen, his grandson by his eldest son Raymond (and also the grandson of Leon II of Armenia) should have succeeded him, but instead Bohemond's younger son, Bohemond IV, took control in defiance of Raymond Roupen's rights. The Templars, who were disputing ownership of Baghras with Leon, supported Bohemond: the Hospitallers remained officially neutral until 1205, when they became open supporters of the Armenian faction.[99] In 1203, Armenian troops were able to enter Antioch, but the Templars had fortified their positions within the city and they drove the Armenians out. Bohemond, the Templars and their Aleppan allies then carried out raids in the area around Baghras, prompting Leon to take possession of territory which included the Templar castles of Roche de Roussel and Roche Guillaume.[100]

The efforts of papal legates to achieve a settlement failed and, in 1207, the Armenians again nearly succeeded in an attempt to take Antioch. By 1210, matters were clearly getting out of hand and Innocent III, who had hitherto adopted a conciliatory approach, was prepared to sanction a more aggressive response against Leon. When the Templars sent reinforcements into the area, the Armenians destroyed a number of villages and confiscated Templar possessions. They also attacked a Templar relief force, killing one of the party and wounding several others, including William of Chartres, the Master of the Temple. Innocent consequently excommunicated Leon and ordered John of Brienne to organise a punitive expedition against the Armenians. The Templars sent as many mounted and footsoldiers as they could spare and John, though he did not go himself, provided fifty knights. This force joined troops from Antioch and raided the area around Baghras, possibly besieging the castle itself. Faced by this threat, Leon agreed to return the castle to the

[98] See Cahen, *La Syrie*, pp. 590–635.

[99] J. S. C. Riley-Smith, 'Templars and Teutonic Knights', p. 102; J. S. C. Riley-Smith, *Knights of St John*, pp. 154–5.

[100] Innocent III, 'Opera omnia', vol. CCXV, cols. 504, 689–90; *Gestes des Chiprois*, p. 16; 'Eracles', vol. II, p. 257; J. S. C. Riley-Smith, 'Templars and Teutonic Knights', pp. 102–3; J. S. C. Riley-Smith, *Knights of St John*, p. 153.

Templars (though at an unspecified date) and a truce was arranged.[101]

The Templars had to wait for Baghras until 1216, when the Armenians finally succeeded in taking Antioch. But Raymond Roupen's regime soon proved unpopular in the city and in 1219 a conspiracy returned control to Bohemond. Raymond resisted briefly in the citadel but then fled, leaving a Hospitaller garrison which Bohemond besieged.[102] The Hospitallers' right to hold the citadel was subsequently confirmed by the papal legate Pelagius. The precise date of the Order's capitulation cannot be established; three letters from Honorius III, dated winter 1225–6, indicated that by this date Bohemond had retaken the citadel and the Hospitallers were entitled to use force in response.[103] It is unlikely, however, that the siege of the citadel had continued for six years. By the mid-1220s Bohemond's position was quite secure, and it was over thirty years before his grandson, Bohemond VI, would again face civil disobedience on a large scale.

The Embriaco lords of Gibelet have been described as the 'most resolute opponents' of the princes of Antioch. They also enjoyed an extremely close relationship with the Hospitallers. In 1212, for example, Guy I of Gibelet became a *confrater*, and in 1274 Guy II placed his family under their protection.[104] In 1258, the Embriacos rebelled against the rule of Bohemond VI.[105] Supported by many of the local barons and the Hospitallers, they destroyed land around Tripoli. Bohemond, with the assistance of the Templars, attempted to repulse the assault but was defeated and wounded. Peace was only restored when Bohemond was able to arrange for Bertrand Embriaco, a cousin of Guy I and the leader of the revolt, to be murdered by some serfs.[106]

This incident, not surprisingly, left much bitterness and in 1278

---

[101] Innocent III, 'Opera omnia', vol. ccxvi, cols. 310–11, 430–2; 'Eracles', vol. ii, pp. 137, 317–18; J. S. C. Riley-Smith, 'Templars and Teutonic Knights', pp. 103–7.

[102] 'Eracles', vol. ii, p. 318; J. S. C. Riley-Smith, 'Templars and Teutonic Knights', p. 107.

[103] *Cartulaire général de l'ordre des Hospitaliers de St-Jean de Jérusalem (1100–1310)*, ed. J. Delaville Le Roulx (4 vols., Paris, 1894–1906), nos. 1824, 1834, 1837.

[104] J. S. C. Riley-Smith, *Knights of St John*, p. 162.

[105] In 1256 the Embriacos, who were of Genoese origin, had been angered by Bohemond VI's opposition to the Genoese in the War of St Sabas. At one point during the war, Bohemond ordered Bertrand Embriaco to lead a charge against a Genoese force; Bertrand turned his lance the wrong way round and advanced shouting, 'I am Bertrand of Gibelet!' (*Gestes des Chiprois*, p. 151). This disagreement undoubtedly contributed to the 1258 dispute. See also Richard, 'Les Comtes de Tripoli', p. 216.

[106] *Gestes des Chiprois*, pp. 157–9.

hostilities were resumed. Guy II of Gibelet's brother was in competition with a nephew of the bishop of Tortosa (the regent for Bohemond VII) for a woman's hand in marriage, and this provided the spark for renewed violence. The situation was slightly changed, however, since William of Beaujeu, the Master of the Temple, provided thirty brothers to support the Embriaco cause: Guy II of Gibelet had, in fact, recently become a *confrater* of the Templars. The Hospitallers remained aloof from the initial exchanges. After Templar properties in Tripoli had been damaged, the brethren, presumably accompanied by the Embriacos, besieged the city though without success. On their way back to Gibelet, this force attacked a number of coastal sites, but they then had to repel an assault on Gibelet itself by troops from Tripoli. A fierce battle resulted in heavy casualties on both sides and a one-year truce was agreed. The following year Bohemond retaliated against further Templar aggression by attacking their sea castle at Sidon. On 16 July 1279 the new Master of the Hospital, Nicholas Lorgne, was able to re-establish peace. This lasted until 1282 when Guy of Gibelet, again with Templar support, made a series of abortive attempts to seize Tripoli. His army finally gained entry, but it did not receive the necessary support from its allies. Guy was forced to take refuge[107] and, despite guarantees offered by Bohemond, was subsequently killed, along with other ringleaders, at Nephin. Bohemond no doubt felt that he was right to follow his father's example here: the removal of the Embriacos appears to have ended the insurrection in the area.[108]

## CONCLUSION: CHRISTIAN AND MUSLIM STRATEGY

We have seen that low-level warfare, exemplified by raids, counter-raids and skirmishes, was probably a regular feature of life in the Latin East. In addition to its nuisance value, however, this form of warfare could make a significant contribution to major military campaigns, which aimed at either the defence or

---

[107] His place of retreat was, according to contradictory accounts, the Hospitallers' or the Templars' buildings. The latter is more likely.

[108] *Gestes des Chiprois*, pp. 203–8, 210–12; *Histoire de l'île de Chypre*, vol. III, pp. 663–7; for the chronology, see Richard, 'Les Comtes de Tripoli', p. 217–19; for an indication of possible Mamluk involvement in this dispute, see R. Irwin, 'The Mamluk Conquest of the County of Tripoli', in *Crusade and Settlement*, ed. P. W. Edbury (Cardiff, 1985), pp. 247–9.

capture of territory or, more especially, the strongpoints of that territory. In western Europe, commanders organised campaigns which did not require them to face the risks associated with battle, and warfare therefore consisted of raiding, to reduce an opponent's supplies and lessen his resolve, followed by the besieging of a strongpoint.[109] This combination of raids and sieges was one which was regularly employed by Muslim armies, particularly in the second half of the thirteenth century.

The term 'strategy' implies a degree of central planning and control which was seldom, if ever, enjoyed by the authorities in the Latin East during this period. The activities of the feudatories, the Military Orders and the Italian communes were not necessarily intended to be divisive, but they helped to create an environment in which even a strong central power would have found great difficulty in imposing its will. For much of the thirteenth century, however, the Latin Kingdom was governed by a series of regents and lieutenants, and it has been shown that they were frequently unable to prevent factional disputes from developing into all-out conflict. It is not, perhaps, surprising that in 1276 Hugh of Antioch-Lusignan left Acre in disgust, having declared the kingdom to be ungovernable.[110]

The extent to which the Latins could organise a co-ordinated military strategy was, therefore, restricted. Contemporary writers expressed certain simple ideas, however, and Latin strategy, in theory, may be summarised as follows. In attack, they hoped by means of sieges to capture enemy strongpoints and thereby extend their sphere of influence. They also made use of raids to inflict damage upon their enemies, although they were unable to integrate such expeditions into a large-scale campaign which would be primarily concerned with the acquisition of territory. Despite the great risks which were associated with battles, the Latins in the east do appear to have been willing to face their opponents, or at least Christian ones, in open conflict. The presence of crusade expeditions in the area also led, on a number of occasions, to a battle being fought. The results of a battle could, therefore, have important consequences in the struggle for territory. The triumph of the Ibelin army at the battle of Agridi

---

[109] J. Gillingham, 'Richard I and the Science of War in the Middle Ages', in *War and Government in the Middle Ages*, ed. J. Gillingham and J. C. Holt (Cambridge, 1984), pp. 81–4 and *passim*.

[110] *Gestes des Chiprois*, p. 206; and see J. S. C. Riley-Smith, *Feudal Nobility*, pp. 224–6.

in 1232, for example, was the ideal start to a campaign which continued with the capitulation of a number of fortresses, probably defended by weakened garrisons because of the losses which had been sustained in the field. But the armies of the Latin East rarely fought alone against Muslim troops and they appear to have made no effort on their own to increase their lands at the expense of the Muslims.[111] The dependence of their offensive strategy on outside help is therefore clear.

When the Latins were faced by Muslim aggression, however, they usually had to cope without outside assistance. So they chose to defend each strongpoint individually, rather than attempt to organise a field army which might try to drive back their enemies, or to persuade them to abandon their efforts to capture a site. The Latins' defensive strategy, which will be examined in more detail in later chapters, was therefore subject at all times to the limitations which were imposed by their resources. Specifically, their garrisons and their strongpoints had to be adequate if their strategy was to be workable.

---

[111] It might be argued that an exception to this was the Latins' involvement in the battle of La Forbie, in 1244. However, this was a conflict which had more to do with inter-Muslim rivalry in Egypt and Syria than the Latins' efforts to defend, or expand, their territories. The Latin army was only one part of a force, consisting mainly of Muslim troops from Damascus, Homs and Kerak, which was heavily defeated by the sultan of Egypt, as-Salih Aiyub, and his Khorezmian allies. The Latins were able to recover from this defeat, despite their losses, because Aiyub's attentions remained, for the most part, focussed on his Muslim opponents. He was able to occupy Damascus in 1245, but the Khorezmians showed themselves to be increasingly unreliable. In 1246, Aiyub defeated them in a battle near Homs. See Irwin, *Mamluk Sultanate*, pp. 18–19, and Gibb, 'The Aiyubids', pp. 705–10.

*Chapter 2*

# THE LATIN ARMIES

## INTRODUCTION

A contemporary writer who described the fall of Acre in 1291 stated that there were 700–800 mounted troops and 14,000 footsoldiers defending the city.[1] This army was extraordinarily diverse. In the final stages of the Muslim assault, the brother knights of the Military Orders fought alongside poorly armed pilgrims; mercenary troops serving only for pay joined with the feudatories and townspeople who defended their properties and their very existence. The effort was in vain. The Christians of the Latin East had failed to gather an army capable of repulsing their Muslim enemies. It was a problem which had beset the Latins throughout this period and they were therefore restricted, in their defensive strategy, to garrisoning their strongpoints, since they were unable to raise an adequate field army at the same time to protect their lands.

The Christian army could be recruited from many different sources. The feudal levy and the troops of the Military Orders provided most of the kingdom's own army. Support was also provided by soldiers from Cyprus. These basic elements were augmented by troops from western Europe. The crusades produced a short-term increase in the size of the Latin armies, but their achievements were not always of long-term value for the Latin East. Organisations such as the confraternities could provide additional numbers, primarily from visitors to the Holy Land. Throughout the century the arrival of individuals and small groups of crusaders offered a further means by which the Latins could increase the number of troops they had available. This could also be achieved by using mercenaries and other paid

---

[1] *Gestes des Chiprois*, p. 241.

47

soldiers, either recruited by the Latins or provided for them by western rulers, such as the French kings or the papacy.

*Knights and sergeants*

The quality of troops used by Christian armies in the Latin East varied considerably. Crusade expeditions probably continued to attract a popular element which would have been of little use as a fighting force. At the other extreme were the mounted soldiers who used their fiefs, or the payments they received, to maintain both themselves and their retinues. Many contemporary writers did not recognise any more complex divisions within an army than this, but both the mounted and foot elements contained distinct groups of personnel. The foremost amongst the mounted troops, and the basis of the Latin armies, was the knight (*miles/chevalier*).[2]

The social and economic standing of the *milites* distinguished them from the rest of the mounted force. The process of becoming a knight had ecclesiastical and secular implications which placed the recipient within a specific rank of medieval society;[3] this social division was further reinforced by the economic pressures of knighthood. Costs of maintenance for a knight's equipment were prohibitive.[4] The largest burden was

---

[2] The general term *miles* itself covered a range of warriors, whose sub-divisions became increasingly institutionalised in Europe during the thirteenth century. Knights banneret, who appeared in England and France during the first half of the century, were ranked above simple knights, knights bachelor or shield knights. See Contamine, *War in the Middle Ages*, pp. 67–8; see also M. H. Keen, *Chivalry* (New Haven, 1984), p. 168, and below, p. 178.

[3] Keen, *Chivalry*, pp. 64–82 and *passim*; see C. Erdmann, *The Origin of the Idea of Crusade* (Princeton, 1977), pp. 57–8. For the morality of knighthood expressed in the foundation of the Templars see M. C. Barber, 'The Social Context of the Templars', *Transactions of the Royal Historical Society*, 5th Series, 34 (1984), pp. 27–31, 36–7 and *passim*.

[4] Scholars have generally assumed that certain standards, particularly of equipment, had to be maintained, but in the Latin East this does not always seem to have been possible. In the mid-thirteenth century a lord might summon a vassal to serve who only owned one horse and, if this were unfit, the vassal might ask his lord to equip him with a spare horse, 'until mine is healed or I have obtained another one...' ('tant que le mien seit garis ou que je en ais un autre recouvré...'). A fief of the value of 900–1,000 besants was considered adequate to support a knight. See P. W. Edbury, 'Feudal Obligations in the Latin East', *Byzantion*, 47 (1977), p. 337; John of Jaffa, 'Livre', pp. 284–5, 357–8.

provision for his horses, involving not only the mounts which he would ride into battle, but also his packhorses and mules.[5] Templar knights were entitled to three horses, and a fourth at the discretion of the Master. In 1206, it was decreed that Hospitaller knights should have four horses. At Arsuf in 1260, a number of knights owed, in addition to personal service, four horses.[6] The importance of the horse was reflected in the payment by lords in both western Europe and the Latin East of *restor* if their vassal's mount was lost during a campaign, and the efforts of western governments to supply the east with horses, exemplified by the Sicilian Kingdom from 1265 to 1284.[7]

Both mounted and foot sergeants (*servientes/serjans*) operated in the Latin armies. Commanders often placed a fair degree of reliance on them, particularly if they were well armed and well organised and, in theory and in practice, contemporary writers recognised the importance of their role.[8] There were some differences between the appearance of a knight and that of a sergeant. The latter's equipment would have been lighter: amongst the Templars, sergeants were consequently not expected to fight with as much bravery as the brother knights.[9] The Hospitallers' mounted sergeants had two horses at their disposal; the Templars' sergeants were only entitled to one.[10] The Military Orders distinguished their knights and sergeants even more clearly by the colours they wore over their armour. Knights of the Temple wore white mantles and surcoats, but their sergeants wore black ones.[11] The distinction may not have been made by the Hospitallers until the mid-thirteenth century, when Alexander IV stated that the brother knights should wear a black mantle and, in war, a red surcoat with a white cross. In 1278, however, the Hospitallers abandoned this discrimination and decided that all

---

[5] For the various mounts, see *Cartulaire des Hospitaliers*, no. 2213, pt 112.

[6] *La Règle du Temple*, ed. H. de Curzon (Paris, 1886), no. 138; *Cartulaire des Hospitaliers*, nos. 1193, 2985.

[7] Contamine, *War in the Middle Ages*, p. 97; see, for example, *Cartulaire des Hospitaliers*, no. 2985 (the knights and sergeants at Arsuf). Thousands of horseshoes were also sent to the Latin East (Pryor, 'Exports', p. 140 and *passim*).

[8] See, for example, 'Eracles', vol. II, p. 401; Fidenzio of Padua, 'Liber recuperationis', pp. 29–30.

[9] *Règle du Temple*, nos. 141, 419. However, heavily armed Templar sergeants were expected to perform as if they were knights. See also below, p. 87.

[10] *Cartulaire des Hospitaliers*, no. 1193; *Règle du Temple*, no. 143. Five of the Templars' officials who were sergeants were allowed two horses.

[11] *Règle du Temple*, nos. 138, 140–1.

their brethren should be equipped with a red surcoat during a campaign. The reasons for this change are unclear; perhaps the Hospitallers were finding it difficult to recruit sufficient numbers of brother knights.[12]

### Archers, crossbowmen and engineers

Contemporary accounts often failed to differentiate between the various types of infantry in the army. However, one group of soldiers often referred to specifically was the archers and crossbowmen, whose performance in battle could be a critical factor in the success or failure of the Latins. Individual crossbowmen, moreover, could be lethal marksmen. During the War of St Sabas, for example, a crossbowman firing from a Genoese tower was prepared to try to murder the count of Jaffa.[13] In the west, mounted crossbowmen had been used by John I of England and Philip Augustus, whilst Frederick II employed Muslim mounted archers.[14] During the two-year period (1250–2) after his release from captivity in Egypt, St Louis spent over 39,000 *livres* on mounted crossbowmen and mounted sergeants. This compares with a total expenditure during the same period (excluding household costs) of nearly 60,000 *livres* on foot crossbowmen and sergeants. The expenditure on the mounted crossbowmen and sergeants was only a small proportion of total non-household expenditure on war and shipping for these two years, which came to over 450,000 *livres*.[15]

The sources unfortunately do not allow a detailed study of the roles performed by engineers and their assistants in the Latin East, but they were an essential and distinct element of an army. It was they, not the knights and other troops, who maintained and operated the various siege engines in use. Information gathered from the Scottish wars of Edward I indicates their importance:

---

[12] Alexander IV, *Registre*, ed. C. Bourel de la Roncière *et al.* (3 vols., Paris, 1902–53), no. 2938; *Cartulaire des Hospitaliers*, no. 3670. For the Hospitallers' manpower shortages, see no. 3308 (vol. IV).

[13] *Gestes des Chiprois*, p. 149. He was persuaded not to fire by a Genoese consul.

[14] Contamine, *War in the Middle Ages*, pp. 70–1.

[15] 'Dépenses de Saint Louis', *RHF*, vol. XXI, pp. 513–14. It is not clear whether these sums are expressed in *livres parisis* or *livres tournois*. It is impossible, without further information, to suggest how many mounted crossbowmen St Louis may have engaged to remain with him in the Holy Land.

their pay was as high as 9d a day compared to the 12d received by a knight. Moreover, the engines stored in a fortress could rapidly fall into disrepair if the garrison did not have men capable of servicing them.[16] During St Louis's four-year sojourn in the Holy Land, carpenters, miners, engineers and other labourers were employed, but the sums spent on them (amounting to less than 3,000 *livres* during the period 1250 to 1252) suggest that their numbers were quite small.[17]

RESOURCES IN THE LATIN EAST

### The feudal levy

The feudatories who owed military service still formed the nucleus of the Latin East's armies during the thirteenth century. In western Europe, commutation had led to a decline in personal service, but in the Latin states the service which was owed for the fief continued to be performed in person.[18] The Military Orders had taken over responsibility for defending much of the Latin East's territory, but in terms of manpower this had not necessarily increased their obligations in the area, nor decreased those of the feudatories. The Hospitallers obtained Arsuf, for example, from Balian of Ibelin in the early 1260s. Military service was still owed by the vassals who had previously served Balian. All but one of the fiefs at Arsuf seem to have been evaluated in terms of money.[19] It has been suggested that the opportunities to create large numbers of *fief rentes* in the east in the first half of the thirteenth century would have helped to offset the loss of territories in 1187. The *servitium debitum* was probably, therefore, sustained at around 670 knights, as John of Jaffa estimated for the period before the battle of Hattin.[20] If this is accepted alongside

[16] A. Z. Freeman, 'Wall-Breakers and River-Bridgers: Military Engineers in the Scottish Wars of Edward I', *Journal of British Studies*, 10 (1971), pp. 1–2, 5.

[17] 'Dépenses de Saint Louis', pp. 513–14; for the role of engineers in the Lombard–Ibelin conflict, see below, pp. 223–4.

[18] Contamine, *War in the Middle Ages*, p. 91; Edbury, 'Feudal Obligations', pp. 336–7, 344–5.     [19] *Cartulaire des Hospitaliers*, no. 2985.

[20] J. S. C. Riley-Smith, *Feudal Nobility*, p. 7; John of Jaffa, 'Livre', p. 426. See Smail, *Crusading Warfare*, pp. 89–90. Riley-Smith argued (*Feudal Nobility*, p. 10) that in the second half of the thirteenth century, with the decline in revenues from commerce and the loss of coastal sites to the Muslims, the number of knights serving in the feudal host would have fallen sharply. John of Jaffa's estimate covers only the Kingdom of

the estimate that about 750 brother knights were maintained by the Military Orders,[21] it is clear that the secular knights who held fiefs in the east remained of considerable importance. The feudal jurists writing in the mid-thirteenth century described in detail the terms under which the knights served and their texts have recently been surveyed from this standpoint. Many of Dr Edbury's points are central to an understanding of the feudal summons during this period. A lord would not always serve with his own retinue, but *servise de cors* would almost invariably be performed personally. Many feudatories, however, owed the service of more than one knight, which led to some sub-infeudation and the employment of mercenaries. It was also possible that some knights, including those who held fiefs, would serve voluntarily. A typical feudal retinue would thus include vassals, rear-vassals, mercenaries and other retainers of the lord's household. In the development of feudal institutions, two factors were especially important: a shortage of manpower and persistent warfare. These meant that 'service, not financial profit, was what was wanted from fiefs'. Edbury concluded with the suggestion that, by the thirteenth century, these feudal institutions had become anachronistic in the context of territorial losses and long periods of peace, compared to constant warfare and lack of manpower in the twelfth century.[22] But as already noted, a lack of territory had probably been balanced in terms of the *servitium debitum* by the use of the *fief rente*. Moreover, although it is true that continuous warfare no longer afflicted the Latin states (excepting the possibility of regular low-level conflict) and also that the Military Orders had relieved some of the strain on the feudal summons, a lack of troops, particularly in periods between the major crusading expeditions, would still have been a matter of concern. The personal obligations of the fief remained the best way to maintain an army. Commutation of services remained inappropriate, since the isolated nature of the Latin East, coupled

---

Jerusalem. One could also expect feudal service in Antioch and Tripoli to produce several hundred knights.

21 This figure breaks down into 300 for the Hospitallers, about the same number for the Templars and rather less for the Teutonic Knights: J. S. C. Riley-Smith, *Knights of St John*, p. 327; J. S. C. Riley-Smith in Ibn al-Furat, *Ayyubids*, vol. II, pp. xvii–xviii and 173, note 2. There is nothing to be added to Riley-Smith's analysis of the available data.

22 Edbury, 'Feudal Obligations', pp. 331–2, 339, 341, 351–2, 355–6; see also J. S. C. Riley-Smith, *Feudal Nobility*, pp. 8–10.

with its lack of manpower, would have made it extremely
difficult to gather an army quickly by any other means. Service
could therefore, in theory, be owed for up to a year within the
kingdom whilst for service beyond a kingdom's boundaries, as in
the case of Cypriot knights serving on the mainland for example,
the obligation (from 1273) was four months.[23] The feudal lord
would provide victuals for service outside the kingdom.[24] The
importance of the feudal levy in the Latin East was stressed by
Hugh of Antioch-Lusignan, when he stated that in 1197 Aimery
of Lusignan had sent Cypriot vassals to relieve the siege of Jaffa.
It is unlikely that any other form of recruitment could have
enabled such a prompt reaction to this situation.[25]

John of Jaffa's consideration of the value of the fief and the
service which was expected from it led him to examine the use
which was made of *servise des compaignons*. If a fief owed two
knights, then one method for the lord to fulfil his obligation was
by sub-infeudation. His right to alienate his demesne was restricted,
however, and thus it was preferable to employ a soldier on a
monetary basis. For a 3,000-besant fief which owed the service of
three knights, the lord could sub-infeudate 1,000 besants for one
knight, leaving 2,000 besants for himself and for the *compaignon*,
who would serve for pay.[26] The nature of the *compaignons'*
relationship with the lord, and the problems of finding suitable
knights in the Latin East, were further illuminated by John of Jaffa
when he described what might happen if a *compaignon* fell ill. The
lord could agree that his vassal's *compaignon* would join the feudal
host later, or the vassal might be obliged to find another knight.

---

[23] John of Jaffa, 'Livre', p. 346; 'Eracles', vol. II, pp. 463–4.

[24] According to John of Jaffa, personal service outside the kingdom could only be
requested for three reasons: for negotiations relating to the marriage of the lord or one
of his children, to defend the honour of the lord or for the need of the lordship or the
common profit of the land (John of Jaffa, 'Livre', p. 347). The earlier 'Livre au roi'
simply stated that service beyond the kingdom's boundaries should be 'for the profit
of the kingdom or for the needs of the land' ('por le proufit dou reaume ou por le
besoing de la terre'; 'Livre au roi', RHC Lois, vol. I, p. 626).

[25] 'Document relatif au service militaire', RHC Lois, vol. II, p. 428.

[26] John of Jaffa, 'Livre', pp. 284–5. The term *sodoier* is used, but this soldier is not truly
a mercenary. Mercenaries were normally employed for a specific expedition and,
more importantly, enjoyed a relationship with their employer which was wholly
financial. See Contamine, *War in the Middle Ages*, pp. 98–9. Troops who were
employed on the terms of *servise des compaignons* seem to have been regular members
of the lord's retinue, and were not simply recruited for a single campaign. Their
relationship to their lord would have been little different from that of a rear-vassal and
the social structure of the feudal *auxilium* thus remained essentially unaltered.

However, the vassal might not be able to recruit a knight either at the rate he was paying his *compaignon* or at the common rate for the kingdom ('ne por les soz comuns de cest reiaume'). In such circumstances, the vassal had to give the money which he would have spent to his lord, who could then try to employ another knight, or put the money to some other use.[27]

The recruitment of the feudal host relied largely on the *servise de cors* and *servise des compaignons* which the feudatories and the knights they retained owed. The feudal relationship did not simply produce obligations on the part of the vassal, however: it also obliged the lord to maintain the vassal's rights. This concept was most eloquently expressed by the jurists in their treatment of the *Assise sur la ligece*, although their ideas were hardly ever borne out by events in practice.[28] In the first of the jurists' works, the requirement of the lord to protect his vassals' lands from the Muslims was described. If the Muslims had seized a vassal's land and the lord was either unable or unwilling to drive them away, then the vassal was no longer obliged to serve the lord for his fief.[29] The feeble response of the Christians to the Muslim onslaught, particularly in the second half of the thirteenth century, could thus, in theory, have affected the nature of the lord's feudal relationship with his vassal. Many of the feudatories – all of whom, according to the *Assise sur la ligece*, were subject to this system of mutual rights and obligations[30] – had alienated their properties to the Military Orders, but some had retained their fiefs. Jaffa, for example, was held by its counts until it was captured by Baybars in 1268. Members of the Ibelin family remained titular counts, but they may have felt disinclined to continue serving in the feudal levy. The possibility of feudatories wishing to withdraw their services because of a previous lack of support from their peers in a military crisis cannot be discounted.

The vassals could owe different types of military service. At Arsuf in 1260, six knights were mentioned as owing service, compared to twenty-one sergeants. The precise terms under which a sergeant performed military service are unclear. John of Jaffa seemed to make no distinction between the military

---

[27] John of Jaffa, 'Livre', pp. 356–7.
[28] J. S. C. Riley-Smith, 'Assise sur la ligece', pp. 179–204.
[29] '…les Sarasins averont saisie sa terre…et que li rois n'a poer de chasser ceaus Turs ou nel vora faire, qu'il n'est puis tenus de luy servir de riens por celuy fié' ('Livre au roi', pp. 625–6). [30] J. S. C. Riley-Smith, 'Assise sur la ligece', p. 180.

obligations of a sergeant holding a fief and those of a knight, whilst Philip of Novara recognised that the rules of succession were the same for both.[31]

John of Jaffa stated that additional sergeants should only be recruited from the churches and the burgesses when the kingdom was in great need. The use of the expression 'grant besoin' suggests that this was a form of the *arrière-ban*, a general summons of all those fit to carry arms. The large number of mounted sergeants who owed feudal service in the Latin East may not, therefore, have been included in the author's total of 5,025 sergeants. Urban communities in the west owed more specific obligations, such as those of the French towns which were expressed in the late twelfth-century *Prisia servientum*.[32] It is possible that a development of this form of service took place in the Latin East in the thirteenth century.

Evidence for use of the *arrière-ban* in the Latin East during this period is scarce. At the time of the Muslim siege of Jaffa in 1197, Count Henry of Champagne requested aid from the 'burgesses and the communes' ('borgeis et as comunes'), in order to relieve the garrison.[33] The *arrière-ban* may have been used in an attempt to defend Caesarea at the time of the Fifth Crusade.[34] On St Louis's first crusade, the king waited at Damietta for the count of Poitiers, 'who was bringing the *arrière-ban* of France' ('qui amenoit l'ariere-ban de France'). [35] However, the use of the term in this context seems inappropriate. A better example, and one from the Latin East, is the army that was gathered for the battle of La Forbie in 1244. William of Châteauneuf, the Master of the Hospital, described it as including 'the army and all the Christians of the Holy Land, assembled by public proclamation under the patriarch'.[36] The patriarch's role here is an interesting one. Innocent IV, in a letter to the ecclesiastics of the Holy Land in the previous year, had referred to the status of the new patriarch,

---

[31] *Cartulaire des Hospitaliers*, no. 2985; John of Jaffa, 'Livre', pp. 346–7; Philip of Novara, 'Livre de forme de plait', pp. 542–3; see Edbury, 'Feudal Obligations', pp. 337–8.

[32] John of Jaffa, 'Livre', p. 426; see Smail, *Crusading Warfare*, pp. 90–3. He concluded (p. 91) that these additional sergeants were probably footsoldiers. See also Contamine, *War in the Middle Ages*, pp. 83–5.    [33] 'Eracles', vol. II, pp. 219–20.

[34] *Ibid.*, p. 334. The text refers to a summons of the communes and other (unspecified) men. See J. L. La Monte, *Feudal Monarchy in the Latin Kingdom of Jerusalem, 1100 to 1291* (Cambridge, Mass., 1932), p. 160.

[35] Joinville, *Histoire de Saint Louis*, p. 98.

[36] '...generalique exercitu Christianorum Terrae Sanctae, sub patriarcha publico edicto congregati' (Matthew Paris, *Chronica maiora*, vol. IV, p. 310).

Robert of Nantes, 'in the Christian army for the protection of the Holy Land',[37] and he played an important part in the period following the defeat at La Forbie.[38] We will return later to the patriarch's involvement in the organisation of the Latin East's defences in the second half of the thirteenth century: he was constantly employed by the papacy to direct funds to their proper use. But he did not appear again so clearly as a leading member of the Christian army.

## The Military Orders

The feudal host on its own would have been wholly incapable of mounting an effective defence of the Latin East. Fortunately, there were other permanent institutions which could offer support in the area. The Military Orders had taken over increasing responsibility for the Latin East's protection since the first half of the twelfth century. They were able to provide the manpower and, because of their estates in Europe, the other resources (including grain, horses, mules and fodder) which were needed to maintain their armies.[39] They also received assistance from the papacy and bequests from the faithful; these would have contributed towards the large amounts of cash which were required to pay mercenaries and fiefholders.[40] However, during the thirteenth century increasing doubts were expressed as to whether the Orders were using their western properties primarily to finance their operations in the east.[41] From the end of the twelfth century, the Templars and Hospitallers were joined by the Teutonic Knights, though the Germans were also concerned to establish themselves in eastern Europe.[42] The importance of the three Orders in the military structure of the Latin East continued to grow until the end of the period.

[37] '...in exercitu christiano pro subsidio Terre Sancte' (Innocent IV, *Registre*, ed. E. Berger (4 vols., Paris, 1884–1921), no. 12; see also no. 13 (to Robert of Nantes)).

[38] B. Hamilton, *The Latin Church in the Crusader States* (London, 1980), p. 264.

[39] Smail, *Crusading Warfare*, pp. 95–7; J. S. C. Riley-Smith, *Knights of St John*, pp. 441–3. Riley-Smith pointed out that the Hospitallers' dependence on their estates in Europe left them vulnerable to economic, political and administrative difficulties in the west.

[40] For example, Alexander IV, *Registre*, no. 848; Barber, 'Social Context', pp. 42–5; J. S. C. Riley-Smith, *Knights of St John*, p. 328.

[41] Forey, 'Military Orders', pp. 325–8.

[42] For the organisation of the Teutonic Knights and their activities in the Latin East in the thirteenth century, see I. Sterns, 'The Teutonic Knights in the Crusader States', in *A History of the Crusades*, gen. ed. K. M. Setton, vol. v (Madison, 1985), pp. 315–78, *passim*.

The armies which the Military Orders maintained were recruited from a wide range of sources and were as diverse as all the armies of the Latin East. The principal element, however, was the brother knight: it has already been suggested that the Templars and Hospitallers each supported about 300 of these in the east, whilst the Teutonic Knights certainly had rather fewer.[43] Many contemporary writers exalted the virtues of the knights of the Military Orders, whom they regarded as the elite troops of the Christian armies. By the beginning of the fourteenth century, some of the performances of these soldiers – at the siege of Saphet in 1266, for example – had already become almost legendary.[44] The distinction between mounted brother sergeants ('frater vero serviens, qui de armis servit'/'les freres sergens qui servent d'armes') and brother knights ('fratrum militum'/'frere chevalier')[45] would probably have been unimportant on campaign. There is no evidence that the brother sergeants had any role to play which was independent of the more heavily armed brother knights although, as already noted, the Templars' *Rule* did not require sergeants to show the degree of bravery which was expected of the knights. Support in battle was also provided by squires.[46]

Brother knights and sergeants were not, however, the only elements of the Military Orders that provided personal and direct aid to the Holy Land. Some soldiers volunteered for temporary membership of a Military Order. The idea of voluntary service in the Latin East, without joining the ranks of a crusade, was one which appealed to many men in the thirteenth century. In 1244, for example, there were a hundred knights or footsoldiers from western Europe serving in the Latin East, whilst James of Ibelin claimed that Cypriot knights were used to serving on the mainland as volunteers.[47] Temporary service with one of the Military Orders, particularly in view of the prestige which they enjoyed, would probably have been especially popular. Dr Barber has recently considered an example from a thirteenth-century folk

---

[43] See above, pp. 51–2, and note 21. Many contemporary accounts refer only to the Templars and Hospitallers in the organisation of the Latin armies. The military commitment of the Teutonic Knights fell far short of that of the first two and the number of their brethren can therefore be assumed to have been smaller.

[44] 'Processus Cypricus', ed. K. Schottmüller, in *Der Untergang des Templer-Ordens*, vol. II (Berlin, 1887), pp. 162, 387–8.     [45] *Cartulaire des Hospitaliers*, no. 1193.

[46] *Règle du Temple*, no. 179; see above, p. 49.

[47] See above, p. 26; 'Document relatif', pp. 431–2.

tale, in which the count of Ponthieu served the Templars for a year.[48] In 1237 Gregory IX referred to the need for confessional arrangements for those who served in the Templars' sites, either freely or for pay.[49]

Paid troops were undoubtedly an important feature of the armies of the Military Orders, both on campaign and for the efficient day-to-day running of the organisation. On the Fifth Crusade, Honorius III knew that the Orders were employing knights, sergeants, crossbowmen and other troops. Also on the Fifth Crusade, 2,500 out of 4,000 crossbowmen were believed to have been mercenaries[50] and it is likely that many of them found employment with the Military Orders. Two of the Hospitallers' officials, the Master Crossbowman and Master Sergeant, were not actually members of the Order; they may have been laymen who took charge of some of the Order's mercenary troops.[51] Earlier, we saw that in 1260 the Military Orders were finding it difficult to recruit mercenaries to garrison their castles.[52] In 1268, Hugh Revel, the Master of the Hospital, stated that there were now only 300 brothers serving in the east, whereas the Hospitallers had previously supported 10,000 men. The significance of the second figure is not clear, but it would certainly have included many mercenaries.[53] In 1281, 600 mounted troops repulsed a Muslim assault on Margat. In the same year Nicholas Lorgne, the Master of the Hospital, informed Edward I of England that the castle was well guarded by both Hospitallers and other soldiers. When the Muslims captured Margat in 1285, 25 Hospitallers, probably the total strength of the brethren in the castle, were allowed to leave with their horses and arms.[54] The rest of the garrison presumably consisted largely of mercenaries. The Hospitallers had clearly been maintaining large numbers of troops in their last stronghold in northern Syria. In a letter describing the siege of Acre in 1291, John of Villiers, the Master of the Hospital, mentioned 'no sodoiier', though it is unclear whether this was a reference to the mercenaries of the Order, or to the city as a whole.[55]

Turcopoles, who were native troops or westerners using native

---

[48] Barber, 'Social Context', pp. 41–2.      [49] Gregory IX, *Registre*, no. 3520.
[50] *Cartulaire des Hospitaliers*, no. 1633; Oliver of Paderborn, 'Historia', p. 259.
[51] J. S. C. Riley-Smith, *Knights of St John*, pp. 325–6.      [52] See above, p. 41.
[53] *Cartulaire des Hospitaliers*, no. 3308 (vol. IV).
[54] *Gestes des Chiprois*, pp. 209–10; *Cartulaire des Hospitaliers*, no. 3766; Ibn 'Abd al-Zahir, 'Vie de Kalavun', in J. F. Michaud, *Histoire des Croisades*, vol. VII (Paris, 1822), p. 696.
[55] *Cartulaire des Hospitaliers*, no. 4157.

equipment, were also employed by the Military Orders. They were not used simply to counter the Muslims' methods of combat, but also to augment the limited number of troops available to the Latin armies.[56] They were commanded by the *Turcopolier*. It is not clear whether this official was a knight or a sergeant, but he was certainly an important figure. The Templars' *Turcopolier* was entitled to four mounts and on reconnaissance trips he could command up to nine knights.[57] Turcopoles were assigned to the retinues of leading officers of the Hospital and Temple.[58] According to one account of the battle of La Forbie in 1244, large numbers of turcopoles employed by the Templars and Hospitallers were killed in the conflict.[59] Both the Templars and Hospitallers used turcopoles during the War of St Sabas.[60] And we shall shortly see that turcopoles were a part of the garrison of a major Templar castle.

The Military Orders would also have augmented their forces with the vassals who owed them military service. As already noted, the acquisition of Arsuf by the Hospitallers in the 1260s provided that Order with the service of six knights and twenty-one sergeants. Their obligations to the Hospital would have been the same as those previously owed to their lord, Balian of Ibelin, and Arsuf's contribution to the *servitium debitum* was therefore unaffected by this transaction. The Hospital agreed to fulfil the feudal obligations of the lord of Arsuf, with the exception of the *servise de cors* which was owed by Balian.[61] It is uncertain whether the Military Orders themselves owed service to the crown.[62]

At the Templars' castle of Saphet in northern Galilee, the garrison in about 1260 was estimated to be more than 1,700 men, rising in wartime to 2,200. Only a quarter of the peacetime force were full-time combatants; the further breakdown of the soldiers' numbers provides valuable, though still incomplete, information explaining the use made by the Templars of the troops which were at their disposal. 'The everyday needs of the castle require 50 knights (probably brother knights) and 30 brother sergeants

[56] Smail, *Crusading Warfare*, pp. 111–12; J. S. C. Riley-Smith, in Ibn al-Furat, *Ayyubids*, vol. II, p. 237, note 3.

[57] J. S. C. Riley-Smith, *Knights of St John*, p. 325; *Règle du Temple*, nos. 169–70.

[58] *Cartulaire des Hospitaliers*, no. 1193; *Règle du Temple*, nos. 77, 99, 101, 110, 125.

[59] Salimbene of Adam, 'Chronica', *MGHS*, vol. XXXII, p. 177.

[60] *Gestes des Chiprois*, pp. 153–4.

[61] *Cartulaire des Hospitaliers*, nos. 2985, 3047.

[62] J. S. C. Riley-Smith, *Knights of St John*, pp. 456–7.

with horses and arms, 50 turcopoles with horses and arms and 300 crossbowmen...'.[63] There is no mention here of vassals of the Order performing castle-guard at Saphet, although it is known that such obligations existed elsewhere.[64] Any feudal obligations to the Templars were perhaps only fulfilled when the castle was under threat. It is noteworthy that as many turcopoles as brother knights were serving at Saphet, a further indication of the importance of such troops to the Templars. The turcopoles and the large number of crossbowmen were no doubt serving for pay. If there were about 300 brother knights maintained by the Templars in the Latin East, then the presence of one-sixth of them within Saphet gives some idea of the importance of that castle to the Order. Additional support at times of crisis may have been provided by the Hospitallers.[65] Conversely, one writer believed that Templars had assisted the Hospitallers at the siege of Arsuf in 1265.[66]

The Military Orders were prominent in every aspect of military life in the Latin East during the thirteenth century. Their reputation was generally very good, and criticisms such as those expressed by the French crusader and poet Philip of Nanteuil after the debacle at Gaza in 1239, or Joinville regarding the Templars' arrogance at Mansurah, were rare.[67] The leaders of the Orders enjoyed an influential position in the Christian hierarchy. They were generally to the fore in discussions of strategy, whether these concerned the policy of the Latin states or the progress of a crusade.[68] A typical example of such discussions took place in 1239, when the Grand Commander of the Temple and the Master of the Teutonic Knights attended a meeting in Acre before the crusade led by Theobald of Champagne set off south towards Ascalon and Gaza.[69]

It is perhaps not surprising, considering the commitment which all the Military Orders made to the defence of the Holy Land, that

---

[63] 'In stabilimento cotidiano castri sunt necessarii l milites et xxx servientes fratres cum equis et armis et l Turcopoli cum equis et armis et balistarii ccc...' (*De constructione castri Saphet*, p. 41).

[64] At Arsuf and Beirut, for example (J. S. C. Riley-Smith, *Feudal Nobility*, p. 8).

[65] 'Maius chronicon Lemovicense a Petro Coral et aliis conscriptum', *RHF*, vol. xxi, p. 773.

[66] John Vitoduranus, 'Chronica', *MGHS rer. Germ. NS*, vol. iii, p. 17.

[67] 'Rothelin', p. 549; Joinville, *Histoire de Saint Louis*, pp. 118–20.

[68] J. S. C. Riley-Smith, *Knights of St John*, pp. 128–30.

[69] 'Rothelin', pp. 531–2. See below, p. 73, and note 122.

their interests clashed occasionally. Their differences, however, sometimes became long-term political ones which adversely affected the unity which the Latin settlement required for its survival. It has been seen that when the Hospitallers favoured Raymond Roupen during a conflict in northern Syria, the Templars supported Bohemond of Antioch.[70] During the crusade of Frederick II, the Teutonic Knights were alone amongst the Orders in their support for the emperor,[71] but later the Hospitallers supported Frederick's marshal, Richard Filangieri, in his conflict with the Commune of Acre.[72] In the War of St Sabas the Hospitallers supported the Genoese and their allies, whilst the Templars joined most of the feudatories and favoured the Venetians.[73] By the late 1270s, however, the Templars were siding with the Genoese Embriaco family against the lord of Tripoli.[74] These internecine squabbles were grave and suggest that the Orders were, for various reasons, constantly at odds with one another. But they were still prepared to co-operate in actions directed against the kingdom's external enemies. Both the Templars and the Hospitallers invariably provided troops for raiding expeditions. The decision to fight on the side of the Damascenes against Egypt in 1244 may not have suited the Hospitallers, but it did not prevent them from providing hundreds of soldiers, many of whom were lost at La Forbie.[75]

Members of the Military Orders excelled amongst the Christians in their approach to warfare in the Latin East. The Orders' experience of campaigning in the region amounted to over 150 years by the time of the final loss of the Holy Land. The quality of their troops was largely a result of their ability to carry out in practice what they had learned in theory. They did not attempt to execute complex manoeuvres but they applied common sense and collective discipline to their fighting methods, attributes which were often absent from the rest of the Christian army. The most detailed account of their military code is contained in a set of statutes dated to the twelfth century from the *Rule* of the Templars, but it continued to develop in statutes which were promulgated in the thirteenth century.[76]

[70] See above, pp. 42–3.    [71] 'Eracles', vol. II, pp. 372–3.
[72] *Gestes des Chiprois*, pp. 125–7.    [73] *Ibid.*, pp. 151–5; 'Rothelin', pp. 633–4.
[74] *Gestes des Chiprois*, pp. 204–8, 210–11; *Histoire de Chypre*, vol. III, pp. 663–7. The Embriacos had previously been supported by the Hospitallers. See above, p. 43.
[75] 'Eracles', vol. II, pp. 429–30; 'Rothelin', p. 564.
[76] *Règle du Temple*, nos. 77–181 and *passim*; Melville, *La Vie des Templiers*, p. 85.

When the Templars were camped, for example, their movements were carefully regulated. If the alarm was raised inside the camp, their response should be ordered but positive; those nearby should go to investigate, armed with shield and lance, whilst the rest should assemble.[77] In July 1219, during the Fifth Crusade, a concerted Muslim assault against the crusader camp routed the footsoldiers, and French secular troops were unable to repulse the attack. Muslim mounted and footsoldiers had entered the camp and the crusaders' position was seriously threatened until the Templars, led by their Marshal who carried their standard, the *bausan*, were given permission to charge. Supported by the Teutonic Knights and other nobles and knights, they forced the Muslims to withdraw, inflicting on them heavy losses although Christian casualties were also numerous. The Templars' performance was praised by Oliver of Paderborn, who may have witnessed their charge.[78] Their discipline contrasted with the lacklustre efforts of the Ibelins and their allies at Casal Imbert in 1232, when inattentive sentries allowed the Lombards to take the Ibelin camp by storm.[79] Another example of a camp being inadequately protected came during St Louis's first crusade. At Damietta, the guard was maintained by mounted troops. The Muslims were able to wait until the horses had passed, before entering the camp and causing considerable damage. St Louis eventually found it necessary to order the cavalry to mount their guard on foot.[80]

On Christian raiding expeditions, the Military Orders played a crucial role. Again, they were suited to such a position because of the discipline which was imposed by their statutes. The Templars were required to restrain themselves as far as possible, although they were allowed to test and water their mounts, with permission, and to leave the ranks if a Christian was threatened by a Muslim. At night they should remain silent. If a cry was raised,

---

[77] *Règle du Temple*, nos. 148, 149, 155, 380. The Templars should not go out of the camp without permission.

[78] Oliver of Paderborn, 'Historia', pp. 209–11; 'Gesta obsidionis Damiate', in *QBSSM*, pp. 99–100; 'Fragmentum de captione Damiatae', in *QBSSM*, pp. 180–1 (dated August). For the Templars' instructions on the delivery of a charge, see below, pp. 158–9.

[79] 'Eracles', vol. ii, pp. 396–7; *Gestes des Chiprois*, pp. 90–1. On the protection of a camp, see also Fidenzio of Padua, 'Liber recuperationis', pp. 32–3. He argued that sentries should be posted some distance from the camp, in order to keep watch over its approaches. They should be on guard both night and day.

[80] Joinville, *Histoire de Saint Louis*, pp. 96–8.

those nearby should take their shield and lance and mount their chargers; they should then await the orders of the Marshal.[81] James of Molay, the last Master of the Temple, argued against the unification of the Hospital and Temple by pointing out that on raids the two Orders separately protected the front and rear of the army; if the Orders were amalgamated then obviously this practice could no longer be maintained.[82] An attack in August 1219 on a Muslim camp at Fariskur showed the discipline and courage which could be demonstrated by the Orders. The Muslims pulled back from their camp, allowing the combined effects of wine and heat to destroy the order of the Christian army. When the Muslims took the offensive, most of the Christians panicked and fled in disarray. Only John of Brienne, the Military Orders and a few other knights marched together as the rearguard, thus preventing a major Christian defeat. But their casualties were still heavy. The Templars and Hospitallers may have lost as many as 200 knights between them, whilst the Teutonic Knights lost 30. Some 250 other knights were killed and King John's armour was scorched by Greek fire.[83]

The Military Orders were not immune to rash behaviour themselves, however. In 1260, for example, Stephen of Saisi, the Marshal of the Templars, was dismissed from the Order because his conduct on a raid had led to a heavy defeat for the Christian troops. Stephen was reinstated by the pope, but his subsequent career in the west was also controversial.[84] In 1266, the indiscipline of the advance guard of a Christian raiding party, which included the Hospitallers and Teutonic Knights, allowed it to fall into an ambush organised by Muslim troops from Saphet.[85]

On the few occasions when Christians fought with Muslims in battle, the Military Orders were normally prominent in the action. It has already been noted that their losses at La Forbie were heavy. At Mansurah on St Louis's first crusade, the Templars tried to dissuade Robert of Artois from chasing the Muslims into the

---

[81] *Règle du Temple*, nos. 156–63.
[82] *Le Dossier de l'affaire des Templiers*, ed. G. Lizerand (Paris, 1923), p. 10.
[83] Oliver of Paderborn, 'Historia', pp. 213–17; James of Vitry, *Lettres*, ed. R. B. C. Huygens (Leiden, 1960), pp. 120–2, 128–9; 'Fragmentum de captione Damiatae', pp. 187–90; 'Gesta obsidionis', pp. 101–3. For Greek fire, see below, p. 214, n. 8.
[84] *Gestes des Chiprois*, pp. 163–4; 'Annales de Terre Sainte', pp. 449–50; Abu Shama, 'Livre', vol. v, p. 204; see Urban IV, *Registre*, nos. 336, 2858.
[85] *Gestes des Chiprois*, pp. 181–2; 'Eracles', vol. ii, p. 455; 'Annales de Terre Sainte', pp. 452–3; Ibn 'Abd al-Zahir, 'Life of Baybars', vol. ii, p. 607; see below, p. 198.

town. Their efforts failed, but they still followed Robert's precipitate charge and lost many brethren as a result.[86] The Orders did not hesitate to provide troops to help defend a Christian strongpoint. The Hospitallers lost forty brothers at the siege of Tripoli in 1289.[87] The Templars also fought at Tripoli, whilst an eye-witness to the fall of Acre praised their willingness 'to shed their blood for the name of Christ and the defence of the Christian faith ...'.[88]

In the thirteenth century, the presence of the Military Orders in the Latin East was most clearly expressed in the numerous castles and strongpoints which they maintained. The Templars constructed two major castles in Palestine; one was wholly original, the other had been previously ruined. At Château Pèlerin in the winter of 1217–18, members of the Order were joined by the Teutonic Knights, Walter of Avesnes and a number of pilgrims, in the construction of a castle on a promontory not far from their fortress of Destroit. The building was completed by May 1218. It soon proved its worth, resisting al-Mu'azzam's assault in 1220, whilst Frederick II was discouraged from attacking it in 1229, since it was 'strong and well guarded'.[89] In December 1240, the Templars began to rebuild the castle of Saphet. Two and a half years later the work was finished, at a cost of 1,100,000 Saracen besants; the castle proved to be a great asset to the Christians in the area until it was captured by the Muslims in 1266.[90]

Many of the sites taken over by the Military Orders in the thirteenth century reflected the nobles' inability, or unwillingness, to deal with the problems of defending their properties. In 1228, the Teutonic Knights purchased seventeen villages from Jacob of Mandelee; they may have already begun work on the site of Montfort, which was to become their principal castle in the Latin East.[91] Leopold of Austria helped them with a gift of 6,000 marks,

[86] 'Rothelin', pp. 604–6; Matthew Paris, *Chronica maiora*, vol. v, pp. 148–51, 154, 166–7.
[87] *Cartulaire des Hospitaliers*, no. 4050. They had also lost large numbers of horses and quantities of arms; John of Villiers gave instructions that these should be replaced on the next passage from the west.
[88] '...suum sanguinem fundere pro Christi nomine et pro deffensione fidei christiane...' ('Processus Cypricus', pp. 155–6; see also p. 394).
[89] Oliver of Paderborn, 'Historia', pp. 169, 244–5, 254–6; 'Eracles', vol. ii, pp. 325–6, 373–4 (variant reading). [90] *De constructione castri Saphet*, pp. 38–41.
[91] *Tabulae ordinis Theutonici*, nos. 63, 65; *Historia diplomatica Friderici secundi*, vol. iii, pp. 92, 97, 117–21; *Gestes des Chiprois*, p. 34 (which suggests that work at the site started in 1226).

which was remembered by Gregory IX when he urged the west to offer further donations to the Order.[92] Bohemond IV of Antioch also arranged for an annual payment of 100 besants from the courts of the *chaine* and the *fonde* at Acre.[93] A good example of an Order taking over defensive duties from a lord no longer able to bear the burden was the Hospitallers' acquisition of Arsuf from Balian of Ibelin in the early 1260s. They agreed to pay a rent of 4,000 Saracen besants a year, which contrasts with the sums the Templars spent on the restoration of Saphet, although it is not known how much the Hospitallers had to spend on refurbishing the site. It may therefore have been regarded by contemporaries as something of a bargain, although its capture by Baybars in 1265 proved costly to the Order.[94] Further north, Julian of Sidon found himself in the same predicament as Balian of Ibelin and sold Sidon and Beaufort to the Templars in 1260. He had also been negotiating with the Hospitallers, who only gave up their possessions in the lordship of Sidon in 1262.[95] Not all properties which were passed to the Military Orders in this period were a straight sale or lease arrangement with a secular lord. After Richard of Cornwall (the brother-in-law of Frederick II) had rebuilt Ascalon, he handed it to the imperial castellan of Jerusalem. In August 1243, the emperor granted Ascalon to the Hospitallers and promised to pay the expenses which were necessary for the defence of the castle. The grant was confirmed by Conrad three months later and the formal transfer took place in April 1244.[96] In 1255 Pope Alexander IV presented Mt Tabor to the Hospitallers, following recognition of the threat which it faced from the Muslims. The pope suggested that the Order should maintain forty 'equites' (probably meaning brother knights) there.[97] It is not known, however, whether the site was ever fortified.

---

[92] Oliver of Paderborn, 'Historia', p. 207; *Tabulae ordinis Theutonici*, no. 72.

[93] *Tabulae ordinis Theutonici*, no. 64.

[94] *Cartulaire des Hospitaliers*, nos. 2972, 2985, 3047, 3071.

[95] 'Eracles', vol. II, p. 445; 'Annales de Terre Sainte', p. 449; *Gestes des Chprois*, p. 162; *Cartulaire des Hospitaliers*, no. 3029.

[96] *Gestes des Chprois*, p. 123; *Cartulaire des Hospitaliers*, nos. 2301, 2308, 2320. By 1247, John of Jaffa had received the county of Jaffa and Ascalon from Henry of Cyprus. This led to a dispute between the count and the Hospitallers over the right to dispose of Ascalon. A settlement was reached by the beginning of 1257. Ascalon had fallen to the Muslims in 1247. See P. W. Edbury, 'John of Ibelin's Title to the County of Jaffa and Ascalon', *English Historical Review*, 98 (1983), pp. 126–7.

[97] *Cartulaire des Hospitaliers*, nos. 2726, 2729, 2811.

In northern Syria, the Military Orders were already well established by the beginning of this period and they received little new territory, apart from in Armenia. The Hospitaller castles of Crac des Chevaliers and Margat, and the Templar sites of Baghras, Tortosa and Chastel Blanc, combined with numerous lesser fortresses to dominate the region at the expense of their weak, faction-ridden Muslim neighbours. Their strength was increased by the right which was sometimes conferred on them to make war and peace as they wished. A sequence of documents concerning Jabala and the fortress of the Château de la Vieille indicated the privileges they could be given. In 1210 Raymond Roupen granted the town and castle, though they were not in Christian hands, to the Hospitallers and 'I also gave to that House freedom to make war and truce with the Saracens...'. This arrangement was confirmed in 1215, but by 1221 it was clear that the Templars and Hospitallers were disputing ownership of Jabala. And in 1233 the patriarch of Antioch had to warn the two Orders that they should not make separate truces with the Muslims of the area.[98]

The Military Order of St Lazarus was a small body of leper knights. Their disease must have given them a strange position within the army, but they do not appear to have had any problems with recruitment: Templars who contracted leprosy were amongst those who would join the Order.[99] In 1244, the entire force of lepers was killed at La Forbie.[100] Their numbers were obviously restored, however, since they were referred to (rather disparagingly) by Joinville at the time of St Louis's stay in Palestine. During the rebuilding work at Jaffa, the Master of St Lazarus organised a raid against a Muslim camp near Ramla. He had not informed anyone else of his intentions, and his force was heavily defeated by the Muslims, with only four of his men being able to escape.[101] In 1257, the Order was granted 200 marks by Alexander IV – a sum which contrasted with the 10,000 marks received by the Templars and the 2,000 marks given to the Hospitallers around this time.[102] The leper knights were able to

---

[98] 'Dedi eciam eidem domui liberam potestatem ad faciendum guerram et treugam cum Saracenis...' (*ibid.*, no. 1355; see also nos. 1441, 1725, 1739, 2058).

[99] *Règle du Temple*, nos. 429, 443.

[100] Salimbene of Adam, 'Chronica', p. 177.

[101] Joinville, *Histoire de Saint Louis*, pp. 294–6.

[102] Alexander IV, *Registre*, nos. 848, 1726, 2341.

take on some responsibilities for the defence of the Latin Kingdom. They guarded the Gate of St Lazarus at Acre, for example. One scholar has suggested that the Order merged with the Hospitallers in 1259, but the Master of St Lazarus may have been at the siege of Acre in 1291.[103] The history of the Order in the second half of the thirteenth century seems likely to remain shrouded in mystery.

The Military Orders, therefore, had a leading role to play in all the Christians' efforts to maintain their territories in Palestine and Syria. Their arguments with one another and their tendency to side with opposing groups in the politics of the Latin East aggravated many disputes and thereby weakened the Latin states, but without them there would probably have been no Christian presence in the area in the thirteenth century. A Muslim chronicler was referring to Saphet, but could have been speaking of the Orders who garrisoned such fortresses, when he described it as 'an obstruction in the throat of Syria and a blockage in the chest of Islam...'.[104]

### RESOURCES FROM THE WEST

### *The Crusades*

In September 1270, Baybars demolished Ascalon. Six months earlier, he had received news of St Louis's plans for a second crusade and he feared that the site might be refortified by the French ruler.[105] This crusade, as Baybars was soon to learn, posed no threat to the Muslims in the region, but the sultan's reaction is nonetheless interesting. The Muslims were clearly concerned at the prospect of a large addition to the Christian forces in the area. But the nature of the crusade in the thirteenth century prevented it from satisfying the military needs of the Christians in the Latin East. It gave a short-term impetus to their efforts but did nothing to alleviate their long-term manpower crisis. The crusade could, in fact, leave the inhabitants of the area with additional problems

---

[103] Prawer, *Histoire du royaume*, vol. II, p. 343; J. Prawer, 'Palestinian Agriculture and the Crusader Rural System', in his *Crusader Institutions* (Oxford, 1980), p. 150; R. Röhricht, *Geschichte des Königreichs Jerusalem (1100–1291)* (Innsbruck, 1898), p. 1014. The leper knights were presumably based at Acre; in 1258 the Master of the Templars stayed at their house in the city, in preference to his own Order's accommodation which was too near to the Pisan quarter – this being the time of the War of St Sabas (*Gestes des Chiprois*, p. 153). [104] Ibn al-Furat, *Ayyubids*, vol. II, p. 89.
[105] Ibn 'Abd al-Zahir, 'Life of Baybars', vol. II, pp. 737, 741.

to solve. Christians would have taken the cross in Europe to fight the infidel and earn salvation. They left their homes and families and expended considerable sums of money to finance their expeditions. When they arrived in the Holy Land, they naturally wanted to do something to justify their journey. Unfortunately their actions were often far from welcome to the occupants of the Latin East, whose aims were more limited and more pragmatic. The Latins might therefore have to placate the Muslim rulers who had been subjected to the zealous militaristic behaviour of the western armies, whilst their troops might have to be further dispersed in an attempt to garrison the fortifications established or rebuilt by the crusaders.

Some contemporaries began to realise that the crusade, in its present form, was not the best way for Europe to aid the Holy Land. The Franciscan Fidenzio of Padua argued that an adequate long-term reinforcement was necessary because nothing would be gained if the Holy Land were conquered and then immediately abandoned. He therefore recommended that each bishopric, abbey or city should send one, two, three or more knights to serve in the east. Other authors of *De recuperatione* memoranda added ideas such as the formation of a new Military Order, the employment of troops used to fighting in their own countries and the careful colonisation of the newly conquered territories. As early as 1235, Gregory IX had suggested that after the crusade of 1239 the west should maintain a force in the Holy Land for ten years.[106] In practice, however, the crusade remained unaltered and thus generally unsatisfactory as a means by which Europe could help the Latin East. St Louis had recognised some of the problems of the area when he established a garrison of French troops there and the success of this venture will be examined later. The idea of permanent garrisons maintained by the west for the defence of the Latin East had proved most fruitful with the creation of the Military Orders. The formation of national companies, and confraternities, added much-needed reinforcements. Those who were best able to analyse the plight of the Latins supported these organisations. William of Beaujeu, the Master of the Temple, argued at the Council of Lyons in 1274 for the provision of an advance expedition numbering 250–300 knights and 500 in-

---

[106] Fidenzio of Padua, 'Liber recuperationis', pp. 58–9; S. Schein, 'The Future *Regnum Hierusalem*. A Chapter in Medieval State Planning', *Journal of Medieval History*, 10 (1984), pp. 98–100; Gregory IX, *Registre*, nos. 2664–5.

fantry.[107] With hindsight such a strategy could be considered a prerequisite for the survival of the Latin East, but permanent forces were, in practice, never adequate to justify the theoreticians' hopes that the Holy Land could be successfully defended by them.

The crusade was the instrument of the papacy and it was one which the popes often used for their own ends (against the Hohenstaufen, for example) rather than for the aid of the Holy Land.[108] They were, however, well aware of the conditions which existed in the area. They received regular reports from both ecclesiastics and secular leaders. Moreover, some, including Urban IV (James Pantéleon, a former patriarch of Jerusalem) and Gregory X (Theobald Visconti, who as archdeacon of Liège had been on crusade) had personal knowledge of the kingdom's problems. Innocent III had not been to the Latin East but his proclamation of the Fifth Crusade showed that he appreciated the threat which resulted from the Muslims' recent fortification of Mt Tabor.[109] The papacy's awareness of the Holy Land's problems might be taken to suggest that there was a cynical attitude towards the diversion of crusade funds, particularly for papal concerns in Sicily, whilst Baybars ravaged the Latin East. But few other western rulers showed any genuine interest in the crusade, which meant that, however well-intentioned popes such as Innocent III and Gregory X might have been, their appeals for aid often went unheeded.

The crusade was a voluntary enterprise and all rulers must have hesitated at the massive commitment required to finance a large-scale expedition. St Louis's outlay on his first crusade was about 1·5 million *livres tournois*, at a time when the average income of the French monarchy was 250,000 *livres*, most of which was required for internal expenses. The French Church had originally agreed to the levying of a twentieth for three years, but this was voluntarily increased to a tenth. A further two-year tenth was levied in 1251, following St Louis's capture in Egypt. Despite widespread problems of collection, these clerical taxes raised nearly 1 million *livres* – that is, nearly two-thirds of the total sum which was expended. Tenths and twentieths had also been imposed on the Church outside France, but these produced virtually nothing. The remaining 500,000 *livres* was obtained, in

---

[107] James I, King of Aragon, *Chronicle*, trans. J. Forster (London, 1883), vol. II, p. 648.
[108] Purcell, *Papal Crusading Policy*, pp. 70–86 and *passim*.
[109] Innocent III, 'Opera omnia', vol. CCXVI, col. 818.

part, by improvements in the collection of royal revenue. There was also increased exploitation of sources of irregular income, including confiscation of the properties of heretics, extortion of money from the Jews and revenue obtained from royal rights, such as licensing elections of certain bishops and abbots and the right to a portion of the revenues of certain vacant benefices. Finally, 'gifts' for the crusade made by towns in the royal domain have been estimated to have produced 274,000 *livres tournois*. The transfer of funds to the east appears to have presented no particular problems and the system continued to function until the beginning of 1253, when it broke down because of political, rather than fiscal, difficulties – most importantly, the crisis following the death of Louis's regent, Blanche of Castile, in late 1252.[110]

Transportation of both men and supplies also required careful consideration. In 1246, Louis contracted for thirty-six ships from Genoa and Marseilles. At the same time, major improvements were being made to the port facilities at Aigues-Mortes. Meanwhile, an advance party was sent to Cyprus to prepare the army's victuals: Joinville's description of the scene which greeted him when the main force arrived on the island indicated the success of this effort, with supplies of wine, wheat and barley in abundance.[111] Yet despite the huge sums of money which had been spent, organisation collapsed as the crusade progressed south towards Cairo. Like the Fifth Crusade, St Louis's expedition was beaten by the climate and the Muslims' resources, supported by their knowledge of the area's geography.

It was not only the crusades into Egypt which required considerable organisation and expenditure. The great achievements of crusaders in the Latin East during this period were their building enterprises, and these needed both men and money if they were to be successful. St Louis spent over 95,000 *livres* on fortifications in the Latin East after the failure of his crusade.[112] Fortifications which were constructed or repaired with the aid of crusaders included Château Pèlerin, Sidon, Jaffa, Caesarea, Ascalon and the city defences of Acre.

When a large crusade expedition was organised to help the

---

[110] Jordan, *Louis IX*, pp. 78–104, *passim*.
[111] *Ibid.*, pp. 70–7; 'Eracles', vol. II, p. 436; Joinville, *Histoire de Saint Louis*, pp. 72–4.
[112] 'Dépenses de Saint Louis', p. 515. Again, it is not clear whether the amount referred to is in *livres parisis* or *tournois*.

Latin states, the Christians in the area thus received an injection of manpower, supported by other resources, which they would have been incapable of mustering on their own. We have seen that the number of knights usually sustained on the mainland of the Latin East probably amounted to a total force of about 2,000 men. An examination of the numbers involved in a crusade indicates the potential impact of such armies. On the Fifth Crusade the eye-witness Oliver of Paderborn estimated that there were 1,200 mounted troops excluding turcopoles and other mounted, innumerable foot (which the Muslims compared to locusts) and 4,000 archers.[113] Another contemporary suggested, before the army left for Egypt, the rather larger figure of 3,000 knights and mounted sergeants, 20,000 foot sergeants and 30,000 others, including women.[114] Some of the problems encountered in trying to establish the size of medieval armies are indicated by a further estimate of 20,000 knights and 200,000 foot,[115] but the earlier assessments probably give a rough idea of the actual size of the army. By the treaty of San Germano in 1225, Frederick II agreed to maintain 1,000 knights on crusade for two years and to provide facilities for 2,000 more to travel. Each knight would be equipped with three horses. The army which assembled near Brindisi in the summer of 1227 may have exceeded this figure.[116] In 1239, the crusade led by Theobald of Champagne set off south from Acre with a force of 4,000 knights, including those supplied by the Latin Kingdom. There were considerable numbers of other troops present on this campaign.[117] St Louis's first crusade was well documented by contemporaries and two of the best eye-witness accounts tally closely in their estimates for the size of his army. Joinville suggested a force of 2,800 knights, whilst Jean Sarrasin, a royal chamberlain, believed that there were 2,500 knights, 5,000 crossbowmen and other troops both mounted and

---

[113] Oliver of Paderborn, 'Historia', p. 259.  [114] 'Eracles', vol. II, p. 323.

[115] 'Annales Ceccanenses', MGHS, vol. XIX, p. 302. The size of this crusader army fluctuated dramatically, not only because of mortality but also according to the number of soldiers who arrived from or departed for the west. As the crusade progressed so the number of replacements declined. See Powell, Anatomy of a Crusade, pp. 166–71, and see below, p. 252.

[116] Richard of San Germano, 'Chronica', MGHS, vol. XIX, p. 344; J. H. Pryor, 'Transportation of Horses by Sea during the Era of the Crusades', The Mariners' Mirror, 68 (1982), pp. 23–4; Van Cleve, 'The Crusade of Frederick II', p. 446.

[117] 'Rothelin', p. 532. The author of De constructione castri Saphet (p. 34) gave the much lower figure of 1,500 fully armed knights. However, this appears to represent only the crusading element of the army.

on foot.[118] The smaller expedition led by the Lord Edward in 1271 included a force under his personal command of 200 to 300 knights and twice as many footsoldiers.[119]

The crusader armies which came to help the Latin East offered, therefore, a considerable increase in the size of the Christian forces. A crusade such as Theobald of Champagne's probably doubled the number of troops which the Latins had available. Smaller expeditions, of which the Lord Edward's is only one example, still provided hundreds of men to augment those who were normally garrisoning the area's strongpoints. The crusades into Egypt threatened the Muslims with up to twice the number of troops normally resident in the Latin East. But the crusade in the thirteenth century achieved little of value for the maintenance of the Latin settlement. How far were the native Latins able to determine the use which was made of this resource?

The decision of the Fifth Crusade to attack Egypt, after a period of castle-building and raiding Muslim positions which bordered the Latin Kingdom, seems to have been taken by John of Brienne following a conference which he held with the leading figures of the Military Orders and the Kingdom. There may not have been any crusaders present at this meeting, although this seems unlikely. The earlier decision to raid Muslim territory had been made at a *parlement* in the tent of the king of Hungary, attended by all the prominent figures of the crusade and the leaders of the Latin East. At the later conference, John of Brienne not only recognised the potential value of a large-scale assault on Egypt, but also argued that the crusade would serve little purpose if it remained in Palestine:

It is my opinion that we cannot accomplish very much at all against the Saracens in this land. However, if you consider that it would be a good idea, then I would gladly go into the land of Egypt, to besiege Alexandria or Damietta. If we are able to capture one of these cities, then I believe that we could, from this, have the kingdom of Jerusalem.[120]

With such an army, an offensive campaign was considered the

---

[118] Joinville, *Histoire de Saint Louis*, p. 82; 'Rothelin', p. 571.

[119] Beebe, 'Edward I and the Crusades', p. 54.

[120] 'Il m'est avis que nous ne porons mie grantment esploitier en ceste tiere sor Sarrasins. Et se vous veés qu'il fust boin à faire, jou iroie volentiers en la tiere d'Egipte, assegier Alixandre ou Damiete, car se nous poons avoir une de ces cités, bien m'est avis que nous en poriemes bien avoir le roialme de Jherusalem' (*Chronique d'Ernoul*, pp. 414–15); see also 'Eracles', vol. II, pp. 322–3, 326.

most appropriate means to defend and possibly extend the borders of the Latin Kingdom. But in the case of the Fifth Crusade, the best opportunity to achieve these objectives may have been lost when the legate Pelagius, and others, refused to accept a generous settlement offered by the Muslims.[121]

The strategy adopted by Theobald of Champagne's crusade suggested a desire to protect the kingdom through the building of a frontier strongpoint in the south at Ascalon, and then the lessening of any possible threat from the east by an attack on Damascus. Neither of these schemes, which had been agreed at a stormy conference at Acre, was carried out. This was principally because of the refusal of Henry, count of Bar, and others, to accept the discipline which Theobald and the Military Orders attempted to enforce. A Christian Arabic chronicler who commented on the failure of this crusade wrote that the crusaders 'did not know the locality of the land nor the ruse of the Muslims in fighting nor their stratagems'.[122] The outcome of the first phase of Theobald of Champagne's crusade (a heavy defeat at the battle of Gaza) demonstrated many of the problems that the leaders of the Latin states faced when trying to make use of an army which was supposedly intended to help them. Crusaders did not understand the circumstances of the region they had volunteered to fight in and they were often unwilling to submit to wise counsel.

St Louis's first crusade had probably always intended to attack Egypt, though the evidence is inconclusive.[123] The Lord Edward's crusade was hampered by a lack of manpower which Edward himself recognised: not having enough men to face Baybars, he

---

[121] In August 1219, the Muslims were prepared to give up their possessions in the Kingdom of Jerusalem, except the fortresses of Kerak and Montreal. They also offered a thirty-year truce. John of Brienne, the Teutonic Knights and many of the crusaders favoured acceptance of the offer, but Pelagius, the Templars, the Hospitallers and the Italians rejected it, mainly because of the Muslims' refusal to include the two fortresses (see 'Eracles', vol. II, p. 339; Oliver of Paderborn, 'Historia', pp. 222–4; *History of the Patriarchs*, vol. IV, p. 64).

[122] *History of the Patriarchs*, vol. IV, p. 196; see also 'Rothelin', pp. 531–2, 539–40. Building work at Ascalon was undertaken later in the crusade. The decision to fortify Ascalon was a sound one. As-Salih Isma'il, who had just taken control of Damascus, had shown himself willing to recognise al-'Adil II, the sultan of Egypt. The (temporary) restoration of good relations between Cairo and Damascus raised the possibility of a united Muslim front against the Latin East. In this context, it was important to protect the south of the Latin Kingdom from a possible attack from Egypt. See Jackson, 'The Crusades of 1239–41', pp. 38–9.

[123] Strayer, 'The Crusades of Louis IX', pp. 494–5.

opted for some raiding against Muslim positions in the vicinity of Acre and, it would appear, an unsuccessful attempt to capture the important Muslim stronghold of Qaqun.[124] The crusades generally presented a series of *faits accomplis* to the inhabitants of the Latin East, most of which would have come as a disappointment. Invasions of Egypt were regarded with approval, but the Fifth Crusade failed after control of its direction had become blurred following the arrival of Pelagius. And St Louis's crusade was halted at Mansurah when the exuberance of crusaders again overcame the cautious advice of the Military Orders. In general, the desire of the crusaders to fight the infidel had to be accommodated by the Latin East's leaders, though they would probably have preferred appeasement to aggression.

It is clear from the financing of St Louis's crusade that the Church provided most of the monetary resources for such an enterprise. Funds were not only given to help major crusade expeditions, however. Tenths which had originally been levied for specific campaigns became a regular aspect of papal financial policy. The money collected was employed in various ways. It could be used in Europe to assist individual crusaders; it could be sent to the Holy Land to be spent in whatever way was deemed appropriate; or it could be returned to the papal treasury and subsequently diverted to other projects.[125] Documents from Innocent IV's pontificate show the means by which individual crusaders were able to join St Louis's expedition. William Longsword, an English crusader whose effigy can be seen in Salisbury Cathedral, died in heroic circumstances at Mansurah, if the account of Matthew Paris is to be believed.[126] His journey was financed in part by the redemption of vows of other *crucesignati* in the diocese of Lincoln and elsewhere, who 'on account of the weakness of their bodies or other just causes are unable to go over the sea to that land in person…'.[127] In another case in which money payments by the faithful enabled men to fulfil their vows to go personally on crusade, Innocent told Odo of Châteauroux, the cardinal-bishop of Tusculum and papal legate, to provide the

[124] *Gestes des Chiprois*, pp. 199–201; Ibn 'Abd al-Zahir, 'Life of Baybars', vol. II, pp. 762, 770–1.
[125] Purcell, *Papal Crusading Policy*, pp. 137–57; Richard, *Latin Kingdom*, pp. 376–7.
[126] Matthew Paris, *Chronica maiora*, vol. v, pp. 152–4. See also 'Rothelin', pp. 605–6.
[127] '…propter impotentiam corporum vel alias justas causas in terram predictam nequeunt personaliter transfretare…' (Innocent IV, *Registre*, nos. 2758; see also nos. 2759, 3723–4).

74

lord of Château-Chinon with 500 marks from the redemption of other crusaders' vows. A companion of the lord of Château-Chinon, who also hoped to go on crusade, was to receive 50 marks.[128]

Financial assistance for individuals who were prepared to offer their services to the Holy Land was not restricted to those who journeyed in the ranks of a crusade. We have already seen that individual pilgrims were a constant feature of the potential resources of the Latin East. In January 1264, Urban IV received news about the poor condition of the Latin states and therefore ordered the levying of a hundredth for five years, which was to be collected by Giles, the archbishop of Tyre, and John of Valenciennes, the lord of Haifa. There does not seem to have been any great enthusiasm in Europe for a new crusade, but in July 1264 Urban assured the rulers of the Latin Kingdom that aid would soon be on its way; at the same time he sent part of the hundredth in order that work could be done on the defences of Jaffa.[129] Urban also wrote in July to the count of Blois, urging him to take the cross. The count and his wife, Alice, were given a subsidy to help them to undertake the journey.[130] In 1287 or 1288 the countess of Blois arrived in Acre with a large number of troops, one of the last pilgrims to visit the Holy Land whilst it was in Latin hands. She built a tower at Acre, and a chapel. The following year she died in the city.[131]

## Confraternities

The need for continual support for the Holy Land beyond that provided by the crusades was not only recognised by individuals such as Alice of Blois. Groups of men, often from urban centres in Europe, formed charitable institutions which allowed them to spend some time serving the armies of the Latin East.[132] Unfortunately, evidence of only eight confraternities has sur-

---

[128] *Ibid.*, nos. 3450, 3451.     [129] Urban IV, *Registre*, nos. 473, 868, 869.

[130] *Ibid.*, no. 690.

[131] 'Annales de Terre Sainte', pp. 459–60; *Gestes des Chiprois*, p. 245; Marino Sanuto the Elder, 'Liber secretorum fidelium crucis', ed. J. Bongars, in *Gesta Dei per Francos, sive orientalium expeditionum et regni Francorum Hierosolimitani Historia a variis, sed illius aevi scriptoribus litteris commendata*, vol. II (Hannau, 1611), p. 229.

[132] On the confraternities, see J. S. C. Riley-Smith, 'A Note on Confraternities in the Latin Kingdom of Jerusalem', *Bulletin of the Institute of Historical Research*, 44 (1971), pp. 301–8.

vived, but it can be presumed that there were many more. This material assumes additional importance because it provides almost unique information on the role of reasonably equipped foot-soldiers, who were possibly the largest single group within the Latin army. In general, the confraternities did not represent the burgesses of the Latin states, since their members were either foreign residents or crusaders.

Three confraternities demonstrate the different forms that these groups could take, and the functions which they might have been expected to perform. At Châteaudun, Odo of Châteauroux encouraged the formation of a confraternity as part of the preparations for the first crusade of St Louis; its statutes were confirmed by Innocent IV. Professor Riley-Smith has pointed out that the confraternity's purchase of crossbows probably indicates that it was made up of burgesses, rather than knights. The later history of the group cannot be traced.[133] The Confraternity of the Holy Spirit may also have been founded to enable its members to join a crusade, the Fifth, but it definitely survived after this and had its statutes confirmed by Pope Alexander IV in 1255. It also participated in the final defence of Acre in 1291. It was important enough for one contemporary writer to refer to it, paired with the Templars, as one of the eight groups which led the resistance to the Muslims at the siege of Acre. The members of the confraternity were Italians, so they may have joined merchant ships going to the Latin East and then spent some months in voluntary service with the Latin armies – possibly by arriving on one passage and leaving on the next, which would have given them between five and seven months in the Holy Land. The size of the confraternity is not known, nor is the quantity of troops that it provided, although some details suggest it may have been a fair number. Members of the confraternity were expected to carry arms if they were able to equip themselves, but if they could not then these would be provided. (This also suggests that members were probably burgesses, many of whom would not normally carry weapons.) Money was available to ransom members of the society who were captured by the enemy. Sections in the rules concerning division of booty and the need for discipline in battle – interesting in itself, for troops probably serving on foot – also imply that membership of the confraternity

---

[133] Innocent IV, *Registre*, no. 2644; J. S. C. Riley-Smith, 'A Note on Confraternities', p. 307.

was quite large. During a conflict, troops were expected to rally under the confraternity's banner.[134]

The Confraternity of St Andrew, founded before 1187, was rather different from the societies considered so far. Not only was it based in the Latin East, but membership was open to 'nobles, knights and burgesses' ('li riche home et li chevalier et li borgeis'), a point which seems to have caused some surprise amongst contemporaries.[135] It played a leading role in the feudatories' efforts to resist the demands of Frederick II. But it is not known whether it enabled inhabitants of the Latin East who did not owe feudal service to help the armies of the kingdom.

### The French regiment

A document from Edward I's reign noted that after his crusade, members of the English Confraternity of Saint Edward the Confessor were ordered 'to the custody ... of the tower which the king caused to be built there' (at Acre).[136] St Louis, at the end of his crusade, also wished to make a permanent contribution to the defence of the Holy Land. He therefore established a body of troops which was to be maintained by revenues from the French monarchy. The history of this regiment is sketchy and its numbers fluctuated, whilst support from France was at times neither regular nor adequate. But the force remained in the Latin East until the fall of the kingdom. It provided much needed reinforcements for the army and played a significant part in many of the military events of this period. Moreover, some of its leaders became important figures in the government of the Latin East.

The original force which St Louis left comprised a hundred knights, with crossbowmen and mounted and foot sergeants. It was commanded by Geoffrey of Sergines, a committed crusader and a close associate of St Louis. Geoffrey was also appointed seneschal of the kingdom,[137] an important position and one which was subsequently held by other members of the French regiment.

---

[134] Alexander IV, *Registre*, no. 346; 'De excidio urbis Acconis libri II', ed. E. Martene and U. Durand, in *Veterum scriptorum et monumentorum amplissima collectio*, vol. v (Paris, 1729), col. 766.

[135] 'Eracles', vol. II, pp. 391–2; J. Prawer, 'Estates, Communities, and the Constitution of the Latin Kingdom', in *Crusader Institutions*, p. 62.

[136] *Calendar of Patent Rolls preserved in the Public Record Office. Edward I. AD 1272–81*, p. 296.

[137] 'Eracles', vol. II, p. 441; 'Rothelin', p. 629; J. S. C. Riley-Smith, *What Were the Crusades?* (London, 1977), pp. 65–6.

The value of this new force to the kingdom's armies was soon illustrated. It is reasonable to assume that it was present when its leaders were mentioned: in the winter of 1255–6, for example, it helped to repel a Muslim assault on Jaffa after a successful Christian raid in the area.[138] In 1263 Geoffrey was wounded during a Muslim raid on Acre,[139] but his injuries were presumably not serious because in the following year he was present during a Christian raid near Ascalon.[140] It was probably also in 1264 that Oliver of Termes (who was to be associated with the French regiment for much of the next decade) came to Acre and in November of that year he took part in a raid on Bethsan.[141] Oliver was a man with a 'questionable past', having been involved in resistance to the French crown in Languedoc in the early 1240s. But he appears to have been successfully rehabilitated.[142]

During the 1260s, the solvency of the regiment was in some doubt. In early 1263, Urban IV had to write to Louis, encouraging him to maintain his support for Geoffrey.[143] Two or three years later, Clement IV was similarly aware of the high costs incurred by Geoffrey. It was therefore arranged that some of the hundredth which was being collected for the Holy Land should go to him.[144] In 1265, Geoffrey was to receive 500 *livres* from a group of friars which was raising money in France to help the Holy Land.[145] In the mid-1260s Geoffrey, Oliver and Erard of Valéry, who had recently travelled to the east, tried to ensure regular payments from France in the form of loans taken out in the east and subsequently repaid by the French crown.[146] These still proved

---

[138] 'Rothelin', pp. 630–2.

[139] *Gestes des Chiprois*, pp. 167–8; 'Eracles', vol. II, p. 447.

[140] 'Annales de Terre Sainte', p. 451; *Chronique d'Amadi*, pp. 206–7.

[141] 'Annales de Terre Sainte', p. 451.

[142] B. Z. Kedar, 'The Passenger List of a Crusader Ship, 1250: Towards the History of the Popular Element on the Seventh Crusade', *Studi Medievali*, 3rd Series, 13 (1972), pp. 276–8. See also Jordan, *Louis IX*, pp. 15–17, 67. Professor Kedar pointed out (p. 277) that the date of Oliver's arrival in the Latin East is not entirely clear. The narrative sources indicate 1264, but a letter from Clement IV suggests that Oliver may not have left Europe until some time after mid-1265 (Clement IV, *Registre*, ed. E. Jordan (Paris, 1893–1945), no. 898). Oliver was certainly in the Latin East in November 1265 ('Emprunts de Saint Louis en Palestine et en Afrique', ed. G. Servois, *Bibliothèque de l'Ecole des Chartes*, 19 (1858), p. 123).    [143] Urban IV, *Registre*, no. 183.

[144] Clement IV, *Registre*, nos. 812–14.

[145] L. Borrelli de Serres, 'Compte d'une mission de prédication pour secours à la terre sainte', *Mémoires de la Société de l'Histoire de Paris et de l'Ile de France*, 30 (1903), pp. 254–7, 264.    [146] 'Emprunts de Saint Louis', pp. 123–31.

insufficient, however, and in 1267 William of Agen, the patriarch of Jerusalem, wrote to the commander of the Templars in Paris asking for further assistance. The letter indicated the extent to which French soldiers were active in the Holy Land at this time. The patriarch wished to hire fifty French knights (who had come to the east in 1265 with the counts of Nevers and Nanteuil and Erard of Valéry) for eight months at a cost of 60 *livres tournois* per knight. An additional forty-eight French knights had been retained at a cost of 1,800 *livres tournois* for five months. Although both these groups were hired by the patriarch on behalf of the papacy, they may well have served with their colleagues in the French garrison. The payments for both groups indicate an annual salary for a knight of 90 *livres tournois*. Geoffrey of Sergines was spending 10,000 *livres tournois* a year on his force, which suggests that it had been maintained at around the figure of 100 knights with which it had been created in 1254. But not all Geoffrey's expenses were being paid by the French crown. The patriarch noted that the regiment's commander had been obliged to borrow 3,000 *livres tournois* to pay his troops and would be forced to alienate his own properties in order to repay this loan.[147] The regiment's difficulties at this time extended to its military activities. In 1266 some of its members, who were acting as part of an advance guard for a raiding party, were ambushed by Muslims on the plain of Acre.[148]

Geoffrey of Sergines's position as the leader of the French troops allowed him to play an influential part in the kingdom's political life. From 1259 to 1261 he was lieutenant in the kingdom, appointed by Plaisance of Cyprus following the death of John of Arsuf. When Plaisance herself died in 1261, Geoffrey was appointed regent for Hugh of Cyprus, perhaps being re-appointed following the death of Isabella of Cyprus in 1264. After the High Court had selected Hugh of Antioch-Lusignan as the new regent, in about 1265, Geoffrey was the first to offer him homage. Geoffrey then became lieutenant for Hugh of Antioch-Lusignan until 1267.[149] He was thus one of the most important

---

[147] *Ibid.*, pp. 284–5, 291–2; 'Eracles', vol. II, p. 454; *Gestes des Chiprois*, p. 176 (where sixty knights are said to have accompanied the counts of Nevers and Nanteuil and Erard of Valéry).

[148] *Gestes des Chiprois*, pp. 181–2; 'Eracles', vol. II, p. 455; *Chronique d'Amadi*, p. 208.

[149] J. S. C. Riley-Smith, *Feudal Nobility*, pp. 217, 318, 320; 'The Disputed Regency of the Kingdom of Jerusalem, 1264/6 and 1268', ed. P. W. Edbury, *Camden Miscellany*, 27 (1979), p. 41.

Christian figures during the first Mamluk onslaught on the Latin Kingdom and he was involved in much of the correspondence to and from the region at this time. His concern for military affairs was not limited to the maintenance of the French regiment. In July 1264, Urban IV expressed concern about the condition of the defences of Jaffa. Part of the hundredth which was being collected should be used to effect improvements: the money was to be sent to the patriarch and Geoffrey of Sergines in order that the castle might be repaired and made ready to defend itself.[150]

Geoffrey died in April 1269, after a career in the east which had earned him eulogies from the papacy and from a contemporary poet, Rutebeuf.[151] The activities of the French regiment are, regrettably, rather obscure in the period following his death. He was succeeded as seneschal by Robert of Crésèques, but the connection of the latter with the French regiment is unclear. His action in a battle with Muslim troops outside Acre in 1269 (when he rejected advice to retreat, saying that he had come to the Holy Land to die for God) does not sound that of a responsible leader and it may be that Oliver of Termes had taken over control of the regiment, although a contemporary Muslim writer stated that whilst Oliver had led the army, St Louis's 'governor' at Acre had been killed in the battle.[152] Meanwhile, Erard of Valéry had returned to Europe, playing an important role in the battle of Tagliacozzo in 1268.[153] There is no information on the regiment during the next few years and it is possible that it went into temporary abeyance in view of St Louis's crusade to Tunis. Erard of Valéry, for example, had agreed to serve on crusade with St Louis for one year and to provide thirty knights in return for 8,000 *livres tournois*.[154] In the winter of 1270–1, Oliver, Erard and John of Grailly (a future commander of the French troops) were all in Sicily with the Lord Edward before his departure for the Holy Land.[155]

By 1272, however, the presence of the regiment in the Latin

---

[150] Urban IV, *Registre*, no. 869; see also no. 473.

[151] 'Annales de Terre Sainte', p. 454; Urban IV, *Registre*, nos. 53–5; Clement IV, *Registre*, nos. 812–14; *Onze poèmes de Rutebeuf concernant la croisade*, ed. J. Bastin and E. Faral (Paris, 1946), pp. 22–7.

[152] *Cartulaire des Hospitaliers*, nos. 3323, 3326; *Gestes des Chiprois*, pp. 183–4 (dated 1267); 'Eracles', vol. II, p. 458; 'Annales de Terre Sainte', p. 454; Ibn 'Abd al-Zahir, 'Life of Baybars', vol. II, pp. 727–9.

[153] Herde, 'Taktiken muslimischer', pp. 87–8; *Gestes des Chiprois*, pp. 188–9.

[154] 'Liste des Chevaliers croisés avec Saint Louis en 1269', RHF, vol. XX, p. 305.

[155] Beebe, 'Edward I and the Crusades', pp. 49–50.

East was again apparent. In that year John of Grailly was appointed seneschal[156] and Oliver of Termes was preparing to return to the Latin East. By the summer he was ready and in 1273 Philip III and Gregory X sent large numbers of troops, possibly to reconstitute completely the French presence in the Holy Land. Giles of Sanci arrived with 400 crossbowmen; Peter of Aminnes brought 300 crossbowmen, whilst Oliver himself travelled with 25 mounted troops and 100 foot archers.[157] Gregory hoped that Oliver would continue to serve in the east but he died in August 1274,[158] and the regiment may have been leaderless again until 1275 or 1276 when William of Roussillon arrived in the kingdom, with 'mounted troops and footsoldiers from the king of France, and he was their commander' ('gens à chevau & à pié de par le roy de France, & fu lor cheveteine'). His force consisted of 40 knights, 60 mounted sergeants and 400 crossbowmen – a sizeable addition to the armies of the Latin East.[159] He died in 1277, but the succession of Miles of Haifa as the regiment's new leader seems to have been immediate.[160] The latter's name suggests that he may have been a native of the Latin East.

Also in 1277, Odo Poilechien became seneschal of the kingdom, presumably replacing John of Grailly, and it has been suggested that in 1286 Odo was commander of the French regiment.[161] This does not appear to have been the case, however. Odo was French, but he was a member of the force which had arrived in Acre to support Roger of San Severino as *bailli* for Charles of Anjou, the latter having purchased the rights to the Latin Kingdom of Maria of Antioch. In 1282, when Roger left the Latin East, Odo himself became the *bailli*,[162] but four years later Henry II of Cyprus came to Acre to claim the throne. The French regiment opposed Henry and, with some other men-at-arms, it joined Odo inside the castle of Acre. The leaders of the Military Orders were eventually able to achieve a settlement without bloodshed and Odo surrendered the castle. Only the French troops were mentioned specifically as the opponents of Henry, which indicates that they had been able

---

[156] 'Eracles', vol. II, p. 463.

[157] Gregory X, *Registre*, ed. J. Guiraud and E. Cadier (Paris, 1892–1960), nos. 796, 798, 802–3 (all undated); 'Eracles', vol. II, pp. 463–4.

[158] Gregory X, *Registre*, no. 493; 'Eracles', vol. II, p. 466.

[159] *Gestes des Chiprois*, pp. 202–3; see also 'Eracles', vol. II, p. 467.

[160] 'Eracles', vol. II, p. 478.       [161] Richard, *Latin Kingdom*, p. 378.

[162] 'Eracles', vol. II, pp. 478–9; *Gestes des Chiprois*, p. 214. See J. S. C. Riley-Smith, *Feudal Nobility*, pp. 220–7.

to retain a considerable presence in the east.[163] Their opposition to Henry does not appear to have affected their status, however, or that of their leader. By September 1288 when Pope Nicholas IV wrote to the Christian leaders, John of Grailly, who had returned to the Latin East the previous year, was described as 'captain of the men...of Philip, king of France' and he had also been re-appointed as seneschal.[164]

John of Grailly and his troops played a prominent role in the final years of the Latin settlement. John, like Geoffrey of Sergines before him, was one of the kingdom's leading figures and he was in regular communication with the papacy.[165] In 1289, as 'commander of the men of the king of France and seneschal of the kingdom of Jerusalem' ('chevetaine des gens dou roy de France & seneschau dou royaume de Jerusalem'), John was present at the siege of Tripoli; on this occasion, the French regiment provided both knights and sergeants.[166] Two years later at the siege of Acre, the regiment was required to defend the Tower of the Legate, near the south-east corner of the city walls. It was supported by English troops commanded by the Burgundian knight Otto of Grandison. After much of the city wall had been breached, a mounted Muslim force attacked the tower. The French defended courageously and suffered heavy casualties, both wounded and dead: amongst the former was John of Grailly himself. Eventually the regiment could no longer prevent the Muslims' advance and with Otto of Grandison it was forced to withdraw.[167] Opinion on the merits of the last commander of the French regiment seems to have been mixed, however: one writer claimed that John, having fled from the siege of Tripoli, did exactly the same at the siege of Acre.[168]

The French regiment was therefore an important part of the Latin army during the second half of the thirteenth century, playing a role which, in some respects at least, was comparable to that of the Military Orders. Unlike the Military Orders, however, it did not have to bear the burden for defence of individual

[163] *Gestes des Chiprois*, p. 219; *Histoire de l'île de Chypre*, vol. III, pp. 671–3.
[164] Nicholas IV, *Registre*, ed. E. Langlois (2 vols., Paris, 1886–93), no. 620; *Gestes des Chiprois*, p. 237; Marino Sanuto, 'Liber', p. 229.
[165] See Nicholas IV, *Registre*, nos. 620, 2252–3, 2258, 2269, 4393, 4400.
[166] *Gestes des Chiprois*, pp. 235, 237.
[167] *Ibid.*, pp. 251–2; see Beebe, 'Edward I and the Crusades', pp. 263–5.
[168] Thaddaeus of Naples, *Hystoria de desolacione et conculcacione civitatis Acconensis*, ed. P. Riant (Geneva, 1873), pp. 25–6.

strongpoints. It was thus able to operate as an itinerant force, taking part in raiding expeditions, battles and the defence of various sites. This last function may help to explain the financial embarrassment it was suffering in the 1260s, when it would have been involved in efforts to contain the threat of Baybars and the Muslim armies. A number of its captains, most notably Geoffrey of Sergines and John of Grailly, became prominent figures in the government of the Latin Kingdom. The regiment appears to have been based at Jaffa during its early years,[169] probably then moving to Acre. It may have found accommodation in quarters erected by St Louis during his period in the Holy Land. The presence of French troops in the Latin East maintained the tradition of French involvement which had begun with the First Crusade.

### Papal support

The papacy, unlike the French crown, did not attempt to maintain a permanent force in the Latin East, but it consistently provided resources for the Latin armies. The sums of money which were paid to individual crusaders or in support of crusades were the obvious forms of papal support for the Holy Land, but we have already seen that funds gathered by the papacy could be employed in other ways. The provision of troops was possible either by the employment of men in the west who would then be sent to the east, or by the use of papal funds to hire soldiers who were already in Palestine.

During the early 1260s, and despite the mounting pressures on the Latin states, most of the papacy's crusading energies were concentrated on Sicily.[170] Nonetheless, the direct supply of troops to the Latin East is evident from the 1260s and, moreover, this does not seem to have been at the expense of sending money to be used in the region. The papacy may have realised that troops were needed immediately, rather than delaying until a crusade could be organised. In October 1266, Clement IV referred to the losses of Arsuf, Caesarea and Saphet and ordered that the cross should be preached quickly, but that first money should be provided for the transportation of 500 crossbowmen on the March passage. In February of the following year the Pisans were instructed to send ten galleys to the Holy Land in March. In May,

---

[169] *Onze poèmes de Rutebeuf,* p. 25.
[170] Purcell, *Papal Crusading Policy,* p. 86 and *passim.*

ships were to be equipped 'in subsidium Terre Sancte' with money which had been collected.[171] During the 1270s, support for the Latin Kingdom in the form of troops continued to be provided by both Philip III of France and the papacy. This may even have been a concerted action, since the troops who arrived in the east in 1273 and 1275–6 under the command of Giles of Sanci and William of Roussillon (already referred to in connection with the French regiment) were financed, at least in part, by the Church.[172] In 1289–90, Pope Nicholas IV sent galleys from Venice and Genoa to the east where the patriarch of Jerusalem was to be responsible for their maintenance. Considerable difficulties arose, however. The equipment of many of the ships proved to be sub-standard and Nicholas advised that the patriarch should only hire ten or twelve vessels out of an original fleet of twenty. The smaller force should be properly provided for with arms and men: the rest of the fleet would then be free to go.[173] This demonstrates the importance of naval support for the defence of the region, the willingness of the papacy to help the Latin East, but the problems which could be faced in practice, and the role played by the patriarch as the representative of the papacy in the area.

The papacy often sent money to the Holy Land which could then be used as those in the area saw fit. In 1208, for example, Innocent III arranged a payment of 1,000 *livres* of Provence, to be used by the patriarch, the Templars and the Hospitallers. In 1209 Innocent inquired about the sum which had been dispatched the previous year, but he also sent another 850 *livres*. The recipients were told to spend the money in whatever way they considered would most benefit the Holy Land. In contrast to these sums, Innocent provided 30,000 *livres* towards the cost of the Fifth Crusade.[174] In the 1260s and 1270s, too, the papacy's activities included the provision of money as well as troops. In 1267, when William of Agen wished to employ the fifty knights that the counts of Nevers and Nanteuil and Erard of Valéry had brought to the Latin East, the pope's approval had to be sought.[175] William's successor as patriarch was Thomas Agni. In the summer

---

[171] Clement IV, *Registre*, nos. 1146, 1171, 1191.

[172] 'Eracles', vol. II, pp. 464, 467.

[173] Nicholas IV, *Registre*, nos. 2252–8, 2269, 4385–90; *Gestes des Chiprois*, p. 238 (presumably the same fleet).

[174] Innocent III, 'Opera omnia', vol. CCXV, cols. 1427–8; vol. CCXVI, cols. 37–8; vol. CCXVII, col. 270.     [175] 'Emprunts de Saint Louis', p. 292.

of 1272, when he was preparing to journey to the east, Gregory X warned him about hiring poor-quality troops. In October 1272 Thomas arrived at Acre with 500 mounted and foot troops, purchased with Church funds and presumably of satisfactory quality.[176] Four years later, in one of the few recorded acts of a short pontificate, Hadrian V sent 12,000 *livres tournois* to the patriarch, leaving him and other leading figures in the kingdom to decide how the money could best be spent.[177] The patriarch also had to deal with Church funds which were directed towards the fortification of strongpoints in the Latin East. We will consider this point later.

The large-scale crusade expeditions could not fulfil the strategic requirements of the Latin East. Apart from providing manpower for building enterprises, they were able to achieve little else of value. But the supply of men, materials and funds from the west was a constant feature of the period's military history. It was simply that the quantities available were insufficient for the Latins to create a strategy which might have been capable of stemming the Muslim advance.

MERCENARIES AND PAID TROOPS

Troops serving for pay were an important element in the Latin armies. The French regiment was paid for by revenues from Europe and the obligation of *servise des compaignons* meant that paid troops served amongst the feudal levy. Many of the soldiers who served with the Military Orders were paid, probably including those who were employed for long-term duties such as castle-guard. We have seen that the Military Orders employed mercenaries during a crusade and for the defence of a strongpoint during a siege campaign.[178] Troops who came to the Holy Land, such as those who accompanied Erard of Valéry, could be employed for a specific length of time, in their case eight months. But most of the documented examples of mercenary troops relate to campaigns between Christian armies.

Both sides in the Lombard–Ibelin war used mercenaries. In 1229 when Frederick II sold the *bailliage* of Cyprus to five nobles,

---

[176] Gregory X, *Registre*, no. 797; 'Eracles', vol. II, p. 462.
[177] 'Eracles', vol. II, p. 477.
[178] On the Military Orders' employment of troops serving for pay, see above, pp. 58–60.

they were provided with German, Flemish and Lombard *sodoyers*, whilst other troops were hired at Acre and elsewhere. It is interesting that such troops were available for hire in Acre. On the Ibelin side, before the battle of Agridi in 1232, Genoese ships were offered commercial privileges and property on Cyprus in return for their support. During the siege of Kyrenia after this battle, John of Beirut hired thirteen Genoese vessels with funds provided by the king. This enabled the Ibelins to besiege the castle by land and sea. Mercenary sergeants were also employed during this siege. When the Ibelins besieged Tyre in 1242, mercenaries and galleys were employed by Philip of Novara, Balian of Ibelin and Philip of Montfort. The Genoese and Venetians both supported this enterprise, the latter receiving commercial privileges in return for their aid.[179] In 1258, during the War of St Sabas, the Venetians and Pisans hired many troops at Acre to serve on their galleys; they were paid 10 Saracen besants a day and 9 at night.[180] During the conflict in northern Syria between Bohemond VII and the Embriacos, the latter engaged a number of mercenary sergeants prior to an attack on Tripoli in 1282. Most of these soldiers were Genoese.[181]

### ARMS AND ARMOUR IN THE LATIN EAST

Contemporary authors recognised that combat in the east posed problems – particularly the high temperatures and a mobile enemy – for troops whose equipment and methods of fighting had evolved in western Europe. But there does not seem to have been any attempt to modify arms and armour in order to deal with these difficulties. Armour in the thirteenth century was in a transitional period before the emergence of full plate armour. A comparison of texts from a section of the *Rule* of the Templars which has been dated to the twelfth century and John of Jaffa's mid-thirteenth-century legal treatise shows how little development had taken place in this period. The basis of the knight's clothing was the hauberk, a coat of chain mail. Some plate-armour protection for the legs was provided by the *chauces de fer*, and *espalieres* protected the shoulders. A padded tunic, the *ganbisson*, could be worn underneath the hauberk, whilst over it

---

[179] *Gestes des Chiprois*, pp. 51, 98–9, 108–9, 112, 130–1; *Urkunden der Republik Venedig*, vol. II, pp. 355–6.      [180] *Gestes des Chiprois*, p. 154.
[181] *Ibid.*, p. 210.

a surcoat was worn. This equipment was virtually standard for a knight. The sergeants who fought with the Templars were expected to be similarly protected, although their hauberks might be lighter without gauntlets and some of them would not wear much plate armour.[182] Complete effigies from the thirteenth century, allowing for problems of dating,[183] appear to confirm that there was no distinction between armour worn by the Latins in the east and the west.

The head was a particularly vulnerable part of the body. In the thirteenth century there were various methods of covering it. Most knights used the chain-mail coif, often with a steel cap beneath it; this protection could be augmented by one of a range of helmets. The Templars' *Rule* referred to sergeants wearing a *chapeau de fer*, an iron hat which was also worn by Joinville at Mansurah in 1250. A Genoese knight wore a similar hat outside Acre in 1253.[184] Broad-rimmed helmets known as 'kettle hats' were popular with footsoldiers and were worn by troops at the siege of Acre in 1291, according to an early fourteenth-century miniature (see plate 1, p. 13). A similar hat was drawn by the contemporary Villard of Honnecourt.[185] A low cylindrical helmet was another means of protection, exemplified by the early thirteenth-century effigy of Geoffrey of Mandeville in the Temple Church, London.

The most common form of protection for the knight, however, was the *heaume*, which as the 'pot helm' had been available at the end of the twelfth century.[186] An example of a pot helm was discovered at the Teutonic Knights' castle of Montfort.[187] In the thirteenth century, it was widely used in the form of the *heaume à visière*, that is, with a visor covering the face. The failure of a knight to wear such protection at the battle of Nicosia in 1229 enabled John of Beirut to kill him with a blow to the mouth. It is noteworthy that in the same battle Frederick II's five *baillis* wore distinguishing marks on their *heaumes*.[188] At the siege of Damietta during the Fifth Crusade, John of Arcis was easily

---

[182] *Règle du Temple*, nos. 138, 141, 419; John of Jaffa, 'Livre', p. 170.
[183] B. Kemp, *English Church Monuments* (London, 1980), pp. 19–20.
[184] *Règle du Temple*, no. 141; Joinville, *Histoire de Saint Louis*, pp. 134, 140.
[185] Villard of Honnecourt, *Facsimile of the Sketch-Book*, ed. R. Willis (London, 1859), plate 3. See also A. Borg, *Arms and Armour in Britain* (London, 1979), p. 11.
[186] Smail, *Crusading Warfare*, p. 107.
[187] B. Dean, *The Crusaders' Fortress of Montfort* (Jerusalem, 1982), pp. 36–8.
[188] John of Jaffa, 'Livre', p. 170; *Gestes des Chiprois*, p. 59.

identified by the defenders of the city: he was wearing a peacock's feather on his *heaume*.[189] The *heaume à visière* is illustrated in a number of contemporary seals from the Latin East, including those of Balian of Arsuf (see plate 2) and John of Montfort.[190] Such a helmet, compared to the pot helm, at least allowed the possibility of breathing reasonably freely without having to remove it completely. St Louis appears to have had difficulty with his breathing towards the end of the battle of Mansurah. It is not clear whether he was wearing a *heaume à visière* or a pot helm, but in any event, he was persuaded by Joinville to take off his helmet in order to get some fresh air. Joinville gave St Louis his own *chapeau de fer* for protection.[191]

It seems that the chosen form of protection varied according to personal taste and, no doubt, cost. A thirteenth-century miniature depicting St Louis's crusade to Egypt illustrates some of the possibilities (see plate 3). One knight is wearing a *chapeau de fer*, another is protected by a form of *heaume*, whilst a third on a ship appears to wear nothing on his head but a mail coif (perhaps with a steel cap underneath). The clothing of St Louis is interesting. He appears to have plate armour on his knee but he has no facial cover, simply wearing a crown over a mail coif. His shield, surcoat and the horse's coat are all decorated with the *fleurs de lis*. The shield, which is fairly small and triangular, is typical of the thirteenth century.[192]

The knight also had to carry a wide range of weapons. The sword, dagger, lance and *mace turquese*, a spiked iron head on a long handle, were referred to in the *Rule* of the Templars and by John of Jaffa. Joinville's account of the battle of Mansurah included an incident when the author was struck by a Muslim lance and pressed down on to his horse's neck; this prevented him from using the sword which he wore on his belt. But he also carried a sword on his horse and when he was able to draw this his attacker fled.[193] The horse itself was also provided with some

[189] 'Eracles', vol. II, p. 337.
[190] G. Schlumberger, *Sigillographie de l'Orient Latin* (Paris, 1943), pp. 64–5 and plate 18, no. 7.     [191] Joinville, *Histoire de Saint Louis*, p. 134.
[192] H. Buchthal, *Miniature Painting in the Latin Kingdom of Jerusalem* (Oxford, 1957), pp. 90–1. A similarly shaped shield to St Louis's may be seen on the effigy of William Longsword in Salisbury Cathedral. For the general history of protective armour during this period, see G. F. Laking, *A Record of European Armour and Arms through Seven Centuries*, vol. I (London, 1920), pp. 108–25.
[193] *Règle du Temple*, no. 138; John of Jaffa, 'Livre', p. 170; Joinville, *Histoire de Saint Louis*, pp. 120–2.

Plate 2. Seal of Balian of Arsuf

protection. As we saw earlier, knights were expected to own as many as four horses[194] and their immense value made it imperative that good care was taken of them. Horses in the Latin East wore plate armour and an iron headpiece.[195] An account of the preparations for Theobald of Champagne's crusade showed how much effort was necessary to gain the maximum benefit from equipment: 'to look at armour, grease hauberks, clean *heaumes*, sharpen swords and knives and shoe, cover and arm horses'.[196]

Amongst the lesser troops of the Latin armies the arms and armour used appear to have depended largely on what the individual could afford. This would consist of a selection from that available to the knight, with the addition of the bow or crossbow, which could be used by both mounted troops and footsoldiers. Some sergeants, even those on foot, were extremely well armed. Fidenzio of Padua noted the need for footsoldiers who used lances, bows and crossbows, with others holding shields to deflect Muslim arrows. It was also important that they should have armour or clothing to protect themselves.[197] But some footsoldiers, such as those depicted by Villard of Honnecourt using a bow and a lance, had very little protective covering.[198]

---

[194] See above, pp. 48–9.     [195] John of Jaffa, 'Livre', p. 170.
[196] '...armeures regarder, hauberz ouller, heaumes forbir, espees et coustiax esmondre, chevax ferrer, couvrir et armer' ('Rothelin', p. 532).
[197] Fidenzio of Padua, 'Liber recuperationis', pp. 29–30.
[198] See Villard of Honnecourt, *Sketch-Book*, plate 49.

Plate 3.  Miniature depicting St Louis's crusade to Egypt

For mounted troops, the heavy and cumbersome arms and armour caused difficulties which were exacerbated by the terrain and climate of the Latin East. The knights were required to expend vast amounts of energy on the battlefield. Their clumsy

90

combat technique in a mêlée was exemplified at the battle of Nicosia. Balian of Ibelin struck the Lombard standard-bearer so hard that he fell from his own horse: John of Beirut also fell off his horse when he killed a Lombard knight.[199] A knight who was thrown from his horse, or was obliged to dismount, was often virtually powerless. At Agridi in 1232, for example, Berart of Manepeau was knocked from his mount by Anceau of Brie. Seventeen of Berart's colleagues dismounted to help him recover, but they were all killed by foot sergeants.[200]

Some of the terrain in the area would have been almost impossible for the heavily armed Christian knights to fight on. Much of the coastline of the Latin Kingdom was covered by sand dunes which extended, in some places, many miles inland. An investigation of the likely battle sites of Gaza in 1239 and La Forbie in 1244 indicates that in both cases the Christian mounted troops would have been fighting on sand dunes, making their task almost impossible.[201] In August 1219, the crusaders' retreat from Fariskur in the Nile delta was made on sand which seriously hampered their movements.[202] At Nicosia in 1229, rather different conditions caused problems, for the recently ploughed field produced so much dust that it was almost impossible to see. John of Beirut was only able to assess the situation once most of the Lombard force had fled and the dust had settled.[203]

Problems associated with the climate in the area were particularly evident during crusade expeditions. Humbert of Romans, writing in the early 1270s, was aware of men's worries about conditions in the east, particularly with regard to the climate, their food and the terrain.[204] At Fariskur on the Fifth Crusade, the weight of arms carried by the footsoldiers and the need to drink undiluted wine because of a lack of water combined with the heat to cause, it was said, insanity and death.[205] The battle of Mansurah was fought in February 1250, when the heat would have been less oppressive than in summer, but some of St Louis's sergeants were still desperate for a drink.[206] During the

---

[199] *Gestes des Chiprois*, pp. 59–60.   [200] *Ibid.*, p. 103.

[201] And see 'Rothelin', pp. 541, 543, and Salimbene of Adam, 'Chronica', p. 177.

[202] James of Vitry, *Lettres*, p. 121.   [203] *Gestes des Chiprois*, pp. 58–9.

[204] Humbert of Romans, 'Opus tripartitum', trans. L. and J. S. C. Riley-Smith, in *The Crusades. Idea and Reality*, p. 108.

[205] Oliver of Paderborn, 'Historia', pp. 214–15; 'Fragmentum de captione Damiatae', p. 189; John of Tulbia, 'De Domino Johanne, rege Jerusalem', in *QBSSM*, p. 132.

[206] Joinville, *Histoire de Saint Louis*, p. 126.

Lord Edward's crusade in 1271, men died because of the heat, their thirst and the food which they had eaten.[207] In all these instances their heavy equipment must have made their problems even worse. The Templars were permitted to wear a short linen shirt during the summer, 'because of the great warmth of the hot season in the eastern lands'[208] but in general there seem to have been few allowances made for the conditions in the region. The equipment which the Christians used appears to have caused them considerable handicap and it is surprising that they were so little influenced by their surroundings: perhaps the constant influx of troops from western Europe helps to explain this apparent lack of integration.

[207] *Gestes des Chiprois*, p. 200; Ibn 'Abd al-Zahir, 'Life of Baybars', vol. II, p. 762.
[208] '...por la grant ardour de la chalour qui est el pais d'orient...' (*Règle du Temple*, no. 20).

*Chapter 3*

# CASTLES AND STRONGPOINTS

### INTRODUCTION

The Latin states were able to defend their territories against external threat and civil disorder by means of the army and the strongpoints. The dependence of the kingdom's troops on the fortified sites is striking. The constant problems caused by a manpower shortage, except at the time of a crusade, meant that the gathering of a large field army was rarely, if ever, possible in the Latin East during the thirteenth century. Most of the available soldiers, rather, were dispersed among a series of individual garrisons which were, to some extent, augmented by forces such as the Military Orders, the French regiment or groups of *peregrini*. The relationship of a garrison to its strongpoint thus provided the basis of the kingdom's military strategy and the framework for much of the military history of the period.

This relationship is illustrated by two documents dating from the 1240s. In September 1244, just before the battle of La Forbie, the principal ecclesiastics of the Holy Land, the leaders of the Military Orders and a number of lords wrote to Innocent IV explaining the difficulties caused by a lack of troops: 'the knights of the land are dispersed in all directions, near the castles they are guarding; they cannot easily be assembled because they are unable to leave the castles undefended...'.[1] Ascalon was besieged following the battle of La Forbie. The garrison 'realised that they were unable to have any help or aid from the Christians who were in the country, because the latter were themselves entirely occupied in guarding their own fortresses'.[2] So they fled from

---

[1] '...milites etiam terre sunt hinc inde dispersi prope castra munientes, qui non valent de facili congregari, eo quod non possunt castra relinquere immunita...' (*Chronica de Mailros*, p. 158).

[2] '...veoient qu'il ne povaient avoir nul secorz ne nulle aide des Crestienz qui estoient ou paiz, car cil meismes estoient tuit emblaé de garder leur fortresces ou il estoient' ('Rothelin', p. 565).

Ascalon, abandoning it to the Muslims. The limited numbers of troops available were therefore employed in the defence of strongpoints. However, the division of the Latin army into a number of garrisons did not simply influence the kingdom's defensive strategy. Strongpoints could also perform a more aggressive role, as a base for raids into hostile territory, for example, and in a general sense to 'threaten' the enemy. Their physical presence, and that of the garrisons within them, were the most obvious expressions of Latin dominance in the region.

We shall consider, first, the efforts which were made to establish and maintain castles and other strongpoints. Then we shall look at the functions which the sites performed. In both respects, the analysis of materials from a wide range of sites will be preferred to the consideration of individual castles. The latter approach has been adopted by most scholars who have dealt with this subject. But even for major castles such as Crac des Chevaliers or Château Pèlerin, where the survival of the monument has made possible detailed architectural studies, the paucity of written material, with gaps often amounting to decades, makes a more general study of castles in such a manner rather unsatisfactory. The sites examined include both fortified towns and castles, since in the thirteenth century the roles played by the two were quite similar: with a few exceptions which will be noted, any fortified site could only perform an effective role if its garrison was strong enough.

### THE ACQUISITION AND BUILDING OF STRONGPOINTS

During the thirteenth century, the Military Orders increasingly took responsibility for the maintenance of the kingdom's strongpoints, particularly in more exposed areas.[3] Examples of sites which the Orders established, or acquired control of during this period, include Château Pèlerin, Montfort, Ascalon, Sidon, Beaufort and Mt Tabor. During the two and a half years of building work at Saphet, knights, sergeants, crossbowmen and other armed men were recruited, whilst labourers and slaves were also sent. Pack horses carried arms, food and other supplies. A Muslim writer suggested that there were 1,000 Muslim prisoners

---

[3] See also above, pp. 64–6.

involved in the work, but less than 200 Christians. News reached Isma'il of Damascus that the Muslims planned a revolt; he warned the Templars, who took prompt action to quell the uprising. Expenses at Saphet after the major building work had been completed were still 40,000 besants a year, which suggests that minor repairs and alterations were a constant feature of castle life.[4]

Crac des Chevaliers underwent considerable work in the thirteenth century, financed by a number of exemptions and grants from the papacy and others. In 1218, for example, Andrew of Hungary made an annual grant to the Hospitallers at Crac of 100 marks, confirmed shortly afterwards by Honorius III. In 1255, Alexander IV granted exemption of certain payments at Crac, because of the constant labours, countless dangers and massive costs which the Hospitallers faced in garrisoning the castle.[5] The problems of castle maintenance will be examined in more detail later.

The Military Orders also accepted responsibility for much smaller castles. Two good examples of this are Montdidier and Tour Rouge, sites in the lordship of Caesarea which were owned by the Abbey of St Mary Latin. In 1236, the Templars were paying rents for both locations to the abbey, but they were expected shortly to leave so that the Hospitallers could move in. The Hospitallers were unable to take possession of the sites until 1248, however, when they agreed to pay the abbey a yearly rent of 800 besants, to cover Montdidier, Tour Rouge and the abbey's lands in nearby Qaqun.[6]

In chapter 2 we saw that during the Antiochene war of succession, Raymond Roupen granted property to the Hospitallers which was not actually held by Christians at the time.[7] Such gifts would encourage efforts to reconquer territory which had been lost to the Muslims. In January 1257, for example, a grant was made by Julian of Sidon to the Teutonic Knights of 'my fortress which is called Cave de Tyron, and all its rights'. The site had

---

[4] *De constructione castri Saphet*, pp. 38, 41; Ibn al-Furat, *Ayyubids*, vol. II, pp. 88–9. The use of Muslim slaves on building enterprises may have been common practice. In 1263, the Hospitallers and Templars refused to agree to a proposed exchange of Muslim and Christian prisoners; the Orders were using their Muslim captives as labourers and craftsmen and, if they had to be released, it would be necessary to employ men as replacements (*Gestes des Chiprois*, p. 167; 'Eracles', vol. II, p. 447).

[5] Deschamps, *Le Crac*, pp. 279–90; *Cartulaire des Hospitaliers*, nos. 1602, 1616, 2727.

[6] *Cartulaire des Hospitaliers*, nos. 2141, 2482; Pringle, *The Red Tower*, pp. 12, 37, 85–6.

[7] See above, p. 66.

probably fallen to Muslim troops around 1253, perhaps at the time of their assault on Sidon.[8]

The Military Orders also played a valuable role in the defence of sites over which they did not exercise full control. In 1218, the Teutonic Knights supported the Templars in the latter's construction of their castle of Château Pèlerin.[9] This work was carried out at the same time as the rebuilding of Caesarea, where the Teutonic Knights had been granted two towers in 1206.[10] At Acre, the Orders frequently vied with one another, and other groups, for the privilege of defending an area of the city. In October 1281, for example, Roger of San Severino settled, in favour of the Hospitallers, a dispute between them and the Pisans over the guarding of sentry positions, walls and towers from St Anthony's Gate to the Accursed Tower.[11] At Tripoli, efforts to maintain and improve defensive positions continued until the fall of the city in 1289: the Tower of the Bishop was old, but the Tower of the Hospital was 'strong and new'.[12]

The crusades were a useful source of manpower for building projects during the thirteenth century and work was often done in conjunction with the Military Orders and local nobility. At Acre in particular, many of the towers, such as the one established by Alice of Blois towards the end of the period, bore the names of their patrons.[13] At Sidon in 1227–8, construction work was done by crusaders who felt frustrated at having to wait for Frederick II.[14] When Richard of Cornwall decided to rebuild the castle at Ascalon in 1240, the Orders and the barons obtained both the workers and the materials which were needed for the task, before they came to the site.[15] St Louis worked for over a year on the fortifications of Caesarea, from March 1251 to May 1252. No contemporary account described this project in great detail, but it was undertaken with advice from the Templars and Hospitallers.[16] In the second half of 1253, St Louis was advised by the barons to

---

[8] *Tabulae ordinis Theutonici*, no. 110; see Joinville, *Histoire de Saint Louis*, p. 302. See above, chapter 1, note 22; for the attack on Sidon, see below, p. 127.

[9] Oliver of Paderborn, 'Historia', p. 169.

[10] 'Eracles', vol. II, pp. 325–6; *Tabulae ordinis Theutonici*, no. 40.

[11] *Cartulaire des Hospitaliers*, no. 3771.     [12] *Gestes des Chiprois*, p. 236.

[13] 'Annales de Terre Sainte', pp. 459–60; *Gestes des Chiprois*, p. 245.

[14] *Chronique d'Ernoul*, pp. 458–9, 460–1; 'Eracles', vol. II, p. 365. The crusaders' efforts were concentrated on the sea castle; they built two towers and a length of wall.

[15] *Gestes des Chiprois*, p. 123.

[16] Joinville, *Histoire de Saint Louis*, pp. 256–8, 282; Matthew Paris, *Chronica maiora*, vol. V, p. 257; 'Rothelin', pp. 627–8.

refortify the town of Sidon, rather than attempt to build a new castle on the Jaffa–Jerusalem road. He took their advice and constructed high walls and towers, and great quarried fosses.[17] Crusaders could not always be relied on for support, however. At Jaffa in 1239, following a heavy defeat in the battle near Gaza, some of the participants in Theobald of Champagne's crusade agreed to provide both money (7,000 marks) and manpower to help with the construction of Saphet. In the event, they left the Holy Land as soon as they reached Acre, their promises having been forgotten.[18]

Most of the local nobility could not afford to maintain their castles in the thirteenth century, so they handed them over to the Military Orders, which possessed the resources to cope in an increasingly hostile environment. In the period immediately before the campaigns of Baybars, the Hospitallers were granted Arsuf and the Templars received both Sidon and Beaufort, indicating that this was a critical time for the feudatories.[19] The Hospitallers had also recently been granted Mt Tabor by the papacy.[20] However, it would be wrong to suggest that all the feudatories gave up their responsibilities. Deschamps argued that it was entirely exceptional for one of the local barons, John of Beirut, to undertake the building of a castle. John, in a rousing speech to Frederick II, said that when he was given Beirut in exchange for becoming constable of the kingdom, the site was a ruin. The Templars and Hospitallers and the local barons declined to have anything to do with it, so John was compelled to do all the work himself, using the rents which he had from Cyprus and elsewhere and alms which were offered.[21] There are, in fact, other examples of nobles who built and maintained their own fortifications. Tiberias was rebuilt and presumably garrisoned by Odo of Montbéliard before it was captured by the Muslims in 1247.[22] John of Ibelin, the son of John of Beirut, strengthened the

---

[17] Joinville, *Histoire de Saint Louis*, pp. 302, 308, 336. According to this author, the proposed site for the new castle was on a hill, about fifteen miles inland on the road from Jaffa to Jerusalem. The native barons were concerned that it would be difficult to supply the site, because of its distance from the sea and the Muslims' domination of the hinterland. [18] *De constructione castri Saphet*, pp. 34–7.

[19] 'Eracles', vol. II, p. 445; *Gestes des Chiprois*, p. 162; *Cartulaire des Hospitaliers*, nos. 2972, 2985, 3047, 3071.

[20] *Cartulaire des Hospitaliers*, nos. 2726, 2729, 2811.

[21] Deschamps, *Le Crac*, pp. 84–6; *Gestes des Chiprois*, pp. 41–2.

[22] 'Eracles', vol. II, pp. 432–3.

castle of Arsuf in 1241[23] although his son, Balian, handed over control of the city and castle to the Hospitallers in the early 1260s. Jaffa, on the other hand, was maintained by its lord, John of Jaffa, until his death in 1266; it was to be captured by Baybars two years later. John was able to refortify the position with the help of crusaders and grants of revenue from western Europe. In the period after the fall of Ascalon in 1247, Jaffa was the most southerly strongpoint in the Latin Kingdom, and an important base for attacks into Muslim territory. Jaffa's role in this respect, and the efforts which were made to maintain the site, will be considered in more detail later.[24] A late example of baronial castle-building was the island fortress at Maraclea, ten miles north of Tortosa, which was constructed by its lord Bartholomew some time between 1277 and 1285. The detailed information about the site is only to be found in Muslim accounts. Bartholomew received help from the count of Tripoli, the Hospitallers of Margat and other Latins, but after the work had been completed the sultan Kalavun demanded the castle's destruction because of the threat which it posed. The demolition was undertaken by both Muslims and Christians.[25]

There was very little castle-building undertaken by the crown in this period, reflecting the relative weakness of the monarchy and the problems of long minorities and absentee rulers. John of Brienne was an exception to this. In March 1212 he purchased all the property that the Abbey of St Josaphat held at Tyre, since the land was needed for the construction of a new fortress. It was presumably this castle that the Lombards were forced to retreat into during the siege of Tyre in 1242.[26] Frederick II was another example of a royal builder. In 1229, he undertook some rebuilding work at Jaffa; he found it hard to persuade the Military Orders to support this project because of his conflict with the papacy.[27]

ARCHITECTURE AND DESIGN

The locations where the Latins established their strongpoints were diverse. Some, occupied in the twelfth century, had been the sites

[23] *Gestes des Chiprois*, p. 124; 'Annales de Terre Sainte', p. 440.
[24] See below, pp. 139–44.
[25] Ibn 'Abd al-Zahir, 'Vie de Kalavun', in Michaud, *Histoire*, vol. VII, pp. 698–700; Deschamps, *Comté de Tripoli*, p. 323.
[26] *Chartes de Terre Sainte provenant de l'abbaye de Josaphat*, ed. H. F. Delaborde (Paris, 1880), no. 46; *Gestes des Chiprois*, p. 132.    [27] 'Eracles', vol. II, pp. 372–3.

of earlier fortresses and the Franks adapted the surviving structures to suit their own requirements. In the thirteenth century sites which were occupied included caves, islands, coastal positions and spurs extending from the end of mountain ranges. A number of castles were virtually the same size as towns – Saphet, for example, was nearly as large as the town of Arsuf. The man-made defences of castles and towns were also similar, with use being made of towers, fosses, machicolations, arrow-slits, posterns and outworks such as barbicans.

The choice of a site for a castle was determined by a variety of factors. A location had to be found which would be difficult for an opposing force to besiege but, at the same time, not so inaccessible that the castle's only function could be to protect its garrison. The Latins, however, recognised that strongpoints were critical for their survival in the east. They also saw that the problems created by a lack of manpower could, to a certain extent, be allayed by a site's position, since the stronger the castle, the fewer men were required to defend it. Further, they acknowledged the threat posed by Muslim siege techniques. Pragmatism and an awareness of the physical geography of the area therefore caused the Latins to take advantage of good natural defences. However, we should not conclude that their main priority was to find sites which were out of the Muslims' reach. Even a site such as Montfort, which is now quite difficult to visit, was at the junction of a highway which linked Tyre and the north with the Sea of Galilee, the Jordan Valley and Jerusalem.[28]

Choosing a naturally protected position was one means of making a castle easier to defend. Another was the manner in which the castle itself was built. The first castles constructed by the Latins in the east consisted of a tower-keep built within a larger fortified enclosure. This form of the castle was common in western Europe from the eleventh to the thirteenth centuries; its use in the east shows that the Latins were not immediately influenced by the structure of the Byzantine fortresses which they encountered. The tower-keep offered great solidity, but its shape made it difficult for its occupants to conduct an active defence against an assault.[29]

A typical example of this type of fortress is Tour Rouge,

---

[28] Dean, *The Fortress of Montfort*, pp. 12–13.
[29] T. E. Lawrence, *Crusader Castles* (London, 1986), pp. 63–77; Pringle, *The Red Tower*, p. 15; Smail, *Crusading Warfare*, pp. 227–8.

recently excavated by Dr Pringle. The tower was probably constructed in the first half of the twelfth century. As noted earlier, it was in use in the thirteenth century; it was cleaned up at some time in this later period (possibly after the Hospitallers had taken over the site in 1248) and may have been refortified. The tower measured approximately 20 by 15 metres at its base, with walls 2·2 metres thick. It had two storeys, the lower covered by two barrel vaults and the upper with six bays of groin vaults. The tower no longer survives to its original height, but the roof was probably about 13 metres above ground level. The site was surrounded by a wall, roughly square and measuring approximately 60 metres on each side.[30]

Castles which relied heavily on the passive strength of the tower-keep were not built only in the twelfth century. The keep at Montfort, for example, was almost certainly constructed after 1226.[31] However, the *castrum* form of the castle was exclusive to the twelfth century. It consisted of walls enclosing a square bailey, with towers at each corner which usually (but not always) projected from the line of the walls. At a number of sites, such as Coliat in Syria and Belvoir in Galilee, towers were also built in the middle of each wall. Belvoir enjoyed additional protection; it had a second *castrum* within its outer one.[32] The *castra* have, in the past, been regarded as imitations of Byzantine models,[33] but this view has been rejected by most recent scholars. It has been shown that similar structures existed in western Europe before the First Crusade.[34] Moreover, the choice of the *castrum* form was a reflection of the need for rapid construction, and the locations (often open country) of many of the sites.[35]

During the thirteenth century the Latins built, or rebuilt, a number of castles on concentric principles, with an inner wall which was able to command the outer one. At Crac des Chevaliers, for example, the central block of the castle, which was

---

[30] Pringle, *The Red Tower*, pp. 14, 124–8; see above, p. 95.

[31] R. D. Pringle, 'A Thirteenth Century Hall at Montfort Castle in Western Galilee', *The Antiquaries Journal*, 66 (1986), p. 55. See below, pp. 108–11.

[32] Benvenisti, *Crusaders*, pp. 280–2, 297–8; T. S. R. Boase, 'Military Architecture in the Crusader States in Palestine and Syria', in *A History of the Crusades*, gen. ed. K. M. Setton, vol. IV (Madison, 1977), pp. 143–4.

[33] Lawrence, *Crusader Castles*, pp. 77–8.

[34] Smail, *Crusading Warfare*, pp. 232–3.

[35] *Ibid.*, pp. 234–6; Benvenisti, *Crusaders*, pp. 280–1; Boase, 'Military Architecture', p. 144.

probably erected by the Hospitallers shortly after they acquired the site in 1142, consisted of an irregular polygon, rounded at the north end, with a number of rectangular projecting towers. Around 1200, an outer wall incorporating a sequence of semicircular towers was constructed, at a distance of between 15 and 20 metres from the earlier wall. Once this work had been completed, a number of improvements were also made to the inner wall, including the strengthening of the central tower on the west face and the extension of the defences at the southern end.[36]

Oliver of Paderborn, in his account of the Fifth Crusade, provided some details of the building of Château Pèlerin. The site was a promontory, which Oliver realised could only be threatened from the east; the fortifications were concentrated in this area. There were three lines of defence. A moat with a low wall on its east side was followed by a second wall which rose approximately 16 metres above the moat. This wall contained three rectangular gate towers. A short distance to the west was an inner wall. This was constructed with massive blocks of masonry and included two towers, 30 metres high and positioned between the three gate towers in the second wall. Oliver also referred to an ingenious device which enabled soldiers to move up and down the inner wall with impunity. Château Pèlerin was never taken by assault.[37]

The process of a siege involved the gradual wearing down of the various elements by which the strongpoint was defended. Some of these defences were unimportant, as medieval 'optional extras', but others were fundamental to the design of the castle. Moreover, not all strongpoints could rely on any form of natural defence. Most of the coastal sites in the Latin East were easily approached and besieged, so their man–made barriers had to be doubly effective. At Ascalon and Arsuf, the use of an artificial *tel*, or mound, enhanced the defensive qualities of the site. Caesarea, on the other hand, relied almost entirely on its walls for

---

[36] Boase, 'Military Architecture', pp. 153–5.

[37] Oliver of Paderborn, 'Historia', pp. 169–71; Boase, 'Military Architecture', pp. 157–9; Benvenisti, *Crusaders*, pp. 178–80. Saphet, too, was probably constructed on concentric principles. The contemporary account of the building of the castle refers to two sets of walls (*De constructione castri Saphet*, p. 40). An analysis of previous descriptions of the site, coupled with an inspection of the visible remains, has shown that most of the medieval towers on the outer wall were probably rounded, whilst those on the inner wall appear to have been rectangular. The keep seems to have been round; but the surviving remains in this area probably date from the Mamluk reconstruction started by Baybars in 1267 and subsequently completed by Kalavun. See Pringle, 'Reconstructing the Castle of Safad', pp. 141–7.

n. All three sites had two lines of defence: the town walls ...u a citadel. The citadel of Arsuf was independent of the town, divided from it by a steep slope leading to a ditch. At Caesarea the citadel was sited on a promontory which formed the south wall of the harbour and could be isolated from the rest of the town. But it was vulnerable to attack from the site of the cathedral, which was located to the east within the city walls, on top of the remains of some Roman buildings.

The position of Ascalon's citadel in the thirteenth century is uncertain, but it is worth consideration since its builder, Richard of Cornwall, wrote in some detail of his work at the site:

with a double wall encircling it and properly equipped with high towers and ramparts, square hewn stones [ashlar] and cut columns of marble, everything which is applicable to a castle had been completed, except the ditch around it, which with the approval of the Lord was to be finished, without any weakness, inside the month from Easter Day.

When the work was completed, the castle was garrisoned and supplied with engines, food and other requirements.[38] The citadel, apparently built on the concentric principle, has been assumed to have been situated in the south-west area of the site where remains are fairly extensive, but recently it has been argued that the north-west corner is a more likely location. The *tel* in this area, which is divided from the rest of the site with evidence of a rock-cut ditch, dominates its surroundings to a far greater extent than the south-western area. There is also evidence of a glacis on the north wall, constructed with smooth ashlar masonry. This differs visibly from earlier structures at the site and is similar to thirteenth-century work found at Caesarea, for example. Access to the shore from the north-west is no worse than it is to the south. Overall, this northern area of the site seems far more compatible with Richard's description of a concentric castle than do the remains in the south. The destruction of Ascalon in 1247 and again in 1270 prevents further evidence of Richard of Cornwall's fortifications from being traced: it seems that when he rebuilt the castle, most of the town was left in a state of ruin and the

---

[38] '...duplici muro cum altis turribus et propugnaculis et lapidibus quadris et incisis columpnis marmoreis decenter ornato et circumeunte, omnia quae ad castrum pertinent et rite erant perfecta, praeter fossatum circa castrum, quod annuente Domino infra mensem a die Paschae perficeretur sine omni defectu' (Matthew Paris, *Chronica maiora*, vol. IV, p. 143; see also 'Rothelin', p. 556).

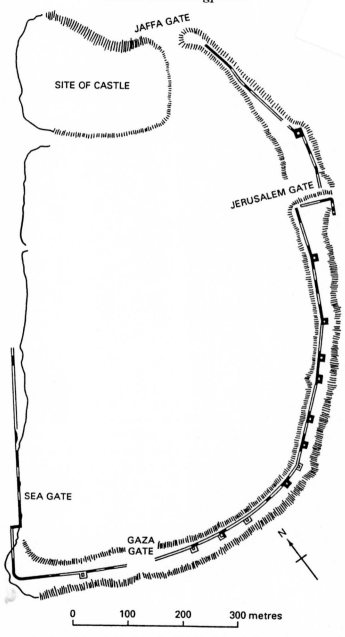

Figure 5. Ascalon (after R. D. Pringle, 'Richard I and the Walls of Ascalon')

Plate 4.  Ascalon: tower on east wall, showing the use of antique granite
through-columns

extent of resettlement there is uncertain (see figure 5).[39] One other
interesting feature which can still be seen is the use made of
antique marble and granite through-columns to strengthen the
walls, similar to that described in Richard's account of his work
(see plates 4 and 5). Re-used marble and granite columns are found
at many sites in the Latin East and the strengthening value of such
stone, at Caesarea and Arsuf as well as Ascalon, is apparent where
the later wall, when exposed to the elements, has gradually receded
leaving the columns bare. Richard of Cornwall's reference to the
practice of re-using antique columns shows the importance which
was attached to it as a means of augmenting the defences of a site
and, especially, as protection against Muslim mining techniques.
Columns were not the only means of strengthening a wall. When

[39] Benvenisti, *Crusaders*, pp. 125–6, 128; Pringle, 'Richard I and the Walls of Ascalon',
pp. 144–6. Otherwise, comments are based on visits to Ascalon in the summer of 1984.
Prior to Baybars's destruction of Ascalon in 1270, parts of the walls of the citadel were
still standing (Ibn 'Abd al-Zahir, 'Life of Baybars', vol. II, p. 737).

Plate 5.    Ascalon: an example of the use of antique marble through-columns

the traveller Willbrand of Oldenburg visited Beirut in 1212, he noted that the walls and towers had iron clamps incorporated into them.[40]

The moat round a town's outer defences prevented small raiding parties from gaining easy access to the town, as well as providing a first line of defence against a more serious aggressor. At Caesarea, the outer defences are well preserved. The town walls are of smooth ashlar construction and in their current state of preservation rise at least to the top of the glacis throughout their length. Access to the town was via entrances which, as potential weak points in the defensive system, were heavily fortified. Those on the east and north sides of the town still survive. A person wishing to enter via the east gate was confronted by the blind wall of a tower, which incorporated arrow-slits into its design. The moat was crossed, to the right of the gate tower, by a drawbridge. Those who used it were exposed to fire from arrow-slits in towers along the line of the wall, in addition to the slits in the face of the wall directly in front of them. When the far side of the drawbridge was reached, it was necessary to turn left through a gate into a hall within the tower

---

[40] Willbrand of Oldenburg, 'Peregrinatio', in *Peregrinatores medii aevi quatuor*, ed. J. C. M. Laurent (Leipzig, 1864), p. 166.

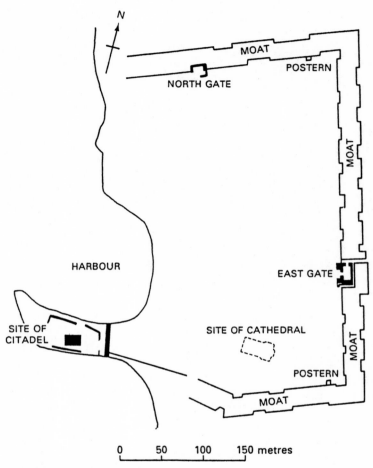

Figure 6. Caesarea

which was commanded by a gallery on an upper level. A further turn to the right was then required in order to leave the tower and pass into the town. If this route was used as the main entrance into Caesarea in peacetime, then it must have caused some congestion, but it would have made entry by an unauthorised person extremely hazardous.

Arrow-slits were an essential means for defenders of a strongpoint to repel an attack. At Caesarea they were incorporated

Plate 6.   Caesarea: the town walls on the east side, looking north from the east gate

into the glacis and, from the surviving evidence above this level, they were also employed in the walls and towers to provide the maximum possible angles of fire (see figure 6 and plate 7). Belvoir, a twelfth-century castle, included arrow-slits in the glacis of its inner defences. It also has well-preserved slits in its walls which indicate the cramped posture which an archer had to adopt to make use of them. These slits are virtually identical with some found at thirteenth-century Muslim sites such as Subeibe and Mt Tabor.[41] At Saphet, subways enabled archers to conceal themselves in advanced positions and fire without being observed by the enemy. They did not, therefore, require protective clothing.[42]

   Defence against a siege was not conducted just from within the strongpoint. It was sometimes possible to leave the protection of the castle and carry out sorties against the besiegers, but this was

---

[41] Information in this and the previous paragraph comes from my own observations at the sites mentioned. For more details on arrow-slits at Caesarea, see Pringle, *The Red Tower*, pp. 68–9. Even arrow-slits could not provide adequate protection at the siege of Tripoli in 1289. Kalavun had so many troops that he was able to order twenty archers to fire against each arrow-slit. The Christian crossbowmen did not dare to return fire, for fear of being hit (*Gestes des Chiprois*, p. 236).

[42] *De constructione castri Saphet*, p. 40, and note.

Plate 7.   Caesarea: postern and arrow-slit in the town wall

obviously not very satisfactory if it required the constant opening and closing of gates. Posterns were therefore built into the walls, normally to allow the defenders to enter the moat, as at Belvoir and Caesarea, for example. At Caesarea, a postern still survives intact, leading into the moat on the north side of the town wall (see plate 7).[43] A problem with the postern was that, as well as allowing defenders out, it was also a means for attackers to get in, so it must have been well blocked at all times when it was not in use. Tight security at gates and posterns was essential; both the Templars and Hospitallers would dismiss a brother from the Order who left a castle by the wrong door – in the case of the latter, if he 'will go out through any place other than the gate of the castle…'.[44]

Montfort, a castle in western Galilee about twelve miles north-east of Acre is, it would appear, an entirely thirteenth-century structure; its features are worth considering here.[45] (See figure 7 and plates 8 and 9.) The castle occupies a spur which rises about

---

[43] Information from my own observations at Belvoir and Caesarea.
[44] *Règle du Temple*, no. 228; '…istra per autre part que per la porte deu chastell…' (*Cartulaire des Hospitaliers*, no. 3844, pt 12).
[45] This description of Montfort is based largely on my own inspection of the site. See Pringle, 'A Thirteenth Century Hall', pp. 52–6, and see above, pp. 64–5.

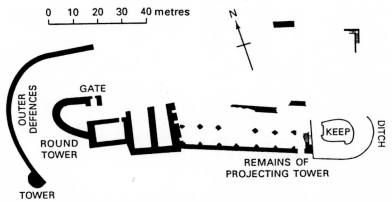

Figure 7. Montfort (after R. D. Pringle, 'A Thirteenth Century Hall')

Plate 8. Montfort: from the west, showing outer defences

180 metres above the Wadi Qurn. Unfortunately much of the site has been levelled and, as at Caesarea, the structure of the upper defences is not always clear. Enough remains, however, to suggest some of the reasons behind the form of the castle. The strongest and highest point of its defences was the D-shaped keep, situated at the east end of the site. It was divided from the remainder of the spur, which rises away to the east, by a rock-cut ditch about

Plate 9.   Montfort: from the north, showing the round tower, gate and
outer defences at the west end of the castle.

twenty metres wide. It could also be isolated from the rest of the
castle to the west; a large cistern situated below the keep would
have enabled it to maintain an independent existence for some
time. Additional cisterns were placed below other structures on
the site.[46]

Just to the west of the keep are the remains of a projecting
tower on the south wall. There are no surviving outer defences on
the south side of the castle, but on the west and north sides an
outer wall did provide additional protection. Whether there was
no outer wall on the south face or it has simply disappeared is
unclear, but since no remains at all have been found it is to be
presumed that there were no outworks on this side. The slope on
the south side of the spur is steep and further reinforcement may
not have been felt necessary. The north-western area of the site,
on the other hand, sloped gently down to the valley and was
therefore particularly vulnerable to attack. Defences were
established at various levels. A round tower was constructed at the
western end of the spur, with a rectangular gate tower slightly to
the east along the line of the north wall, the latter incorporating
a well-preserved arrow-slit facing north. Below the round tower

[46] Dean, *The Fortress of Montfort*, p. 9.

the outer wall survives almost complete on the west slope of the spur: there is evidence of another tower in the south-west edge of the outer wall. Along the north side the line of the outer wall can still be discerned although it is incomplete. It extends up to forty metres from the main area of the castle. Both the outer and inner lines of defences at the castle were built using rough-quality rubble masonry. The keep, on the other hand, was constructed with large blocks of ashlar.[47]

Montfort is a good example of man-made defences adding to the natural strength of a site.[48] To the east, where the rising ground of the spur meant that the whole site was overlooked, the rock-cut ditch and the keep afforded protection. Other vulnerable areas were defended by two sets of walls: Montfort was thus apparently conceived on a semi-concentric principle. The spur gave defenders the advantage of height on the south, west and north sides, whilst if the outer defences were breached, the garrison could gradually fall back to the self-contained keep where it still enjoyed a height advantage over the rest of the castle. Montfort, because of its geographical position and its sturdy construction, was regarded by the Teutonic Knights as a suitable base for their operations in the Latin East. But however strong castles may have appeared, the Muslim armies were able to break resistance with effective siege techniques and by sheer weight of numbers. Montfort fell to Baybars in 1271. It has been suggested, quite plausibly, that the site retains an unusual relic from its final defence. A neat cut has been made in the face of the south wall, about three metres long and two metres deep, possibly as part of mining operations against the castle.[49] Perhaps the castle capitulated before the mine was completed: it is difficult to think of any other reason why such a cut should have been made.

### MAINTENANCE OF THE STRONGPOINTS

In times of both peace and war, strongpoints had to maintain a credible state of preparedness. We have already seen that constant improvements were made to the defences of strongpoints such as Crac des Chevaliers and Saphet. These improvements may have been designed to combat an expected Muslim assault; they may

[47] Pringle, 'A Thirteenth Century Hall', pp. 54–5.
[48] Dr Smail noted a number of similar cases in the twelfth century (Smail, *Crusading Warfare*, pp. 218–26).     [49] See Dean, *The Fortress of Montfort*, p. 8.

have been repairs after an attack on the castle; or they might have been restoration of damage caused by earthquakes, which were common in the region. Between their purchase of Beaufort from Julian of Sidon in 1260 and the fall of the castle in 1268, the Templars constructed new fortifications on the plateau about 250 metres from the south wall, presumably to strengthen that side of the fosse. When the castle was besieged by the Muslims in 1268, this was the first position to be abandoned by the Templars as they fell back to the older citadel.[50]

Support from western Europe often helped the Latins to maintain their strongpoints. Money payments were especially welcome. After most of the building work at Château Pèlerin had been completed, Honorius III wrote to England in 1222 asking for more money to be sent there.[51] The fortress of Cursat in northern Syria also benefited from a papal grant – not surprisingly, as it belonged to the patriarch of Antioch. Cursat had suffered during Muslim attacks on the area around Antioch, so Innocent IV gave Patriarch Opizo dei Fieschi a three-year grant of revenue from the churches of Cyprus and Antioch, in order that he could make the necessary repairs.[52] The papacy might also offer advice on the most sensible use of revenue. In 1257, Alexander IV wrote to the patriarch of Jerusalem and the archbishop of Tyre, in connection with bequests which the faithful in the Latin East had made for the fortification of Jerusalem and Ascalon. Alexander realised that there was no immediate prospect of these sites being recovered but he urged that the money should be used to fortify other cities and castles, and for the general defence of the kingdom in whatever ways were deemed appropriate.[53]

The commander of a fortress had to ensure that there were adequate supplies of food and drink, arms and manpower. Sieges could develop into campaigns of attrition in which the maintenance of supplies became a problem, often for the attackers as well as the defenders. And it was essential, even in peacetime, that castles were well provisioned. The Templar commanders at Antioch and Tripoli, for example, were required to ensure that garrisons were supplied with leather, corn, wine, iron and steel.[54]

---

[50] Deschamps, *Royaume de Jérusalem*, p. 196; Ibn 'Abd al-Zahir, 'Life of Baybars', vol. II, pp. 643–4.

[51] Honorius III, *Regesta*, ed. P. Pressutti (2 vols., Rome, 1888–95), no. 4098.

[52] Innocent IV, *Registre*, no. 7393; Alexander IV, *Registre*, nos. 1087, 1175.

[53] Alexander IV, *Registre*, no. 1939.     [54] *Règle du Temple*, no. 126.

In 1268, the Templars abandoned Baghras without a fight and the Muslims who entered the site found 'crops, provisions, and such things as are usually stored in a castle of this kind...'.[55] In the near-eastern climate, the supply of water was critical and the Latins used various means to ensure that supplies were freely available.[56] At Saphet, there was a lack of water whilst the building work was being done, but a Muslim revealed a source of supply to the Christians. It seems that the supply thereafter was plentiful; there were many water mills working outside the castle, as well as others operated by wind and animals.[57] At Montfort, the Teutonic Knights were able to use a source of water outside the castle in peacetime,[58] in addition to the cisterns which they maintained within the walls.

Every castle would have large storerooms, small mills for grinding flour, wine and olive presses and kitchens, remains of which have been found at Belvoir, Montfort and Château Pèlerin.[59] But strongpoints were also heavily dependent on the surrounding area for supplies. In the near vicinity of Saphet there were 260 villages with a total population of 10,000, besides a large town with a market. Grapes, figs, herbs and olives are examples of the produce which was abundant in the region.[60] Oliver of Paderborn noted that the area around Château Pèlerin was extremely fertile.[61] The same was true at Margat, where the Hospitallers were able to harvest 500 cartloads of crops a year. Willbrand of Oldenburg went on to claim that the castle had stocks to sustain it for five years, even against a siege: in fact it resisted Kalavun for only six weeks in 1285.[62] Sometimes there might even be too much food and not enough men, as occurred during the siege of Beirut in 1231–2. The Ibelins had plenty of food and arms but they had to wait for reinforcements before they were able to conduct an active defence of the castle.[63] Food supplies were clearly not a problem at Château Pèlerin during the siege by al-Mu'azzam in 1220. Four thousand warriors were fed daily; there were many others who had come to defend the castle

---

[55] Ibn 'Abd al-Zahir, 'Life of Baybars', vol. II, pp. 679–80.
[56] Deschamps, *Le Crac*, pp. 90–3.     [57] *De constructione castri Saphet*, pp. 39, 42.
[58] Benvenisti, *Crusaders*, p. 334.     [59] *Ibid.*, p. 289.
[60] *De constructione castri Saphet*, pp. 42–3.
[61] Oliver of Paderborn, 'Historia', p. 171.
[62] Willbrand of Oldenburg, 'Peregrinatio', p. 170; *Gestes des Chiprois*, pp. 217–18; Ibn 'Abd al-Zahir, 'Vie de Kalavun', in Michaud, *Bibliothèque*, vol. IV, pp. 548–9.
[63] *Gestes des Chiprois*, pp. 78–9, 86.

at their own expense or, interestingly, to sell food.[64] It is not clear how these merchants were able to enter the castle: perhaps they were Italians who had come down the coast by ship from Acre. Throughout the thirteenth century, the Muslims found it virtually impossible to threaten the Christian sea lanes,[65] so it would have been comparatively easy for a site such as Château Pèlerin to be resupplied, or reinforced, from the sea.

Castles were not always well supplied, however. Montfort suffered from serious problems in this respect towards the end of its period in Christian hands. In 1270, the Teutonic Knights acknowledged the poor condition of their castle and came to an agreement with the Hospitallers, which allowed the Germans to farm the fortified *casal* of Manueth for one year. They were to hold no other rights there.[66] The Teutonic Knights obviously had serious difficulties in supplying the garrison at Montfort from their own territory, though whether this was because of poor harvests or as a direct result of Muslim activity is not clear. It was the latter threat which affected the supplies of Crac des Chevaliers in the same year, when Baybars raided the castle with 200 mounted troops. After a brief engagement with a Christian force from the castle, the Muslims returned to camp and there followed an extension of the raid which was recognised as being of great significance by the Muslim chronicler Ibn 'Abd al-Zahir: 'The horses grazed on the grass and plants. This was one of the causes of the capture of this castle, since it had no provisions except what grew on its territories, upon which the Sultan's horses had grazed all this time.' Crac was, indeed, heavily dependent on its lordship for supplies[67] and when the Muslims besieged the castle in 1271, the effects of the previous year's raid must have been felt.

During the Ibelin siege of Dieudamour (1229–30), the Lombard defenders began to suffer from a lack of food – so much so that they were forced to eat their horses. The Ibelins, however, did not maintain the siege effectively and the Lombards were able, by a sortie, to capture the Ibelin camp and, it was specifically noted, acquire some food which enabled them to maintain their defence for far longer than would otherwise have been possible.[68]

---

[64] Oliver of Paderborn, 'Historia', p. 255.
[65] See above, chapter 1, note 12. An exception was the siege of Ascalon. See below, pp. 217, 223.      [66] *Cartulaire des Hospitaliers*, no. 3400.
[67] Ibn 'Abd al-Zahir, 'Life of Baybars', vol. II, pp. 729–30; see also J. S. C. Riley-Smith in Ibn al-Furat, *Ayyubids*, vol. II, p. 236, note 5.
[68] *Gestes des Chiprois*, p. 63.

# Castles and strongpoints

Table 1. *The reported size of garrisons in the Latin East, 1192–1291*

| Castle | Garrison |
|--------|----------|
| Acre (1291) | 700–800 mounted (knights), 14,000 foot[a] |
| Antioch (1268) | 8,000 warriors in the citadel[b] |
| Arsuf (1265) | A garrison of 2,000; 1,000 taken prisoner, 90 Hospitaller brothers killed or captured.[c] Alternative numbers of Hospitallers given by sources are 80,[d] 180 Hospitallers and Templars[e] or 410 Hospitallers.[f] They had lost nearly all the Convent[g] |
| Ascalon (1244–7(?)) | 100 knights, or an unspecified number of knights and sergeants sent to relieve the siege[h] |
| Beirut (1231–2) | Force of 100 armed men – knights, sergeants and squires – sent into the citadel by the Ibelins[i] |
| Chastel Blanc (1271) | 700 men – it is unclear if this was the garrison[j] |
| Château Pèlerin (1220) | 4,000 warriors fed daily, others were there at their own expense[k] |
| Château Pèlerin (1237) | (force from) 120 brothers, archers and crossbowmen[l] |
| Crac des Chevaliers (1212) | 2,000 men[m] |
| Crac des Chevaliers (1255) | Alexander IV stated that 60 *equites* were to be maintained there by the Hospitallers[n] |
| Jaffa (1197) | 40 knights, or a number of knights and sergeants sent there by Aimery of Lusignan[o] |
| Jerusalem (1239) | 20 knights in the Tower of David[p] |
| Jerusalem (1239) | One knight and 70 foot in the Tower of David[q] |
| Kyrenia (1232–3) | 50 knights and 1,000 crossbowmen/sailors[r] |
| Maraclea (c. 1277/85) | 100 warriors[s] |
| Margat (1212) | 1,000 men[t] |
| Margat (1281) | 600 mounted troops came out and drove off a Muslim assault[u] |
| Margat (1281) | The castle well-defended by brethren and other armed men[v] |
| Margat (1285) | 25 Hospitallers allowed to leave the castle with their horses and arms: this was probably the full Hospitaller contingent[w] |
| Mt Tabor (1255) | Alexander IV said that 40 *equites* were to be kept there by the Hospitallers[x] |
| Saphet (c. 1260) | 'In peacetime more than 1,700 people are maintained [at the castle], and in time of war 2,200. The everyday needs of the |

Table 1 (*cont.*)

| Castle | Garrison |
|---|---|
| | castle require 50 knights and 30 brother sergeants with horses and arms, 50 turcopoles similarly equipped, 300 crossbowmen, 820 workmen and other servants, and 400 slaves [y] |
| Saphet (1266) | 27 brothers and 10 Templars killed after the siege, but not the Hospitallers, and 767 warriors and 4 Franciscans. Alternative figures suggest that there were 3,000 other people there.[z] Or, 2,000 men were taken and slaughtered.[aa] There were native (Syrian) troops in the garrison[bb] |
| Tripoli (1289) | 40 Hospitaller brothers were lost[cc] |

[a] *Gestes des Chiprois*, p. 241. This appears to be one of the more acceptable sets of figures. See below, pp. 212, 219, 222.

[b] Ibn 'Abd al-Zahir, 'Life of Baybars', vol. II, p. 658. A large number of people died because of the overcrowding in the citadel.

[c] 'Chronica minor auctore minorita Erphordiensi', *MGHS*, vol. XXIV, p. 204; John Vitoduranus, 'Chronica', p. 17; Marino Sanuto, 'Liber', p. 222.

[d] 'Annales de Terre Sainte', p. 452 (text 'A').

[e] John Vitoduranus, 'Chronica', p. 17.

[f] 'Annales de Terre Sainte', p. 452 (text 'B').

[g] *Cartulaire des Hospitaliers*, no. 3173. This document (a letter from Clement IV to the king of Armenia) also refers to Hospitaller losses at Caesarea in 1265.

[h] 'Annales de Terre Sainte', p. 442; 'Eracles', vol. II, p. 433. (These dates cover the possible extent of a Muslim blockade of Ascalon, followed by a short siege. However, it is by no means certain (and, indeed, seems unlikely) that the blockade continued for some three years.)

[i] *Gestes des Chiprois*, p. 85.

[j] Ibn 'Abd al-Zahir, 'Life of Baybars', vol. II, p. 743.

[k] Oliver of Paderborn, 'Historia', p. 255.

[l] Albert of Trois Fontaines, 'Chronicon', p. 942.

[m] Willbrand of Oldenburg, 'Peregrinatio', p. 169.

[n] *Cartulaire des Hospitaliers*, no. 2727.

[o] 'Document relatif au service militaire', p. 428; 'Eracles', vol. II, p. 219.

[p] 'Annales prioratus de Dunstaplia', ed. H. R. Luard, in *Annales monastici*, vol. III (Rolls Series, 36; London, 1866), p. 150.

[q] *History of the Patriarchs*, vol. IV, p. 195. There were two attacks on Jerusalem in the space of six months. This figure relates to the size of the garrison after the first attack, which way by as-Salih Aiyub's troops. See below, p. 243 and note g.

[r] *Gestes des Chiprois*, p. 108.

[s] Ibn 'Abd al-Zahir, 'Vie de Kalavun', in Michaud, *Histoire*, vol. VII, p. 698.

### Notes to table 1 (cont.)

*t* Willbrand of Oldenburg, 'Peregrinatio', p. 170.

*u* *Gestes des Chiprois*, pp. 209–10. For the date of this attack, see below, p. 128, note 114.

*v* *Cartulaire des Hospitaliers*, no. 3766.

*w* Ibn 'Abd al-Zahir, 'Vie de Kalavun', in Michaud, *Histoire*, vol. VII, p. 696.

*x* *Cartulaire des Hospitaliers*, no. 2726.

*y* 'In cotidianis expensis dantur victualia mille et septingentis personis et plus, et tempore guerre duobus milibus et ducentis. In stabilimento cotidiano castri sunt necessarii l milites et xxx servientes fratres cum equis et armis et l Turcopoli cum equis et armis et balistarii ccc, in operibus et aliis officiis dccc et xx, et sclavi cccc' (*De constructione castri Saphet*, p. 41).

*z* 'Maius chronicon Lemovicense', pp. 773–4.

*aa* Ibn 'Abd al-Rahim, 'Vie de Kalavun', in Michaud, *Bibliothèque*, vol. IV, p. 497.

*bb* *Gestes des Chiprois*, p. 179. This would have been the turcopole element of the garrison.

*cc* *Cartulaire des Hospitaliers*, no. 4050.

A regular supply of arms was also essential for the maintenance of a strongpoint. It was imperative that stocks could be sustained in time of conflict, so strongpoints had to be capable of producing weapons themselves. At Saphet, for example, the manufacture of crossbows, arrows, siege engines and other kinds of arms was a constant activity.[69]

In 1239–40, Muslim troops led by an-Nasir Da'ud overcame the Christian defenders at Jerusalem. It was said that Frederick II had failed to provide adequate quantities of men, food, armour, engines and other (unspecified) items which were needed to mount an effective defence of a castle.[70] Problems with the victualling of a garrison could reduce the capacity of a strongpoint to withstand assault, but lack of sufficient numbers to garrison a site was an even more serious matter. It is important, therefore, to give some idea of the size of garrisons before we go on to consider the functions of the strongpoints in this period. This will also emphasise the extent to which the entire Latin army was committed to defending the strongpoints. (See table 1.)

There are three main problems with these statistics. First, almost all of them contain at least some element of ambiguity and most are an incomplete statement of the total garrison strength.

[69] *De constructione castri Saphet*, pp. 40–1.

[70] '...avoient malvaissement garni le chastel de genz et de viandes, et d'armeurez, et d'anginz et de toutes manierez de choses qui apartiennent au chastel deffendre' ('Rothelin', p. 530).

There are seldom references to the number of footsoldiers and other lesser persons in a garrison. Secondly, many appear to be arbitrary totals: the figures '100' and '1,000' seem very common and units of 1,000 cannot be regarded as accurate, since they may have been used simply to imply a large number of men. Thirdly, the statistics for one fortress often come from different dates, when circumstances might have changed. Allowing for these reservations and the question of the reliability of the sources for some of these figures, some suggestions can still be made.

The detailed breakdown given for the garrison of Saphet in 1260 is particularly valuable, although even here there are problems and ambiguities. The figures given may well represent the ideal state of the castle, rather than the number of men that were actually there. But the total of this ideal force comes to 1,650 and as it is said that daily expenses were for more than 1,700, in the early 1260s Saphet was probably close to full strength. It is immediately clear that the fighting force of the castle was only one element of the garrison as a whole and, numerically, a minor one. Just over a quarter of the men stationed there were full-time combatants: although this is an isolated example, it seems reasonable to assume that this would have been normal in any strongpoint. If the circumstances required it, however, many of the workmen and other servants would presumably have been able to fight too.

The figures relating to the combatants themselves are equally revealing, though they must be used with caution as there is so little with which to compare them. The presence of 300 crossbowmen indicates that they were a crucial part of a castle's garrison in the thirteenth century. The mounted troops numbered 130, that is about 8 per cent of the total garrison. From the figures quoted for the sieges of Arsuf and Acre, it seems that the mounted troops of a garrison would normally have constituted between 5 per cent and 10 per cent of its total strength. Of the horsemen at Saphet, the 50 *milites* and 30 *servientes fratres* (sergeants) would appear to have been Templar troops. This, as was noted earlier,[71] means that possibly a sixth of the total of Templar brethren in the east was committed to the garrisoning of Saphet, demonstrating the importance of the castle to the Order and to the region as a whole.

[71] See above, p. 60.

Table 2. *The possible size of some castle garrisons*

| Castle | Mounted knights | Total mounted | Total fighting force | Total garrison |
|---|---|---|---|---|
| Saphet | 50 | 130 | 430 | 1,650 |
| Crac | 60 | 160? | 520? | 2,000 |
| Margat | 30? | 80? | 260? | 1,000 |
| Mt Tabor | 40 | 105? | 340? | 1,300? |

The numbers suggested by Alexander IV for the garrisoning of Crac and Mt Tabor, and Willbrand of Oldenburg's numbers for Crac and Margat in 1212, can be interpreted in the light of the information for Saphet. This has its dangers but it does, at least, have some additional evidence to support it. Alexander's remarks about the *equites* to be maintained at Crac and Mt Tabor were probably a reference to brother knights like the *milites* at Saphet, where they constituted about 40 per cent of the mounted contingent. The number of Templar brothers at Saphet was particularly large, but Crac, Mt Tabor and Margat would have warranted a proportionately similar commitment by the Hospitallers. Working from the Saphet statistics, approximate figures can be attained (see table 2). Those with question marks have been calculated.

For Margat the possible numbers are obtained by working backwards from Willbrand's total, from which it would seem there might have been about thirty Hospitaller brothers in the fortress. This is close to the twenty-five Hospitallers who were allowed to leave Margat with their arms when the castle fell in 1285. It is possible, therefore, that the Hospitallers had nearly a third of their brethren in the east engaged in garrisoning the two sites of Crac and Margat, but considering the great importance of these castles to the Order, this would not have been so surprising. Projected figures for Mt Tabor show how substantial a strongpoint this might have been for the Hospitallers.

From these figures it seems that larger fortresses and other strongpoints in the Latin East would have had garrisons of around 1,000 men, of whom 200–300 would have been a permanent fighting force. But this figure would obviously vary considerably from one site to another. As far as the Military Orders were concerned, twenty to thirty brethren was a large force: the Templars' provision of thirty brothers to assist Guy of Gibelet in the 1270s may be seen in this context.[72]

Much of the remaining evidence which is not too ambiguous comes from instances when garrisons appear to have received additional support, normally to deal with an assault of some kind. As the Muslims increasingly dominated the hinterland, any effort to assist a beleaguered garrison would normally have had to come from the sea, as at Jaffa in 1197, Beirut in 1232 (a Christian siege), Ascalon in 1247 and Acre in 1291.[73] The Hospitallers often devoted large numbers of troops to the defence of a coastal strongpoint. The lowest estimate of the Hospitaller brethren at Arsuf is eighty, in itself a very large number of men. The Hospitallers' loss of forty brothers at the siege of Tripoli in 1289 is clear evidence of the Order's willingness to commit itself even when its own properties were not directly threatened. The statistics relating to the fall of Saphet in 1266, on the other hand, suggest that no great influx of Templars had taken place, although the garrison was clearly larger than the 1,700 of about the year 1260. The author of *De constructione castri Saphet* suggested a total in wartime of 2,200 men. This increase of 500 would presumably have been achieved largely through the employment of mercenary troops. It is interesting, as already pointed out, that there may have been Hospitallers at Saphet, whilst one writer suggested that Templars were present at the fall of Arsuf.

The force of 100 knights, sergeants and others which was sent into Beirut in 1232 dramatically altered the course of the siege.[74] A garrison of 50 knights and 1,000 crossbowmen and marines was able to repel attackers for ten months at Kyrenia in 1232–3, before deciding to capitulate with no hope of relief.[75] These two examples of strongpoints being defended against Christian opposition indicate that a fairly small garrison could achieve some success against Christian siege methods but, as we shall see later, when faced by a Muslim army such a force stood little chance.

---

[72] See above, p. 44.
[73] We have already seen that throughout this period the Muslims were unable to threaten the Christian shipping routes. Indeed, the Mamluk conquest of the Latin East was undertaken entirely by land-based armies; no support was provided by the Egyptian fleet. See above, chapter 1, note 12, and Pryor, *Geography, Technology, and War*, p. 131. [74] *Gestes des Chiprois*, pp. 85–6. [75] *Ibid.*, pp. 108, 116.

Regardless of their size, garrisons had to be well disciplined. Earlier, we saw that at both Templar and Hospitaller sites brothers were always expected to use the proper entrances and exits.[76] Discipline was particularly important at strongpoints which were close to enemy territory – most of which were controlled by the Military Orders. The gates of such fortresses were kept shut at night, and brothers were not permitted to leave. In 1212, a traveller saw guards (four Hospitallers and twenty-eight others) posted at Margat.[77]

We may therefore conclude that the actual fighting force in a garrison was small and, particularly, that very few mounted troops were available. In peacetime, it seems unlikely that any garrison would have contained more than about 500 full-time combatants. This force was likely to be strengthened at times of crisis, assuming that such reinforcement was practicable. A study of the functions of the strongpoints in the thirteenth century will indicate the extent to which these small garrisons could hope to influence events in their area.

## THE FUNCTIONS OF THE STRONGPOINTS

### *Contemporary and modern views of the strongpoints' functions*

Contemporary writers' comments about the roles performed by fortresses in the Latin East were often understandably vague. Andrew II of Hungary, who travelled east with the Fifth Crusade, noted the excellent location of Margat when he endowed it with revenues from his salt mines: 'it is positioned advantageously in front of the pagans...'. With regard to Crac des Chevaliers (which was also to receive a grant) he was even more graphic: 'every day they firmly drive back the attacks of the Amalekites and preserve that part of the Holy Land against the enemies of the cross of Christ and the blasphemers of His name...'.[78] The papacy appears to have been particularly fond of ambiguous pronouncements concerning the part which, it believed, castles ought to play

---

[76] See above, p. 108.
[77] *Cartulaire des Hospitaliers*, no. 2213, pt 52; Willbrand of Oldenburg, 'Peregrinatio', p. 170.
[78] '...recte in frontibus paganorum situm est, sustentationem perpetuam...'; '...cotidianos Amalechitarum insultus viriliter repellunt, qui partem Terre Sancte contra inimicos crucis Christi et blasphematores nominis ejus potenter retinent...' (*Cartulaire des Hospitaliers*, nos. 1603, 1602).

in the defence of the Latin East. Crac was 'to defend and to guard against the attacks of the pagans ...', for example. Innocent IV saw the expenses of the Hospitallers at Ascalon as 'for the purpose of guarding against the enemies of the Catholic faith'.[79] In 1230, Gregory IX appealed for aid to be given to the Teutonic Knights in their building of Montfort. According to Gregory, the fortress, which was located on the border with the Muslims, was an immense help to the Christians in the area.[80]

Naturally, many of these statements by the papacy and others were not intended to give a realistic impression of the functions of individual castles in the Latin East. Rather, they were stereotyped images which were meant to bolster morale amongst the Christians in both western Europe and the Latin East and, more practically, to encourage the provision of funds for the Holy Land.

Modern writers have tried to be rather more precise about the roles of castles. Many have followed Deschamps, whose ideas will be considered later, and looked at them in terms of their supposed ability to defend frontiers. Smail preferred to concentrate on some other points in a statement which may be the final word on the strongpoints' functions in the twelfth century:

frontier defence was a role which a castle, or even a group of castles, could only imperfectly fulfil ... They were used in attack, and played a notable role in the Latin conquest of Antioch, Tripoli, Tyre, and Ascalon. In Transjordan and southern Palestine they were used to establish Latin control in areas of strategic importance, and ... became centres of colonization and economic development. They served as residences, as administrative centres, as barracks, and as police posts. Above all, they were centres of authority.[81]

In the thirteenth century the context had altered, but the functions of the strongpoints can still be examined in similar terms.

## The administrative and policing function

The centre of administration in a lordship, whether it was held by a lay lord or by one of the Military Orders, was the town where the lord's chief castle stood. The existence of a *bourg*, a semi-

---

[79] '...a paganorum incursibus defendere ac tueri ...'; 'contra inimicos catholice fidei defendendum' (*ibid.*, nos. 2727, 2394).
[80] *Tabulae ordinis Theutonici*, no. 72; Prawer, *Histoire du royaume*, vol. II, p. 182.
[81] Smail, *Crusading Warfare*, p. 60.

agricultural, semi-urban community, around a castle was important, particularly on the coast, where a port and market could provide revenue for the lord. This may help to explain why a fair number of coastal positions could still be maintained by a lay ruler, whereas so many inland fortresses, with less opportunity to exploit trade and commerce, were alienated to the Military Orders. The town would probably also be the seat of a bishopric,[62] so the castle was one essential factor in the administrative set-up of a lordship. In the west the castle was the focal point for all the inhabitants of the seigneurie, and its role in administration seems to have been virtually total.[83] In this respect the castle was rather less important in the east, because of the survival, under the Latins, of many parts of the former Muslim administration. When the Latins came to the east, they found a highly developed local administrative structure which they chose not to alter.[84] The castle would still, however, have performed a number of important functions which can better be described as administrative than military.

Outside the main administrative centre of the seigneurie, castles would undoubtedly have played an executive role in the countryside. In the lordship of Sidon, for example, stood Beaufort, the Cave de Tyron and the small fortress of Belhacem.[85] They may have all performed management tasks for the lord at one time or another. The castle of Qaqun in the Sharon Plain was a centre from which it was possible to administer the southern part of the lordship of Caesarea.[86] By the mid-thirteenth century Saphet, perhaps along with the Hospitaller site at Mt Tabor, was controlling the remains of the principality of Galilee, performing an administrative role which in fact began, in the case of Saphet, whilst it was being built. The building costs to the Templars were 1,100,000 besants, 'beyond the returns and revenues of the castle…'.[87] The Teutonic Knights used Montfort as a central store for their revenues; another store was at Acre.[88] At a local level,

---

[82] J. S. C. Riley-Smith, *Feudal Nobility*, p. 25.

[83] M. Bloch, *Feudal Society* (London, 1962), p. 401.

[84] J. S. C. Riley-Smith, 'The Survival in Latin Palestine of Muslim Administration', in *The Eastern Mediterranean Lands in the Period of the Crusades*, ed. P. M. Holt (Warminster, 1977), pp. 9–12.

[85] J. S. C. Riley-Smith, *Feudal Nobility*, p. 25.

[86] Pringle, *The Red Tower*, p. 13.

[87] '…preter redditus et obventiones dicti castri…' (*De constructione castri Saphet*, p. 41).

[88] *Tabulae ordinis Theutonici*, no. 100.

many villages would have made use of fortified warehouses or towers to gather their harvests or other produce. At Calansue, another settlement in the Sharon Plain, a collection of twelfth-century buildings probably performed an important role in the Hospitallers' administration of their estates in the surrounding area. A number of vaulted structures were presumably used to store agricultural produce; a nearby tower would have provided the Hospitallers, and the local inhabitants, with protection against Muslim raids. The site passed from Christian to Mamluk control in 1265.[89] It also appears that some mills, like the one at Recordane which was held by the Hospitallers, were fortified in the thirteenth century.[90]

At other sites, the castle played an even more active role in the trade, industry and social life of the area. In the early years of the Latin settlement, the Hospitaller fortress of Bethgibelin was involved in attempts to colonise the countryside.[91] In the thirteenth century, colonisation activities continued and the role of the castle in this respect was frequently an important one. Land ownership in the Latin Kingdom during this period was by no means static and, with the re-acquisition of areas previously held by Muslims, security was essential if newly acquired territories were to be permanently settled. This security could be provided by a garrisoned castle. Moreover, the castle's occupants would also benefit from the colonisation of the area, because the product of the civilian presence, whether agricultural or industrial, would either be used directly by the castle or would come in the form of revenue, as at Saphet.

At some sites, repopulation by civilian Latins proved impossible. Throughout the period Ascalon was frequently (in theory at least) under Frankish control, but despite the rebuilding of the castle in 1239–40, the area around it appears to have remained desolate. At Caesarea, on the other hand, the construction of a castle was seen as a first step towards the repopulation of the town.[92] St Louis's work at the site in 1251–2 included not only the building of the citadel, but also the strengthening of the *bourg* with walls, fosses, and sixteen towers.[93]

[89] Pringle, *The Red Tower*, pp. 14, 42–3, 56.
[90] Benvenisti, *Crusaders*, pp. 249–51.
[91] Prawer, 'Colonisation Activities in the Latin Kingdom', in *Crusader Institutions*, pp. 119–26.  [92] Oliver of Paderborn, 'Historia', pp. 168–9.
[93] 'Rothelin', pp. 627–8.

The extent of his efforts indicates that at least some of the town area had been re-occupied.

In the case of Château Pèlerin, Oliver of Paderborn emphasised the Muslims' abandonment of colonised areas, rather than the possibility that Christian-organised settlement might be able to exploit the Muslim withdrawal. The fertile area between Château Pèlerin and Mt Tabor had previously been occupied by Muslim agriculture, but with the building of the new fortress, 'no one could safely plough or sow or reap because of fear of those living in it'. One presumes, however, that the Christians would not have wished to leave such a rich area barren and the existence of a burgess court there suggests that this had not happened.[94] Christian settlement had again followed as a result of the building of a strongpoint and the security which this had brought to the area.

Strongpoints were not solely concerned with the Muslim threat from outside the kingdom's borders. It has been shown that in the twelfth century an unbridgeable gulf existed between the Latins and the indigenous population which manifested itself particularly at times of stress.[95] The same was probably true in the thirteenth century. In 1229, for example, popular insurrection led to the Christian garrison in Jerusalem being besieged by 15,000 Muslims.[96] In 1263, the possibility of an uprising involving native peasants who lived near Casal Robert was noted in a document settling a dispute between the archbishop of Nazareth and the Hospitallers.[97] Throughout the century, it is possible that there were minor native uprisings about which information is lacking. Even more likely is that garrison troops occasionally had to perform other policing duties such as the settlement of local disputes and conflicts, although the *rays* or headman remained responsible for most aspects of justice at the village level.[98]

Major sites such as the Hospitaller castles of Crac and Margat, which were religious houses as well as fortresses, should not be regarded as austere and purely functional. When Andrew II of Hungary visited the two sites in early 1218, he must have been

---

[94] '...nec arare nec seminare nec metere quisquam secure poterat propter metum habitantium in eo' (Oliver of Paderborn, 'Historia', pp. 171–2). See also John of Jaffa, 'Livre', p. 420.

[95] Smail, 'Crusaders' Castles', pp. 141–3, developed in context in *Crusading Warfare*, pp. 40–63, *passim*.                         [96] See below, p. 241.

[97] *Cartulaire des Hospitaliers*, no. 3051.

[98] J. S. C. Riley-Smith, *Feudal Nobility*, pp. 47–8.

impressed by the frescoes which had recently been added to the chapels.[99] At Montfort, the Teutonic Knights constructed a hall at the foot of the spur on which the castle was situated; this may have been used as a guest house.[100] Moreover, it was not only visiting Latins who would make use of the castles as residences. The point has often been made that the Latin nobles preferred to live in the larger towns, and undoubtedly this was increasingly true as the Muslims gained control of the countryside. But they also made use of their castles to reside in, and for other purposes. In 1282, during the civil conflict in northern Syria, the Gibelet faction was advised to attack Tripoli, since Bohemond was known to be spending some time at Nephin. Guy of Gibelet was probably imprisoned at Nephin after the failure of his revolt: a court was convened there on 6 February 1282 to hear his confession. In attendance were the count of Tripoli, the lords of Maraclea and Botrun and numerous ecclesiastics. The gathering may have been merely to hear Guy speak and there is no evidence of any sentence being passed, though he was subsequently killed at the castle.[101] The *Rule* of the Temple implied that Château Pèlerin was the major prison of the Order in the Latin East and it was used on a number of occasions. One case can be dated between 1218 and 1268. At Antioch three Templar brothers, including one called brother 'Paris', killed some Christian merchants: having been expelled from the Order they were whipped at Antioch, Tripoli, Tyre and then into Acre, before they were taken to Château Pèlerin where they were to remain in perpetual imprisonment. They all died there.[102]

## Defensive functions

The physical barriers presented by a castle or strongpoint could, on their own, be enough to repel some types of Muslim threat. We have already seen that the growing sophistication and relative isolation of some strongpoints in the thirteenth century were, to some extent, reactions to a lack of manpower and strong fortifications could compensate for insufficient numbers. At

---

[99] J. Folda, 'Crusader Frescoes at Crac des Chevaliers and Marqab Castle', *Dumbarton Oaks Papers*, 36 (1982), pp. 195–6, 208–10.

[100] Pringle, 'A Thirteenth Century Hall', pp. 71–2, 75.

[101] *Histoire de l'île de Chypre*, vol. III, pp. 662–3, 666–8; *Gestes des Chiprois*, pp. 211–12 (which stated that he was starved to death).

[102] *Règle du Temple*, no. 554. For other examples, see nos. 593, 603.

Saphet, for example, few men were required to defend the castle effectively, but large numbers were needed to besiege it.[103] A similar situation existed at Dieudamour. It was positioned on a very steep slope and required a substantial force to maintain a siege.[104]

Strongpoints were sometimes used as a shield against a minor Muslim raid. The defenders would be quite content to remain behind the castle walls and watch the raiders expend their energy. They would not try to drive off the attack because they realised that there was no real threat to the strongpoint itself – and by retaining control of the strongpoint, the Latins ensured that they retained control of the region. Many castles and towers remained empty for much of the time, but they would undoubtedly have been utilised by the inhabitants of the area when there was a Muslim incursion. A strongpoint's walls were a valuable asset, even for those who normally lived outside them. During the 1260s, Baybars attacked Acre on a number of occasions and, although he was able to do much damage to the area outside the city walls, the peasants and villagers of the surrounding countryside would have been able to save themselves by going into the city. But in May 1267 Baybars flew the banners of the Templars and the Hospitallers and of Tyre and was able to approach the city without being recognised. Many peasants were constructing defensive works outside the walls and 500 of them fell victim to the Muslims, who rode right to the gates of the city. By virtue of their cunning, they had been able, on this occasion, to prevent the defences of Acre from providing any personal protection.[105] In 1253, a small force which St Louis had sent to begin refortification work at Sidon was faced by a heavy Muslim raid. The Christians realised that they could not combat such an onslaught in the open, so they retreated into the sea castle, 'which is very strong and surrounded by the sea on all sides'. A few other people were able to protect themselves there too, but the castle was not large enough to accommodate all the local inhabitants and the Muslims, faced with no opposition, were able to kill 2,000 and take considerable booty.[106]

---

[103] *De constructione castri Saphet*, p. 42.    [104] *Gestes des Chiprois*, p. 63.

[105] *Ibid.*, pp. 182–3. The raids of Baybars against Acre are dealt with in more detail in chapter 5 of this study.

[106] '...qui est mout forz et enclos est de la mer en touz senz' (Joinville, *Histoire de Saint Louis*, p. 302). The Muslims also damaged the town's defences; it was these which were rebuilt by St Louis in the second half of 1253. See above, pp. 96–7.

When Christians within a castle were faced by a serious attempt to capture it they were, again, sometimes able to rely largely on the fortifications for protection. Not all attempts to capture a Christian strongpoint were successful and when they did fail the strength of the defences was often an important factor. In 1260, for example, a Mongol force besieged Sidon but Julian, its lord, was able to retreat into the land castle, whilst a number of the town's inhabitants were picked up by two Genoese galleys and ferried to the sea fortress. The Mongols rampaged through the town and smashed its walls, but they were unable to capture either of the castles: nevertheless, the damage which had been done forced Julian to sell the town to the Templars soon after.[107] Further north, Crac and Margat both faced a number of assaults and abortive sieges in the thirteenth century, before they finally succumbed in 1271 and 1285 respectively. Crac was raided by al-'Adil in 1207,[108] besieged by al-Ashraf in 1218[109] and raided by Baybars in 1270.[110] Margat was besieged by the army of Aleppo in 1206,[111] and raided in 1231.[112] In the winter of 1269–70, Baybars twice advanced towards Margat, but on each occasion bad weather forced him to turn back to Hama.[113] Finally, Margat was besieged by a Muslim army from Crac in 1281.[114] Both these Hospitaller castles had strong garrisons but their survival indicates that their fortifications, too, were exceptionally sturdy.[115]

Withdrawal into a fortress could enable an army to regroup and recover after a battle. On Theobald of Champagne's crusade, after the defeat near Gaza of a force led by the counts of Bar and Montfort, Theobald's army turned round and returned to its

---

[107] *Gestes des Chiprois*, p. 162; 'Eracles', vol. ii, pp. 444–5; Hayton, 'La Flor des Estoires de la Terre d'Orient', *RHC Arm.*, vol. ii, p. 174; see Richard, *Latin Kingdom*, p. 374; for the sale to the Templars, see above, p. 65.

[108] Al-Makrizi, *Histoire d'Egypte*, p. 287; Abu'l-Fida, 'Annales', p. 83.

[109] Kamal al-Din, 'L'Histoire d'Alep', trans. E. Blochet, *Revue de l'Orient Latin*, 5 (1897), p. 55; Abu Shama, 'Livre des deux jardins', vol. v, p. 166.

[110] Ibn 'Abd al-Zahir, 'Life of Baybars', vol. ii, pp. 729–30.

[111] Ibn-Wasil, 'Mufarridj al-Kurub fi Akhbar Bani Aiyub', in al-Makrizi, *Histoire d'Egypte*, p. 286, note 1.       [112] Kamal al-Din, 'L'Histoire d'Alep', p. 79.

[113] Ibn 'Abd al-Zahir, 'Life of Baybars', vol. ii, p. 729.

[114] *Gestes des Chiprois*, pp. 209–10; 'Annales de Terre Sainte', p. 457; Abu'l-Fida, 'Annales', p. 158; Bar Hebraeus, *Chronography*, trans. E. A. W. Budge, vol. i (London, 1932), p. 463. This last attack should be dated to the beginning of 1281 (Cahen, *La Syrie du Nord*, p. 720).

[115] At the time of the final siege of Crac in 1271, villagers had taken shelter in the castle. They were released by the Muslims to ensure the supply of agricultural produce to the site (Ibn Shaddad, in Deschamps, *Le Crac*, p. 133).

camp at Ascalon, presumably safe from Muslim marauders.[116] In 1244, the armies of the Latin East met their heaviest defeat of the thirteenth century in open battle at La Forbie. The losses were considerable, but some were able to escape the carnage, including the patriarch of Jerusalem, the constable of Acre and Philip of Montfort. Their flight from the battle was not wholly precipitate, however, for they found refuge at the recently constructed castle of Ascalon first, before making their way back to Acre.[117] Had Ascalon not been refortified by Richard of Cornwall, the defeated forces would have had to march up the coast to Jaffa, exposed to the ravages of pursuing Muslim troops or Muslim peasants.

The inert strength of the strongpoint itself was augmented by the ability of its garrison to combat raids and sieges; and the location of the castle, combined with the strength of the garrison, determined how far it was capable of controlling an area – that is, its strategic value. It has been argued that in this respect the significance of almost every strongpoint could be established by a consideration of its geographical position.[118] This view has been convincingly rejected with regard to the twelfth century,[119] but the question of the extent to which castles in the Latin East acted as a means of frontier defence and opposed the progress of an external enemy has been an area of persistent controversy amongst military historians.

A successful strategy involves, amongst other things, the ability to influence one's opponent to one's own advantage and, in this sense, some castles were unquestionably of greater strategic value than others. In the cases of Crac and Margat, for example, the strength of their garrisons and their proximity to the Muslims at Ba'rin and Hama allowed the Hospitallers considerable influence over their Muslim neighbours.[120] Willbrand of Oldenburg noted in 1212 that Margat, being situated on a mountain, was especially useful for warding off the Assassins and other Muslims – so much so that they were obliged to pay the Hospitallers 2,000 marks a year in tribute.[121] But it is clear from contemporary evidence that few of the Latin strongpoints were of any genuine strategic value.

---

[116] 'Rothelin', p. 548.
[117] *Ibid.*, pp. 564–5; Matthew Paris, *Chronica maiora*, vol. IV, p. 342.
[118] Deschamps, *Le Crac*, pp. 16–42, and *passim*; Deschamps, *La Défense du comté de Tripoli*, pp. 59–81, and *passim*.
[119] Smail, 'Crusaders' Castles', pp. 135–8; Smail, *Crusading Warfare*, pp. 60–2, 204–9.
[120] See below, pp. 187–8, 201, for details of the Hospitallers' activities against Ba'rin and Hama.        [121] Willbrand of Oldenburg, 'Peregrinatio', p. 170.

The only possible exceptions to this were the two Hospitaller castles mentioned above (with the support of others in the region) and the Templar castles of Saphet (which, as already noted, Muslims acknowledged to be 'an obstruction in the throat of Syria and a blockage in the chest of Islam...')[122] and (perhaps) Château Pèlerin. Oliver of Paderborn considered that Château Pèlerin posed a serious threat to Mt Tabor; but the two sites are about twenty-five miles apart and it is therefore unlikely that, as Oliver suggested, the Templars' building of Château Pèlerin led to the destruction of Mt Tabor by Muslim forces.[123] Saphet was able to restrict Muslim access to the fertile area west of the Jordan, as well as perhaps further progress westward towards the Christian positions on the coast. There are no specific examples of such a function being performed by the castle, but the Muslims were clearly aware of its potential. The author of *De constructione castri Saphet* described the strategic role that Saphet was able to play:

before the building of the said castle Saracens, Bedouin, Khorezmians and Turcomans frequently made incursions all the way to Acre and throughout the rest of the Christians' land. But the construction of Saphet created a means of resistance and an obstacle. The Muslims would not dare (unless they were a great multitude) to cross over the River Jordan in order to harm the Christians. Merchant caravans are now progressing safely all the way from Acre to Saphet, and everyone is practising agriculture and land settlement freely.[124]

The threat which had existed of small-scale raids in this fertile area of Christian territory had been removed by the rebuilding of the castle at Saphet. Its large garrison was obviously able to dominate the area and prevent these attacks from taking place. But the author of *De constructione* acknowledged that Saphet could not oppose an intrusion by a large Muslim force.

Strongpoints were unable to defend the frontiers of the Latin states. Smail went so far as to say, with reference to the twelfth century, that 'when warfare was fought on a scale likely to endanger the Latin occupation, no fortress or group of fortresses

---

[122] Ibn al-Furat, *Ayyubids*, vol. II, p. 89.

[123] Oliver of Paderborn, 'Historia', pp. 171–2. Oliver stated that Château Pèlerin was six miles from Mt Tabor.

[124] '... ante edificationem dicti castri Sarraceni, Biduini, Coramini et Turcomani faciebant insultus frequenter usque Accon et per terram aliam christianorum. Sed edificato castro Saphet positum est repugnaculum et obstaculum ne ad nocendum publice transire audeant a flumine Iordanis usque Accon, nisi esset maxima multitudo, et ab Accon usque Saphet vadunt secure honerati saumarii et quadrige, et agricultura et terre colonia libere ab omnibus exercetur' (*De constructione castri Saphet*, p. 43).

could restrain the passage of an invading force'.[125] The same was true in the thirteenth century, but in some respects the Latins' position was even worse. In the twelfth century, the major Muslim threat came from Damascus. Even for some periods of the thirteenth century, the Latins were reasonably well protected against any low-level Muslim attack from east of the Jordan: it has been seen what Saphet was able to do and further north, Beaufort may have been able to play a similar role.[126] However, from the time of the Mamluk usurpation, Egypt was the major Muslim power base in the area and the principal threat to the survival of the Latin Kingdom. Despite this threat, Christian forces in the south were concentrated almost entirely at coastal positions such as Jaffa, Arsuf and Caesarea. These sites could not be expected to hinder the progress of large numbers of Muslim troops and it is therefore not surprising that the conquests of Baybars in the south were able to continue largely unchecked. The Christians had no hope of resisting a major Muslim assault and, indeed, there is no suggestion that they ever attempted to do so. The situation was made worse by the absence, in normal circumstances, of a field army, and it has been shown that this encouraged a sense of isolation within each individual strongpoint.[127] The consequences of a lack of manpower were at the root of many of the Latin East's strategic problems during the thirteenth century.

The Latins' strongpoints were not completely ineffectual, however. Some of them were able to counter the threat of minor Muslim raids and in the hundred-year period under consideration, this could mean a lifetime of peaceful existence for many inhabitants.

### Aggressive functions

During the early years of the twelfth century, a number of sites played a role that was at least as significant in attack as it was in defence, particularly those that were located near Tripoli, Tyre and Ascalon. They limited the effectiveness of the nearby Muslim garrisons and enabled the Christian forces to maintain constant pressure on their opponents.[128] In the thirteenth century, manpower difficulties and the increasing strength of the Muslim

---

[125] Smail, 'Crusaders' Castles', p. 137.
[126] See Deschamps, *Royaume de Jérusalem*, pp. 192–6.
[127] See above, pp. 93–4.    [128] Deschamps, *Le Crac*, pp. 18–19.

states meant that such an aggressive role was generally not practicable. But certain castles and their garrisons were still able, in various ways, to take the initiative against their Muslim neighbours.

Strongpoints were used by troops as a base at various stages of a campaign. Many expeditions were prepared at Acre. These included the Fifth Crusade in May 1218,[129] Theobald of Champagne's crusade in 1239 (when the army was camped both inside and outside the city)[130] and the crusade of the Lord Edward in 1271.[131] Acre was an ideal place to make ready. It was the great trading centre of the Latin East, as well as being home to most of the important barons, prelates and other leaders. When Theobald of Champagne's army marched down the coast from Acre, two other strongpoints also had an important role to play. Many soldiers remained at Château Pèlerin, unable to go any further because of sickness and disease. The rest of the army moved on to the castle at Jaffa, which they made their base for the next four days. It was from there that first Peter of Brittany and then the counts of Bar and Montfort set out on raids which would lead this crusade towards a major setback at the battle of Gaza.[132]

A castle without a strong garrison – and, in theory, a castle without a garrison at all – could still be used when Christian troops carried out an offensive enterprise. In northern Syria the Templar position of Roche de Roussel was not strong enough to influence enemy policy on its own. But as one of a network of strongpoints held by the Military Orders in the north, it was useful as a base from which to enter enemy territory. In 1237, a large force led by the Templars gathered there before an attack on the Muslim town of Darbsak. The Christians suffered a heavy defeat, however, with William of Montferrand, the commander of Antioch, amongst the dead.[133]

Garrisons, or parts of garrisons, could occasionally function independently of their castle. This would normally occur when,

---

[129] Oliver of Paderborn, 'Historia', pp. 175–6. The fleet stopped at the harbour of Château Pèlerin on its way from Acre to Damietta.

[130] 'Rothelin', pp. 529, 531–2.

[131] Walter of Guisborough, 'Chronica', p. 207. This account includes details of an assault on Nazareth by the Lord Edward (pp. 207–8) which are not contained in sources written in the Latin East.     [132] 'Rothelin', pp. 532–3, 535, 538.

[133] Kamal al-Din, 'L'Histoire d'Alep', pp. 95–6; Matthew Paris, *Chronica maiora*, vol. III, pp. 404–5; Abu'l-Fida, 'Annales', p. 112; J. S. C. Riley-Smith, 'Templars and Teutonic Knights', p. 110.

as part of a field army, they combined with other troops in order to attack the enemy. But it was necessary to be very circumspect when doing this. In 1187, the defeat at Hattin had so decimated the Latin army that Saladin and his troops were able to occupy many Christian strongpoints which were virtually undefended.[134] In the thirteenth century the Latins must have been in something of a quandary, because their manpower shortages meant that, despite the inherent risks, it was essential to extract the maximum possible use from the troops that were available. The Military Orders committed large numbers of troops to most of the military activity in the area, and many of these must have been taken from their normal duty of protecting the kingdom's castles. Unfortunately, it is seldom clear from where these troops had been mustered. Individual seigneurs were also mentioned as taking part in military campaigns, often well away from their own lordships: presumably they would have been accompanied by at least some of their vassals.

It was possible for troops to be gathered from virtually everywhere if the occasion demanded. In 1233 the Hospitallers led an assault on Ba'rin, for which 80 knights had arrived from Jerusalem, under Peter of Avalon, and 100 knights from Cyprus, led by John of Beirut, at a time when his faction was well placed in its conflict with the Lombards. The army also included the Master of the Temple, with 'tout son covent' and 30 knights from Antioch. The Hospitallers themselves provided 100 knights, 400 mounted sergeants and 1,500 foot sergeants.[135] Later we will see that raids undertaken by Christian armies, even though they had little long-term value, became increasingly important in the strategy which had to be adopted in the second half of the thirteenth century. A large-scale raid, this time in Galilee, took place in 1260. The Templar garrisons from Beaufort, Château Pèlerin, Saphet and Acre all sent contingents; the force also included John II of Beirut, John of Gibelet and many knights of Acre. It was heavily defeated by the Muslims near Tiberias.[136]

---

[134] *La Continuation de Guillaume de Tyr (1184–1197)*, pp. 56–87, *passim*. Some sites in the north, such as Tyre, Tripoli and Antioch, remained well garrisoned.

[135] 'Eracles', vol. II, pp. 403–4. 'Covent' is the Master's Convent. It would probably have been made up of Templars from the headquarters of the Order. See J. S. C. Riley-Smith, *Knights of St John*, pp. 230, 279 and *passim*.

[136] 'Eracles', vol. II, p. 445; *Gestes des Chiprois*, p. 163; 'Annales de Terre Sainte', pp. 449–50; al-'Ayni, 'Le Collier', p. 217; Abu Shama, 'Livre des deux jardins', vol. v, p. 204.

Another example of a force involved in action away from its base occurred as a result of the Templars' participation in the civil conflict centred on Tripoli and Gibelet in the 1270s and 1280s. Templar support for the Embriacos encouraged the latter to send troops to Tripoli who would be augmented by the Templar commander of that city. It was also arranged that a Templar contingent from Tortosa would be present at Tripoli when the Gibelet force arrived. On this occasion, however, the promised Templar support failed to materialise.[137]

Individual fortresses which were well positioned and had a strong garrison were able to carry out aggressive operations against the enemy; again, these normally took the form of raids. The evidence relating to such activities is slightly different in northern Syria from that concerning expeditions undertaken in Palestine. In the south, it is generally in the form of theoretical statements which cannot be directly related to any specific incident. An exception to this is a brief reference to two raids carried out by Julian of Sidon, both dated to 1260. The first of these was against Philip of Montfort at Tyre, when Julian raided outside the city with knights and turcopoles before returning to Sidon. In the second, troops from Beaufort and Sidon assaulted some Mongol encampments, causing the furious Mongol general, Kitbugha, whose nephew had been killed in the attack, to besiege Sidon, though without any success.[138] These are interesting examples of a lord expressing his authority in military terms and using a major castle of his seigneurie as the base for his efforts.

The construction of the Templar castles of Château Pèlerin and Saphet had cleared the immediate areas of the Muslim threat and, in theory, made them available for Christian colonisation and agricultural activities.[139] Aggressive tactics had a part to play in this process. In the case of Saphet,

In fact, the land from the River Jordan all the way to Damascus is left uncultivated and unoccupied because of fear of the castle of Saphet. From the castle itself are launched great attacks and plunderings and ravagings as far as Damascus, and there the Templars have achieved yet more miraculous victories over the enemies of the faith, which could not easily be recited since they would require a large book to be made.[140]

---

[137] *Histoire de l'île de Chypre*, vol. III, pp. 663–7; *Gestes des Chiprois*, p. 211.
[138] *Gestes des Chiprois*, pp. 162–3; Hayton, 'Flor des Estoires', p. 174; see above, p. 128.   [139] See above, pp. 125, 130.
[140] 'A flumine vero Iordanis usque Damascum remanet terra inculta et quasi vasta propter metum castri Saphet, unde fiunt grandes insultus et depredationes et vastationes usque

Allowing for exaggeration and the absence of any supporting evidence, the Templars had forced their Muslim neighbours on to a far more defensive footing as a result of their activities from Saphet, and raids had been carried out into Muslim territory. Positive measures had been an important element in the efforts of the Templars to exert their authority over the area.

In northern Syria, the Military Orders were able to dominate their Muslim neighbours for much of this period. Hospitaller policy (centring on Margat and Crac, but with many other dependent sites) was far more unified and effective than it could have been elsewhere. At least until the middle of the thirteenth century, these castles and their garrisons enjoyed a level of influence in the region which was unequalled anywhere else in the Latin East. Most of their campaigns were directed against the accessible Muslim positions of Homs, Hama and Ba'rin and took the form of raids which were motivated by the desire to maintain payments of tribute. This will be considered later,[141] but it should be noted how persistent was the Military Orders' dominance over their neighbours. In the 1270s, following the loss of Crac des Chevaliers, Chastel Blanc and Baghras, the situation altered, so that it had some parallels with that which was apparent in the south as early as the 1240s: Margat was still able occasionally to perform aggressive functions but these were isolated instances compared to the large-scale ventures that had been organised earlier in the century.

It was not necessarily just to fight with the Muslims that Christian garrisons would move beyond the immediate vicinity of their own castles. They were sometimes involved in tasks such as castle-building. As already noted, sometime between 1277 and 1285 the Hospitallers from Margat assisted Bartholomew, the lord of Maraclea, in the construction of an island fortress. They were joined there by the count of Tripoli and other Latins.[142] Garrisons could also support other strongpoints at times when neither site was being directly threatened. There appears to have been co-operation between the Hospitallers at Crac des Chevaliers and the Templars at Chastel Blanc, for example. In 1266, Muslim troops defeated a force of fifty Frankish archers and crossbowmen which

Damascum et ubi facte sunt plures miraculose victorie per fratres Templi contra fidei inimicos, quas non esset facile recitare, quia inde posset fieri magnus liber' (*De constructione castri Saphet*, p. 43). [141] See below, pp. 187–8, 201.
[142] See above, p. 98.

was travelling from Chastel Blanc to Crac.[143] The fact that this was a Templar site apparently helping one which belonged to the Hospitallers is especially interesting: perhaps the force mentioned was a group of mercenaries that had only recently been hired by the Hospitallers of Crac.

### CASTLES AND THE FEUDAL REGIME

During the first hundred years of the Latin settlement there were occasional disputes amongst lords, but the extent of such conflicts was restricted by the power which the crown enjoyed: 'the kings of Jerusalem succeeded in dominating the feudal society subject to them'.[144] And it does not appear that the role of castles was generally of any great significance in the disputes which did develop.[145] But in the thirteenth century, and particularly after the crusade of Frederick II, a succession of regents and lieutenants, governing on behalf of absentee monarchs and minors, made the position of the crown much weaker. At the same time the Italian communes, the Military Orders and the lay baronage became embroiled in a series of conflicts, some of which also involved the participation of outside forces, including various Muslim factions and the Armenians. Castles had an important part to play in a number of these conflicts.

In the principality of Antioch, a dispute over the right of succession raged throughout the early years of the thirteenth century: some aspects of the quarrel have already been considered in chapter 1. A significant feature of this conflict was the position of the Templar castle of Baghras. The refusal of Leon of Armenia to return it to the Templars encouraged them to side with Bohemond of Antioch, whilst the Hospitallers, on the other hand, were rewarded for their loyalty to the Armenians with grants of territories such as Jabala, although the site was not in Christian hands at the time.[146] Further north, another grant was made by Leon to the Hospitallers in an attempt to create a march between himself and the Seljuq Turks. In April and August of 1210, the Hospitallers received land which included the castles of Castellum

---

[143] Ibn 'Abd al-Zahir, 'Life of Baybars', vol. II, p. 585.
[144] Richard, *Latin Kingdom*, pp. 95–6.
[145] Custody of the royal castles was an issue during the regency of Raymond of Tripoli; they were given into the hands of the Military Orders. See Smail, 'Crusaders' Castles', pp. 145–7.  [146] See above, pp. 42–3, 66.

Novum and Camardias and the towns of Silifke and Karaman. The gift of the last of these, situated about fifty miles northwest of Camardias and again not in Christian hands, suggests that Leon was keen to encourage the Hospitallers in expansionist activities, but they only remained in the area for about fifteen years. As at Jabala the rights which they received were extensive, including the power to make peace and war with the Muslims and to take all spoils, regardless of whether or not the king was present.[147]

The dispute between Frederick II and the Ibelins in Cyprus and the Latin Kingdom involved castles in a more obviously military, rather than political, role.[148] On the mainland, the Ibelins were able to maintain their grip on Beirut and Acre, whilst the imperial forces made use of Tyre as their main strongpoint. Beirut was the centre of John of Beirut's lordship and it was also an important factor in the commencement of the conflict, since Frederick had demanded that it should be returned to the crown.[149] In the autumn of 1231 he sent a large force, commanded by Richard Filangieri, to the east; this began the siege of Beirut whilst Filangieri went on to receive the submission of Tyre. If Beirut had fallen to the Lombards, then their position would have become far stronger *vis-à-vis* the baronage, but the successful defence of the castle by an increasingly strong and confident Ibelin force prevented its capture. On Cyprus, a succession of sieges in the period 1229–33 meant that the ownership of castles was constantly changing, but the Ibelin forces were eventually able to ensure that they were in firm control of the island, particularly after their capture of Kyrenia in 1233. However, the Lombards maintained an influential presence on the mainland, largely because of their control of Tyre. They held the city for ten years and they were still able to launch an assault on Acre in 1241. In the following year, however, the baronial party decided to attack Tyre. Its fall caused the final expulsion of the imperialists from Syria: they no longer had any suitable bases from which to continue their activities.[150] Tyre, however, was again of importance during the War of St Sabas in the 1250s and 1260s. By 1258 the two groups

---

[147] *Cartulaire des Hospitaliers*, nos. 1344, 1349–51. See J. S. C. Riley-Smith, *Knights of St John*, p. 132.

[148] On this conflict, see *Gestes des Chiprois*, pp. 58–68, 77–114, 116–17; 'Eracles', vol. II, pp. 376–7, 380, 385–402; *Chronique d'Amadi*, pp. 140–79, 182. See above, pp. 37–9.

[149] *Gestes des Chiprois*, p. 41.

[150] *Ibid.*, pp. 128–35, *passim*; 'Eracles', vol. II, pp. 426–7; *Urkunden der Republik Venedig*, vol. II, pp. 356–7. See J. S. C. Riley-Smith, *Feudal Nobility*, pp. 198–211.

involved in the conflict had polarised: the majority of the baronage and the Templars favoured the Venetians and Pisans, whilst Genoa's principal supporters were Philip of Montfort (the lord of Tyre) and the Hospitallers. The Genoese made use of Philip's main strongpoint as the base for a number of assaults on Acre, such as a land and sea operation which failed in June 1258.[151]

Some features of the conflict in northern Syria between the Embriacos, lords of Gibelet, and the princes of Antioch have already been considered,[152] but the particularly interesting role of the castles in its second phase justifies a re-examination. Tripoli was the principal strongpoint in the area and the key to Bohemond's control of his county. It is therefore not surprising that the Embriacos should have directed most of their energies against this target. In 1278, it was attacked by a force which included a strong contingent of Templars. Bohemond's troops chose to rely on the strength of the city's walls for protection. A naval assault led by the Templars in 1279 was a failure, but it still provoked a retaliatory raid on Sidon, with the attack apparently concentrated on the sea castle. The site was robbed and severely damaged and a number of Templars and others were taken prisoner. In 1282 there were three further attacks on Tripoli, but these ended in disaster. On the first occasion a knight, Paul Eltefahha, signalled to the Embriacos' fleet that they should come ashore, but they failed to observe the signal and the attempt was aborted. The second time, the Embriacos believed that dawn was breaking, so they turned back. When they did successfully enter Tripoli, the promised Templar support was not there, so the Embriacos were forced to surrender.

The main Embriaco base was Gibelet itself and it is clear that all the attempts to capture Tripoli started from this point. In 1278 Bohemond attempted to besiege the town, but was met by the Embriacos in a violent engagement outside the walls. This is noteworthy, as it has been suggested that at this time the town's defences were rather weak. If this was the case then it would have been quite appropriate for the Embriacos to face this attack in the open, rather than to rely on the strongpoint's passive strength to combat the threat.

Two other sites just down the coast from Tripoli also became involved in the conflict. The lord of Botrun had been on the side

---

[151] *Gestes des Chiprois*, pp. 152–5; 'Rothelin', pp. 633–4. See above, pp. 39–41.
[152] See above, pp. 43–4.

of the Embriacos in the 1258 dispute, but by the 1270s he was firmly allied to the count of Tripoli. In 1278, on the way back to Gibelet after their assault on Tripoli, the Templars attacked the manor of Botrun and undoubtedly caused great damage. Burchard of Mt Sion, writing seven years later, noted that the castle was in a state of ruin, though in 1282 Rostain, the lord of Botrun, was one of those who witnessed the confession of the lord of Gibelet. Nephin also played a major role in the course of the dispute. In 1278, after the destruction of Botrun, the Templar-led force came to Nephin and attempted to besiege it. Twelve brothers and Paul Eltefahha gained entrance to the castle, but the sergeants inside were able to close the gates and trap them. They surrendered and were taken off to prison in Tripoli. Paul Eltefahha was obviously subsequently released, as he played an important co-ordinating role in the events of 1282. Nephin was also involved in the final stages of the conflict. The Embriacos decided to attack Tripoli because Bohemond was known to be spending some time at Nephin; Guy of Gibelet's confession was taken there; and it was also his final prison and place of execution. From Tortosa to Sidon, the strongpoints had a role to play in this conflict between a lord and his vassal.[153]

### THE CASTLE AND TOWN OF JAFFA

It was pointed out earlier that attempts to study individual sites have tended, largely because of the inadequacies of written sources, to produce a very sketchy impression of the various forms and functions of the castle in this period. For this reason a more general approach has been preferred here, but the castle of Jaffa will now be examined in detail. The absence of visible remains from the 200 years of the Latin settlement has discouraged many scholars, most of whom have been more concerned with the architectural aspects of sites, from considering the range of written materials which are available. These materials are, in fact, sufficient to provide a reasonably satisfying picture of some aspects of the history of this one site during the thirteenth century. In 1197, Muslim troops besieged and captured Jaffa, despite

---

[153] *Gestes des Chiprois*, pp. 158, 204–8, 210–12; *Histoire de l'île de Chypre*, vol. III, pp. 663–8; Burchard of Mt Sion, 'Descriptio Terrae Sanctae', p. 27; Du Cange, C. du Fresne, *Les Familles d'Outremer*, ed. E. G. Rey (Paris, 1869), p. 259; Deschamps, *La Défense du comté de Tripoli*, pp. 208–9.

Christian efforts to relieve it.[154] The news of its loss provoked a reaction from Innocent III.[155] But in 1204 the site was returned to the Christians as part of a truce agreed with the sultan al-'Adil.[156] Around 1235 it came into the possession of Count Walter of Brienne, though possibly without his being given any feudal rights in the county. Walter was captured at the battle of La Forbie in 1244 and died, at an unknown date, in prison in Egypt. By June 1247, the regent Henry of Cyprus had granted Jaffa to John of Ibelin, the nephew of John of Beirut.[157] As we have seen, the mid-thirteenth century was a time when many of the feudatories had to give up their lordships, but John was able to retain control of Jaffa until his death in 1266. In 1268 Jaffa was captured by the Muslims.

The Military Orders had occupied a number of sites in the town in the period before the Muslim conquest in 1197. In 1194, Henry of Champagne granted a position to the Hospitallers 'located near to the castle of Jaffa, with two towers'.[158] The Teutonic Knights were granted land there in March 1196.[159] But there is no evidence that the Military Orders' presence continued into the thirteenth century. It seems likely that, despite its return to Christian hands in 1204, Jaffa remained deserted until 1228 – when Frederick II rebuilt the castle it was necessary for him to uncover the foundations before work could commence.[160] In the

---

[154] 'Eracles', vol. II, pp. 218–19, 221; *La Continuation de Guillaume de Tyr (1184–1197)*, pp. 191, 193; Ibn al-Athir, 'Kamel Altevarykh', vol. II, pp. 85–6; 'Document relatif au service militaire', p. 428; Arnold of Lübeck, 'Chronica Slavorum', p. 204.

[155] Innocent III, 'Opera omnia', vol. CCXIV, col. 309.

[156] Al-Makrizi, *Histoire d'Egypte*, p. 284.

[157] Edbury, 'John of Ibelin's Title', pp. 115, 123–4. Edbury argues (pp. 124–5) that Henry may have granted Jaffa to Walter in his capacity as heritor, rather than as regent, and that Jaffa was not at this time part of the royal domain. However, Frederick II – presumably in his capacity as regent for Conrad – appears to have appointed a castellan at Jaffa, following his work at the site in 1228 (*Historia diplomatica Friderici secundi*, vol. III, p. 133: a document dated April 1229, confirming Pisan privileges in the kingdom, in which Frederick referred to 'our *baillis*' of Tyre and Jaffa, as in the present so in the future' ('baiulis nostris Tyri et Joppen tam presentibus quam futuris')). On the debate over the status of Jaffa in the mid-thirteenth century, see also J. S. C. Riley-Smith, *Feudal Nobility*, pp. 125, 214–15; H. E. Mayer, 'John of Jaffa, his Opponents and his Fiefs', *Proceedings of the American Philosophical Society*, 128 (1984), pp. 140–8. Mayer rejects Edbury's contention that Walter of Brienne was never count of Jaffa; but he accepts the argument that Jaffa was not part of the royal domain (whilst acknowledging, on the second point, that both he and Edbury are 'dealing in likelihoods').

[158] '...juxta castellum Joppen sitam, cum duabus turribus' (*Cartulaire des Hospitaliers*, no. 954).  [159] *Tabulae ordinis Theutonici*, no. 32.

[160] 'Eracles', vol. II, p. 373; see also Edbury, 'John of Ibelin's Title', pp. 122–3.

following year two towers were constructed by Gerald, the patriarch of Jerusalem.[161] However, no further work at the site was recorded for over twenty years, until the time of St Louis's first crusade.

St Louis spent over a year at Jaffa, from May 1252 to June 1253. Just before Louis's arrival, John of Jaffa undertook repairs to ensure that the castle could withstand an assault. His efforts were admired by Joinville, who was particularly impressed by the display of shields on the ramparts of the citadel. St Louis therefore fortified the new *bourg* around the castle: details of the work which was undertaken show that the town area was largely undefended at this time. Walls were built which reached the shore to the north and south and incorporated twenty-four towers into their design, suggesting a size which was at least comparable with Caesarea. The two moats (presumably one round the town walls and the other round the walls of the castle) were repaired and cleared of mud. There were three main gates, one of which was built by the legate, Odo of Châteauroux: along with a section of wall, this work cost him 30,000 *livres*. Louis himself was involved in less glamorous work such as earth-moving, 'in order to gain the indulgence' ('pour avoir le pardon').[162] In April 1253, before Louis's work at Jaffa had been completed, Innocent IV had offered an indulgence of forty days to those who helped with the construction of the port of Jaffa; he had recognised that this work was of great importance for the future security of the Holy Land.[163]

The complete rebuilding of Jaffa's castle and its town walls would have encouraged colonisation activities at the site. The probable provision of a port would have brought trade and revenue into the town. But John of Jaffa soon found himself in financial difficulties. By 1256 his problems had come to the attention of the papacy: Alexander IV acknowledged that John was unable to provide for the defence of Jaffa on his own. A thousand marks from money which a previous patriarch of Jerusalem had deposited with the Templars was to be paid to the

[161] 'Annales de Terre Sainte', p. 438; *Gestes des Chiprois*, p. 77; see also *La Continuation de Guillaume de Tyr (1184–1197)*, p. 193.

[162] Joinville, *Histoire de Saint Louis*, pp. 282–4, 306–8; see also 'Rothelin', p. 629; in William of St Pathus, *Vie de Saint Louis* (p. 110), it is suggested that spiritual privileges were also gained for work at Caesarea; see also al-'Ayni, 'Le Collier', p. 227.

[163] Innocent IV, *Registre*, no. 6463.

current patriarch, James Pantaléon; the money was to be spent on the castle. The involvement of the patriarch in military affairs is again of note. In the following year, however, the Templars were told by Alexander that they should make the payment direct to the count.[164]

The work of reconstruction was continued, with help from Europe, into the 1260s. John was unable to maintain the site on his own, but he resisted the temptation to sell it to the Military Orders. In 1264 the papacy, in the person of Urban IV, intervened once more, since it was feared that the weakness of Jaffa's fortifications could allow an enemy force to seize control of the castle. Part of the five-year hundredth which was being collected in Europe was to be directed to the work of refortification, but the money was not to be given to John. As we have already noted, on this occasion the payment was to be directed to the patriarch of Jerusalem and Geoffrey of Sergines.[165] It is interesting that John's desire to hold on to Jaffa meant that, as far as arrangements for the defence of his property were concerned, he was obliged to accept outside intervention. It seems, however, that the money was well spent, since in 1266 Baybars expressed disapproval at the fact that siege engines had been set up in the castle,[166] presumably to augment the defences.

Few other strongholds in Palestine and Syria attracted so much attention from the papacy during this period. This is not surprising, since for much of the thirteenth century Jaffa was the most southerly fortified point which was held by the Christians. The size of its garrison is not known, but its location meant that it was often used by other forces as a base from which to carry out operations against enemy positions. The castle was the headquarters during the expedition into southern Palestine of Theobald of Champagne's crusade.[167] On other occasions, Jaffa proved to be well placed for strikes inland. In 1242, a force from the castle journeyed north-east and raided Nablus, where a slaughter of both Muslim and Christian inhabitants took place. In an attempt to avenge this attack, as-Salih Aiyub sent 2,000 Egyptian troops to join an-Nasir Da'ud and other soldiers at Gaza.

---

[164] Alexander IV, *Registre*, nos. 1492–3, 2174–5.
[165] Urban IV, *Registre*, nos. 473, 869; see above, p. 80.
[166] Ibn 'Abd al-Zahir, 'Life of Baybars', vol. II, p. 590.
[167] 'Rothelin', pp. 532–3, 538.

Castles and strongpoints

The Muslim force mounted a siege of Jaffa, which continued until Aiyub instructed the Egyptians to withdraw.[168]

By the 1250s, when John of Jaffa's building work was in progress, the garrison may have been augmented by at least the occasional presence of the French regiment led by Geoffrey of Sergines.[169] In 1255, the leaders of the Latin Kingdom negotiated a truce with Damascus, but Jaffa was left out of it. Consequently, during the winter of 1255–6 a force which included Geoffrey of Sergines assembled there, before raiding Muslim territory. The defences constructed by the count and St Louis proved adequate when the Muslims counter-attacked. The Christians chose at first to stay behind the castle walls to protect themselves rather than going out to face the Muslims. When the Christian force of 200 knights and 300 archers, crossbowmen and sergeants did emerge, it defeated the Muslim army, despite being heavily outnumbered.[170] Forays of this type may have been more common than the sources suggest: further military action would help to explain the need for regular repair work during the 1250s and 60s. In 1264 the French regiment was again involved in a raid out of Jaffa, accompanied on this occasion by the Templars and Hospitallers in activities which, it was hoped, would persuade the Muslims to return Gerard of Picquigny, John of Jaffa's castellan, who was a prisoner-of-war. The force moved south towards Ascalon, burning all the countryside. But the raid does not seem to have had the desired effect, since Gerard was subsequently the guest of Baybars at a military review held by the Muslims. He was only later released at the whim of the sultan.[171]

John of Jaffa died in 1266[172] and two years later Jaffa was captured by the Muslims. There is nothing left to suggest the grandeur of St Louis's walls, or the many construction projects which occupied the count, and others in the kingdom, during the middle years of the thirteenth century. Some structures in the monastery of St Peter may date from this period but there is little else to see, apart from noting that the site dominates its immediate

[168] *History of the Patriarchs*, vol. iv, pp. 268–9; al-Makrizi, *Histoire d'Egypte*, pp. 479–80.
[169] See above, p. 83.  [170] 'Rothelin', pp. 630–2.
[171] 'Annales de Terre Sainte', p. 451; Ibn 'Abd al-Zahir, 'Life of Baybars', vol. ii, pp. 516–17, 530.
[172] He was probably succeeded by his son James, and not Guy, as has generally been assumed; see P. W. Edbury, 'The Ibelin Counts of Jaffa: A Previously Unknown Passage from the "Lignages d'Outremer"', *English Historical Review*, 89 (1974), pp. 606, 609–10.

surroundings and offers more natural protection than a position such as Caesarea. Only the written materials indicate the efforts which were made to sustain the strongpoint and its value to the Latins in the east.

## CONCLUSION

The inability of the Latins, without major assistance from the west, to create and maintain an effective field army on a permanent basis meant that their strongpoints were crucial to the strategy which they used to defend the Latin East. Throughout the century, constant efforts were made by crusaders, the native baronage and the Military Orders to build strongpoints which could then be guarded by garrison troops. There were some sites which were able, under normal circumstances, to control their neighbourhood and to repulse minor Muslim attacks. Moreover, garrison troops, particularly when acting in unison with troops from other strongpoints (or with itinerant forces such as crusaders, or members of the French regiment) were able, on occasion, to function outside their own strongpoints in order to inflict damage on enemy territory. But castles could not defend the frontiers of the Latin states against a large Muslim army. The continuation of the Latin presence was therefore increasingly reliant on the survival of independent, and isolated, fortified sites. The passive strength of the fortifications relieved some of their problems, but the Latins were unable to defend the borders of their kingdom and their strongpoints were lost, one by one, in a process which would eventually end the Latin settlement.

## Chapter 4

# BATTLES

## INTRODUCTION

Historians of medieval warfare have devoted far more time to the study of battles than to other important topics, such as sieges and raids. For this period of the Latin East's history, however, battles do not warrant quite such a central position. The gradual reduction of the kingdom from about 1260 to 1291 was achieved through a series of siege campaigns undertaken by Baybars and his successors. During this period, and indeed throughout the thirteenth century, the resident Latins did not try either to arrest their decline or to expand their territories by confronting the Muslims in open battle, since they normally had insufficient troops available to maintain an army in the field and at the same time protect their strongpoints. However, when a crusade was organised, the additional numbers tended to operate as a field army and battles were not infrequent. They were then fought by Christian troops who showed little understanding of how best to combat the tactics of their Muslim opponents. The consequences of this lack of understanding were serious. The crusades of Theobald of Champagne and St Louis, for example, both suffered major setbacks as a result of defeat, or costly victory, in battle. The methods and performances of Christian armies in battle during this period are therefore by no means insignificant aspects of the Latin East's military history. The battlefield tactics of the Muslims will be given fuller treatment when they have a bearing on the techniques employed by the Christian soldiers in and around the Latin East.

The dividing lines between various types of military activity are not always easy to draw. For the purposes of this study, a battle can be defined as an engagement in which at least one of the opposing forces decides to seek military success through a direct confrontation, in the open, with its enemies. Many Christian raids of the second half of the thirteenth century were ended by the Muslims' willingness to pursue such a direct encounter. In the case of sieges, a vigorous defence of a strongpoint could encourage the defenders to ignore the protection of the site and face their enemies in the open.[1] This might produce a confrontation which contemporary writers described in terms of a battle (at Jaffa in 1256 or Gibelet in 1278, for example)[2] or it might lead to the aggressors being repulsed, or achieving success, without a major conflict taking place. Battles in the Latin East during the thirteenth century took two distinct forms, as they did in the twelfth: besides the pitched battle, there were battles during the course of a march, in which the initiative generally lay with the Muslim forces, because of the mobility of their mounted archers.[3]

We have already seen that some scholars have tried to reconstruct individual battles which took place in the Latin East during this period.[4] However, the attempts of contemporaries to give an overall impression of what happened in a battle must be used with extreme caution. Even an account by an eye-witness, who would normally have been a combatant, is unlikely to show much awareness of events beyond the author's immediate vicinity: a good example of such an account is Joinville's description of Mansurah, in which he offered little perspective on the conflict as a whole.[5] In any case it seems that, despite the efforts of commanders to form up their troops so that they could perform as units, battles in this period tended to disintegrate into a confused mass of isolated incidents, as can be seen in Philip of Novara's description of the battle of Nicosia in 1229.[6] Another difficulty to be overcome is the assessment of the reliability of various accounts of one engagement. The relatively full account which the writer of 'Eracles' gave of the battle near Gaza in 1239 would appear to be acceptable. But if this is compared with the very detailed information contained in the 'Rothelin' account, which may have been written by an eye-witness, it becomes almost impossible to reconcile the two versions.[7] We shall therefore try to establish the general form which battles took in

---

[1] See below, pp. 236, 239.
[2] For Jaffa, see 'Rothelin', pp. 631–2; for Gibelet, see *Gestes des Chiprois*, pp. 205–6.
[3] Smail, *Crusading Warfare*, pp. 140, 156–97.
[4] See above, pp. 2–4, 5–6, 15 and note 40.
[5] Joinville, *Histoire de Saint Louis*, pp. 118–40.
[6] *Gestes des Chiprois*, pp. 58–60.
[7] 'Eracles', vol. II, pp. 414–15; 'Rothelin', pp. 541–6, and p. 546 note 'B'.

the Latin East during this period, by examining the methods which were most consistently used by the main protagonists. Contemporary descriptions of conflicts will be supplemented by the remarks of an eye-witness who produced a study of Christian tactics against Muslims, the Franciscan Fidenzio of Padua. His views are important since he had detailed first-hand knowledge of the Muslim armies: he had been present with them at the siege of Antioch in 1268, for example.[8] In conclusion, a more detailed examination will be made of the battle near Gaza in 1239. This is not to establish the particular course of this conflict, but rather to compare a contemporary description of a single encounter with the more general remarks which will have been made.

SIZE OF ARMIES AND LENGTH OF COMBAT

*Numbers of combatants in battles*

Some of the statistics for combatants which were reported (not necessarily accurately) are given below, in table 3.

As in the case of the size of castle garrisons, there are problems here concerning the arbitrary nature of figures, their ambiguity and their reliability, particularly with regard to the size of Muslim forces. Even from such statistics, however, it is apparent that most conflicts involved small numbers of men. A typical Christian force appears to have numbered hundreds, not thousands, which is consistent with the size of armies believed to have been maintained in the Latin East at this time.[9] The Christian army at La Forbie in 1244 was therefore close to the limits that the kingdom could expect to call on. Christian forces, even those which were augmented by the presence of crusaders, were usually so small that some doubt has to be expressed about suggestions that Muslim armies numbered tens of thousands of men. We saw earlier, however, that the total strength of the Aiyubid army was approximately 22,000 men, whilst Baybars's army may have numbered 40,000.[10] These figures suggest that Christian forces could expect to be outnumbered when they faced Muslim armies in open battle, although the precise extent of the Muslims' numerical superiority remains a matter of conjecture. Certainly the Muslims were capable of raising large numbers of troops

---

[8] Fidenzio of Padua, 'Liber recuperationis', p. 29.      [9] See above, pp. 51–2.
[10] See above, pp. 32–3.

Table 3. *The size of armies in battles in and around the Latin East*

| Battle | | Number of combatants |
|---|---|---|
| West bank of Nile (1218) | CHRISTIAN: | 30 knights |
| | MUSLIM: | 7,000 mounted, 15,000 foot; or 4,000 or 15,000 foot. 3,000, or alternatively 1,500, were drowned[a] |
| East bank of Nile (1219) | MUSLIM: | Losses were constantly in thousands. More than 5,000 were killed on 31 March. More than 5,000 attacked the crusaders on 31 July[b] |
| Fariskur (1219) | CHRISTIAN: | Losses included 200 from the Military Orders, and 2,000 commoners.[c] Alternative numbers lost were 250 secular knights, 30 Templars, 13 Hospitallers and innumerable others[d] |
| After raid on Burlus (Egypt) (1220) | CHRISTIAN: | Many Teutonic Knights and about 20 secular knights were captured[e] |
| Advance of crusaders up the Nile (1221) | CHRISTIAN: | About 1,200 knights (excluding turcopoles and other mounted), 4000 archers (2,500 of whom were mercenaries) and innumerable foot, were on the journey south. |
| | MUSLIM: | 7,000 mounted[f] |
| Nicosia (1229) | CHRISTIAN: | The presence of turcopoles and mercenaries meant that the Lombards considerably outnumbered the Ibelins[g] |
| Casal Imbert (1232) | CHRISTIAN: | 24 Ibelin knights were taken, others were killed or wounded[h] |
| Agridi (1232) | CHRISTIAN: | 60 Lombard knights killed, 40 were taken. The total Ibelin mounted force was 233, with at least 50–60 foot sergeants. The Lombard force consisted of 2,000 horse[i] |
| Darbsak (1237) | CHRISTIAN: | Losses more than 100 Templar knights, 300 crossbowmen, secular troops and foot[j] |
| Between Jaffa and Damascus (1239) | CHRISTIAN: | Force of 200 knights, besides other armed men[k] |
| Gaza (1239) | CHRISTIAN: | 600 knights, 70 knights banneret, crossbowmen, mounted and foot sergeants and others. Or, 400 knights, Templars and Hospitallers and footsoldiers[l] |
| | MUSLIM: | 2,000 horsemen, or 1,050 Turks[m] |

## Table 3 (*cont.*)

| Battle | | Number of combatants |
|---|---|---|
| La Forbie (1244) | CHRISTIAN: | 600 knights, 600 Military Orders, and turcopoles, other horse, foot and crossbowmen.[n] Also perhaps 300 knights from Antioch, 300 from Cyprus[o] |
| | MUSLIM: | 4,000 Damascenes, 20,000 Khorezmians, 3,000 Egyptians[p] |
| On march to Mansurah (1249) | MUSLIM: | 600 mounted[q] |
| Mansurah (1250) | CHRISTIAN: | Losses with the count of Artois were about 300 knights, 80 Templar troops and others.[r] Another source reported that the army included crossbowmen and mounted sergeants[s] |
| Egyptian counter-attack at Mansurah (1250) | MUSLIM: | 4,000 mounted, innumerable foot, with the Egyptian army in reserve[t] |
| Battle at siege of Jaffa (1256) | CHRISTIAN: | 200 knights, 300 archers, crossbowmen and sergeants. They lost 20 sergeants, 1 knight |
| | MUSLIM: | 2,000 Muslims killed[u] |
| Towards Tiberias (1260) | CHRISTIAN: | 900 knights, 1,500 turcopoles, c. 3,000 infantry[v] |
| Careblier (1266) | CHRISTIAN: | More than 500 killed of the advance guard, which included Hospitallers, Teutonic Knights, French knights and others, both mounted and foot[w] |
| Acre (1269) | CHRISTIAN: | 130 mounted, excluding squires; 400 were lost, including the squires[x] |
| | MUSLIM: | Emir from Saphet with 500; Baybars with 4,000[y] |
| Gibelet (1278) | CHRISTIAN: | Total force of 100 mounted including 30 Templars, knights, valets and turcopoles, and squires and foot, against 200 mounted, besides foot and squires[z] |
| Homs (1281) | MUSLIM: | 80,000 total Mongol force (including some Franks).[aa] An alternative (Christian) source reported 50,000 Muslim mounted, 40,000 Mongol mounted[bb] |
| Tripoli (1282) | CHRISTIAN: | Some knights, 25 mounted sergeants, and 400 footsoldiers[cc] |

## Notes to table 3

[a] 'Eracles', vol. II, p. 333, gives the figures 7,000 and 15,000, with 3,000 drowned; *History of the Patriarchs*, vol. IV, p. 51, gives 4,000 mounted and 4,000 foot; Oliver of Paderborn, 'Historia', p. 190, says 1,500 were drowned.
[b] 'Gesta obsidionis', pp. 90, 99.
[c] James of Vitry, *Lettres*, pp. 121–2.
[d] 'Fragmentum de captione Damiatae', p. 190.
[e] Oliver of Paderborn, 'Historia', p. 252.
[f] *Ibid.*, p. 259.
[g] *Gestes des Chiprois*, p. 58.
[h] *Ibid.*, p. 91.
[i] *Ibid.*, pp. 97, 103, 104.
[j] Matthew Paris, *Chronica maiora*, vol. III, p. 405.
[k] 'Rothelin', p. 533.
[l] *Ibid.*, p. 539; *Gestes des Chiprois*, p. 119; 'Eracles', vol. II, pp. 414–15.
[m] The first figure (from *History of the Patriarchs*, vol. IV, p. 195) was the size of the force which al-'Adil II, the sultan of Egypt, had dispatched to Gaza to protect the frontier. The second figure (from 'Eracles', vol. II, p. 414) had been reported to the Christians by a spy.
[n] J. S. C. Riley-Smith in Ibn al-Furat, *Ayyubids*, vol. II, p. 173, note 2.
[o] Salimbene of Adam, 'Chronica', p. 177.
[p] 'Eracles', vol. II, pp. 428–9.
[q] 'Rothelin', p. 597.
[r] Joinville, *Histoire de Saint Louis*, p. 120.
[s] 'Rothelin', p. 606.
[t] Joinville, *Histoire de Saint Louis*, p. 146.
[u] 'Rothelin', p. 632.
[v] Abu Shama, 'Livre des deux jardins', vol. V, p. 204.
[w] 'Eracles', vol. II, p. 455; *Gestes des Chiprois*, p. 182.
[x] *Gestes des Chiprois*, pp. 183–4.
[y] 'Annales de Terre Sainte', p. 454 (figures taken from texts 'A' and 'B').
[z] *Gestes des Chiprois*, p. 205.
[aa] Al-Makrizi, *Histoire des Sultans Mamlouks de l'Egypte*, trans. M. E. Quatremère (Paris, 1845), vol. II (a), p. 35.
[bb] *Cartulaire des Hospitaliers*, no. 3782.
[cc] *Gestes des Chiprois*, pp. 210–11.

when the occasion demanded – for example, when confronting a crusade into Egypt or, as will be seen later, during siege campaigns. On the battlefield, however, Christian forces were sometimes only opposed by contingents of the Muslim army.[11] In western Europe, the small states produced small forces and the

---

[11] For example, the battle outside Acre of 1269 (Ibn 'Abd al-Zahir, 'Life of Baybars', vol. II, pp. 727–8). For the number of troops involved in sieges, see below, pp. 214–223.

same is undoubtedly true when considering the normal size of armies that would be put into the field in and around the Latin East.[12]

The Latin armies were made up of three basic elements: mounted troops (which included knights and mounted sergeants), infantry and archers. The role which each section of the army had to play depended on a number of variables, including the nature of the opposition, the relative size of the Latin army, the type of terrain and the circumstances in which the decision to risk a battle was taken. Unfortunately, contemporary writers often failed to distinguish between the various types of combatant. When knights were mentioned, the author may have meant a combination of knights and others such as mounted sergeants, turcopoles and mounted squires. The same problem exists in references to contingents of the Military Orders. We know that they maintained a range of troops amongst both their own brethren and their auxiliaries, but it is often impossible to apply this knowledge to a single force, since details are so sketchy. There are also few statistics to indicate the number of footsoldiers in an army and their quality, as well as quantity, could vary enormously. At Agridi in 1232, the arrival of 50–60 *sergans à pié* was considered critical, but the total Ibelin mounted force was only 233. Many of the foot sergeants were professional soldiers, but crusade expeditions, in particular, frequently had to support considerable numbers of simple *peregrini* who had journeyed out of religious devotion or in the hope of acquiring some booty. Such groups would have produced major logistical difficulties for the crusader armies, but to chroniclers they were just as much a part of the force as were the *sergans à pié*. This means that even if the large numbers of footsoldiers suggested in some sources are to be accepted (and perhaps the frequent allusion that they were innumerable is not such an exaggeration) the actual number of effective Christian infantry must have been considerably lower.

An integral part of almost any Christian army that went into action in this period was the archers and crossbowmen. They had a particularly important role to play against Muslim troops and their value was recognised by Fidenzio of Padua, who suggested that all Christian soldiers should be able to use the bow in order

---

[12] Verbruggen, *Art of Warfare*, pp. 6–10. Calculations to show the size of the Latin armies during the period 1098–1125 suggest forces of between 200 and 1,200 knights, and between 900 and 9,000 footsoldiers (*ibid.*, p. 7).

to combat Muslim tactics.[13] Their importance to the army was also acknowledged by contemporary chroniclers; an estimate of their number was often given, alongside that of the mounted troops.

### Length of combat

The length of a typical combat was another subject which appears to have tempted contemporary writers to exaggerate in order to impress the reader. Some of the battles fought on the Fifth Crusade, when the Muslims attacked the crusader position on the east bank of the Nile, purportedly went on for days. A major conflict on 31 March 1219 lasted for ten hours, from dawn till night.[14] In May, a battle was fought which went on for three days and nights[15] and a conflict in July continued for two days.[16] However, these examples are unusual, since the Muslims were attacking an entrenched defensive position. It is unlikely that a pitched battle could continue for any great length of time. The extreme heat that often prevailed in the area, the weight of armour and other clothing that men wore, the relatively small number of combatants and the sheer physical effort of fighting would all have encouraged a short combat time. The possible effects of a blow, on deliverer as well as recipient, have already been noted.[17]

### Preparations for battle and battle formations

The initial stages of a battle were significantly influenced by the terrain, and the formations which were adopted by the opposing armies. We have already considered some of the problems of terrain. Sand dunes and dusty ploughed fields presented different, but equally serious, problems for the heavy chargers of the Christian knights and the heavily laden Christian infantry – problems which were often made even more difficult by the climate.[18] In the twelfth century, a battle site with plenty of space had advantages for both Christian and Muslim commanders, since it provided a good area for the heavy Christian knights to

[13] Fidenzio also advocated the use of mounted archers in Christian armies ('Liber recuperationis', pp. 29, 30). See above, p. 50.
[14] 'Gesta obsidionis', p. 90; Oliver of Paderborn, 'Historia', pp. 205–7.
[15] John of Tulbia, 'De Domino Johanne', p. 127.
[16] 'Gesta obsidionis', p. 94.     [17] See above, pp. 89–91.
[18] See above, pp. 91–2.

operate in, whilst at the same time allowing the Muslims to use their lighter, more mobile mounted archers.[19] As early as the First Crusade, Christian troops used natural obstacles to prevent possible attacks against the flanks of the army.[20] However, commanders were often restricted in their choice of terrain. In 1253, a detachment of St Louis's army was sent to attack Banyas. Joinville and other troops were obliged to take up a difficult position on the slopes above the Grotto of Pan between the town and the castle of Subeibe. They were exposed to Muslim troops advancing from the castle above them. After suffering heavy casualties, the crusaders' position became untenable and they were forced to retreat on to the plain, by way of the southern slope of the hill on which Subeibe is situated.[21]

The initial battle formation of the army, whether it was on the march or fighting a pitched battle, was important, not least because once an encounter had started it was extremely difficult for commanders to maintain order and discipline. But it is seldom possible to establish how armies were organised, even at the start of a conflict. The positions of infantry and bowmen, in particular, are generally a matter of speculation. In the case of the mounted forces, in the west the *conrois* (tactical units often based on family or feudal relationships) would line up next to one another, thus forming *batailles*.[22] At the battle of Agridi in 1232, the Ibelin force of 233 mounted troops assembled in five *batailles*. The first was led by Hugh of Ibelin, Anceau of Brie commanded the second, Baldwin of Ibelin the third and John of Caesarea the fourth. Much of the Ibelin strength seems to have been held back in the rearguard, which included John of Beirut and the king of Cyprus. It should have also included Balian of Ibelin, but he positioned himself to one side of Hugh and Anceau in the front line.[23] When the Egyptians attacked the crusaders soon after the battle of Mansurah in February 1250, the latter were assembled in at least nine *batailles*, though again their precise disposition is unclear. A

---

[19] Verbruggen, *Art of Warfare*, pp. 185–7.

[20] Smail, *Crusading Warfare*, pp. 170–4.

[21] Joinville, *Histoire de Saint Louis*, pp. 312–18. The geographical details have been established by an inspection of the site.

[22] Verbruggen, *Art of Warfare*, p. 75; Contamine, *War in the Middle Ages*, p. 229. Accounts of battles in the Latin East do not allow the nature of the *conrois* and *batailles* to be determined: the two expressions seem interchangeable, as does *eschelle*.

[23] *Gestes des Chiprois*, pp. 97, 101–2. The account in *Chronique d'Amadi* (pp. 169–70) suggests that the Ibelins were organised in only four *batailles*.

reserve force commanded by the duke of Burgundy was guarding the crusaders' camp.[24]

Formation was equally important on the march. In the attack on the Muslim camp at Fariskur in August 1219, the crusaders marched *sic cuneis*.[25] In the absence of any other information, this suggests the use of a wedge formation in order that, by manoeuvring, the Christians could always present a full face to the Muslims, regardless of the direction from which the latter might attack. When the crusaders progressed southwards to Mansurah in July 1221, the Nile was on the right, with ships on it; on the left were the footsoldiers, whilst the mounted troops formed a link between the two. The archers and spearmen stayed together, whilst the unarmed common people (who were, for once, mentioned by Oliver of Paderborn) were close to the river bank. The experienced combatants (*peritiores*) were in the van and rearguard, warding off any attacks, whilst it was publicly proclaimed that no-one should slip beyond the front or rear of the army. In this formation and by enforcing strict discipline, the crusaders were able to avoid heavy losses on the march southwards.[26] Unfortunately, this is the only instance when such a full impression of a Christian formation on the march is given. When St Louis's force marched up the Nile, it is known that the advance guard was attacked and that this contained a large number of Templars, but there is no further information on the deployment of the army.[27] It has already been seen that the troops of the Military Orders were frequently positioned at the front and rear of a force.[28]

KNIGHTS AND OTHER MOUNTED TROOPS

*Discipline and morale*

The knights were not necessarily the single largest unit in Christian armies of this period, but they remained the most influential. They were capable, in theory, of devastating a Muslim force with a single charge. The excellence of their protective armour made them impervious to much of the Muslims'

---

[24] Joinville, *Histoire de Saint Louis*, pp. 146–52.
[25] James of Vitry, *Lettres*, p. 120.
[26] Oliver of Paderborn, 'Historia', pp. 260–1.
[27] Joinville, *Histoire de Saint Louis*, p. 102; 'Rothelin', pp. 597–8.
[28] See above, p. 63.

weaponry, whilst the discipline of their training could be expected to enhance the quality of the army as a whole. Many of these points will be examined below. But the principal characteristic of the knights was a tendency to think and act as individuals, or as members of a very small unit. This is perhaps not surprising since, as was seen in chapter 2 of this study, the knights in the armies of the Latin East were recruited from many different sources. In some circumstances, as in the early stages of a charge, for example, knights could perform collectively. But they were rarely entirely subordinate to the needs of the army. Throughout the period, and in diverse circumstances, Christian armies were therefore hampered by the personal ambitions and consequent actions of individual knights.

These problems manifested themselves at all levels of the armies. For the commanders, difficulties of decision-making in, or just before, a battle could undermine the unity of a force. We have already noted the occasion outside Acre in 1269, when Robert of Crésèques refused to retire into the city, saying that he had come to the Holy Land to die for God. Oliver of Termes and a few others were able to escape before the Christians suffered a heavy defeat at the hands of a Muslim army.[29] There was an instance of prevarication at the battle of Mansurah in 1250. At the height of the conflict, St Louis called a council, to decide whether to move towards the river. This manoeuvre would have had two benefits. First, the army would have gained the support of the duke of Burgundy and the force which was guarding the crusader camp. Secondly, it would have given the sergeants an opportunity to drink. The movement was agreed on, but when news came that the counts of Poitiers and Flanders, and others, were so hard pressed that they could not follow, Louis's council advised him to stay. The king was reproached for this decision, so he determined again to go towards the river, but then news came of the difficulties of his brother Robert in Mansurah, so he decided to advance towards the town instead.[30] Even with a monarch present, decision-making was a difficult and potentially disastrous process.

At moments of crisis for an army, the fortitude of the knights was often inadequate. When the crusaders attacked the Muslim camp of Fariskur in August 1219, not only the footsoldiers but the

---

[29] See above, p. 80.     [30] Joinville, *Histoire de Saint Louis*, pp. 126–8.

Cypriot knights and even some Hospitallers lacked the courage to face the Muslim assault. Another account of this battle also reported that some of the Christian knights fled; the Military Orders and other knights had to try to protect the rear.[31] On the retreat towards Damietta in 1221, panic prevented any hope of an orderly withdrawal. Just before the flight began, the crusaders rather unwisely burned their tents, thereby indicating to the Egyptians that they were about to move. Many of the crusaders chose to try to forget their troubles and were too drunk even to make the journey.[32] At the same stage on St Louis's first crusade, Joinville painted a vivid picture of the onset of panic in the army. As the crusaders began their retreat, a group of engineers led by Joscelin of Cornaut was ordered to destroy the bridge over the river. However, they failed to perform this task and amid increasing chaos the crusaders on land started to fire on their comrades on the ships, in an attempt to make them wait for them.[33] In these last two instances, the crusaders were probably already doomed, but their panic made their fate inevitable. Moreover, the knights were obviously not alone in losing their grip on the situation. At the battle of Mansurah, on the other hand, despair overwhelmed some of the crusader knights – and this contrasted with the courage and ingenuity of the footsoldiers. As St Louis and those with him attempted to repel the Muslim attack, many knights stood on the opposite bank bewailing the fate of their king, whilst the infantry tried desperately to cross the river.[34]

A lack of discipline could also result in displays of over-exuberance in which the careful planning of commanders was ignored or forgotten. At the initial landing near Damietta on St Louis's first crusade, Joinville, heading towards the beach by boat, was ordered to disembark near the standard of St Denis. But he disregarded this instruction and landed instead in front of 6,000 mounted Turks.[35] Any pre-arranged plans appear to have given way to a wild scramble to reach the shore. At the battle of Mansurah, Robert of Artois was widely blamed for his pursuit of the Muslims into the town, although Joinville (perhaps not surprisingly, as he was discussing his hero's brother) did not

---

[31] Oliver of Paderborn, 'Historia', p. 214; James of Vitry, *Lettres*, pp. 121, 129.
[32] Oliver of Paderborn, 'Historia', pp. 270–1.
[33] Joinville, *Histoire de Saint Louis*, pp. 166–8.  [34] 'Rothelin', p. 607.
[35] Joinville, *Histoire de Saint Louis*, p. 86; 'Rothelin', p. 590.

completely exonerate the Templars from all criticism. It is clear, however, that this was an occasion when, as St Louis was said to have stressed, good discipline was essential: when one force had crossed the river, it should have awaited the arrival of the next. The first *batailles*, which included Robert of Artois and the Templars, instead chased the Muslims into the narrow streets of Mansurah where, unable to manoeuvre, they were overwhelmed by their lighter and more mobile opponents.[36]

Discipline and morale had, therefore, to be maintained if an army was to perform efficiently. The rules and training of the Military Orders enabled them to act as a cohesive force within the army.[37] Contemporary writers occasionally referred to efforts to maintain soldiers' confidence. The morale of some sergeants at Banyas in 1253 was salvaged, according to Joinville, by his own courageous behaviour. He dispensed with his horse when the sergeants complained that he could retreat, if necessary, and this gesture seems to have given them renewed faith.[38] For a Christian force, particularly one which was on crusade, encouragement could come from religious invocations or symbolism. Prior to two Muslim attacks against the army on the Fifth Crusade, the legate Pelagius urged the troops on with a rousing sermon, before they went into battle on behalf of Christ. In May 1219, the crusaders gathered round a *carrocium*, a type of wagon containing the consecrated host. It caused the Muslims to have some doubts about launching an attack.[39] In the midst of battle, too, religious faith was important. After the Muslims had dealt with the crusaders inside Mansurah in 1250, they attacked the rest of the force which had crossed the Ashmun river. Facing up to this challenge, St Louis not only ordered his men to hold together and stand firm, but he also implored them to trust in Jesus.[40] Such displays of religious fervour could have undesired consequences, however. Muslim writers who reported on the battle of La Forbie noted that the Christians marched under their crosses, ac-companied by their priests; this may have aroused some of the doubts which were expressed by al-Mansur Ibrahim of Homs about fighting with Christians against fellow-Muslims.[41]

---

[36] 'Rothelin', pp. 602–6; Joinville, *Histoire de Saint Louis*, pp. 118–20.
[37] See above, pp. 61–4.  [38] Joinville, *Histoire de Saint Louis*, pp. 314–16.
[39] 'Gesta obsidionis', pp. 78, 105–6, 91–2. For earlier examples of the use of a *carrocium*, see Erdmann, *Origin*, pp. 53–6.  [40] 'Rothelin', p. 606.
[41] Al-Makrizi, *Histoire d'Egypte*, p. 489; Yafi'i, 'Compilation des chroniques égyptiennes' in J. F. Michaud, *Bibliothèque des Croisades*, vol. IV (Paris, 1829), p. 445.

Examples of the unreliability of knights can be contrasted with instances when they did show resolve under pressure. During the Lombards' destruction of the Ibelin camp at Casal Imbert in 1232 (something which, admittedly, the Ibelins could have avoided if they had maintained a better watch over the site) the defenders fought tenaciously and managed to hold out till morning, even though many were not mounted, or were only half-dressed and lacking weapons.[42] Both Muslim and Christian writers recognised the bravery of the Latins at La Forbie in 1244. Their Muslim allies fled, but the Christians fought on until they were overwhelmed by sheer weight of numbers. Very few of them escaped the carnage.[43]

### The charge

The armour worn by the knights was in many respects a handicap. Fighting demanded a tremendous physical effort and the knight's armour made him cumbersome in comparison with a Muslim opponent. But the mail and plate armour which was worn did have some advantages. When under attack, the knights were well protected, so that amongst the Military Orders, the brother knights were expected to show a greater degree of bravery than the more lightly armed sergeants.[44] When the knights were the attackers, the collective weight of their charge was the most potent weapon available to a medieval army and in western Europe this tactic was central to Christian methods.[45]

The Templars' *Rule* provided the brothers with instructions on the delivery of a charge. The force would be organised into a number of *eschelles*, including one, under the command of the *Turcopolier* which, in addition to the turcopoles, contained most of the brother sergeants. None of the units was allowed to start to charge without the permission of the Marshal, the official who controlled the military wing of the Order. The Marshal himself would take the standard, the *bausan*, from the Under Marshal. Then he would select as many as ten brother knights whose duty would be to protect both him and the standard when the charge began. The other brothers were instructed to attack behind, in front, to the right and to the left of the banner; but they should

---

[42] *Gestes des Chiprois*, pp. 90–1; 'Eracles', vol. II, pp. 396–7.
[43] Yafi'i, 'Compilation', p. 445; 'Rothelin', p. 564.    [44] See above, p. 49.
[45] Verbruggen, *Art of Warfare*, pp. 72–4, 94–5 and *passim*.

always be ready to offer assistance to the knights who surrounded the Marshal. A reserve banner would be given to a Commander of the Knights and he was expected to stay as close as possible to the Marshal, ready to take over the leadership of the charge if the Marshal were injured or otherwise unable to continue.

Prior to the commencement of the charge, each knight would have one squire in front of him carrying his lance and another behind tending to the spare horses. When the charge started, the squire who was looking after the reserve warhorse should ride after his master (presumably to offer assistance if the knight's horse were killed or incapacitated). The other squire would take his master's mule and join the *Gonfanonier*, a brother sergeant who was responsible for the Order's squires. The squires with the *Gonfanonier* would then form themselves into an *eschelle* and follow the rest of the Templar force.[46]

This was the theory; and we have already seen how the training of the Military Orders enabled them to perform basic manoeuvres (including, during the Fifth Crusade, a charge) to good effect.[47] But the Templars, who were amongst the most experienced soldiers in the Latin East, must have realised that the charge was not necessarily a suitable tactic in battles against Muslim opponents. The Muslim approach to engagements with Christian armies during this period could render the charge at best ineffectual and at worst dangerous to the Christians themselves. But, since battles were normally fought by Christian armies which were largely made up of crusaders from western Europe, the charge, or a modified form of it, remained an essential element in Christian battle plans. In Europe, knights were accustomed to lining up in their *batailles*, prior to an ordered charge against a solid target. This could not be done in the east so the charge, rather than being a pre-emptive act, took place after continual Muslim harassment and therefore lacked the structural unity which some scholars have perceived in it in the west.

It is clear from the examples available that Muslim commanders were aware of the potential threat of the charge and had

---

[46] *Règle du Temple*, nos. 103, 143, 161, 164–6, 170, 177–9; see also M. Bennett, 'La Règle du Temple as a Military Manual or How to Deliver a Cavalry Charge', in *Studies in Medieval History presented to R. Allen Brown*, ed. C. Harper-Bill (Woodbridge, 1989), pp. 14–15. Within the Hospitallers, the Master Esquire of the Convent had charge of the squires and grooms, and the *Gonfanonier* (as the name suggests) was responsible for the standard of the Order (J. S. C. Riley-Smith, *Knights of St John*, pp. 321–2).

[47] See above, pp. 61–4.

developed tactics to deal with it – tactics which enabled them to use the energy of the manoeuvre to their own advantage. That these methods were not just coincidentally employed is confirmed by Fidenzio of Padua, who described the Muslim technique, when faced by a Christian charge: 'The Saracens retreat and scatter; they rush, some here, others there. Afterwards, at the sound of a trumpet...they are reunited and they attack the Christians, striking the men and their horses with many arrows and killing them.' The lighter Muslim horses were able easily to outdistance the Christian mounts if they were chased: the difficulty for the Christians was that 'they do not know how to gather themselves together again' ('nesciunt se recolligere').[48] But this had been an unsolved problem throughout the thirteenth century. During the crusaders' retreat from Fariskur in August 1219, some of the rearguard who were protecting the rest of the retreating army decided to charge, because of the damage which was being caused by Muslim archers; when they did so, the Muslims opened their ranks and then closed up again, once the Christians had gone straight through. The Muslims then closed in themselves on the crusaders, using cudgels, swords, javelins and Greek fire.[49] At the battle of Mansurah in 1250, Muslim pressure again resulted in a Christian charge. Following the defeat of Robert of Artois, the Muslims were able to surround St Louis's forces and began firing great quantities of arrows, which struck both men and horses. At this point in the battle, St Louis did not have any crossbowmen with him to return the fire, so he had to charge in order to deal with the Muslim threat. It appears, however, that the size of the Muslim force prevented this from being a particularly successful attack. Joinville remarked that in this battle he was hit five times, whilst his horse received fifteen wounds. This shows that whilst Muslim arrows lacked penetration, their concentrated fire could have a debilitating effect.[50] A final example again illustrates the established Muslim tactics in dealing with the charge. As Robert of Crésèques (who had only recently arrived in the east) faced the

---

[48] 'Sarraceni cedunt et ad invicem dividuntur et vadunt, alii huc, alii vero illuc; postmodum vero ad sonum buccine...congregantur et insultum faciunt in Xpistianos, et percuciunt viros et equos ipsorum multis sagittis et occidunt eos' (Fidenzio of Padua, 'Liber recuperationis', p. 30). The Muslim tactic described by Fidenzio seems to be a form of the *al-karr wa-l-farr* exercise, in which the Muslims used the feigned retreat. See N. Elisséeff, *Nur ad-Din* (3 vols., Damascus, 1967), vol. III, pp. 743–5.

[49] James of Vitry, *Lettres*, pp. 121, 129; 'Fragmentum de captione Damiatae', pp. 188–9.

[50] 'Rothelin', pp. 606–7; Joinville, *Histoire de Saint Louis*, p. 132.

Muslim forces outside Acre in 1269, the latter hesitated as the two sides closed, so Robert charged. The Muslims opened their ranks and allowed the crusaders to pass through, before attacking them from the rear and eventually inflicting a defeat.[51]

There were occasions when a Christian charge did enjoy some success. Earlier, we saw that a charge by the Templars during the Fifth Crusade forced the Muslims to abandon their assault on the crusader camp.[52] Similarly, the battle fought by a force under Peter of Brittany in 1239 produced a successful charge. The Muslims advanced towards the crusaders firing rapidly, but when the latter charged, they forced the Muslim archers back on to the rest of the Muslims who were following behind. As the Muslims were now unable to use their bows, a close mêlée developed, a conflict which was to be concluded by the decisive intervention of a crusader reserve force.[53] The battle of Gaza on the same campaign provides one of the best examples of a Christian charge, and its consequences, during this period; it will be examined in detail later. The charge when used against Muslim opponents was a powerful but unwieldy tactic, a reaction to the pressure which resulted from the Muslims' ability to maintain the initiative during the first stages of a battle. The more flexible Muslim cavalry could use a Christian charge to their own advantage, but this did not prevent Christian troops from consistently employing a tactic which was recognised by contemporaries such as Fidenzio of Padua as inappropriate to the requirements of warfare in the east.

The Muslims, unlike the Christians, were able to modify their tactics according to the opponents that they were facing. Against the Mongols, for example, they were prepared both to face up to a charge and to use it themselves. It is difficult to establish the precise course of the battle of 'Ain Jalut in 1260, but one eye-witness stated that the future sultan Baybars, with an advance guard, 'repulsed the vigour of their [the Mongols'] first charge'. As a result of this, the other Muslims were able to advance and gain the victory.[54] The account of al-Makrizi also suggested a conflict determined by the charge, as one wing of the Muslim force was broken in disorder, but the situation was saved by the

---

[51] *Gestes des Chiprois*, p. 184.     [52] See above, p. 62.
[53] 'Rothelin', p. 535.
[54] Ibn 'Abd al-Zahir, 'Life of Baybars', vol. II, p. 339.

Mamluk sultan Kutuz who charged in amongst the Mongols.[55] At Homs in 1281, the Mongol and Muslim forces again lined up for a pitched battle, each side deployed with a left, right and centre. The Mongol charge broke the Muslim left, but the Muslim right held and this eventually decided the battle.[56] Homs, like 'Ain Jalut, was a conflict in which the outcome was determined by the success or failure of the charge, and its immediate penetration. This is very different from Muslim battles against Christians, when the Muslims normally had to avoid being confronted in the early stages of a battle by the powerful Christian charge.

The Christians in the Latin East did have some opportunities to use a pre-emptive charge during this period, but only against Christian opponents. We have already seen that the Lombard–Ibelin conflict was significantly influenced by two battles, at Nicosia in 1229 and Agridi in 1232. Few details survive of the battle at Nicosia, but it seems that the two sides simply lined up in their *batailles* and charged. Philip of Novara added that once the efforts of the clergy to mediate had failed, each knight directed his energies against the enemy he hated the most.[57] At the battle of Agridi, the charge of the first Lombard *bataille* led by Walter of Manepeau was carried out so badly that it took him past the Cypriot rearguard. After trying to attack the fourth Ibelin *bataille*, Walter and his men fled. This indicates how difficult it was to correct a misdirected charge by a body of knights. The charge of the second Lombard *bataille* was more effective, but the third Cypriot *bataille* was able to offer help to the first, which had taken the full brunt of the assault. The battle subsequently developed as a series of confused individual combats, in which some great feats of arms were performed.[58] The charge, though apparently carried out from a position of complete order, had merely been the prelude to an untidy mêlée.

Christian efforts to regroup after a charge would have relied heavily on the use of banners and standards: these were also important as symbols to maintain the morale of an army, particularly as many, like the *carrocium*, were imbued with

---

[55] Al-Makrizi, *Histoire des Sultans*, vol. I (a), pp. 104–5; see also Thorau, 'The Battle of 'Ayn Jalut', pp. 238–9.
[56] Al-Makrizi, *Histoire des Sultans*, vol. II (a), pp. 36–8; *Cartulaire des Hospitaliers*, no. 3782.     [57] *Gestes des Chiprois*, p. 58.     [58] *Ibid.*, pp. 103–4.

religious significance.[59] Their use has already been noted in the case of the Confraternity of the Holy Spirit;[60] such rallying points were important for infantry as well as for mounted troops. The statutes of the Military Orders stressed how critical the standard was in battle, both for the positional sense of the army and as a final symbol of defiance. We have seen that the Templar standard, the *bausan*, was carefully protected when the brothers were preparing to charge. If a Templar lost contact with the banner of his unit then he was expected to attach himself to the nearest banner he could see. When the Christians faced the prospect of defeat in battle, the banners assumed additional importance. No Templar was permitted to flee from the field as long as the *bausan* was flying: if it was impossible to reach the Templar banner then a brother should join a unit under another standard, and follow that. But if a Templar or Hospitaller abandoned the banner, he would be dismissed from the Order. The banner itself had to be flying at all times: hence the protection it was afforded, because 'if the banner is lowered, those who are far away do not know why it is down...and men who lose their banner are very frightened, and it could result in a very great defeat...'.[61]

## Close combat

The charge, if executed correctly, would bring the knights into close contact with their opponents and they would use their lances, swords, maces and daggers. However, most of the blows suffered by a knight would, far from causing instant death, simply result in some form of handicap. At Nicosia in 1229, Anceau of Brie had all his weapons (lance, sword and dagger) broken, and suffered so many blows that he could hardly use his hands.[62] The knights' problems in a tight conflict were made worse by their heavy equipment which could cause them great difficulty, particularly if they were unhorsed. During the retreat from the Muslim camp at Fariskur in 1219, the Muslims' arrows were hitting not only the knights but also their horses: when a horse

[59] See Erdmann, *Origin*, pp. 35–53.   [60] See above, pp. 76–7.
[61] '...se le confanon se baisse, cil qui sont loing ne sevent por quoi il est baissiés...et les gens qui perdent lor confanon sont mult esbai, et porroit torner a mult grant desconfiture...' (*Règle du Temple*, no. 611; see also nos. 164–8, 232, 241–2; *Cartulaire des Hospitaliers*, no. 2213, pt 34, and no. 3844, pt 10).
[62] *Gestes des Chiprois*, p. 59.

fell, the rider would either die or be captured.[63] Berart of Manepeau was thrown from his horse by Anceau of Brie during the battle of Agridi. Seventeen of his colleagues dismounted to help him; they were all killed by Ibelin foot sergeants.[64] This indicates not only the difficulties which were experienced in trying to remount, but also the potential vulnerability of knights to footsoldiers when they had dismounted. At the battle of Mansurah, Joinville was thrown from his horse and, although he was able to recover, he suffered a severe battering, particularly when he was knocked to the ground again and ridden over.[65] In the battle fought outside Acre in 1269, after the charge led by Robert of Créseques had failed, the Muslims attacked the Christians' horses and this brought the battle to an end: as soon as one of the Christians was forced on to his feet, his chances of survival were remote.[66]

A Christian army could be severely disadvantaged in close combat when it was attacked in the flanks. Such an attack was an especial worry when a Christian force was on the march, but the threat was apparent at all times, since Muslim tactics involved efforts to surround the Christians. The danger of an assault from the side was demonstrated, during the Fifth Crusade, in the initial stages of the crusaders' attack on the Muslim camp in August 1219: it was such an assault which caused the Cypriot knights to flee, a flight which led to panic spreading rapidly throughout the army.[67] The vulnerability of the flanks increased the importance of the advance guard and rearguard to the army since, if they were well organised, they could help to ward off the Muslims' attacks.[68]

The effects of close combat can be illustrated by the injuries which Joinville suffered at the battle of Mansurah. First, he was wounded between the shoulders by a Muslim lance. Then he was thrown from his horse and, though he managed to get up, he was knocked to the ground again, losing the shield which was protecting his neck as the Muslims rode over him. But he was still able to continue in the battle, apparently without receiving

---

[63] 'Fragmentum de captione Damiatae', p. 189.     [64] See above, p. 91.
[65] Joinville, *Histoire de Saint Louis*, p. 122.     [66] *Gestes des Chiprois*, p. 184.
[67] Oliver of Paderborn, 'Historia', p. 214; James of Vitry, *Lettres*, p. 121. It appears that the crusaders' attack on the camp had begun in a well-organised 'wedge' formation (see above, p. 154); this had obviously broken down.
[68] See above, p. 63.

attention. He suffered further wounds, however, from the barrage of arrows with which the crusaders had to contend. He was struck five times, despite the protection of a Muslim's padded tunic he had found and which he used as a shield. When the conflict was over, he desperately needed rest because of the wounds which he had suffered, but he managed hardly any as the Muslims renewed their attack before dawn the next day. Because of his injuries, he was unable to wear a hauberk: this was also the case during the next Egyptian attack a few days later, when he added that he was not carrying a shield either. Whether these wounds were treated in any way is unclear, but Joinville now became very ill, blaming it on his injuries. Later, as the crusaders fled, a jousting hauberk was placed on him to provide protection from Muslim arrows. His sickness remained a problem throughout the time that he was a captive of the Muslims and when he arrived in Acre he suffered a further serious attack of fever.[69] The likelihood of wounds becoming infected was a constant threat in the aftermath of battles during this period. Illness and disease were persistent hazards and it seems from this account that Joinville's failure to have his injuries treated properly made his condition far worse and brought him close to death.

Despite the inability of knights to protect themselves when knocked from their mounts in battle, they were prepared, in certain circumstances, to fight on foot.[70] At the battle of Nicosia in 1229, when John of Beirut found himself with only a few foot archers and faced by fifteen Lombard knights, he chose to dismount and lead his troops into the courtyard of a monastery, where they were able to keep their opponents at bay with lances until help came.[71] During the first crusade of St Louis, when the crusaders arrived off Damietta in 1249, the knights (only some of whom were mounted) plunged into the water alongside the footsoldiers. When they reached the shore, they placed their shields in the sand with their lances pointed at the Muslims.[72] Finally, when the Muslims attacked the crusaders at Mansurah

---

[69] Joinville, *Histoire de Saint Louis*, pp. 120–4, 132, 140–2, 150, 164, 172, 176, 208, 220, 224, 226.

[70] This method of fighting was occasionally used by knights from western Europe. See Contamine, *War in the Middle Ages*, pp. 230–1.

[71] *Gestes des Chiprois*, p. 59.

[72] 'Rothelin', pp. 590–1; Joinville, *Histoire de Saint Louis*, p. 86. This defensive formation is similar to the one advocated by Fidenzio of Padua for use by Christian infantry. See below, p. 171.

many of the knights who faced the onslaught chose to dismount to fight, including the count of Anjou and his knights. In the *bataille* of the count of Poitiers, the entire force except its leader had dismounted. At the end of the conflict, St Louis praised the successful defensive action that had been fought by the troops on foot.[73]

Even a small number of knights could be of considerable value in battle. On 23 June 1219, during the Fifth Crusade, the Muslims launched a major assault on the crusaders' position on the east bank of the Nile. This attack was driven off by John of Arcis, accompanied by just four knights and a number of retainers. One Christian was killed. The reported size of the Muslim force (5,000–8,000 men) was surely exaggerated but the role of this small body of knights was, nonetheless, regarded by the chroniclers as decisive.[74] The battle of Nicosia in 1229 again demonstrated the importance of the individual knight; the Lombard army had designated twenty-five knights to attack only John of Beirut.[75] The principal chronicler of the Lombard–Ibelin conflict, Philip of Novara, undoubtedly accentuated the importance of individuals, but his account does at least show the kind of cohesion and added strength that the presence of a knight was believed to bring to a force. In the same war, Balian of Ibelin performed great feats of arms in defending a pass against the Lombards during the battle of Agridi in 1232.[76] At the battle of Mansurah, a group of only six men (including Joinville) attempted to prevent the Muslims from crossing a bridge over a stream, since this would have created a situation in which St Louis was under attack from two angles. This defensive action appears to have been successful, whilst the small Christian force also charged a group of Muslim infantry which was harassing two sergeants.[77]

Against poorly equipped Muslim infantry, in fact, the knight might expect to do considerable damage. In the Muslim attack on the crusaders on the west bank of the Nile in October 1218, as the Muslim mounted and foot attacked from different directions, the crusaders concentrated their attack on the latter and slaughtered

---

[73] Joinville, *Histoire de Saint Louis*, pp. 146, 150, 154.
[74] 'Gesta obsidionis', p. 92; John of Tulbia, 'De Domino Johanne', p. 128; 'Liber duellii christiani in obsidione Damiate exacti', in *QBSSM*, pp. 153–4.
[75] *Gestes des Chiprois*, p. 59.    [76] *Ibid.*, pp. 102–3.
[77] Joinville, *Histoire de Saint Louis*, pp. 128–32. The group was reinforced by the count of Soissons and Peter of Neuville; but their arrival coincided with the departure of Humbert of Beaujeu.

many thousands, whilst others were drowned.[78] At one point during the Egyptian counter-attack at Mansurah, the flight of some mounted Muslim troops enabled the men of the count of Flanders to inflict heavy losses on the Muslim footsoldiers.[79]

### Reserve forces and use of ambushes

Battles involved such comparatively small numbers of men that an effective entry by a reserve or a fresh force could have a decisive influence on the outcome.[80] At the battle of Nicosia in 1229, however, the significance of the arrival of fresh troops was almost certainly overestimated, since they included the chronicler of the battle, Philip of Novara.[81] We shall return later to the part played by a fresh force of 50–60 foot sergeants at the battle of Agridi in 1232.[82] Peter of Brittany planned the careful use of troops in reserve in southern Palestine in November 1239. He divided his force of 200 knights and other armed men in two and placed both groups in hiding. If one failed to halt the Muslim caravan which was approaching, then the other would be able to do so, besides which one force would be able to aid the other. The Muslims fell into this trap and were charged by the troops led by Peter. It is clear, however, that the caravan was accompanied by a large number of armed men and, with the second Christian force unaware of what was happening, Peter saw that the battle was turning in the Muslims' favour. By blowing on a horn, he was able to call the second force into action, as a result of which the Muslims were obliged to flee.[83] A well-placed ambush could produce excellent results, but it could also turn into disaster. During the conflict outside Acre in 1269, an ambush may have been set by the Christians, but it did not work and the Muslim troops were subsequently able to surround their opponents.

In the course of this last conflict, Baybars had also set an ambush, although it was not needed.[84] The use of an ambush was a favourite Muslim ploy, but against well-organised Christian

---

[78] 'Eracles', vol. II, pp. 333–4; see also *History of the Patriarchs*, vol. IV, p. 51, which reported that the crusaders lured the Muslim infantry into their camp.

[79] Joinville, *Histoire de Saint Louis*, p. 150.

[80] See Verbruggen, *Art of Warfare*, pp. 198–200.

[81] *Gestes des Chiprois*, p. 60.      [82] See below, pp. 170–1.

[83] 'Rothelin', pp. 533–5.

[84] Ibn 'Abd al-Zahir, 'Life of Baybars', vol. II, pp. 727–8; Ibn al-Furat, *Ayyubids*, vol. II, p. 138.

troops it was not always effective. When St Louis marched up the Nile in December 1249, the Muslims set an ambush and then sent 500 or 600 of their best troops to attack the crusaders' advance guard, which was principally made up of Templars. But the Muslim attack was driven off with half the force being killed.[85] Christian armies were often wary of the possibility of a Muslim ambush. At Doc in 1203–4, Aimery of Lusignan sent out scouts to establish whether Muslim troops were positioned to attack the Franks in the rear.[86] At Jaffa in 1256, Geoffrey of Sergines was dissuaded from chasing the defeated and fleeing Muslims because of the threat of an ambush.[87] The device was also used by the Muslims against other opponents. In one account of the battle of 'Ain Jalut, Kutuz placed most of his force in an ambush, exposing only himself and a few troops to the Mongol army. The Muslim soldiers with Kutuz were obliged to retreat but the pursuing Mongols fell into the awaiting ambush and were subsequently slaughtered.[88]

### FOOTSOLDIERS

As mentioned above, one of the most obvious features of the footsoldiers was their diversity. They would have included both scantily clad pilgrims and the well-armed professional troops who played a leading role, for example, in some of the Lombard–Ibelin conflicts. Ill-disciplined infantry could hamper the efforts of Christian horsemen to perform efficiently, but well-armed and trained footsoldiers could integrate with the rest of the army and provide valuable support.

The large number of commoners within the ranks of the army on the Fifth Crusade contributed to the decision to attack the Muslim camp at Fariskur in August 1219. Most contemporary writers agreed that the masses had been highly critical of the failure of the knights to attack the Muslims – and this encouraged the crusade's leaders to agree to an assault on the camp.[89] Yet in principle the decision was a sound one, because this Muslim

---

[85] 'Rothelin', pp. 597–8; Joinville, *Histoire de Saint Louis*, p. 102.
[86] *Chronique d'Ernoul*, pp. 358–9; 'Eracles', vol. II, pp. 262–3. As was noted earlier (chapter 1, note 4) details of the conflict near Doc in 1203–4 are sketchy and are only present in Christian sources.    [87] 'Rothelin', p. 632.
[88] Rashid al-Din, *Histoire des Mongols de la Perse*, ed. and trans. M. E. Quatremère, vol. I (Paris, 1836), p. 349.
[89] 'Eracles', vol. II, p. 340; James of Vitry, *Lettres*, p. 120; 'Fragmentum de captione Damiatae', p. 185; 'Gesta obsidionis', p. 101.

position had posed a constant threat to the crusaders' efforts to conclude the siege of Damietta. In the disaster which followed, at least part of the blame lay with the indiscipline of the footsoldiers, although, as we saw earlier, they were not alone in panicking. When the army arrived at the Muslim camp, the masses were seized by hysteria and turned on one another; they proved impossible to restrain.[90] One writer stated that in the subsequent flight none of the footsoldiers survived back to the crusader camp.[91] In another account of this incident, Oliver of Paderborn reported that the infantry were also struggling because of the weight of their equipment.[92] Heavily laden footsoldiers would have been particularly affected by conditions in the region.

Poorly trained footsoldiers were, indeed, vulnerable to Muslim attack, especially if they lacked the support of mounted troops: Fidenzio of Padua stressed that knights should not abandon their infantry.[93] But knights and footsoldiers could complement one another in order to combat Muslim tactics. Unfortunately, there are very few details of the precise interaction of the two elements. During the Fifth Crusade, for example, when the Muslims were driven off after one of their assaults against the crusaders' fosse on the east bank of the Nile, the mounted crusaders came out followed by the footsoldiers. But it is unclear how (if at all) the footsoldiers were organised or what their function may have been. Perhaps it was to collect booty and prisoners.[94] When the Christians were opposite Mansurah on this crusade, they came under great pressure, particularly from Muslim archers. The crusaders therefore deployed their footsoldiers as a barrier. The footsoldiers also fired back the arrows which had been aimed at the crusader army. This afforded protection to the mounted troops, who also gave support to the footsoldiers, although precisely how is, once again, unclear; they may have charged the Muslims from behind the ranks of the infantry.[95] At the battle of Mansurah, the Muslims who were attacking St Louis retreated back to their camp once the crusader foot had successfully crossed the river. One Muslim writer stated that the crusader infantry had been unable to contribute to the course of the battle because it had

---

[90] James of Vitry, *Lettres*, p. 121; John of Tulbia, 'De Domino Johanne', p. 132; 'Liber duellii christiani', pp. 158–9.     [91] *Chronique d'Ernoul*, p. 424.
[92] Oliver of Paderborn, 'Historia', p. 214.
[93] Fidenzio of Padua, 'Liber recuperationis', p. 29.
[94] Oliver of Paderborn, 'Historia', p. 210; 'Fragmentum de captione Damiatae', p. 181.
[95] Oliver of Paderborn, 'Historia', pp. 272–3.

developed so quickly; if they had been able to do so then the outcome might have been radically different, because there were enough infantry to protect the mounted troops.[96] Both Muslim and Christian writers recognised that Christian knights could perform far more effectively if they were supported by well-organised infantry. But knights and footsoldiers were not always complementary. At La Forbie in 1244, following the flight of its Muslim allies, the Christian army's squires and foot sergeants became mixed up with the ranks of knights, so that the latter were unable to attack.[97]

The Christian infantry could, in addition to their operations in conjunction with mounted troops, perform an independent role against both Christian and Muslim opponents – even during the course of a crusade. When the Muslims launched a counter-attack at Mansurah in 1250, the crusaders were faced with the problem of dislodging some stones which Muslim troops were using to conceal themselves. A priest approached them, later assisted by fifty foot sergeants. The mounted Muslims charged this group, but did not dare to approach it too closely. One of the Muslims, moreover, was wounded in the ribs by a lance hurled by one of the sergeants. The Muslims retreated under this pressure and the sergeants were able to remove the stones.[98] It appears that even mounted Muslim soldiers hesitated before engaging in close combat with the better-quality infantry of a Christian army.

Christian footsoldiers' greatest achievements in this period came during the battles fought by the Lombards and Ibelins. The infantry element of the army was held in high esteem in these campaigns – something which may, in part, be explained by the widespread employment of mercenaries. At a key point in the battle of Agridi in 1232, fifty to sixty Ibelin foot sergeants arrived from the town. Good quality infantry could inflict serious damage in the right circumstances; this force was able to dispatch a number of Lombard knights who had been either knocked from their horses or otherwise obliged to dismount. A passage in the 'Eracles' account of the battle (contained also, in a slightly different form, in Philip of Novara's narrative) vividly described the performance of the foot sergeants and the ways in which they were able to influence the course of the engagement:

---

[96] 'Rothelin', p. 607; Djamal al-Din, 'Remède contre le chagrin', in Michaud, *Bibliothèque*, vol. IV, p. 459, and in Michaud, *Histoire*, vol. VII, p. 559.
[97] 'Eracles', vol. II, p. 429.     [98] Joinville, *Histoire de Saint Louis*, pp. 142–4.

there was one thing which greatly helped the Cypriots: they had foot sergeants, which meant that when one of their knights was knocked down, the sergeants helped him up and remounted him on a horse. And when one of the Lombards was struck down, he was either killed or captured by the foot sergeants...

It was because of this, it was said, that Lombard casualties were so heavy; more than sixty knights were killed and forty were taken prisoner.[99]

The battles of Agridi and Mansurah showed that against either Christian or Muslim opponents Christian infantry could function without support from the mounted elements of the army. Fidenzio of Padua, who wrote about the role played by Christian footsoldiers against Muslim troops, considered that if there were too many footsoldiers in the Christian army then they should be organised separately. He went on to discuss the various weapons which were available to infantry troops and the ways in which these should be used against Muslim armies, whose principal threat was the mounted archer. The first line of defence was the lance, a weapon which Fidenzio also recommended for use by mounted troops. Soldiers with lances should be arranged in a ring around the other footsoldiers, with their weapons pointed towards the oncoming Muslim cavalry. The Muslims would thus be prevented from engaging the remainder of the Christian infantry in combat. However, the Christian spearmen would be vulnerable to the firepower of the Muslim archers, so protection should be provided for them by shieldbearers. The infantry should also be armed with swords, and be adequately clothed to minimise the effects of the blows of the Muslim troops.

### ARCHERS AND CROSSBOWMEN

Fidenzio of Padua also considered the functions of the 'ballistarii et sagittarii' amongst a Christian force which was comprised only of infantry. Spearmen could drive the Muslims off if they attempted to close in on the Christian army, but the use of archers and crossbowmen would keep the enemy at a distance and, more significantly, would inflict heavy casualties upon their horses.

---

[99] '...une chose y ot, qui aida moult a Chypreis: ce que il avoient sergens a pié; dont il avenoit que, quant un de lor chevaliers estoit abatus, que li sergent le relevoient, et le remetoient a cheval. Et quant un des autres estoit abatus, piestant l'ocioient li sergent et prenoient...' 'Eracles', vol. II, p. 401; see also *Gestes des Chiprois*, pp. 103–4; and see above, p. 91.

Fidenzio emphasised this point since he realised that Muslim troops were ineffective on foot. Yet without the support of archers, Christian infantry, however well-organised they might otherwise be, were still liable to be overwhelmed by the Muslims. For similar reasons, archers and crossbowmen should be mixed in with a force which included horsemen.[100]

Evidence from battles fought in the Latin East during this period supports Fidenzio's contention that archers and cross-bowmen were critical to the success or failure of a Christian army. Their principal function was to keep an aggressive Muslim force at such a distance that the Muslim mounted archers were largely ineffectual; if the Muslims did attempt to close in, then concentrated Christian firepower might successfully repulse them. These tactics applied both to pitched battles and to battles on the march. If they were to be effective, however, then massed ranks of archers were needed. We saw earlier that there were 4,000 archers on the Fifth Crusade, of whom 2,500 were mercenaries.[101] The number that had been recruited on this occasion cannot be regarded as typical, but it does at least indicate the importance which was attached to this element of the Christian army. Moreover, as specialists and professionals, they would have been unlikely to panic. The value of archers to this crusade was demonstrated by an occasion when they were not present. When the Templars returned from an attack on Burlus in 1220, the crusaders who went to meet them were heavily defeated by the Muslims. Oliver of Paderborn suggested that the crusaders had been ill prepared for battle, since they lacked the support of crossbowmen and archers.[102]

Two further incidents from the Fifth Crusade showed the importance of archers when the Muslims tried to approach a Christian army. First, on 8 July 1219, Muslim foot and mounted soldiers attacked the crusaders' fosse on the east bank of the Nile; every time the Muslims charged, the Christian archers and crossbowmen killed vast numbers of them. Secondly, on 21 September when the Muslims attacked, the performance of the Christian crossbowmen and archers kept their opponents under constant pressure.[103] During the battle of Mansurah on St Louis's

---

[100] Fidenzio of Padua, 'Liber recuperationis', pp. 29–30.
[101] See above, p. 58.    [102] Oliver of Paderborn, 'Historia', pp. 252–3.
[103] 'Fragmentum de captione Damiatae', pp. 174, 193–4. The dating is unclear. For the time of the first attack, compare 'Gesta obsidionis', pp. 93–4.

first crusade, the Muslim cavalry were forced to dismount and erect a barrier, in order to protect themselves from crusader crossbow attacks.[104] On the march, too, archers and crossbowmen had a vital part to play in warding off Muslim assaults. Earlier, we saw that during the march south towards Mansurah in July 1221, the archers were used in partnership with the spearmen.[105] The combined force stayed together, using their closely packed lances if the Muslims approached too close and presumably (although this is not actually stated) complementing this with arrows when the Muslims were further away. This enabled them to protect the baggage from Muslim assaults.[106] Archers and crossbowmen also had an important role to play in civil conflict in the Latin East. Their ability to inflict damage on a force that approached too near was recognised by John of Beirut after the battle at Casal Imbert in 1232. He realised that it was pointless to chase the Lombards, not only because they had already reached the mountain pass, but also because they had crossbowmen and archers with them.[107]

Archers were equally important when Christian forces moved on to the attack in a conflict. During St Louis's first crusade, the crossbowmen contributed to the crusaders' successful establishment of a beachhead at Damietta. As the footsoldiers and knights hurled themselves into the water, so the crossbowmen also worked well, firing rapidly and with great accuracy. This concentrated firepower helped to force the Muslims back and the crusaders were able to land safely.[108] Later in this crusade, at the battle of Mansurah, Joinville reported that the arrival of the king's foot crossbowmen caused the Muslims to flee: the latter retreated as the former were preparing for action, when 'they saw our men set foot in the stirrup of their crossbows' (in order to draw the cord of the bow). Another French chronicler, William of Nangis, suggested that many Muslim horses were killed in this battle by the crusader crossbowmen.[109]

It is clear that Christian archers and crossbowmen had to interact with the other elements of a Christian force if they were to be effective. This was demonstrated in the role which they

---

[104] Joinville, *Histoire de Saint Louis*, p. 142.   [105] See above, p. 154.
[106] Oliver of Paderborn, 'Historia', p. 260.   [107] *Gestes des Chiprois*, p. 92.
[108] 'Rothelin', p. 590; Matthew Paris, *Chronica maiora*, vol. VI, pp. 153–4; William of Nangis, 'Vie de Saint Louis', *RHF*, vol. XX, p. 371.
[109] '…nous virent mettre pié en l'estrier des arbelestes' (Joinville, *Histoire de Saint Louis*, p. 134). William of Nangis, 'Vie de Saint Louis', p. 375.

performed during the Fifth Crusade's march south from Damietta. It is also reflected in the course of the Egyptian counterattack at Mansurah in 1250. The positioning of the Christian *batailles* meant that the count of Flanders, and his soldiers, were some distance from Joinville and his men. When Joinville saw that Muslim mounted and foot soldiers were attacking the count, he ordered crossbowmen to fire on the horsemen. As the latter fled, so the count's men were able to advance and inflict heavy casualties on the Muslim foot. Similarly, when Jocerant of Brançon's *bataille* came under pressure, Henry of Cône instructed the king's crossbowmen to fire on the Muslims; they were again driven off.[110]

In certain circumstances, however, archers might prove to be rather less effective. In the battle of Mansurah, all of the crossbowmen that entered the town with Robert of Artois's force died.[111] In the narrow streets of Mansurah, or indeed in any confined situation, archers were generally of far less value than they were out in the open. Archers could play a decisive part in the success or failure of Christian tactics against a Muslim force.

Heavier artillery was, occasionally, used in battles, though usually in situations where a force was defending an entrenched position – circumstances akin to siege warfare. When the Muslims were attacking the crusaders' encampment on the east bank of the Nile in the summer of 1219, the Templars drove their opponents back with the help of an *albarest de torn*, a large siege crossbow on a stand. In 1253 the Damascenes approached Acre and, according to Joinville, were within range of this powerful form of the crossbow.[112] Shortly before the battle of Mansurah in 1250, St Louis ordered Joscelin of Cornaut and his engineers to construct eighteen engines, which were to be used to bombard the Muslim army on the opposite bank of the river. The Muslims had set up sixteen engines, and the two sides exchanged fire; Joinville did not believe that the crusaders' machines caused any serious injury, but the Muslim engines certainly damaged the Christian position, particularly when they were used to launch Greek fire.[113] Throughout this period, however, larger artillery would have been too inaccurate to be used to any great effect in a battle,

---

[110] Joinville, *Histoire de Saint Louis*, pp. 148–50, 152.    [111] 'Rothelin', p. 606.

[112] 'Fragmentum de captione Damiatae', pp. 180–1; Joinville, *Histoire de Saint Louis*, p. 300; see Contamine, *War in the Middle Ages*, p. 186.

[113] Joinville, *Histoire de Saint Louis*, pp. 106, 112–16.

besides being too cumbersome to be constantly manoeuvred as the circumstances of a conflict changed.

## THE ROLE OF NON-COMBATANTS

We have seen that certain types of conflict could continue for a long time – perhaps on and off for a number of days – and that debilitating injuries, such as those suffered by Joinville, were the most likely result of the type of combat which took place. These considerations, coupled with the difficult conditions in the area, meant that an army's logistical support could be crucial to the outcome of a conflict. It would have included the provision of food, water and equipment and the tending of wounds, but unfortunately there is very little information on this aspect of an army in battle. On the Fifth Crusade, during a battle outside Damietta on 31 March 1219, the women brought water, stones, wine and bread to the fighters, whilst the priests prayed and tended the wounds of the injured. This conflict continued for ten hours.[114] The fact that these tasks were performed by women and priests suggests that they were undertaken on something of an *ad hoc* basis, even on a large crusade expedition. This is surprising, given the time, effort and expense which went into the preparation of a crusade.

## THE AFTERMATH OF BATTLE

Many combatants, like Joinville, would have spent much of their time after a battle trying to rest and hoping that wounds would heal and not become infected. Other more enjoyable conse-quences of a battle included the seizure of booty and the acquisition of ransoms for captured prisoners, though crusader armies appear normally to have enslaved their captives. After the Muslim attack on the crusaders besieging Damietta on 31 July 1219, the Christians obtained both booty and slaves.[115] A similar situation went disastrously wrong for them in August of the same year, however: at Fariskur, the Muslims attacked whilst the crusader footsoldiers were loading themselves up with booty.[116] After the battle fought by Peter of Brittany in 1239, the Christians

---

[114] Oliver of Paderborn, 'Historia', pp. 206–7.
[115] 'Fragmentum de captione Damiatae', p. 181.
[116] *Chronique d'Ernoul*, p. 424.

returned to Jaffa with large amounts of booty and prisoners. On this occasion, the original intention of the crusaders had been to raid, but a battle had had to be fought to attain their objectives.[117] There was a major slave market at Acre and, in addition, Muslim prisoners were held in captivity there. In 1274–5, a number of Muslim sea captains escaped from prison in Acre, having been set free by some of their compatriots.[118]

When the Christians were defeated, there would also be booty taken, and there were many instances when Christian prisoners were taken off in chains, usually to Egypt.[119] But the Muslims were prepared to ransom some of their more important prisoners. In 1260, a substantial Christian force was defeated by some Turcomans at their camp near Tiberias: many were killed, but John II of Beirut was subsequently ransomed for 20,000 besants, as were the commander of the Temple, the marshal of the kingdom (John of Gibelet) and James Vidal, one of the kingdom's leading feudatories. The total ransom may have amounted to as much as 200,000 besants, but the arrangements for its distribution caused much squabbling amongst the Muslims.[120] Some captives were worth even more than this. When St Louis and his force were captured, it was accepted that 800,000 besants would be the ransom for the army (after the sultan had waived 200,000 besants of the million-besant ransom originally agreed), whilst Damietta itself should be the price for the king. Only half of this sum was actually paid, amounting to 208,750 *livres tournois*. As the average yearly income of the French monarchy at this time was about 250,000 *livres*, it is clear that this ransom was an enormous sum to have to pay.[121]

### A CAMPAIGN WITHOUT BATTLE

In the Latin East before 1187, campaigns in which battle was avoided by a field army were an important part of the Latins' defensive strategy. By keeping an army in the field, a Latin

---

[117] 'Rothelin', pp. 533–5.
[118] J. S. C. Riley-Smith, *Feudal Nobility*, p. 62; Ibn 'Abd al-Zahir, 'Life of Baybars', vol. II, pp. 814–15. The sea captains had been involved in an unsuccessful raid on Cyprus in 1271. See below, pp. 190–1.
[119] After La Forbie, for example: al-Makrizi, *Histoire d'Egypte*, pp. 489–90; Joinville, *Histoire de Saint Louis*, p. 294.
[120] 'Eracles', vol. II, p. 445; 'Annales de Terre Sainte', pp. 449–50; *Gestes des Chiprois*, p. 164; al-'Ayni, 'Le Collier', p. 217.
[121] Joinville, *Histoire de Saint Louis*, pp. 186, 256; see Jordan, *Louis IX*, pp. 77–9.

commander could harass his opponent into abandoning an attempt to capture a strongpoint. To the Muslims, on the other hand, a battle-seeking strategy made sense because of the manpower problems of their enemies.[122] In the thirteenth century, however, the native Latins chose not to organise a field army as a part of their defensive policy, opting instead to defend themselves from within their individual strongpoints. When a field army was organised, it was normally a force which had been heavily augmented by crusaders who would wish, in some way, to confront their enemies.

The defeat of St Louis's crusade into Egypt may have encouraged those who stayed with him in the Holy Land to behave more cautiously towards their Muslim opponents. An incident outside Acre in 1253 thus provides, for this period, a rare example of a success achieved through the deliberate avoidance of a direct confrontation. As the Damascenes approached the city, threatening to destroy the gardens if they were not paid 50,000 besants, Christian foot sergeants fired on them with bows and crossbows. There was a joust between a Genoese knight and some Muslims, but the Damascene army did not dare to fight so it set off in the direction of Sidon. The Christians had not attempted to force a battle and the Damascenes had caused no harm to the land outside Acre.[123]

### THE BATTLE OF GAZA, NOVEMBER 1239

As has already been pointed out, the detailed analysis of a single battle will produce unsatisfactory results; to use such an analysis as the basis for more generalised remarks is liable to give a distorted impression. We may, however, look at one detailed account of a conflict, not in an attempt to establish its precise course, but rather to test some of the conclusions which have been reached from evidence relating to other engagements. The events connected with the battle of Gaza, as recorded in the 'Rothelin' source, are particularly interesting as they allow a further consideration of the roles played by the various components of a Christian army in conflict with the Muslims.

The site of the battle was marked with the building of a

---

[122] Smail, *Crusading Warfare*, pp. 138–56; see Gillingham, 'Richard I and the Science of War', pp. 81–3.   [123] Joinville, *Histoire de Saint Louis*, pp. 298–302.

'Victory Mosque' by the emir Shams ad-Din Sunqur[124] and local
inhabitants are still proud of the inscription which records the
defeat suffered by the crusaders. The mosque is in the centre of the
village of Beit-Hanun, which is located in a shallow depression
just north-east of Gaza. To the west is a line of sand dunes, whilst
to the east are some gentle hills. It was to somewhere near this
location that Henry of Bar, Aimery of Montfort and many other
barons led their men in search of booty.

Before the Christian army had even set out from its base at
Jaffa, its leaders had allowed personal ambition and antagonism to
dominate their decision-making. The count of Bar had been
incensed by the successful expedition organised by Peter of
Brittany and it was this which encouraged him to carry out a
second raid, despite appeals for caution from Theobald of
Champagne, the leaders of the Military Orders and Peter of
Brittany himself. Theobald even attempted to use the fealty
which had been sworn to him as the leader of the expedition to
enforce obedience, but it was to no avail and, in the cover
provided by darkness, the army set off. It was a large force,
numbering 600 knights, 70 knights banneret, crossbowmen,
mounted and foot sergeants and many others. Yet even within its
ranks there were some who doubted the wisdom of the
expedition. Walter of Brienne became concerned about the
damage which the horses might be suffering as a result of the
journey and advised caution, but although many advocated a
return to Ascalon it was decided to press on towards Gaza. The
target of the expedition was herds of animals, which had been
moved by local inhabitants who feared the possible effects of the
conflict.

The Christians now contributed to their subsequent downfall
with a number of avoidable mistakes and omissions. Their choice
of a site to make camp was unwise. It was in a valley which would
allow an enemy force to dominate the position from the heights
of the sand dunes and hills. Moreover, there was no means by
which the Christians could reach the higher ground to counter
such a threat. Their situation was made even more perilous by
their apparent failure to post guards or look-outs to watch over
the camp. This enabled the Muslims to investigate the cir-

---

[124] 'An Ayyubid Inscription from Beith-Hanun', ed. Y. Sukenik, *Bulletin of the Jewish
Palestine Exploration Society*, 12 (1946), p. 85 (in Hebrew). I am grateful to Dr M. H.
Burgoyne, who translated the Arabic text for me.

cumstances of their enemies thoroughly before they attacked. Whilst the Christians spent their time eating and sleeping, the Muslims were organising large numbers of troops which, according to Walter of Brienne and the duke of Burgundy, outnumbered the Christians by at least fourteen to one. The Muslim commander, Rukn-ad-Din al-Hijawi, had sent instructions by fire and messenger that every available Muslim should come to fight against the crusaders.[125] When the Christians realised the gravity of the threat which they faced, some of them (including Walter of Brienne and Hugh of Burgundy) decided to flee. Their flight obviously weakened the army, although it is impossible to say by how much. The rest of the force chose to stay, since they recognised that, although the knights might escape, the infantry would be left helpless. On this occasion at least, there was no possibility of the footsoldiers defending a position without the support of mounted troops.

The simple disposition of the two sides was quite clear. It has been noted that the Christians had established themselves in a valley. The Muslim infantry were massed on the sand dunes and hills which overlooked the site, and they were able to cast down various projectiles, particularly arrows, on to their enemies. The Muslim cavalry were placed to block a narrow entrance, in order to trap the Christians where they had made their camp. As the battle developed, the Christian soldiers were forced to make a number of quick decisions, resulting in disorder which the Muslims were able to exploit to their own advantage. The engagement started with the Muslim infantry bombarding the Christians with stones and great quantities of arrows. This caused confusion amongst the Christian ranks: many of their number were wounded and, it was interestingly stated, many horses were killed. The standard response in this situation was to attempt to drive the Muslims off with archers and crossbowmen – and indeed this tactic was adopted. For a time it kept both the Muslim infantry and cavalry at a safe distance, but this could not be maintained because of a shortage of arrows. Once again the Muslims were able to move closer, so the Christian knights resorted to a charge. We have seen in other cases that the charge

---

[125] We saw earlier (p. 148 and note *m*) that al-'Adil II had dispatched 1,050, or 2,000, horsemen to Gaza. This number would have been increased by Rukn-ad-Din al-Hijawi's efforts, though perhaps not to the extent suggested by Walter of Brienne and Hugh of Burgundy.

was normally a reactionary manoeuvre, and this is another good example: the knights had to attack in order to combat the particular threat which they faced. On this occasion, however, the first stage of the charge was remarkably effective. The Muslim cavalry guarding the narrow entrance presented a solid target and a close conflict began in which the Christians gradually gained the advantage. Their chances of success had been increased because the Muslim footsoldiers could no longer strike at them from above. In order to draw the Christians from this protected position, the Muslims therefore employed a feigned retreat. The advantage which the Christians had achieved was now completely thrown away as they chased wildly after the apparently fleeing Muslims. When the latter turned again, the Christians realised their mistake: they faced the Muslim horse in one direction and, in the other, the Muslim foot who had come down from their previous positions. The depleted Christian force was trapped. It tried to regroup in its *batailles*, but this made little difference. The Muslims used their arrows to wear down the Christians before moving closer with swords and maces: few of the Christians were able to escape the subsequent slaughter.

When news of the disaster reached the rest of the army, which had moved to Ascalon, they hurriedly armed themselves and rode towards the battle site. The Teutonic Knights were far quicker than the others and their approach served to drive off the Muslims who were still chasing some of the survivors, but they were unable to free any of the prisoners, who were taken to Egypt. Then they realised the extent of the carnage. Christians lay dead and stripped of all their arms and clothing. A few were still alive, including Anceau of l'Ile who was found naked and covered in wounds. The survivors were carried back to camp on shields, but an operation to rescue the prisoners was ruled out, on the advice of the Templars, the Hospitallers and the native Latins, who argued that such a scheme was bound to result in the deaths of the captives. The army retreated back to its base at Ascalon. When Richard of Cornwall was in Palestine, he found that some of the victims of this battle had been left on the battlefield; their remains were gathered and buried in Ascalon's cemetery.[126]

The battle of Gaza illustrates a number of important points

---

[126] 'Rothelin', pp. 538–48; Matthew Paris, *Chronica maiora*, vol. IV, pp. 144–5; *History of the Patriarchs*, vol. IV, pp. 195–7. Details in this last account are vague, but they do seem to indicate that the Muslims used the feigned retreat.

relating to battles which were fought in and around the Latin East at this time. The reliance of footsoldiers on other elements of an army, the importance of archers and crossbowmen and the typical response of knights to the Muslim threat which they faced are all apparent. Two other more general points are striking, however. Throughout the battle, apart from the brief success enjoyed by the Christian archers and then immediately after the charge of the knights, the tactical initiative always lay with the Muslims. All that the Christian army could do was respond in retaliatory fashion to pre-emptive moves by their opponents. Secondly, the battle reflects a paradox which was noted earlier: the armies of the Latin East could generally only fight when they were reinforced by troops from the west, yet these troops did not understand the kind of conflict in which they were likely to become involved. They tried to respond, particularly through the charge, with the techniques which they knew from the battlefields of Europe, but the Muslims could use the power of the charge to their own advantage, thereby leaving the knights in an even worse situation.

## CONCLUSION

It has been written that the knight, along with the castle, should be regarded as the symbol of medieval warfare,[127] but in the Latin states and their environs the knight, particularly one from the west, would have frequently found his effectiveness seriously reduced. In the thirteenth century the Muslim armies were able to a very great extent to dominate the terms on which battles were fought, and thus the knights were reduced to imprudent gestures in order to try to assert their superiority. Robert of Artois's unnecessary death demonstrated the essential problem for the knight in this period; his reckless decision to chase the fleeing Muslims into Mansurah resulted from his frustration at an inability to combat Muslim tactics – a feeling no doubt shared by many western knights both before and after him. This failure to come to terms with Muslim tactics explains, to a great extent, Muslim successes, and Christian defeats, in battles during this period.

The significance of the battles which have been examined should not be underestimated. At various points in the thirteenth century a Christian army suffered a defeat in battle which had

---

[127] Verbruggen, *Art of Warfare*, pp. 301–2.

important consequences. Theobald of Champagne's crusade was seriously disrupted by the defeat at Gaza. The heavy losses incurred by the crusaders at Mansurah in 1250 were a significant setback for St Louis's force; the battle was considered by Muslim commentators to be the turning point of their army's ultimately successful campaign. From this time, the crusader army was always forced to take the defensive against the Muslim forces. If Robert of Artois and the Templars had not ignored specific instructions and charged after the fleeing Muslims into Mansurah, the expedition as a whole could have had very different results. A successful crusade into Egypt would not only have eased the pressure on the Latin states, but might also have affected the Muslim power-structure in Egypt and in some way hindered the emergence of the Mamluk sultanate in the 1250s. But it has to be stressed that battles were not decisive in determining the fate of the Latin East. With the exception of La Forbie in 1244, the Christians, who were obliged to defend their kingdom for most of the time without significant support from the west, learned from the lesson of Hattin and preferred to maintain themselves behind the walls of their strongholds rather than risk a major engagement with a Muslim army. This was most apparent in the period of Baybars's sultanate: in view of the damage which he did to the Latins through the capture of strongpoints and cities such as Saphet, Crac and Antioch, it might seem surprising that there was no attempt on the part of the Christians to confront the invading Muslims and drive them out of their lands. This is largely explained by the dearth of manpower suffered by the Latins during this period. Only a crusade could have produced an army which might have been capable of taking on the Muslims and there was no great crusade in the 1260s. For the final demise of the Latin East, the significance of battles was fairly limited.

*Chapter 5*

# RAIDING EXPEDITIONS

### INTRODUCTION

The mechanics of warfare in this period and, in particular, the near impossibility of maintaining an adequate fighting force for any great length of time, meant that for both the Latins and Muslims the ultimate objective – the capture of areas which were controlled by the enemy – could not always be pursued. The Latins' military options were further restricted by the problems they encountered in even gathering a field army which could safely operate outside the confines of the strongpoints. It was inevitable, therefore, that much of the military activity in this period should aim for quite limited objectives. The raid, or *chevauchée*, was thus an integral part of war in the Latin East during the thirteenth century. For the Muslims it was one element in their overall strategy which aimed to expel the Latins from the mainland. For the Latins, as they became progressively weaker, raiding expeditions were at times their only means of carrying war to their Muslim neighbours, however desultory these raids may appear to have been.

We saw earlier that there can be a thin dividing line between different forms of military activity.[1] In this respect, the campaign of the Lord Edward in late 1271, directed against the Muslim fortress of Qaqun, has been described as one of 'a few raids in 1271 [which] accomplished nothing...',[2] but some contemporary writers suggested that this particular attack should be regarded as an abortive siege attempt.[3] A superficial examination of the Christian attack on the Muslim camp at Fariskur in August 1219 might indicate that this was a raid, but contemporary accounts showed that the crusaders hoped to encounter and fight with the

---

[1] See above, pp. 145–6.   [2] Strayer, 'The Crusades of Louis IX', p. 517.
[3] For example, *Gestes des Chiprois* (pp. 200–1).

183

Muslims, so in this instance a battle was the prime objective.[4] If these two examples were not raids, then what was one? In the area around the Latin East in the thirteenth century, a raid may be defined as being a military action that had direct aims which did not include either the permanent acquisition of enemy territory or a major engagement with enemy forces. Raids were used as a reprisal against enemy activity; to maintain or exact tribute from a neighbour; to ensure adequate supplies during an expedition; and as a means of damaging enemy morale, by directing an attack against a target which was of symbolic importance but had little military value. Perhaps the best example of this was Baybars's destruction of the church at Nazareth in 1263.[5] For both the Christian and Muslim armies, raiding expeditions were an alternative to a major campaign, which would still weaken the enemy and cause long-term damage and injury. In terms of manpower, time and other considerations, they were a comparatively inexpensive form of warfare. They could, moreover, bring in direct profit to the participants and they did not necessarily need to involve a great number of troops, assuming that no significant encounter with an enemy force was anticipated. Such expeditions would normally involve pillage and destruction on a large scale. Crops and trees would be burned, buildings destroyed, people killed or taken prisoner and considerable amounts of plunder seized. These were the typical consequences of raids – and the impact of such campaigns should not be underestimated.[6]

During the second half of the thirteenth century, when additional troops were available to the Latin states (in the form of a crusade, for example) a raiding expedition of the type outlined above was likely to be the most aggressive action which could sensibly be undertaken. The Muslims, however, were able to use their raids to much greater effect – something which was particularly apparent during the reign of Baybars. A raid against a strongpoint, for example, could prevent the Christians from mounting an effective defence of another site which was under more serious and prolonged attack; it might also be used against cities such as Acre and Tripoli, to debilitate Christian resistance at

---

[4] Oliver of Paderborn, 'Historia', pp. 213–14; 'Eracles', vol. II, pp. 340–1; James of Vitry, *Lettres*, pp. 120–2.

[5] Ibn 'Abd al-Zahir, 'Life of Baybars', vol. II, p. 455.

[6] See below, pp. 207–9.

a stage when a full-scale siege was considered inappropriate. Earlier in the century, however, the Christians, too, found themselves in a position where they might have been able to use raids as a part of a more ambitious overall strategy, rather than as the only pre-emptive aspect of their military thinking. On the Fifth Crusade, raids were one element in a series of attempts by the Christians to weaken the Muslim position in Palestine. These also included an abortive siege of Mt Tabor and castle-building at Château Pèlerin and Caesarea;[7] but there is no suggestion that the various elements were ever intended to be part of a single grand design.

The raid was therefore a central feature of the process of warfare in the Latin East throughout the thirteenth century, but individual expeditions did not attract the attention of contemporary western chroniclers in the way that sieges did. This is hardly surprising, since the loss or gain of a strongpoint in the Latin East or the surrounding area would naturally have been of far greater interest to them than would be the outcome of a small-scale raiding expedition. With a few exceptions, information on raids is therefore restricted to those western and eastern accounts which concerned themselves primarily with events in the eastern Mediterranean lands. There are problems to be faced when reading these accounts. Unless a raid was aimed at a fixed point, it is hard to determine precisely where the expedition went. Moreover, accounts are frequently contradictory, especially when Christian and Muslim sources are compared. Information about the forces which set out on raids is often limited and, in the case of the Muslims, virtually non-existent. A more fundamental problem is the extent to which the raids for which there is evidence are truly representative. In comparison to sieges, for example, it is reasonable to say that something at least is known of most successful assaults on strongpoints in this area during the thirteenth century. But there were probably countless small raiding expeditions of which nothing is recorded.

---

[7] Oliver of Paderborn, 'Historia', pp. 164–72.

## THE TARGETS OF RAIDING EXPEDITIONS

### Christian raids

It is possible to identify two different types of raid. First, there are those which were used, for the most part, by Christian forces operating from the coastal region and certain inland strongholds south of Beirut. Here, raids were directed against small Muslim camps and villages, particularly in the region close to the west bank of the river Jordan, which for much of the thirteenth century was the border area between the Christians and their Muslim enemies to the east. It was only to be expected that this area should be a constant target for Christian troops, less to make any permanent territorial gains than to inflict damage and injury on relatively unprotected Muslim concentrations of population and to seize crops and other possessions. Muslim positions west of the Jordan regularly suffered from Christian raids, at least until the end of the 1260s. In 1203–4, for example, Aimery of Lusignan organised raids into the Jordan valley, as well as a seaborne expedition against the Egyptian town of Fuwah.[8] In 1210, a Christian raid was thwarted because the Muslims had pulled back to the east side of the Jordan.[9]

Bethsan was a fertile site about ten miles south of Belvoir on the edge of the Jordan valley, and it was a frequent target of Christian raids. In 1217, it was sacked by crusaders on a *chevauchée* out of Acre, as the protective Muslim force under the sultan al-'Adil retreated in fear of a possible attack on Damascus.[10] In early 1250, when the progress of St Louis's first crusade had possibly caused a reduction in the number of Muslim troops in Palestine, a force from the kingdom led by John of Arsuf ravaged Bethsan and a Muslim camp in the vicinity, purportedly seizing as many as 16,000 animals in the process, as well as a Muslim emir.[11] Then, in November 1264, a large force which was led by Oliver of Termes and included both Templars and Hospitallers destroyed Bethsan and three neighbouring villages, taking much plunder

---

[8] 'Eracles', vol. II, pp. 260–3; Ibn al-Athir, 'Kamel-Altevarykh', vol. II, pp. 95–6; *Gestes des Chiprois*, p. 17; Abu Shama, 'Livre des deux jardins', vol. V, p. 153.

[9] 'Eracles', vol. II, pp. 309–10.

[10] *Ibid.*, p. 323; Ibn al-Athir, 'Kamel-Altevarykh', vol. II, p. 112; Abu'l-Fida, 'Annales', p. 88; Oliver of Paderborn, 'Historia', p. 164.

[11] 'Eracles', vol. II, p. 437; 'Annales de Terre Sainte', p. 443; *Chronique d'Amadi*, pp. 199–200; Marino Sanuto, 'Liber', p. 218.

and many prisoners.[12] Not all raids in the area were quite so effective, however. In 1260 a substantial force composed of, amongst others, the Templars from Acre, Saphet, Château Pèlerin and Beaufort, John II of Beirut and John of Gibelet, set off in the direction of Tiberias to raid a Muslim camp, but suffered heavy losses.[13] In 1266, the advance guard of a large Christian army which was attempting to carry out another raid towards Tiberias was decisively beaten by the Muslims near the plain of Acre.[14] The campaigns of Baybars drove the Christians back until their presence was almost entirely restricted to a few coastal sites. This meant that by the close of the 1260s Muslim positions in the area immediately west of the Jordan could be considered safe from Christian attack. The last two raids on record in southern Palestine were undertaken by the Lord Edward against St George, about ten miles east of Acre, and Qaqun (which it may be wrong to regard as simply a raid: it is situated about fifteen miles south-east of Caesarea).[15]

In northern Syria the policies of the Hospitallers, in particular, were far more aggressive than those which were followed in the south – in part because in the north the Muslims were disunited and weak.[16] The Christians' comparative strength in this area is reflected in the type of raids which they attempted to carry out, though their methods were by no means wholly successful. They were prepared to attack the larger centres of Muslim population, rather than simply carrying out punitive expeditions against Muslim camps and villages.[17] Assaults were directed, for example, against Ba'rin, Hama and Homs. Ba'rin was first attacked in this period in 1203;[18] it faced further attacks in 1230,[19] 1233[20] and

---

[12] 'Annales de Terre Sainte', p. 451; Marino Sanuto, 'Liber', p. 222.

[13] *Gestes des Chiprois*, p. 163; Ibn al-Furat, *Ayyubids*, vol. II, p. 49; 'Annales de Terre Sainte', pp. 449–50; 'Eracles', vol. II, p. 445.

[14] 'Eracles', vol. II, p. 455; *Gestes des Chiprois*, pp. 181–2; Ibn 'Abd al-Zahir, 'Life of Baybars', vol. II, p. 607.

[15] *Gestes des Chiprois*, pp. 200–1; Ibn 'Abd al-Zahir, 'Life of Baybars', vol. II, pp. 762, 770–1; al-Makrizi, *Histoire des Sultans*, vol. I (b), pp. 89, 101.

[16] J. S. C. Riley-Smith, *Knights of St John*, pp. 136–41; see above, p. 66.

[17] It should be noted that the large Muslim towns and cities in northern Syria were far more accessible to the Christians than sites of equivalent size would have been to the Latins in Palestine.

[18] Abu'l-Fida, 'Annales', p. 81; Ibn-Wasil, 'Mufarridj al-Kurub fi Akhbar Bani Aiyub', in al-Makrizi, *Histoire d'Egypte*, p. 278.

[19] Ibn al-Athir, 'Kamel-Altevarykh', vol. II, p. 180.

[20] 'Eracles', vol. II, pp. 403–5; 'Annales de Terre Sainte', p. 439; *Gestes des Chiprois*, p. 117.

1234,[21] in all of which the Hospitallers played a major role. Hama was attacked by the Latins in 1204, an assault which was successfully driven off, though it appears that the raiders came right to the walls of the city and caused considerable damage.[22] In 1230 the town was attacked again.[23] Homs was attacked in 1204[24] and 1207,[25] but the second assault seems to have been a serious attempt to besiege the city, rather than just a raid. It faced a further attack in 1265 by Bohemond VI, a venture which was supported by the Templars and Hospitallers, but the Muslims probably forced the Latins to retreat before they came too close to the city.[26] Other Christian attacks in the area included two on Jabala, first in 1204[27] and then again in 1230, when it seems that the army managed not only to gain access to the town but actually to hold it for a few weeks, before it was driven off, in the process losing everything which had been taken.[28] Latakia was also attacked in 1204.[29] In 1237, a disastrous raid against Darbsak resulted in heavy Christian losses; the Latin army had seriously underestimated the strength of the opposition.[30]

### Muslim raids

Muslim raiding expeditions in Palestine were generally aimed at major and well-defended Christian positions. Throughout this period, the Muslims persistently directed assaults against Acre. In 1203–4, in response to Christian aggression, a force led by al-Mu'azzam of Damascus moved towards the plain of Acre and

---

[21] 'Annales de Terre Sainte', p. 439. For the dates of the 1233 and 1234 raids, see Cahen, *La Syrie du Nord*, p. 650, note 1.

[22] Ibn al-Furat, 'Tarikh al-Duwal wa'l-Muluk', in Michaud, *Histoire*, vol. VII, p. 766; Abu Shama, 'Livre des deux jardins', vol. V, pp. 153–4; Abu'l-Fida, 'Annales', p. 83; Ibn al-Athir, 'Kamel-Altevarykh', vol. II, p. 96; al-Makrizi, *Histoire d'Egypte*, pp. 284–5.

[23] Abu'l-Fida, 'Annales', p. 107; al-'Ayni, 'Le Collier', pp. 194–5; Bar Hebraeus, *Chronography*, vol. I, p. 396.

[24] Al-Makrizi, *Histoire d'Egypte*, p. 285; Ibn al-Furat, 'Tarikh al-Duwal wa'l-Muluk', in Michaud, *Histoire*, vol. VII, p. 766.

[25] Ibn al-Athir, 'Kamel-Altevarykh', vol. II, pp. 105–6; Bar Hebraeus, *Chronography*, vol. I, p. 364.  [26] Ibn 'Abd al-Zahir, 'Life of Baybars', vol. II, p. 576.

[27] Al-Makrizi, *Histoire d'Egypte*, p. 285.

[28] Ibn al-Athir, 'Kamel-Altevarykh', vol. II, p. 180.

[29] Al-Makrizi, *Histoire d'Egypte*, p. 285.

[30] Kamal al-Din, 'L'Histoire d'Alep', pp. 95–6; Matthew Paris, *Chronica maiora*, vol. III, pp. 404–6.

Muslim raiding parties were sent to attack properties just outside the walls.[31] In mid-1207, again in retaliation for Christian activity, al-'Adil carried out raids in the vicinity of Acre; a truce was subsequently agreed.[32] Then in 1210 al-Mu'azzam returned to Acre with troops, causing a considerable amount of damage and taking much plunder.[33] From the 1260s, Acre became a constant target of Muslim raiding expeditions, often at the same time as more serious attacks were being prepared or carried out against other centres of Christian resistance. In the years of Baybars's ascendancy, Acre found itself facing raids of varying severity on an almost annual basis.[34]

Tyre was another major Christian centre of population and potential resistance and it, too, was subjected to Muslim raids on a number of occasions. In 1228, for example, Muslim raiders were able to take considerable quantities of booty, besides ambushing a Christian force which had come out to protect the commoners and their herds of cows and sheep.[35] Before the Muslim assault on Saphet in 1266, Tyre was one of a number of targets raided by bands of marauding Muslims and, again, a substantial amount of booty was taken.[36] In 1269, there were two Muslim attacks on Tyre; these involved plundering and the taking of prisoners.[37] Château Pèlerin had to face raids from the Muslims in 1264 (as a response to Christian raids) and then again in the following year, after Baybars had captured Caesarea but before he began the attack on Arsuf.[38]

The Muslims followed a similar policy in their raids in northern Syria. Tripoli and Antioch, in particular, frequently found themselves the targets of Muslim aggression. When al-'Adil had finished with Acre in 1207, he moved north and eventually attacked Tripoli, blockading it whilst inflicting severe damage on the surrounding area.[39] Baybars carried out raids against Tripoli on three separate occasions.[40] Antioch also experienced three raiding attacks from Muslim forces in Baybars's

---

[31] 'Eracles', vol. II, pp. 261–3; *Chronique d'Ernoul*, pp. 357–9.

[32] Abu'l-Fida, 'Annales', p. 83; Ibn al-Athir, 'Kamel-Altevarykh', vol. II, pp. 105–6.

[33] Abu Shama, 'Livre des deux jardins', vol. V, pp. 157–8; Marino Sanuto, 'Liber', p. 206.    [34] See below, pp. 204–5.

[35] Abu Shama, 'Livre des deux jardins', vol. V, pp. 185–6; al-'Ayni, 'Le Collier', p. 187.

[36] Ibn 'Abd al-Zahir, 'Life of Baybars', vol. II, p. 586.    [37] *Ibid.*, pp. 706–7.

[38] *Ibid.*, pp. 516, 561.

[39] Ibn al-Athir, 'Kamel-Altevarykh', vol. II, p. 106; Abu'l-Fida, 'Annales', pp. 83–4.

[40] See below, pp. 203–4.

reign before it fell in 1268. In 1262, a large Muslim force, which included troops from Homs, Hama and other positions, struck at the city's port, St Simeon, and caused massive amounts of damage.[41] Antioch was attacked again in 1264, and then again just before it was captured in May 1268.[42] In January 1270, Baybars attacked Crac des Chevaliers in a raid which probably sapped the morale of its defenders besides doing much harm to the surrounding countryside.[43]

### Seaborne raids

Both the Muslims and Christians were prepared to take to the sea to carry out raids against the enemy. The target of seaborne raids for the Christians was Egypt. In 1204, about twenty Frankish boats carried out a successful raid on Fuwah, pillaging the area for between two and five days.[44] In 1211, eighteen ships attacked Burah and al-Hairah; this produced booty and caused much damage to the Egyptians.[45] In 1243, a raid was directed against al-Warrada and then Qatya, east of the Nile delta. The raiders enjoyed some initial successes, before being defeated by a small Muslim force.[46]

In the period leading up to the Christians' capture of Beirut in 1197, an independent pirate emir, Usamah, was able to intercept Frankish ships travelling down the coast to Acre and Tyre. According to Christian accounts, Usamah's galleys captured 14,000 Christians; these were sold into slavery, whilst many others were killed. Once the Muslims had lost Beirut, they were no longer well placed to strike against Christian ships travelling to the Holy Land.[47] However, the Muslims were able to direct some

---

[41] Ibn 'Abd al-Zahir, 'Life of Baybars', vol. II, pp. 423–4; 'Eracles', vol. II, p. 446; *Gestes des Chiprois*, p. 167. The Christian sources suggested that the Muslim troops tried, unsuccessfully, to besiege Antioch.

[42] Ibn 'Abd al-Zahir, 'Life of Baybars', vol. II, pp. 511, 656–7.

[43] See above, p. 114.

[44] 'Eracles', vol. II, p. 263; *Chronique d'Ernoul*, pp. 359–60; Abu Shama, 'Livre des deux jardins', vol. v, p. 153; Ibn al-Athir, 'Kamel-Altevarykh', vol. II, p. 96; *Gestes des Chiprois*, p. 17.

[45] *History of the Patriarchs*, vol. III, pp. 193–5; 'Eracles', vol. II, p. 316; Abu Shama, 'Livre des deux jardins', vol. v, pp. 158–9.

[46] *History of the Patriarchs*, vol. IV, pp. 288–9; see Jackson, 'The Crusades of 1239 – 41', p. 53.

[47] 'Eracles', vol. II, pp. 224, 226; *Chronique d'Ernoul*, pp. 315–16 (13,000 captured); Ibn al-Athir, 'Kamel-Altevarykh', vol. II, pp. 85–6; see above, chapter 1, note 12.

seaborne raids against Cyprus. In 1203, a Muslim emir operating out of the Sidon area seized two boats and five Christians, but was unable to do any further damage.[48] Then, in 1271, Baybars sent a force of galleys to Cyprus, roughly to coincide with his assault against Montfort. But the ships, which had been disguised as Christian vessels, were shipwrecked off Limassol and many of their crews were killed or captured.[49]

From the above it is clear that the more confident and aggressive the military strategy which was adopted, the more likely it was that raids would be directed against the larger and better defended of the enemy's positions. For those who were less sure of themselves, most obviously in this period the Christians of Palestine, a typical raid would be against a small and ill-defended target.

ORGANISATION OF EXPEDITIONS

### *Size and structure of the army*

The information in table 4 is restricted to the raiding expeditions which were carried out by Christian forces: there appear to be very few worthwhile statistics of this kind for the Muslims.

Conclusions from information such as this must, as usual, be tentative; allowances have to be made for ambiguities, the arbitrary nature of some of the figures and the accuracy, or otherwise, of the sources. Yet even with these reservations, it is apparent that in comparison to other statistics relating to the potential and actual size of the Latin armies, some of these expeditions involved large numbers of men. In several instances the force benefited from the presence of crusaders. But a raid such as the one in 1260 which was defeated when it was heading towards Tiberias represented, allowing for the acute shortage of manpower in the Latin East at the time, a major commitment of the kingdom's resources. The same is true of the raid of 1266 towards Tiberias and the one which was undertaken by the Lord Edward and the kingdom's knights in 1271. In all three cases, the numbers quoted have been obtained from Arabic sources – which raises the possibility that there may be an element of exaggeration

---

[48] 'Eracles', vol. II, p. 258; *Chronique d'Ernoul*, p. 354.
[49] Ibn 'Abd al-Zahir, 'Life of Baybars', vol. II, pp. 757–8; *Gestes des Chiprois*, p. 199; 'Eracles', vol. II, p. 460.

Table 4. The size of armies on raiding expeditions in and around
the Latin East

| Raid | Numbers |
| --- | --- |
| Jordan valley (1203) | Mounted, foot, Templars advance guard and Hospitallers rearguard[a] |
| Ba'rin (1203) | 500 knights (led by the Hospitallers), 1,400 infantry, turcopoles and bowmen[b] |
| Fuwah (1204) | 20 boats[c] |
| Burah and al-Hairah (1211) | 18 ships (3 transports, 7 warships and 8 'fire ships'); 100 cavalry, 1,000 infantry/sailors[d] |
| Armenia (1211) | Templars, mounted and footsoldiers, 50 knights provided by John of Brienne and support from Antioch[e] |
| Towards Sidon (1218) | 500 men[f] |
| Ba'rin (1233) | Templars, 100 knights from Cyprus, 80 knights from Jerusalem, 30 knights from Antioch, 100 Hospitaller knights, 400 mounted sergeants, 1,500 foot sergeants[g] |
| Darbsak (1237) | 100 Templar knights, 300 crossbowmen, secular troops and footsoldiers killed[h] |
| From Jaffa (1239) | 200 knights and other armed men[i] |
| Towards Gaza (1239) | 600 knights, 70 knights banneret, crossbowmen, mounted and foot sergeants and others.[j] Alternative figures are 400 knights, Templars and Hospitallers, and footsoldiers[k] |
| Al-Warrada (1243) | 300 archers[l] |
| Between Gaza and Ascalon (1256) | The French regiment and many other Christians, both mounted and on foot. One turcopole was killed[m] |
| Towards Tiberias (1260) | Templars, secular knights, mounted and foot sergeants:[n] suggested numbers (from an Arabic source) are 900 knights, 1,500 turcopoles, 3,000 infantry[o] |
| Around Ascalon (1264) | Templars, Hospitallers, knights of Acre, Geoffrey of Sergines (presumably with French regiment)[p] |
| Around Bethsan (1264) | Templars, Hospitallers, knights of Acre, Oliver of Termes (presumably with French regiment)[q] |
| Towards Homs (1265) | Troops from Antioch, Templars and Hospitallers[r] |
| Towards Tiberias (1266) | Templars, Hospitallers, Teutonic Knights, French knights, Cypriot soldiers, others both mounted and foot. Over 500 mounted and foot killed.[s] An alternative (Arabic) source suggested 1,100 mounted[t] |

Table 4 (*cont.*)

| Raid | Numbers |
|---|---|
| Around Montfort (1269) | Knights, turcopoles and squires; 130 mounted, excluding squires[u] |
| St George (1271) | Templars, Hospitallers, Teutonic Knights, English crusaders, troops from Acre and Cyprus;[v] or 1,500 cavalry, with a large infantry force[w] |
| Qaqun (a siege?) (1271) | Templars, Hospitallers, Teutonic Knights, knights of Acre and Cyprus, English crusaders and footsoldiers[x] |

[a] 'Eracles', vol. II, pp. 259–60; Ibn al-Athir, 'Kamel-Altevarykh', vol. II, pp. 95–6.

[b] Ibn-Wasil, 'Mufarridj al-Kurub fi Akhbar Bani Aiyub', in al-Makrizi, *Histoire d'Egypte*, p. 278.

[c] Abu Shama, 'Livre des deux jardins', vol. V, p. 153.

[d] *History of the Patriarchs*, vol. III, p. 193.

[e] 'Eracles', vol. II, p. 317.

[f] Abu Shama, 'Livre des deux jardins', vol. V, p. 164.

[g] 'Eracles', vol. II, pp. 403–4.

[h] Matthew Paris, *Chronica maiora*, vol. III, p. 405.

[i] 'Rothelin', p. 533.

[j] *Ibid.*, p. 539.

[k] *Gestes des Chiprois*, p. 119; 'Eracles', vol. II, pp. 414–15.

[l] *History of the Patriarchs*, vol. IV, p. 288. It seems unlikely that this was the total Christian force.

[m] 'Rothelin', p. 630. In a subsequent battle outside Jaffa (p. 632) the Christian force numbered 200 knights and 300 archers, crossbowmen and sergeants.

[n] *Gestes des Chiprois*, p. 163.

[o] Abu Shama, 'Livre des deux jardins', vol. V, p. 204.

[p] 'Annales de Terre Sainte', p. 451.

[q] *Ibid.*, p. 451.

[r] Ibn 'Abd al-Zahir, 'Life of Baybars', vol. II, p. 576.

[s] 'Eracles', vol. II, p. 455; *Gestes des Chiprois*, pp. 181–2.

[t] Ibn 'Abd al-Zahir, 'Life of Baybars', vol. II, p. 607.

[u] *Gestes des Chiprois*, p. 183.

[v] 'Annales de Terre Sainte', p. 454; *Gestes des Chiprois*, p. 200 (which does not mention the troops from Cyprus or the Teutonic Knights).

[w] Ibn 'Abd al-Zahir, 'Life of Baybars', vol. II, p. 762.

[x] 'Eracles', vol. II, p. 461; *Gestes des Chiprois*, p. 200 (which does not mention the Teutonic Knights or the footsoldiers).

in them. However, the Christian accounts do indicate that a wide variety of troops had been assembled, which appears to confirm that substantial numbers were involved in these enterprises. It seems, therefore, that such expeditions, however limited their aims and achievements, had come to be regarded by the leaders of the Latin East as a central part of their military policy towards the Muslims. Almost all the raids for which statistical information is available were co-operative ventures to which the various and at times contrary military forces within the kingdom were prepared to commit themselves.

Most raids appear to have been undertaken by forces which consisted of both mounted and footsoldiers. The footsoldiers could perform a useful role in the Christian army, particularly if they were able to work in conjunction with mounted troops. Moreover, some of the infantry would have been archers or crossbowmen, who were of considerable value in combatting Muslim tactics.[50] During a raid, the Christian armies were therefore far better equipped to deal with any Muslim attacks if they had a force made up of both cavalry and foot. But by using infantry in such a capacity they would have lost much of their potential speed of movement and, as a consequence, the element of surprise. So *chevauchées* in the Latin East should not be thought of as being undertaken purely by mounted knights who moved quickly and swooped down on unsuspecting adversaries. They must often have involved a systematic and thorough destruction of persons and property. It is unfortunate that there is no more detailed information on the role played by infantry forces in these raids. It is clear, however, that a typical raid into the Muslim region to the west of the Jordan would have been an exhausting experience for them: they would probably have had to travel at least fifty miles, carrying a considerable weight in arms and other equipment.

It may tentatively be suggested that some Muslim raids were carried out exclusively by cavalry troops, though the evidence is rather vague. In a raid against Acre in 1263, Baybars took with him one in every ten of his mounted troops – but it is unclear whether this represented the entire Muslim contingent.[51] In 1266, when Baybars was again at Acre, he dispatched a cavalry force

[50] See above, pp. 168–74.
[51] Ibn 'Abd al-Zahir, 'Life of Baybars', vol. II, p. 457.

under two emirs to raid Tyre.[52] In 1269, Baybars himself set off
with lightly armed cavalry to raid that city, although two other
Muslim forces of unknown composition were also sent.[53] The
force which Baybars took with him to raid Crac des Chevaliers
in 1270 seems to have been made up only of 200 lightly armed
horsemen, of whom forty engaged and defeated a Christian force
just outside the fortress.[54]

## *Length of an expedition*

One of the difficulties for the aggressors in a siege was to maintain
their numbers at an acceptable level. This at least would not have
been a problem for a raiding expedition since, provided a viable
force could be gathered at the outset, then the subsequent action
was unlikely to last for much more than a week, or two at the
most. There was a limit to the amount of damage and plundering
which could be done in any particular area, besides which the
more time that was spent in any one place, the greater the risk that
the enemy would organise an effective counter-attack. The
Christians' regular use of infantry in their raids would have
further restricted the distances which could be covered and the
time which could profitably be spent away from a base. On the
first *chevauchée* of the Fifth Crusade, directed against Bethsan and
the surrounding area, the Franks were away from Acre for
between three and twelve days.[55] The Hospitallers' raid against
Ba'rin and the surrounding area in 1233 lasted nearly a fortnight,
but for much of this time the army was not engaged in active
campaigning.[56] The seaborne raid on Fuwah in 1204 may have
lasted for two days, or continued for as many as five.[57] The raid
against Burah and al-Hairah is said to have lasted for three days.
The Christian force remained undisturbed by any Egyptian
troops, but the area was probably so devastated after this time that
there was nothing else which could usefully be done.[58]

Muslim raids lasted for a similar length of time. In 1263,
Baybars spent three days in the vicinity of Acre, causing

---

[52] *Ibid.*, p. 586.   [53] *Ibid.*, p. 707.   [54] *Ibid.*, p. 729.

[55] 'Eracles', vol. II, pp. 323–4; Oliver of Paderborn, 'Historia', pp. 164–5.

[56] 'Eracles', vol. II, pp. 404–5.

[57] Abu Shama, 'Livre des deux jardins', vol. V, p. 153; Ibn al-Athir, 'Kamel-Altevarykh', vol. II, p. 96.

[58] *History of the Patriarchs*, vol. III, p. 194. The Egyptian troops were in Syria with al-'Adil.

considerable damage, before he left for Mt Tabor.[59] In 1266, prior to the attack on Saphet, the sultan was again before Acre for about a week[60] and in the following year he was there for four days, once more inflicting damage on the area around the city.[61]

Medieval armies often found it difficult to maintain adequate supplies in the field and this was something that could not be ignored even on a two-day raid. The consequences of inadequate supplies were demonstrated by the raid of the Lord Edward towards St George. The expedition itself – which was undertaken in the middle of July – was not unsuccessful, but a lack of water and the type of food which the troops were obliged to eat combined with the oppressive heat to cause intense suffering and many casualties, particularly amongst the English crusaders.[62] But since raiders would not have wished to be weighed down with large quantities of victuals, expeditions often chose to resort to foraging. On the first raid of the Fifth Crusade, the crusaders were able to obtain fresh supplies during their sacking of Bethsan and then, as they progressed through the surrounding area where they possibly remained for a further five days, they had no difficulty in obtaining both food and fodder for the animals.[63] The account of the raid towards Sidon of Christmas 1217–18 which was recorded by the author of 'Eracles' does not wholly correspond to that in other narratives, but it does contain some interesting information on the means by which an army supplied itself during a raid. Scouts were dispatched in each of the areas which the troops passed through. When they reached villages, they were able to refresh themselves and then to take supplies back to the main force.[64] In 1228, a group of crusaders who were working on the sea fortress at Sidon sent scavengers into Muslim territory in order to obtain victuals. They were able to seize animals, bread and corn, besides taking a number of prisoners.[65] In these last two cases, the raid's purpose was to obtain supplies for the main part of the army during a campaign. The first raid which took place on Theobald of Champagne's crusade in 1239 had the same

---

[59] Ibn 'Abd al-Zahir, 'Life of Baybars', vol. II, pp. 457–60.
[60] *Gestes des Chiprois*, p. 179; Ibn 'Abd al-Zahir, 'Life of Baybars', vol. II, p. 586.
[61] Ibn 'Abd al-Zahir, 'Life of Baybars', vol. II, p. 624.
[62] 'Eracles', vol. II, p. 461; *Gestes des Chiprois*, p. 200; Ibn 'Abd al-Zahir, 'Life of Baybars', vol. II, p. 762.
[63] Ibn al-Athir, 'Kamel-Altevarykh', vol. II, p. 112; Oliver of Paderborn, 'Historia', pp. 164–5.  [64] 'Eracles', vol. II, pp. 324–5.
[65] *Chronique d'Ernoul*, p. 460; 'Eracles', vol. II, pp. 372–3 (variants).

intention. Led by Peter of Brittany, the expedition successfully intercepted a Muslim caravan, thereby earning great acclaim from the lesser crusaders amongst the main force at Jaffa; the raiders brought back large numbers of animals, which had been in short supply.[66]

## Raiding tactics

The element of surprise was an essential aspect of an effective raid. We have already seen that, in this respect, the presence of footsoldiers could have hampered the Christians, but it was still possible to increase the impact of an expedition. Both Muslims and Christians often chose to travel in darkness, aiming to arrive in the target area at dawn, thus avoiding detection by the enemy, as well as benefiting from the lower night temperatures. For the raid which Aimery of Lusignan led from Acre in 1203, the Christian force of mounted troops and footsoldiers set out in the evening when the horses had been fed and then travelled all night, so that by the morning they were in Muslim territory.[67] Similar tactics were employed by the co-operative force headed by the Hospitallers which attacked Ba'rin in 1233. After leaving Crac des Chevaliers in the evening, it travelled all night and reached Ba'rin at dawn, when it immediately began to plunder the suburb.[68] It is about twenty miles from Crac to Ba'rin, so the trip would have been extremely tiring for the infantry, which formed an important part of the Christian force. Both the raids of Theobald of Champagne's crusade travelled by night. On the first, Peter of Brittany was in position to ambush a Muslim caravan as it set out at dawn. The count of Bar and the other nobles and men on his *chevauchée* also set out in the evening and approached Gaza at dawn.[69] The Muslims used this method too, exemplified by Baybars's attack on Acre in 1263. Setting out from Mt Tabor at midnight, by the following morning he was positioned at Acre and ready to do the maximum amount of damage to the city.[70] Careful planning contributed to the success of a Christian raid out of Jaffa into Muslim territory at Christmas 1255–6. Before the departure of the assembled army, scouts were sent out in order to ascertain from which area of Muslim territory it stood to make the most gain. Timing was again important. The troops went out

---

[66] 'Rothelin', p. 535.　　　　　[67] 'Eracles', vol. II, p. 260.
[68] *Ibid.*, pp. 403–4.　　　　　[69] 'Rothelin', pp. 533–4, 538–9, 541–2.
[70] Ibn 'Abd al-Zahir, 'Life of Baybars', vol. II, p. 457.

at night, surrounded by secrecy and, by travelling throughout the night, they came amongst the Muslims between Gaza and Ascalon.[71]

Thoughtful planning of an expedition was therefore important, but it was also essential that good discipline be maintained when a raid was in progress; this applied particularly to marching formation. The Military Orders often had a crucial role to play during raiding expeditions.[72] On the raid into the Galilee region in 1203, the Templars made up the advance guard and the Hospitallers the rearguard. The latter were attacked by the Muslims when they were returning to Christian territory, but the assault was successfully resisted.[73] In 1266, however, poor discipline led to disaster as the raiding party's advance guard (which included the Hospitallers, Teutonic Knights and Geoffrey of Sergines with the French regiment) pushed too far ahead of the rest of the force in their desire to obtain booty; they were ambushed and defeated by the Muslims, losing over 500 men.[74] In 1239, as we have seen, overconfidence about their position contributed to the defeat suffered by the crusaders led by the count of Bar.[75] In both of these last two examples, the Christian troops were clearly intent on a raiding expedition, but the Muslims were able to engage and defeat them in battle. Raids could develop into battles on the march, as in 1266, or even a pitched battle, as occurred in 1239. It was poor organisation and indiscipline which led to engagement and defeat. Commanders would hope to keep such risks to a minimum, however, and most raids were able to avoid a major confrontation.

In some circumstances, it was considered beneficial to divide up the raiding force in order to inflict the maximum amount of damage. This would only be done when there was considered to be no likelihood of an attack by enemy troops. Instances have already been noted – in 1217–18 and 1228 – when small parties were sent out to obtain supplies.[76] In the Galilee raid of 1203, once the Christians had arrived in Muslim territory they spread themselves out in a number of directions.[77] A similar technique was used by the crusaders who raided around Bethsan in 1217.

---

[71] 'Rothelin', p. 630.  
[72] See above, pp. 62–3.  
[73] 'Eracles', vol. II, p. 260.  
[74] *Gestes des Chiprois*, p. 182; 'Eracles', vol. II, p. 455.  
[75] See above, pp. 178–9.  
[76] See above, p. 196.  
[77] 'Eracles', vol. II, p. 260.

## Raiding expeditions

Detachments of men were sent to ravage all the land between Bethsan and Nablus; they seized booty and killed great numbers of Muslims.[78] After their initial raid on Ba'rin in 1233, the Christians dispatched scouts and foragers to plunder the villages in the area.[79] When the Christians attacked Burah and al-Hairah in 1211, the force of 100 knights and 1,000 infantry was divided precisely in two in order to ravage the area more effectively.[80]

### THE REASONS FOR RAIDING

### Retribution

Raids were used as reprisals against enemy activity, whether in retaliation for some damage which had already been done or, if the enemy was in the middle of a campaign, to interfere with its efforts and weaken its resolve. Retaliatory raids were used by both Muslims and Christians and, as we saw in chapter 1 of this study, they helped to create an environment in which low-level warfare was endemic.[81] Mention has already been made of an assault on Cyprus by a Muslim emir in 1203.[82] This raid had taken place at a time of truce and Aimery of Lusignan demanded of al-'Adil that restitution should be made for the damage that had been done. When the latter proved unable to placate Aimery, the Christians chose to take matters into their own hands, so the two sets of raids, first into the Galilee region and then by sea against Fuwah, were a reaction to the piracy of the Muslim emir. The author of the 'Eracles' account stated that much harm was done by the Christians, to avenge the Muslims' seizure of five men on Cyprus.[83] In 1227, some Aleppans seized and killed a Templar knight. The Templars went out and killed many Muslims, besides taking prisoners and booty; they subsequently returned much of their plunder, in the face of threats from the governor of Aleppo.[84]

There were also instances when the Muslims retaliated against a Christian offence, although it is very likely that on some of these occasions, particularly the large number which were reported during the sultanate of Baybars, previous Christian misconduct was used as no more than a pretext for a Muslim attack. Two

[78] Abu'l-Fida, 'Annales', p. 88.  [79] 'Eracles', vol. II, p. 404.
[80] *History of the Patriarchs*, vol. III, p. 193.  [81] See above, pp. 18–19.
[82] See above, pp. 190–1.  [83] 'Eracles', vol. II, pp. 258–63.
[84] Ibn al-Athir, 'Kamel-Altevarykh', vol. II, p. 170.

examples of Muslim retaliation date from earlier in the century. The raid by al-Mu'azzam on Acre in 1203–4 was a further response to Frankish aggression, which itself had been in retaliation for previous Muslim activity. A truce was finally arranged in August 1204.[85] The Christian raid of 1207 against Homs led to retaliation by al-'Adil. Leaving Egypt, he journeyed first to Acre, where Muslim prisoners were returned and a peace was agreed. But problems persisted in northern Syria. Around May 1207, Muslim raids were carried out in the areas around Crac and Tripoli (where a considerable amount of damage was done) before peace was once more restored. It seems to have been as a result of these Muslim raids that the Frankish initiative in northern Syria petered out.[86] In 1242, Christian troops based at Bethlehem and elsewhere carried out a number of raids which caused injury to both people and property. An-Nasir Da'ud responded to these attacks by raiding Bethlehem. The Franks avenged this attack in October 1242, when they sacked Nablus. The sequence of hostilities ended when an-Nasir was forced to withdraw from a siege of Jaffa.[87] Finally, in 1256 Muslim raiding around Jaffa was a response to Frankish attacks between Gaza and Ascalon.[88]

Many of the raiding expeditions of the Mamluk sultan Baybars appear to have been prompted by a desire to punish the Franks for some specific offence which they were alleged to have committed. Baybars's first raid on Acre, in April 1263, was explained, at least in part, in these terms by both Muslim and Christian writers. The two sides had failed to come to an agreement over an exchange of prisoners, largely because of the refusal of the Templars and Hospitallers to release their Muslim captives. Baybars had been further angered by the Hospitallers' construction of a wall at Arsuf. Serious efforts were made to satisfy the sultan's demands, but terms could only be agreed with John of Jaffa, a man who appears to have earned the respect of the Muslims by his aggressive attitude towards them throughout the 1250s. Since no general agreement was reached, Baybars carried

---

[85] 'Eracles', vol. II, pp. 261–3; Ibn al-Athir, 'Kamel-Altevarykh', vol. II, pp. 95–6; *Chronique d'Ernoul*, pp. 357–9.

[86] Ibn al-Athir, 'Kamel-Altevarykh', vol. II, pp. 105–6; al-Makrizi, *Histoire d'Egypte*, p. 287; Ibn al-Furat, 'Tarikh al-Duwal wa'l-Muluk', in Michaud, *Histoire*, vol. VII, p. 767; Abu'l-Fida, 'Annales', pp. 83–4.

[87] *History of the Patriarchs*, vol. IV, pp. 243, 268–9; al-Makrizi, *Histoire d'Egypte*, pp. 479–80; Jackson, 'The Crusades of 1239–41', pp. 51–2. For the siege of Jaffa, see above, pp. 142–3.    [88] 'Rothelin', pp. 630–1.

out a succession of raids against Acre and the area around, even though he had previously ordered that no harm should be done to the Christians.[89] In mid-1264, Baybars was told that the Franks had set out from Jaffa in order to carry out a raid. In retaliation for this action and to make it clear to the Christians that such behaviour would not be tolerated, the sultan ordered an emir to raid Caesarea and Château Pèlerin. Not only were the Frankish assaults stopped, but further threats prompted the return of booty which they had seized on their raids.[90] A raid of 1269 against Tyre was a result of unacceptable behaviour by Philip of Montfort, who had imprisoned and killed a number of Muslims. In the initial assault Baybars's troops exercised some restraint, leaving the crops and returning female prisoners and children that had been taken. When Philip still refused to make reparation, however, the Muslims followed up with a further and more damaging raid against the locality.[91]

### As an expression of influence

Raids could also be used by an aggressor to express authority over a subservient neighbour. This applied particularly, as we have already seen, in northern Syria where the Christians were much stronger, relative to their Muslim neighbours, than they were in the south. At various times during this period, Muslim princes owed tribute to the Christians and some raids were intended to ensure that these payments were maintained. The Assassins, for example, were paying tribute to the Hospitallers of Margat in 1212.[92] In 1231, they were attacked by a combined force of Templars and Hospitallers in order to make sure that tribute payments were continued.[93] An attack by the Hospitallers against Hama in 1230 was successfully repulsed by the Muslims between Hama and Ba'rin: it was suggested that this raid was linked to the refusal of Hama to pay tribute to the Hospitallers.[94] Three years later, Ba'rin formed an alliance with Hama and the sultan of Hama ceased to pay tribute to the Hospitallers, so a substantial

---

[89] Ibn 'Abd al-Zahir, 'Life of Baybars', vol. II, pp. 447–62, *passim*; *Gestes des Chiprois*, pp. 167–8; 'Eracles', vol. II, pp. 446–7; J. S. C. Riley-Smith, *Feudal Nobility*, p. 27.

[90] Ibn 'Abd al-Zahir, 'Life of Baybars', vol. II, p. 516; Ibn al-Furat, *Ayyubids*, vol. II, p. 67.

[91] Ibn 'Abd al-Zahir, 'Life of Baybars', vol. II, pp. 706–7; al-'Ayni, 'Le Collier', pp. 236–7.  [92] Willbrand of Oldenburg, 'Peregrinatio', p. 170.

[93] 'Annales de Dunstaplia', p. 128.

[94] Bar Hebraeus, *Chronography*, vol. I, p. 396.

Christian force was sent to raid Ba'rin. The attack was bought off with the promise that Hama would resume the payment of tribute to the Hospitallers and this ensured that a new peace could be established.[95]

### To damage morale

To be the victim of a raid was obviously in itself a distressing experience. There were times, however, when attackers aimed specifically at the damage or seizure of an object – particularly one of religious importance – in order to damage the enemy's confidence and morale. Both mosques and churches suffered from the attentions of raiders. The attack of the Christians from Jaffa on Nablus in 1242 involved not only the destruction of the mosque, but also the seizure of the pulpit in which the preacher said prayers.[96] There was an even more interesting example of damage to a religious object during the raid by Baybars in 1263. Having failed to come to terms with the Christian envoys, he sent two emirs to raze the church at Nazareth. The sultan's biographer, Ibn 'Abd al-Zahir, noted that there was no effective Christian defence against this action and went on to discuss the importance of the church to the Christian faith. Only one Christian source from the Latin East, the 'Annales de Terre Sainte', recorded the destruction of the church, but the raid must have been a great blow to Christian morale and news of it, not surprisingly, reached western Europe. In a letter to Louis IX, Urban IV stated that the church had been 'reduced to the ground, its celebrated structure having been utterly destroyed'.[97] Churches were also razed during Baybars's raid on Tripoli in 1268.[98]

### As part of an offensive campaign

The Muslim armies were able to use raids during their campaigns to take control of Christian territory. An examination of some of the expeditions which were organised by Baybars demonstrates

---

[95] 'Eracles', vol. II, pp. 403–5.

[96] Al-Makrizi, *Histoire d'Egypte*, pp. 479–80; *History of the Patriarchs*, vol. IV, pp. 268–9.

[97] Ibn 'Abd al-Zahir, 'Life of Baybars', vol. II, pp. 455, 460; Ibn al-Furat, *Ayyubids*, vol. II, pp. 56–7; 'Annales de Terre Sainte', p. 450; Urban IV, *Registre*, no. 344 ('redegit ad solum, ejus structura nobili omnino destructa'). The Church of the Transfiguration on Mt Tabor had also been destroyed. The author of *De constructione castri Saphet* claimed (p. 44) that the building of Saphet provided protection for visitors to both Nazareth and Mt Tabor.

[98] Ibn 'Abd al-Zahir, 'Life of Baybars', vol. II, p. 653.

this use of the raid. First, by raiding a Christian strongpoint, and thereby ensuring that its garrison was fully occupied, it was possible to isolate another site which was to be besieged. This type of raid might also help to distract attention from the main target of a campaign. Baybars used a raid to good effect during the first of his major campaigns in Palestine, that of 1265, when Caesarea, Arsuf and Haifa all fell to the Muslims. Whilst the attack on Caesarea was still in progress, Baybars sent a party of soldiers up the coast to raid Acre, thus reducing the likelihood of any relieving force being sent.[99] The same tactic was used by Baybars in 1266, when the principal target was Saphet. On that occasion, raids were simultaneously directed against Tripoli (where three small fortresses were also captured), Acre, Tyre, Sidon and Montfort, before most of the Muslim troops converged on Saphet.[100] The diversity of raiding was so great that the Latins cannot have had much idea where any major assault might be directed. Moreover, any subsequent efforts to relieve Saphet would probably have been far less effective than might otherwise have been the case.

The Muslims used similar tactics in preparation for the successful siege of Antioch in 1268. They began with a heavy raid against Tripoli, which would surely have distracted Bohemond VI from any immediate concern about the defensive capabilities of Antioch. Then, at Hama, Baybars divided his force into three groups. One was sent to raid Darbsak, situated about twenty-five miles north of Antioch and held by the Templars; a second party was directed against St Simeon, the port of Antioch. This would have hindered any Frankish aid which was sent by sea, a sensible precaution given that Antioch was well beyond the operating range of the Egyptian fleet. Baybars himself moved north past Apamea, then followed the Orontes River, before coming to Antioch.[101] The Muslims' raids had almost completely isolated

---

[99] *Ibid.*, pp. 556, 558.

[100] *Ibid.*, pp. 582–7. The raid on Montfort was also referred to (p. 756) when Baybars was preparing to besiege the site in 1271. See al-'Ayni, 'Le Collier', pp. 221–2; 'Annales de Terre Sainte', p. 452.

[101] Ibn 'Abd al-Zahir, 'Life of Baybars', vol. II, pp. 647–8, 653–4, 656; Ibn al-Furat, *Ayyubids*, vol. II, pp. 116, 121 and 228, note 2; see Pryor, *Geography, Technology, and War*, pp. 117–19. Darbsak had previously been in the possession of the Templars until 1188, when it was captured by Saladin (J. S. C. Riley-Smith, 'Templars and Teutonic Knights', p. 97). The Mongol Khan Hulegu had given the site to Hetoum I of Armenia in 1261 (Cahen, *La Syrie du Nord*, p. 705). Presumably Hetoum had then given it to the Templars.

Antioch and had made it extremely unlikely that a successful defence of the city could be conducted. Baybars prepared in similar fashion for the successful campaign of 1271 (when Chastel Blanc, Crac des Chevaliers and Gibelcar were all taken) with a raid against Tripoli.[102] Once more, this would have weakened the potential resistance to Muslim conquests whilst at the same time causing confusion amongst the Christians. Another diversionary raid took place in 1271. At roughly the same time as the siege of Montfort, Baybars dispatched a seaborne force to attack Cyprus. The author al-'Ayni suggested that this was a serious effort to capture the island, but it seems far more probable, as is implicit in most other accounts, that it was hoped in this way to distract and confuse the Christians. The Lord Edward was on crusade at this time and Baybars probably feared the potential consequences of a major Christian counter-offensive. He would have anticipated that this threat would fade away following the raid on Cyprus. As has already been noted, the Muslim ships were able to approach the island, but they were subsequently wrecked in the harbour of Limassol.[103]

Even Muslim chroniclers occasionally acknowledged that some Christian strongpoints were targets too formidable to be taken in a single siege campaign. Moreover, Muslim commanders, in common with their Christian counterparts, found it virtually impossible to maintain a strong attacking force for any great length of time, particularly at harvest time when men were needed elsewhere. A partial solution to these problems was to wear down Christian resistance gradually at any one point by conducting a series of raiding expeditions against it. This meant that when a determined effort was to be made to capture the position supplies of food and other requirements were unlikely to be adequate to withstand a long siege. Defensive structures, which could have suffered damage during a raid, would not necessarily have been repaired.

Acre was attacked on numerous occasions during the reign of Baybars, though it is quite clear that the sultan never intended to mount a serious assault on its defences.[104] The first time that

---

[102] Ibn 'Abd al-Zahir, 'Life of Baybars', vol. II, p. 742; Ibn al-Furat, *Ayyubids*, vol. II, p. 143.

[103] Ibn 'Abd al-Zahir, 'Life of Baybars', vol. II, pp. 757–8; 'Eracles', vol. II, p. 460; *Gestes des Chiprois*, p. 199; al-'Ayni, 'Le Collier', pp. 239–40. See above, p. 191.

[104] One reason for Baybars's decision not to direct a serious attack against Acre may have been a realisation that the economic well-being of much of his territory was dependent

Baybars came before Acre was in 1263; Ibn 'Abd al-Zahir indicated that this was a reconnaissance, but considerable damage was done to the area outside the city, including the destruction of the fortified mill at Doc which was held by the Templars.[105] The attack on the city in 1265, which has already been noted as a diversionary tactic during the siege of Caesarea, would have had the additional benefit of further weakening Frankish resistance.[106] Baybars was again at Acre in 1266[107] and in May 1267 he attacked the city on two separate occasions, causing damage which included the devastation of the Hospitaller mill at Recordane.[108] In 1269, Baybars was once more at Acre, this time to deal with the Crusade of the Infants of Aragon, though he undoubtedly used the occasion to weaken yet further the city's defences.[109] Tripoli was also subjected to a number of raids which would have weakened its resistance when the time came to besiege it.

The Christians were not strong enough to use raiding expeditions as part of an offensive strategy which also included sieges. On the Fifth Crusade they did use raids as part of a general offensive against the Muslims, but these were never intended to link up with simultaneous or subsequent siege campaigns. However, as the Christians became progressively weaker during the thirteenth century, the raid became increasingly important to them, if only as an expression of aggressive intent. It was essential that they retained the ability to attack their neighbours, particularly when additional troops were available, most obviously crusaders. But it would have been inappropriate for the Christians to have attempted to acquire territory which, because of their shortage of manpower, would almost certainly have been lost again in a short space of time. This meant that, whereas major expeditions in the twelfth century would have been trying to expand the frontiers of the Latin states, by the later years of the thirteenth, large Christian armies were gathered to achieve the short-term results of a raid. The territory which was invaded would remain in enemy hands when the raid had been completed.

The raid of 1266 towards Tiberias, for example, was a large co-

---

on the availability of the city as an outlet for goods. See J. S. C. Riley-Smith, *The Crusades*, p. 203.

[105] Ibn 'Abd al-Zahir, 'Life of Baybars', vol. II, pp. 457–60; Ibn al-Furat, *Ayyubids*, vol. II, pp. 57–9; Urban IV, *Registre*, no. 344.     [106] See above, p. 203.

[107] Ibn 'Abd al-Zahir, 'Life of Baybars', vol. II, p. 586; *Gestes des Chiprois*, p. 179.

[108] Ibn 'Abd al-Zahir, 'Life of Baybars', vol. II, pp. 623–4; *Gestes des Chiprois*, pp. 182–3.

[109] Ibn 'Abd al-Zahir, 'Life of Baybars', vol. II, pp. 726–9; *Gestes des Chiprois*, pp. 183–5.

operative venture. The willingness of all the Military Orders, the French regiment, a large Cypriot force and many others from Acre to take part in this raid indicates the importance which the Christians attached to it. The failure of the raid to achieve anything, because of poor discipline which allowed a Muslim ambush to succeed, must have been regarded as a serious setback, given that such expeditions were virtually the only positive reaction to the campaigns of Baybars during this period. The growing strength of the Muslims was illustrated by two events during the raid. Muslim troops from the recently acquired fortress of Saphet, which provided both a forward base for strikes against Christian coastal positions and an early line of defence, were amongst those who ambushed the advance guard of the Christian army at Careblier, only about eight miles south-east of Acre. Secondly, many of the Latins who escaped the battle were subsequently killed by Muslim peasants who lived in the neighbourhood and were anxious to obtain booty. The Latins were still the masters, but their subjects were not afraid to rise in rebellion if a good opportunity presented itself.[110]

The crusade of the Lord Edward could not, because of the difficult military situation in the area, hope to achieve any long-term gain. But the size of the force which went on the raid towards St George once again showed how significant such an expedition was considered to be, by both the Christians in the Latin East and the crusaders. The army included all the Military Orders, the men of Acre and the English crusaders: for the raid against Qaqun later in 1271, these were certainly joined by Hugh of Antioch-Lusignan and forces from Cyprus, though they were probably on the first expedition as well.[111] As we saw earlier, however, the expedition against Qaqun may have been of rather more consequence than the first raid. Some sources indicated that the crusaders besieged the castle and caused considerable damage before they were obliged to withdraw. Qaqun, moreover, was an important base for the Muslims in their efforts to re-establish their authority on the coastal plain. It had been restored by Baybars in 1266, following the capture of Caesarea and Arsuf in the previous year, and it had become the focal point for a number of Muslim centres of population (such as Tour Rouge and Calansue),

---

[110] *Gestes des Chiprois*, pp. 181–2; Ibn 'Abd al-Zahir, 'Life of Baybars', vol. ii, p. 607; 'Eracles', vol. ii, p. 455.

[111] 'Annales de Terre Sainte', p. 454; *Gestes des Chiprois*, p. 200; 'Eracles', vol. ii, p. 461.

performing both administrative and defensive functions. It was particularly useful as a defence against possible attacks from Château Pèlerin.[112]

## THE RESULTS OF RAIDING

Whatever the reasons for carrying out a raid, the effects of such an expedition seem to have been fairly predictable. They would normally have included devastation of the land of an area and damage to buildings, besides the killing of a number of the enemy. It was also common for prisoners and booty to be taken.

Raiders would seek to plunder and destroy gardens, orchards and crops, besides upsetting the system of irrigation which was essential for the successful cultivation of sugar-cane and for mills and gardens.[113] Such actions would undoubtedly have had a profound impact upon their victims. This could be in the short term, when a harvest was seized by the enemy, or in the long term when, as a result of the burning of fields and orchards, or the tearing up of trees, the land could be barren for a number of years. Oliver of Termes and John of Joinville used an interesting technique to set fire to a cornfield during their retreat from Banyas in 1253. On Oliver's advice, they stuffed burning charcoal into hollow canes and then plunged the canes into the threshed corn.[114] The destruction of the aqueduct at Tripoli by the Muslims is another example of how agriculture could be affected.[115] Most raids aimed in some respect to deal a blow to the agriculture of the enemy and the cumulative effect of this policy must have been considerable. According to one scholar, the effects of raids and the Mamluks' systematic destruction of land were felt for many centuries.[116]

Victims of raids often had to suffer the destruction of their houses and of other buildings. The impact of the destruction of religious sites such as churches and mosques has already been

---

[112] See above, p. 183; Ibn 'Abd al-Zahir, 'Life of Baybars', vol. II, p. 615; Ibn al-Furat, *Ayyubids*, vol. II, pp. 101, 155; Burchard of Mt Sion, 'Descriptio Terrae Sanctae', pp. 83–4. The church at Qaqun had been converted into a mosque. It is unlikely, even if the Christians had succeeded in capturing Qaqun, that they would have attempted to garrison the site. It would have been far too exposed to Muslim attacks and would almost certainly have been swiftly overrun.
[113] See J. S. C. Riley-Smith, *Feudal Nobility*, pp. 49–53.
[114] Joinville, *Histoire de Saint Louis*, p. 318.
[115] Ibn 'Abd al-Zahir, 'Life of Baybars', vol. II, pp. 653–4.
[116] Benvenisti, *Crusaders*, p. 215.

noted. The dismantling of towers and walls by Muslim troops during raids was a useful means to prepare for a possible future siege. It may reasonably be presumed that any unprotected person in the path of a raid was almost bound to suffer. But raiding expeditions did involve more than just the wanton destruction of persons and property. They also presented an opportunity to make some profit in the form of the acquisition of people, or plunder. The raiders would presumably agree amongst themselves upon the taking of prisoners beforehand, since it would involve some organisation and the prevention of the slaughter of everyone who was encountered. Prisoners could be useful as a bargaining counter if members of one's own side had been seized by the enemy. There was little point, beyond this, in holding them captive, since they might just as well be killed, but they could be put to work by their captors as slaves – as in the building of Saphet, for example.[117] Some Muslim captives would no doubt have found their way to the important slave market in Acre.[118] Other prisoners might be more fortunate; in 1269, for example, Baybars sent back some women and children he had captured in the course of a raid on Tyre.[119] Oliver of Paderborn noted that some of the younger captives who had been seized by the crusaders in Palestine in 1217–18 were baptised by James of Vitry.[120]

Raiders could also acquire various kinds of booty. Most accounts simply stated that much booty had been taken but, from the occasions when further information was provided, it seems that both Muslims and Christians concentrated their attentions on animals, seizing what appear to have been fair-sized flocks. Livestock was relatively scarce in the Latin East, and had been in the region since ancient times,[121] so the removal and acquisition of flocks would have been important to both the Muslims and Christians.

Two well-documented raids show what a single expedition might expect to achieve. In 1271, when English crusaders joined the native Latins in a raid towards St George, crops were ravaged and burned, and grain was seized. The village itself was demolished and heavy casualties were inflicted on the local

---

[117] See above, pp. 94–5 and note 4.   [118] See above, p. 176.
[119] Ibn 'Abd al-Zahir, 'Life of Baybars', vol. II, p. 707.
[120] Oliver of Paderborn, 'Historia', p. 167.
[121] Prawer, 'Palestinian Agriculture', p. 185.

population. The Christians also seized both large and small animals.[122] In 1263, Baybars attacked Acre for the first time. On this occasion trees were cut down, and gardens were burned. Walls were destroyed, as well as the Templars' fortified mill at Doc. Many people were killed; others were taken prisoner, including four knights and thirty infantry from the tower, though they may later have been released. The Muslims completed the raid by seizing cattle and other booty.[123]

CONCLUSION

Raids could weaken an enemy and undermine his morale, whilst at the same time offering the opportunity of profit to the raiders with little risk of disaster, providing that the operation was well organised and the force did not encounter a large body of enemy troops. The Muslims used the raid as a part of their overall strategy to weaken the Christians and prepare them for capitulation through later use of the siege. For the Christians, as the thirteenth century wore on so the raid became increasingly their sole means of showing any aggressive intent. It was almost the only positive aspect of their military policy during the second half of the century, particularly when they lacked the support of large numbers of crusaders. The fact that both sides, for whatever reason, placed a great emphasis on the use of raiding expeditions meant that the peculiarly destructive powers of such enterprises were frequently unleashed on the unprotected peoples of the region. Those least able to cope had to face the consequences of Muslim expansionism and the final military gestures of the shrinking Latin states.

[122] *Gestes des Chiprois*, p. 200; 'Annales de Terre Sainte', p. 454; Ibn 'Abd al-Zahir, 'Life of Baybars', vol. ɪɪ, p. 762; Ibn al-Furat, *Ayyubids*, vol. ɪɪ, p. 155.

[123] Ibn 'Abd al-Zahir, 'Life of Baybars', vol. ɪɪ, pp. 455, 457–60; al-'Ayni, 'Le Collier ', pp. 218–19; al-Makrizi, *Histoire des Sultans*, vol. ɪ (a), p. 200; Urban IV, *Registre*, no. 344; 'Annales de Terre Sainte', p. 450. According to this last source, Baybars was accompanied by an army of 30,000 cavalry; this figure is surely a wild exaggeration.

## Chapter 6

# SIEGES

The fate of the Latins in Palestine and Syria was decided by a succession of siege campaigns, which were conducted by Muslim armies throughout the period and with particular effect after the succession of Baybars to the Mamluk sultanate. Other forms of military activity were therefore largely incidental. Raids, when used by the Muslim armies, could help to weaken and isolate a Christian site as part of the preparation for a siege. Battles could, in theory, decimate the limited manpower which was available and, as in the case of Hattin in 1187, have such a decisive impact that many subsequent sieges presented few difficulties to the victorious Muslims. But neither raids nor battles, on their own, had a decisive influence on the military history of the period 1192–1291. Both allowed the possibility of recovery, a process which would normally rely heavily on the protection which the strongpoints were able to provide. If, on the other hand, the strongpoints themselves had succumbed to enemy pressure, then the recovery process was made, at best, considerably more difficult.

Sieges were therefore of fundamental importance in the military history of this period. The ability to control territory was largely determined by the possession of strongpoints and they would, ordinarily, only change hands as a consequence of a military campaign – although some sites were acquired by treaty. It was for this reason that in the thirteenth century the Latin army was geared to operate principally as a series of garrison forces within the strongpoints. Additional troops – particularly crusaders – enabled the Latins to undertake operations which they would not have otherwise attempted. But the strongpoint and the garrison within it were the obstacles which the Muslims had to overcome if they were to recover the Holy Land from the Christians.

In the twelfth century, as well as the thirteenth, the walled towns and castles were the ultimate expression of Latin authority in the region.[1] But the military conditions in the thirteenth century were somewhat different from those of the earlier period. The progressive Muslim expansion, particularly in the second half of the century, ended with the eradication of the Christians through the fall of the remaining Latin strongholds in 1291. It is therefore even more true than it was in the twelfth century that the ability to capture or to defend the strongpoints of the Latin states was decisive. Moreover, at no point did either the Muslims or the Christians attempt to accelerate or halt this pattern of events by resorting to a pitched battle.

In the first half of the thirteenth century, Latin armies which had been augmented by crusading forces did undertake siege campaigns in their efforts to strengthen the kingdom. Beirut, for example, was captured by siege in 1197; in the same year, Toron was besieged, though without success; and in 1217 there was an abortive siege of Mt Tabor. Information from the immediate vicinity of the Latin Kingdom can be supplemented by use of the extensive accounts of the siege of Damietta by the Fifth Crusade and the sources which described the conflict between imperial and pro-Ibelin forces on the mainland and in Cyprus, from the 1220s to the 1240s. These materials vary from a one-line reference to the fall of a castle or city in a set of annals, to a work which is almost entirely devoted to a particular siege, such as Oliver of Paderborn's 'Historia Damiatina', which includes a marvellously detailed eye-witness account of the methods employed by the Fifth Crusade during the siege of Damietta. It is thus possible to examine the Christians' techniques as besiegers, as well as their efforts to resist a Muslim attack.

There are, as ever, problems connected with the sources, which are largely narrative accounts, on which we rely for information. There is not much that can be gained from the simple statement that in any given year a castle or town was besieged by either the Christians or the Muslims; even the dating is often inaccurate. News of the fall of Acre in 1291 was reported by at least seventy sources, though many of this number are, in fact, lacking in detail and largely repetitive. When slightly more information is given, it normally indicates the number of persons who were involved

---

[1] Smail, *Crusading Warfare*, p. 215.

in the siege. These figures must be treated with caution: it is clear that writers were often trying to do no more than create an impression of vast size, or of the dominance which one side enjoyed over the other. Estimates of the number of Muslim troops at the siege of Acre in 1291, for example, varied from 70,000 mounted and 150,000 foot[2] to 600,000 men,[3] yet both may be wild guesses. The so-called 'Templar of Tyre' who produced the former estimate was an eye-witness and therefore in as good a position to know as anyone. But it would have been almost impossible – particularly for a member of the opposing side – to number accurately a force which contained tens, let alone hundreds, of thousands of men. Even more fantastic is the statement that al-Ashraf engaged 666 engines in this siege, surely a reflection of religious fervour rather than numerical accuracy.[4] The question of numbers of men and machines involved in sieges will be examined in more detail later.

A further problem with the sources is that accounts of a particular siege may be a stereotyped model of a typical encounter, rather than a precise report. Many writers were simply too far from the action, and possessed too limited a geographical awareness, to describe a siege in the Latin East with any degree of accuracy. In spite of these reservations, there are materials of good quality, including a number of eye-witness accounts. From these, an attempt will be made to present an overall view of siege warfare in and around the Latin Kingdom. This method appears preferable to a consideration of individual sieges, since it avoids an over-reliance on any particular source, which might create a false impression. Moreover, although a century of warfare is being considered, there appears to have been little change in the methods of attack and defence which were employed.

### SIEGE WEAPONS

The same basic weapons were used by both Muslims and Christians for defence and attack. One means of gaining access to a strongpoint was by climbing over the walls. This could be done by using a ladder (as in one account of the Fifth Crusade's capture

---

[2] *Gestes des Chiprois*, p. 241; *Chronique d'Amadi*, p. 219.
[3] Ludolph of Suchem, 'De itinere Terrae Sanctae', ed. F. Deycks, *Bibliothek des Litterarischen Vereins in Stuttgart*, 25 (1851), p. 43.
[4] 'De excidio urbis Acconis', col. 769.

of Damietta)[5] or a siege tower, a device which was not only exposed to assaults from the walls, but also required fairly smooth ground to approach the target. An alternative solution for an aggressor might be to smash the walls down. This could be achieved by a variety of devices which launched stones and other projectiles. The principal engines in use in the thirteenth century were the mangonel, petrary and trebuchet. The mangonel and petrary worked on the principle of torsion, that is the twisting of cords and ropes to produce force by which to propel the projectile. The most recently developed and most effective of the ballistic weapons was the counterweight trebuchet. It was operated by the sudden release of heavy weights; it was both more powerful and more accurate than the earlier machines, and it could cause extensive damage. Modern experiments using a trebuchet worked by fifty men and with a ten-ton counterweight have demonstrated that the device could hurl a projectile weighing 100–150 kilograms approximately 150 metres.[6]

In addition to ballistic machines which attempted to wreck the walls from a distance, other devices were effective when close access to the walls had been achieved. Once the fosse had been successfully surmounted, machines such as the ram and the bore were immediately brought into use against the walls. Although they are seldom referred to in accounts of warfare in the Latin East, contemporary writers may have considered them such obvious devices as not to have warranted a mention. References to the use of mining, on the other hand, are far more common.

Attackers who were close to the walls of a city or castle clearly required protection from the counter-measures of defenders. The most simple expedient was the mantlet, a wooden shelter. More sophisticated was the 'cat' or 'gattus', a type of penthouse which was used to protect men who were mining, using the ram or the bore, or generally operating in close proximity to the walls.[7]

The weapons which were employed in defence were precisely the same as those used in attack. Defenders sometimes attempted to dig counter-mines against the mining operations of the

---

[5] 'Liber duellii christiani', p. 162.

[6] Oman, *Art of War*, vol. I, pp. 136–7; vol. II, pp. 43–6; Contamine, *War in the Middle Ages*, pp. 103–5. For a contemporary drawing of a trebuchet see Villard of Honnecourt, *Sketch-Book*, plate 58.

[7] For the means by which the besiegers could protect themselves, see Contamine, *War in the Middle Ages*, pp. 102–3, and Oman, *Art of War*, vol. II, pp. 49–50.

besiegers and sorties could be made against enemy positions. Two weapons seem to have been peculiar to the Muslims in this period. Greek fire was a highly inflammable mixture which was not quenched by water;[8] it was used by the Muslims in both attack and defence. Secondly, there was the *caraboha*,[9] a hand-held sling which was used for hurling stones. A Christian writer remarked that *carabohas* inflicted considerable damage at the siege of Acre in 1291. They could be used for rapid firing, thereby causing more widespread injury than bigger engines.[10]

Finally, ships could be important in an area where so many of the strongpoints were situated on the coast. They played a vital role in the siege of Damietta, for example,[11] whilst their employment by the Latins as a weapon of defence was noted at the siege of Acre in 1291 by the Muslim eye-witness, Abu'l-Fida.[12] The Muslim fleet was not normally used against Christian targets, either generally to threaten the shipping routes or, more specifically, to support a Muslim land-based assault against a strongpoint.[13]

### THE NUMBERS OF MEN AND WEAPONS

There is some repetition in table 5 below from an earlier one listing garrison numbers in the Latin East (see pp. 115–16, above). This table does not generally include references to population figures. Few numbers relate to siege engines because, although such devices were referred to at almost every siege, there was seldom any indication of the precise number present. The figures

---

[8] See notes in Rashid al-Din, *Histoire des Mongols*, vol. I, pp. 132–5; M. Mercier, *Le Feu Grégeois* (Paris, 1952), pp. 90–1. As Mercier points out, the Christians tried to protect their engines from Greek fire, but there is no evidence that they used Greek fire themselves. Joinville came under attack from Greek fire during St Louis's first crusade: 'it came straight at us, as big as a barrel of verjuice, and the tail of fire which came behind it was as long as a great lance. It made such a noise as it came that it seemed like a thunderbolt from heaven; it resembled a dragon flying through the air. The great mass of flame shone so brightly that within the camp one could see as clearly as if it were day' ('il venoit bien devant aussi gros comme uns tonniaus de verjus, et la queue dou feu qui partoit de li, estoit bien aussi grans comme uns grans glaives. Il faisoit tel noise au venir, que il sembloit que ce fust la foudre dou ciel; il sembloit un dragon qui volast par l'air. Tant getoit grant clartei que l'on véoit aussi clair parmi l'ost comme se il fust jours, pour la grant foison dou feu qui getoit la grant clartei'; *Histoire de Saint Louis*, p. 112).

[9] See Rashid al-Din, *Histoire des Mongols*, vol. I, pp. 136–7.

[10] *Gestes des Chiprois*, p. 244. See also *Cartulaire des Hospitaliers*, no. 4157.

[11] See Oliver of Paderborn, 'Historia', pp. 175–6, 179–86 and *passim*.

[12] 'Annales', p. 164.     [13] See above, chapter 1, note 12.

Table 5. *The size of armies in siege campaigns*

| Siege | Christian forces | | Muslim forces | |
|---|---|---|---|---|
| | Men | Weapons | Men | Weapons |
| Jaffa (1197) | 20,000 killed.[a] 40 knights were sent by Aimery of Lusignan; an alternative source noted that sergeants, as well as knights, were sent[b] | | | |
| Mt Tabor (1217) | | | 2,000 men in the garrison[c] | |
| Damietta (1218–19) | 1,200 mounted troops excluding turcopoles and other mounted, innumerable footsoldiers and 4,000 archers. Or 1,400 knights; 42,000 others; 400 knights from the Holy Land[d] | 8 mangonels were aimed at Damietta from the west bank[e] | 300 men in the Chain Tower.[f] 45,000 garrison at start of siege.[g] The Muslims tried to send a force of 500 men into Damietta.[h] Total population of 60,000, but this declined to 3,000[i] | |
| Caesarea (1218) | | | | 3 petraries[j] |

Table 5 (cont.)

| Siege | Christian forces | | Muslim forces | |
|---|---|---|---|---|
| | Men | Weapons | Men | Weapons |
| Château Pèlerin (1220) | 4,000 warriors fed daily, excluding those who were there at their own expense | Trebuchet, petrary and mangonel destroyed the Muslim engines | | Trebuchet, 3 petraries and 4 mangonels[k] |
| Jerusalem (1229) | | | 15,000 men on foot attacked the city[l] | |
| Dieudamour (1229–30) | A constant Ibelin force of 100 knights and many footsoldiers was maintained[m] | | | |
| Beirut (1231–2) | The Ibelins sent a force of 100 knights, sergeants and others into the citadel[n] | Imperial forces attacked with 'a great trebuchet', 3 smaller trebuchets and 6 'tunbereaus'. Before the arrival of Filangieri at Beirut, their forces were made up of 300 knights and 200 crossbowmen/mounted sergeants[o] | | |
| Kyrenia (1232–3) | Filangieri left a garrison of 50 knights and 1,000 crossbowmen/sailors[p] | 13 Genoese ships were employed by the Ibelins: and they built 2 siege towers, petraries, mangonels and great | | |

| | | | |
|---|---|---|---|
| Jerusalem (1239) | 20 knights in the Tower of David[r] | | |
| Jerusalem (1239) | 1 knight, 70 foot in the Tower of David[s] | | |
| Ascalon (1244–7 (?)) | 100 knights sent to relieve the siege. An alternative source reported that knights and sergeants were sent[t] | 8 galleys and 2 'galions' from Cyprus; or a total force (including vessels from Acre) of 15 galleys and 50 other ships[u] | 22 galleys, one sailing ship[v] |
| Acre (1257–8) | 800 armed men in the Genoese quarter, besides other people[w] | Over 50[x] or 60[y] ballistic machines in the city | |
| Arsuf (1265) | A garrison of 2,000.[z] 90 Hospitallers were captured or killed, 1000 others taken prisoner.[aa] Or garrison of 1,000 captured and killed, including 80–410 Hospitallers.[bb] Or more than 1,000 knights and sergeants captured[cc] | | |
| Saphet (1266) | 2,000 Christians taken and subsequently slaughtered.[dd] The garrison in war should have been 2,200[ee] | | |

Table 5 (cont.)

| Siege | Christian forces | | Muslim forces | |
|---|---|---|---|---|
| | Men | Weapons | Men | Weapons |
| Beaufort (1268) | | | | 26 engines[ff] |
| Antioch (1268) | 1,000 men able to fight.[gg] Or 8,000 warriors in the citadel[hh] | | | |
| Chastel Blanc (1271) | 700 men; it is unclear if this was the garrison force[ii] | | | |
| Crac (1271) | Estimate (1212) of garrison total of 2,000[jj] | | | |
| Margat (1281) | 600 mounted | | 7,000 mounted and many foot[kk] | |
| Margat (1285) | 25 Hospitallers allowed to leave the castle with their horses and arms; this was probably the full Hospitaller contingent | | Kalavun left a garrison after its capture of 1,000 soldiers, 150 Mamluks, and 400 workmen[ll] | |
| Tripoli (1289) | 40 Hospitaller brothers lost[mm] | | 40,000 mounted, 200,000 foot.[nn] 1,500 stonecutters, miners and workers[oo] | 4 big engines,[pp] or 19 engines[qq] |

| Acre (1291) | Total population of 30,000–40,000; 700–800 mounted and 14,000 footsoldiers.[r] Or 900 mounted and 18,000 foot. Henry of Cyprus brought 300 knights. The numbers fell to 12,000, of which 800 were knights, then Henry fled taking 3,000 with him.[ss] Or Henry of Cyprus brought a relief force of 200 knights, 500 footsoldiers.[t] Or c. 30,000 armed men/pilgrims, 1,200 knights[uu] | 70,000 mounted, and 150,000 foot.[vv] Or 40,000 mounted, 200,000 foot.[ww] Or 200,000 mounted, 'infinite' foot.[xx] Or total force of 600,000[yy] | 14 big engines,[zz] or 300 machines[aaa] |

[a] Roger of Howden, *Chronica*, ed. W. Stubbs, vol. IV (Rolls Series, 51; London, 1871), p. 26.

[b] 'Document relatif au service militaire', p. 428; 'Eracles', vol. II, p. 219.

[c] 'Chronica regia Coloniensis', *MGHS rer. Germ.*, vol. XVIII, p. 243.

[d] Oliver of Paderborn, 'Historia', p. 259; 'Fragmentum de captione Damiatae', pp. 200–1.

[e] *History of the Patriarchs*, vol. IV, p. 44.

[f] *Ibid.*, p. 47.

[g] R. Röhricht, *Studien zur Geschichte des Fünften Kreuzzuges* (Innsbruck, 1891), p. 42; James of Vitry, *Lettres*, p. 131.

[h] Abu Shama, 'Livre des deux jardins', vol. v, p. 176.

[i] James of Vitry, *Lettres*, p. 126.

[j] 'Eracles', vol. II, p. 334.

[k] Oliver of Paderborn, 'Historia', pp. 254–5.

*l* 'Eracles', vol. II, p. 384.

*m* Gestes des Chiprois, pp. 63–4.

*n* Ibid., p. 85.

*o* 'Eracles', vol. II, pp. 385–8. The 'tunbereaus' were presumably a variety of mangonel. According to Philip of Novara, the total force under Filangieri's control was 600 knights, 100 mounted squires, 700 footsoldiers and 3,000 marines. See above, p. 39.

*p* Gestes des Chiprois, p. 108.

*q* Ibid., pp. 108–9.

*r* 'Annales de Dunstaplia', p. 150.

*s* History of the Patriarchs, vol. IV, p. 195. See below, p. 243, and note g.

*t* 'Annales de Terre Sainte', p. 442; 'Eracles', vol. II, p. 433.

*u* 'Annales de Terre Sainte', p. 442; 'Eracles', vol. II, p. 433.

*v* 'Eracles', vol. II, pp. 433–4; 'Annales de Terre Sainte', p. 442 (21 galleys destroyed (text 'A') or 12 galleys and a sailing ship (text 'B')); Gestes des Chiprois, p. 146 (21 galleys and 1 sailing ship).

*w* Gestes des Chiprois, p. 152.

*x* 'Annales Januenses', vol. IV, p. 32.

*y* 'Rothelin', p. 635.

*z* Chronica minor auctore minorita Erphordiensi', MGHS, vol. XXIV, p. 204; John Vitoduranus, 'Chronica', p. 17.

*aa* Marino Sanuto, 'Liber', p. 222.

*bb* 'Annales de Terre Sainte', p. 452 (texts 'A' and 'B').

*cc* 'Eracles', vol. II, p. 450; Gestes des Chiprois, p. 171.

*dd* Ibn 'Abd al-Rahim, 'Vie de Kalavun', in Michaud, Bibliothèque, vol. IV, p. 498; Sifridus of Balnhusin, 'Historia universalis et compendium historiarum', MGHS, vol. XXV, p. 706.

*ee* De constructione castri Saphet, p. 41.

*ff* Ibn 'Abd al-Zahir, 'Life of Baybars', vol. II, p. 643; al-Makrizi, Histoire des Sultans, vol. I (b), p. 51.

*gg* 'Chronique de Primat', RHF, vol. XXIII, p. 20.

*hh* Al-Makrizi, Histoire des Sultans, vol. I (b), p. 53; Ibn 'Abd al-Zahir, 'Life of Baybars', vol. II, p. 658.

*ii* Al-Makrizi, Histoire des Sultans, vol. I (b), p. 84; Ibn 'Abd al-Zahir, 'Life of Baybars', vol. II, p. 743.

*jj* Willbrand of Oldenburg, 'Peregrinatio', p. 169.

*kk* *Gestes des Chiprois*, pp. 209–10.

*ll* Ibn 'Abd al-Zahir, 'Vie de Kalavun', in Michaud, *Histoire*, vol. VII, pp. 696–7. These figures can be compared with those for some Christian garrisons (including Margat). See above, p. 119.

*mm* *Cartulaire des Hospitaliers*, no. 4050.

*nn* 'Annales de Terre Sainte', p. 460 (dated 1290).

*oo* Ibn al-Furat, 'Tarikh al-Duwal wa'l-Muluk', in Michaud, *Histoire*, vol. VII, p. 806; al-Makrizi, *Histoire des Sultans*, vol. II (a), p. 102.

*pp* 'Annales de Terre Sainte', p. 460.

*qq* Ibn al-Furat, 'Tarikh al-Duwal wa'l-Muluk', in Michaud, *Histoire*, vol. VII, p. 806; al-Makrizi, *Histoire des Sultans*, vol. II (a), p. 102.

*rr* *Gestes des Chiprois*, p. 241.

*ss* 'De excidio urbis Acconis', cols. 765, 770.

*tt* Marino Sanuto, 'Liber', pp. 230–1.

*uu* James Auria, 'Annales', *MGHS*, vol. XVIII, p. 337.

*vv* *Gestes des Chiprois*, p. 241.

*ww* 'De excidio urbis Acconis', col. 769.

*xx* 'Chronica S. Petri Erfordensis Moderna', *MGHS*, vol. XXX, p. 425.

*yy* Ludolph of Suchem, 'De itinere', p. 43.

*zz* 'Annales de Terre Sainte', p. 460.

*aaa* John Victoriensis, in *Fontes rerum Germanicarum*, vol. I, ed. J. F. Boehmer (Stuttgart, 1843), p. 327.

are far from comprehensive: in the case of the siege of Acre, in particular, a wide range of estimates was given in the sources. The statistics from Arsuf in 1265 show how much numbers could vary and it would be wrong to make too much of them. There are, however, points which can be noted. First, it is clear that most sieges involved comparatively small numbers of men and machines – in the case of the former, not much larger numbers than those which might be assembled for raiding expeditions.[14] The modest force which was sent to relieve Jaffa in 1197 was said to have failed, not because of its small size but because its commander, Renaud Barlais, proved to be incapable of conducting a satisfactory defence.[15] In conflicts between Christian armies, forces numbering hundreds of men could prove sufficient, either in attack or defence. In order to maintain an adequate blockade of a castle, as at Dieudamour in 1229–30, it appears that hundreds, rather than thousands, of men were required. At the siege of Beirut, the entry of a hundred men into the citadel enabled the Ibelin troops to seize the initiative from the imperial army.[16]

An earlier examination of the size of castle garrisons in the Latin states suggested that even at the very largest sites, total numbers would not have exceeded 2,000 men and only a small proportion of this figure would have been full-time soldiers.[17] The 'Templar of Tyre' reported that at the siege of Acre in 1291 the city could only raise 700–800 mounted troops, a figure which presumably included the Military Orders, mercenaries, pilgrims and others. It is no wonder that the arrival of Henry of Cyprus was greeted with such joy. But forces which could be numbered in hundreds, although effective against a Christian assault which similarly involved small numbers of men, stood little chance against the large Muslim armies which could be assembled.[18] The vast reserves of manpower which Muslim commanders were able to draw upon were perhaps the single most important reason behind the success of the siege campaigns which were conducted in the second half of the thirteenth century. The Christians, by contrast, had constantly to grapple with the problems created by a shortage of troops. At the siege of Acre, it would appear (if the

---

[14] See above, pp. 192–3.
[15] 'Eracles', vol. II, p. 219; *Continuation de Guillaume de Tyr (1184–1197)*, p. 191 (where he is called William Barlais).  [16] *Gestes des Chiprois*, pp. 85–6.
[17] See above, pp. 118–20.  [18] See above, pp. 32–3.

figures for the size of the Muslim army are accurate) that the Christians were outnumbered by at least eleven to one. The similarity in the weapons which the two sides possessed made such a numerical advantage all the more decisive.

The success or failure of a siege could be decided before the assault had even begun. Careful preparations, by both attackers and defenders, were essential. Arrangements for the organisation of the siege train, for example, varied according to the geography of the region, the proximity of friendly sites and the amount of forward planning which had been undertaken. Some siege engines were transported ready-made to the scene but often they were constructed on the spot. At Beirut in 1231, the attacking imperialists had not only many engineers, but also the materials – timber, iron and lead – which were needed to construct machines.[19] At the siege of Ascalon in 1247, the Muslims were not so thorough in their preparations. Their fleet was wrecked in a storm, but this proved to be a blessing in disguise because from the hulks they were able to construct cats, mantlets, covered ways and, with some trees, additional engines which they needed to complete the siege of the castle.[20] Accounts of the campaigns of Baybars show that Muslim commanders had, by then, become very conscious of the need for careful planning. Whilst the sultan examined the defences of Arsuf and Caesarea, prior to the commencement of activities against the latter, wood for siege engines, ammunition and supplies all arrived. Engines and ladders were made; other engines were sent from Muslim fortresses, whilst troops went into the mountains to prepare stakes, presumably as a defence against a possible Christian counter-attack.[21] At the siege of Saphet in 1266, siege engines which had been constructed around Acre and Damascus were transported to the site by camels – but the weight proved unbearable and both emirs and soldiers had to assist.[22] Against Beaufort in 1268, the Muslims again transported timber for engines and for the

[19] *Gestes des Chiprois*, p. 79. For the role performed by engineers in the army, see above, pp. 50–1.     [20] 'Eracles', vol. II, pp. 433–4.
[21] Ibn 'Abd al-Zahir, 'Life of Baybars', vol. II, pp. 554–5; al-'Ayni, 'Le Collier', p. 219; al-Makrizi, *Histoire des Sultans*, vol. I (b), p. 6.
[22] Ibn 'Abd al-Zahir, 'Life of Baybars', vol. II, pp. 587–8, 591.

reinforcement of defensive positions.[23] In the same year the Franciscan Fidenzio of Padua saw for himself, at the siege of Antioch, how meticulously the Muslim army had set up its camp around the city.[24]

Later Muslim campaigns were also characterised by careful planning. For the siege of Margat in 1285, Kalavun ordered engines and inflammable substances for the manufacture of Greek fire to be brought from Damascus: the Muslim soldiers carried the engines on their backs and heads.[25] Al-Ashraf made thorough arrangements for the siege of Acre. Wood was prepared in Syria for the construction of machines and Muslim forces were mobilised from Damascus, Cairo, Hama, Tripoli and throughout Syria, with a variety of engines and arsenals.[26] The Muslims also took great care in establishing themselves once they arrived before Acre. Several days were spent in the preparation of their defences, trenches and palisades and the positioning of their engines around the walls.[27]

There is very little information about the arrangements which defenders made before a siege. As in the case of an attacking force, the presence of engineers sometimes meant that machines could be built on the spot. At Kyrenia, Philip Chenart, the commander of the imperial garrison, had a number of engineers at his disposal, so he constructed trebuchets, petraries and mangonels.[28] In preparation for the siege of Tripoli in 1289, most of the kingdom's military forces gathered to help in the city's defence, including Amalric of Lusignan with many knights and soldiers, the Templars and Hospitallers and the troops of the French regiment. The Venetians, Genoese and Pisans all sent galleys; they may have prevented an even worse slaughter than actually took place.[29]

The outcome of a siege could be affected by the ability of attackers and defenders to maintain acceptable levels of men and supplies, or even to increase them by outside aid. One of the greatest problems for the aggressor was to keep an army together; if this proved impossible then a siege could easily collapse. At the

[23] *Ibid.*, p. 642.     [24] Fidenzio of Padua, 'Liber recuperationis', p. 29.
[25] Ibn 'Abd al-Zahir, 'Vie de Kalavun', in Michaud, *Histoire*, vol. VII, pp. 693–4.
[26] Al-Makrizi, *Histoire des Sultans*, vol. II (a), pp. 121–4.
[27] *Cartulaire des Hospitaliers*, no. 4157; al-Makrizi, *Histoire des Sultans*, vol. II (a), p. 125.
[28] *Gestes des Chiprois*, p. 108.
[29] *Ibid.*, pp. 235–6; James Auria, 'Annales', pp. 323–4. For details of the Christians' preparations at the siege of Acre, see below, p. 254.

siege of Dieudamour, 1229–30, John of Beirut was unable to sustain an adequate besieging force and numbers dwindled, to such an extent that the defenders were able to conduct a sortie which gave them the supplies they desperately needed. The Ibelins therefore agreed to maintain a permanent force at the site of a hundred knights and many footsoldiers: the siege was subsequently completed successfully.[30] During a crusade expedition, the problem was accentuated because many participants were under no contractual obligation to remain with the army. Difficulties arose during the Fifth Crusade, for example.[31]

Efforts could also be made to augment the garrison within a beleaguered stronghold. At the siege of Damietta, al-Kamil tried to increase the strength of the garrison by sending in both supplies and men. His ingenious efforts included the filling of empty animals' carcasses with food; these were then floated down-river, to be hooked with long poles by the defenders and hauled into the city. The crusaders were able to prevent most of these supplies from reaching their destination.[32] At Caesarea in 1218, the Genoese sent, in addition to arms and supplies, fresh troops to bolster the defence, but they proved inadequate and had to be rescued themselves.[33] The presence of at least 4,000 troops within the castle during the siege of Château Pèlerin in 1220 suggests that the normal garrison had been considerably augmented. Moreover, it was believed that al-Mu'azzam later terminated the siege at the prospect of further reinforcements arriving.[34] At the siege of Ascalon, a force of about a hundred men was dispatched by sea from Acre to offer support to the garrison; but the Muslims still managed to capture the site.[35] The maintenance of supplies was particularly important when a siege became a matter of attrition. The Genoese quarter in Acre was besieged for more than a year during the War of St Sabas, but the defenders were never short of food despite efforts to blockade them. It was the Hospitallers who were able to keep their Genoese allies supplied, since their buildings were adjacent to the Genoese quarter. Supplies and troops also reached the Genoese, via the Hospitaller quarter, from their ally Philip of Montfort at Tyre.[36]

---

[30] *Gestes des Chiprois*, pp. 63–4; 'Eracles', vol. II, p. 377.
[31] See below, p. 252.   [32] 'Eracles', vol. II, pp. 344–5.
[33] *Ibid.*, p. 334.   [34] Oliver of Paderborn, 'Historia', pp. 255–6.
[35] 'Eracles', vol. II, pp. 433–4; 'Annales de Terre Sainte', p. 442.
[36] *Gestes des Chiprois*, p. 152.

## THE BESIEGERS

The progress of a successful siege in and around the Latin East during this period varied considerably between two extremes. The attacking force might prove so dominant that it could almost immediately capture the target by a violent frontal assault. If, on the other hand, it did not enjoy any significant advantage, then the siege could become a matter of maintaining an effective blockade which would eventually force the defenders to surrender, often because of famine and a realisation that there was no hope of succour. The Muslims' rapid capture of Antioch in 1268 is a good example of the former type, whilst the siege of Damietta by the Fifth Crusade typifies the latter. Between these two extremes lie the great majority of cases from the thirteenth century.

### The Christians

Siege engines were a standard feature of most assaults. Their potential value was noted at the siege of Mt Tabor in 1217. An attempt was made to gain possession of the site without using engines, possibly because the slope was too precipitous for them to be brought into a satisfactory position. But the attackers were forced to abandon the siege, and it was suggested that the absence of engines had rendered the assault ineffective.[37] At the siege of Damietta, petraries and trebuchets proved to be of no use against the Chain Tower in the middle of the Nile, even though they were tried for many days.[38] The relative inefficiency of the ballistic siege engines at the siege of Damietta is further illustrated by the fact that although large numbers of trebuchets and mangonels were lined up against the city, they had little effect. It was therefore necessary for other methods to be employed, which involved the crusaders moving much closer to the walls and consequently placing themselves under far greater threat from the activities of the defenders.[39] It would appear, from Oliver of Paderborn's account, that only one tower in Damietta had been damaged, by the repeated blows of the trebuchet of the duke of Austria.[40] But the author of the 'Eracles' account believed that

[37] 'Eracles', vol. II, p. 324; James of Vitry, *Lettres*, p. 98.
[38] Oliver of Paderborn, 'Historia', p. 181; James of Vitry, *Lettres*, p. 105.
[39] 'Fragmentum de captione Damiatae', p. 178.
[40] Oliver of Paderborn, 'Historia', p. 237.

damage to one of the great corner-towers, which the defenders were too weak to repair, had been done by the Hospitallers' engine.[41] A Christian Arabic writer did state that the combination of the mangonels and a constant bombardment of arrows resulted in large numbers of casualties.[42] However, most of the references to the suffering of the besieged Muslims at Damietta concerned the effects of plague and famine, which resulted from the length of the siege and the effectiveness of the crusaders' blockade.

Ballistic siege engines did prove their worth in some later sieges in the Latin East. At the siege of Kantara, 1229–30, Philip of Novara emphasised the importance to the Ibelin assault of a trebuchet built there by Anceau of Brie. It was even suggested that the departure of John of Beirut from the siege of Dieudamour to inspect this engine contributed to the successful sortie which was organised by the defenders of that castle. At Kantara, however, the trebuchet clearly had the desired effect. The walls of the castle were almost completely shattered, though the rock on which it stood was very durable and impossible to scale.[43] At the siege of Beirut, engines constructed by the Lombard forces proved to be similarly effective; they had been well placed to inflict the maximum possible damage.[44]

Petraries, mangonels and trebuchets were used at the siege of Kyrenia in 1232–3 and they weakened the walls sufficiently for an assault to be undertaken. This attack failed, however, and John of Beirut, full of remorse for the number of men that had been lost, indicated that he was content for the siege to be concluded by attrition. Philip of Novara knew that expenditure on sergeants and galleys was high, but he believed that this was justified by the strategic value of the site.[45] At Tyre in 1242, the Ibelins attacked with engines and petraries which caused much damage to the citadel.[46] During the War of St Sabas, siege engines were said to have had a devastating impact. In 1257–8, the Genoese quarter of Acre was under siege from the Venetians, Pisans and others. The large number of engines in use – as many as sixty – were firing day and night. The power of these machines was so great that the author of the *Gestes des Chiprois* named some of them: the Genoese used engines which he called 'Bonerel', 'Vincheguerre' and 'Peretin', whilst the Venetians had one called 'Marquemose'.

[41] 'Eracles', vol. II, pp. 337, 345.     [42] *History of the Patriarchs*, vol. IV, p. 44.
[43] *Gestes des Chiprois*, pp. 63, 65.          [44] *Ibid.*, p. 79.
[45] *Ibid.*, pp. 109, 111–12.                [46] *Ibid.*, p. 132.

By the end of the siege in 1258, the city looked as if it had been destroyed by a Muslim army.[47] In the right circumstances ballistic weapons could exert a powerful influence on the outcome of a siege, whether they were used as a decisive element in themselves, as at Kantara, or as part of a general siege plan, as in the case of Kyrenia in 1232–3.

Another aspect of aggressive siege tactics involved weapons which, in order to be effective, needed to be close to the walls of a strongpoint. This often meant that the fosse around the strongpoint had to be filled – which could be a hazardous operation in itself. The simplest device was the ladder. At Mt Tabor in 1217, the crusaders successfully placed a huge ladder against the wall of a tower, but the Muslims managed to burn it with Greek fire.[48] A more complex construction than the ladder was the siege tower. Historians have pointed to the importance of this device in medieval sieges, but in the Latin East it appears to have been used sparingly and to little effect. The crusaders constructed wooden towers at Damietta, but these do not seem to have played a major part in the siege.[49] At the siege of Kyrenia, the Ibelins built two great siege towers that were successfully brought over the fosse and positioned against the wall. But the defenders were able to set fire to them and the infantry within had to be rescued by the Ibelin knights.[50] A rather different type of tower played an important role in the Lombards' siege of Beirut. They built a tower on a site, some distance from the castle, which overlooked the walls; this enabled them to inflict considerable damage on the defenders.[51]

The other important siege engine in use in and around the Latin East was the movable shed or penthouse, known as the 'cat'. At Damietta, where ballistic weapons proved to be comparatively ineffective, the crusaders placed great emphasis on the role that the cat could play – particularly in gaining direct access to the walls, in order to facilitate close-range operations. In July 1219 an attempt was made using a cat, supported by ballistic engines and other machines, to destroy a tower. In August of the same year, the crusaders constructed a massive cat encased in iron with which, they believed, they could capture the city. On both

[47] *Ibid.*, p. 150; 'Rothelin', p. 635; 'Annales Januenses', vol. IV, p. 32.
[48] Abu Shama, 'Livre des deux jardins', vol. V, p. 163.
[49] 'Gesta obsidionis', pp. 92, 95.     [50] *Gestes des Chiprois*, p. 109.
[51] *Ibid.*, p. 79.

occasions, however, the cat was destroyed by the Muslim defenders. In one of these assaults a 'ram', which was also in use, was burned. Some accounts of the siege suggested that cats, in conjunction with other siege engines, were used to fill in the fosse, before they were brought against the walls and towers of the city.[52] The cat was not only employed during sieges. Before the battle of Mansurah on St Louis's first crusade, two devices called 'cats' castles' were used to protect men building a causeway across to the Muslim army on the opposite bank of the river. The machines appear to have been cats incorporated into the design of a tower. The crusaders tried to protect the cats from a Muslim bombardment of stones and Greek fire, but their efforts were in vain and the cats were burned. Another cat was constructed and once more the Muslims were able to set fire to it. John of Joinville very honestly confessed to a sense of relief when this third cat was burned: it meant that he and his men would not have the hazardous duty of protecting it during the night.[53]

When it proved impossible to climb over or break through the walls, a solution could be to go underneath, by means of a mine. One possible use of the mine was to weaken the foundations of the site. The miners would support the hollowed-out stonework with wooden beams: when these were destroyed, normally by fire, the structure would collapse. At the siege of Toron in 1197, both Muslim and Christian writers noted the damage caused by mining. Arnold of Lübeck referred to the presence at the siege of several Saxons who were experienced silver-miners; their efforts almost proved decisive and the Muslim garrison considered surrendering after the Christians had burned out the foundations. The Muslims realised, however, that their safety would not be guaranteed if they capitulated, so they held out until they were relieved by a force under the sultan al-'Aziz 'Uthman.[54] Mining could also be used to enable the attackers to gain access to the strongpoint by bypassing the walls. This technique was tried, though without great success, at the siege of Damietta.[55]

---

[52] 'Gesta obsidionis', pp. 95, 100; 'Fragmentum de captione Damiatae', pp. 175–6, 178–80; John of Tulbia, 'De Domino Johanne', pp. 129, 131; 'Liber duellii christiani', pp. 155, 157–8.

[53] Joinville, *Histoire de Saint Louis*, pp. 106, 112–16. The Muslims used a petrary and an 'arbalestre à tour' (a large siege crossbow) to launch the Greek fire.

[54] Arnold of Lübeck, 'Chronica', p. 207; Ibn al-Athir, 'Kamel-Altevarykh', vol. II, pp. 87–8; *Continuation de Guillaume de Tyr (1184–1197)*, pp. 195–7.

[55] See below, p. 252.

At Beirut in 1231–2, the Lombard forces were able to cause much damage by mining. They also built a covered street,[56] which would have enabled them to move from one part of the siege to another without being exposed to the defenders. At the siege of Kyrenia, the Ibelins constructed movable shelters, which obviously served a similar purpose. During the same siege, the value of the crossbowman was indicated; a large number were present, and both sides suffered heavy casualties.[57] The power and accuracy of the crossbow meant that it could be used to pick out individual targets during a siege campaign, in addition to the important role which, as we saw earlier, it performed on the battlefield. At the siege of Kantara, for example, Philip of Novara reported that a shot by a crossbowman killed one of the five imperial *baillis*.[58]

The geography of the Latin East and the area around it meant that ships often played a significant part in siege warfare. The presence of Christian ships acting in unison with an army at the siege of Beirut (1197) was regarded by western sources as an important factor in the decision of the Muslims to abandon their defensive position.[59] Christian ships also played an important role at the siege of Damietta. A seaborne attack enabled the crusaders to capture the Chain Tower in the middle of the Nile.[60] During the summer of 1219, the crusaders' ships, particularly those from Italy, made a number of attacks on the city and their troops tried to surmount the walls with ladders. Each time, however, they were driven back by the Muslim defenders and suffered considerable damage. On one occasion the wind direction prevented an attack being made.[61] At Beirut in 1231–2, the imperial forces chained their galleys together and established a highly effective blockade. But John of Beirut was able to break this blockade and send a shipload of a hundred men into the citadel. This changed the course of the siege; the Ibelins were far more successful thereafter in countering the imperial assault on the castle.[62] At the siege of Kyrenia, the lack of ships on the Ibelin side lengthened the time it took them to force the defenders into submission. The imperial ships experienced no difficulties in

---

[56] *Gestes des Chiprois*, p. 79.    [57] *Ibid.*, p. 109.    [58] *Ibid.*, p. 68.
[59] 'Chronica regia Coloniensis', p. 161; Roger of Howden, *Chronica*, vol. IV, p. 28; *Chronique d'Ernoul*, pp. 311–13.    [60] See below, p. 251.
[61] 'Gesta obsidionis', pp. 93, 95–6, 101; 'Fragmentum de captione Damiatae', pp. 173–5.    [62] *Gestes des Chiprois*, pp. 84–5; see below, p. 237.

travelling back and forth from Kyrenia to Tyre, thus maintaining the garrison's supplies. John of Beirut therefore engaged thirteen Genoese ships to aid the Ibelin cause.[63] In 1242, the Ibelins used both land and sea forces for their assault on Tyre, including the Venetians who, as we saw earlier, hoped to regain their commercial privileges in that city.[64] In 1258, a Genoese fleet led by Rosso della Turca attacked Acre in the hope of relieving the Genoese quarter in the city and winning the War of St Sabas. The fleet included, in addition to forty-eight galleys, four sailing ships, each of which was equipped with a siege engine, but it was defeated by a Venetian force outside Acre and the Genoese quarter was subsequently overrun.[65]

## The Muslims

Muslim armies relied heavily on the power of their ballistic weapons, either as the prelude to a frontal assault or, unsupported, to bring the defenders to a state where they were forced to capitulate. They also made considerable use of mines, but there is little evidence to suggest that devices such as the cat or the siege tower found any great favour with them. Finally, they took full advantage of the considerable reserves of manpower at their disposal.

At Caesarea in 1218, al-Mu'azzam appears to have required only three petraries to overcome the weak Christian efforts at defence.[66] At the siege of Jerusalem in 1239–40, mangonels were used by an-Nasir Da'ud, prior to a general assault. It seems that Muslim miners were only brought in to raze the Tower of David once the defenders had surrendered.[67] An unusual siege took place in 1241. The Christians had been given the castle of Beaufort by treaty, but its Muslim garrison refused to leave. Muslim troops used engines against the site (with no suggestion of any other form of assault) and their compatriots surrendered.[68] At Caesarea in 1265, siege engines were used at the same time as a general

---

[63] *Gestes des Chiprois*, p. 108.
[64] *Ibid.*, pp. 130–1; *Chronique d'Amadi*, p. 192; *Urkunden der Republik Venedig*, vol. II, pp. 355–7.
[65] *Gestes des Chiprois*, pp. 152–5; see 'Annales Januenses', vol. IV, pp. 34–5.
[66] 'Eracles', vol. II, p. 334.
[67] Al-Makrizi, *Histoire d'Egypte*, pp. 452–3; al-'Ayni, 'Le Collier', p. 196; 'Rothelin', p. 530; Djamal al-Din, 'Remède contre le chagrin', in Michaud, *Histoire*, vol. VII, p. 548.
[68] 'Rothelin', pp. 552–3.

assault on the city walls. The Muslim army then moved on to attack the citadel; this was immensely strong, with granite columns incorporated into its walls, but the assaults of the engines still caused the Christians to surrender in a week.[69] The Muslims used their mangonels at the siege of Saphet in 1266; the Templars' resistance was resolute, however, and the Muslims were obliged to employ a number of other methods of attack.[70] At the siege of Beaufort in 1268, the Muslims were once again successful, apparently with a fairly basic approach. Faced by twenty-six engines, the Templars had to pull back from the citadel which they had recently constructed. The Muslims captured this and the machines were immediately brought up to fire on the other citadel; under such fierce pressure, the defenders were forced to concede.[71] In the sieges of both Crac and Gibelcar, it was the impact of engines coupled with the frontal assaults of the Muslims that determined the outcome.[72] Engines played an important role in the siege of Montfort in 1271[73] and against Margat in 1285 they were again of significance, although some of them were said to have been placed too close to the walls of the fortress, and this allowed the defenders to destroy a number with their own engines.[74]

At Latakia in 1287, the Muslim engines supplemented the damage which had previously been done by an earthquake, and this caused the Christians to surrender.[75] The Muslims concluded the sieges of Tripoli and Acre only after some stiff Christian resistance and they required a wider range of siege techniques than they usually employed. In both instances, however, ballistic weapons undoubtedly played an important part. At Tripoli, the presence of nineteen large and small engines contributed to the weakening of the defences before the city fell to a general

[69] Al-Makrizi, *Histoire des Sultans*, vol. I (b), p. 7; al-'Ayni, 'Le Collier', p. 219; Ibn 'Abd al-Zahir, 'Life of Baybars', vol. II, pp. 555–7. Caesarea's citadel could be attacked from the site of the cathedral; see above, p. 102. Baybars himself used this position to fire arrows against the citadel (Ibn 'Abd al-Zahir, 'Life of Baybars', vol. II, p. 556).

[70] Ibn 'Abd al-Zahir, 'Life of Baybars', vol. II, pp. 590–5; al-'Ayni, 'Le Collier', p. 222.

[71] Ibn 'Abd al-Zahir, 'Life of Baybars', vol. II, pp. 643–5; al-Makrizi, *Histoire des Sultans*, vol. I (b), p. 51.

[72] Ibn 'Abd al-Zahir, 'Life of Baybars', vol. II, pp. 744, 749; al-Makrizi, *Histoire des Sultans*, vol. I (b), p. 85.

[73] Ibn 'Abd al-Zahir, 'Life of Baybars', vol. II, p. 756.

[74] Ibn 'Abd al-Zahir, 'Vie de Kalavun', in Michaud, *Histoire*, vol. VII, p. 694; Abu'l-Fida, 'Annales', p. 161.

[75] Ibn 'Abd al-Zahir, 'Vie de Kalavun', in Michaud, *Histoire*, vol. VII, pp. 708–9.

assault.[76] Similarly, at the siege of Acre, ballistic engines maintained a constant bombardment on the city and helped to weaken the walls and towers before a frontal assault completed its capture.[77]

Mining was the other principal Muslim siege technique. It was almost as successful as were ballistic weapons for the conclusion of a siege. At Ascalon in 1247, mines were used not simply to destroy the walls and towers, but as a means of gaining direct access to the castle. The mine passed through the hill on which the castle was built and came out in the middle of the castle itself. The Muslim troops used this route to enter the strongpoint.[78] Mining was tried against Caesarea in 1265; but St Louis had fortified the site so well that the assault proved ineffectual.[79] Mines were said to have contributed to the fall of Saphet in 1266[80] and they were also used against Montfort five years later.[81] Mining operations were particularly effective at the siege of Margat in 1285. A mine was dug and then set on fire, as a preliminary to a general assault, but a tower which fell to the ground filled the breach that had been made. The mine, however, had penetrated so deep into the fortress that the 'Tour de l'Esperance', a main tower, was believed to be about to collapse. The Christians were therefore obliged to surrender.[82] Mines were dug at the siege of Tripoli in 1289,[83] where they undoubtedly helped to weaken the city walls. They were also employed at the siege of Acre; they were directed against a number of towers, including the tower of the countess of Blois and the barbican of King Hugh, in the vicinity of the Accursed Tower where Muslim attacks were concentrated.[84]

At sieges where considerable Christian resistance was encountered – Ascalon, Arsuf, Saphet, Tripoli and Acre, for example – the Muslims varied their tactics and used weapons

---

[76] Abu'l-Fida, 'Annales', p. 162; al-Makrizi, *Histoire des Sultans*, vol. II (a), p. 102; *Gestes des Chiprois*, pp. 236–7 (which also blames the defenders for abandoning the city).

[77] *Gestes des Chiprois*, p. 243; al-Makrizi, *Histoire des Sultans*, vol. II (a), p. 125; Abu'l-Mahasin, 'Livre des étoiles resplendissantes relativement aux rois d'Egypte', in J. F. Michaud, *Bibliothèque des Croisades*, vol. IV (Paris, 1829), p. 570; 'De excidio urbis Acconis', col. 769.       [78] 'Eracles', vol. II, pp. 433–4.

[79] Ibn 'Abd al-Zahir, 'Life of Baybars', vol. II, p. 556.       [80] *Ibid.*, p. 593.

[81] *Ibid.*, pp. 756–7. There is what appears to be the beginning of a mine, dug in the south wall of the site. See above, p. 111.

[82] Ibn 'Abd al-Zahir, 'Vie de Kalavun', in Michaud, *Bibliothèque*, vol. IV, p. 549 and in Michaud, *Histoire*, vol. VII, pp. 694–5; *Gestes des Chiprois*, pp. 217–18 (dated 1284).

[83] Ibn al-Furat, 'Tarikh al-Duwal wa'l Muluk', in Michaud, *Histoire*, vol. VII, p. 806; *Gestes des Chiprois*, p. 236.

[84] *Gestes des Chiprois*, pp. 244–5; Marino Sanuto, 'Liber', p. 230.

which brought them closer to the walls of the strongpoint.[85] As noted about the Christians, this often involved overcoming the problem of how to fill in the fosse which surrounded the strongpoint. At the siege of Ascalon, the Muslims constructed cats, mantlets and covered ways; these would have been of value because the fosse had been filled and the Muslims' assaults had brought them close enough to the walls to be threatened by the defenders.[86] At the siege of Arsuf, in a somewhat confused account by Baybars's biographer, Ibn 'Abd al-Zahir, it is apparent that the Muslims found it difficult to reach the fosse prior to approaching the walls of the citadel, and the Franks were able to destroy their efforts by fire. The Muslims solved their problems by digging tunnels through which they poured sand to fill the fosse.[87] At Saphet, it seems that, rather than weakening the walls before an assault, the Muslims used an assault first, probably to force the defenders back so that stonemasons could begin drilling at the base of the walls and towers. At the same time the gate was burned by 'dart-casters' with containers of tar.[88] A miniature, dated c. 1300, from an Old French translation of 'De excidio urbis Acconis' gives an impression of how Muslim stonemasons may have worked on the walls of Acre, once the city's fosse had been filled in.[89] The *caraboha*, the hand-held sling used by the Muslims, was most effective at short range: at both Tripoli and Acre it was used in conjunction with other devices which indicated that the aggressors were fairly close to their targets. At Tripoli, *carabohas* were mentioned along with wooden protection, 1,500 stone-cutters, and sappers.[90] At Acre, having overcome the fosse, the Muslims built ramparts to protect the *caraboha* throwers.[91]

In so many of the sieges during this period, a violent Muslim frontal attack ended a campaign rapidly and decisively. It is therefore fortunate that an eye-witness account of such an assault survives, that of the Muslims against Acre on 18 May 1291, recorded by the author of the *Gestes des Chiprois*:

---

[85] This apparent variation in tactics against a more determined Christian defence may, to some extent, be explained by the detailed accounts which survive of all these sieges.

[86] 'Eracles', vol. II, pp. 433–4; 'Rothelin', p. 565.

[87] Ibn 'Abd al-Zahir, 'Life of Baybars', vol. II, pp. 562–4.

[88] *Ibid.*, pp. 590–1; al-'Ayni, 'Le Collier', p. 222.

[89] See plate I, p. 13, above.

[90] *Gestes des Chiprois*, p. 236; Ibn al-Furat, 'Tarikh al-Duwal wa'l Muluk', in Michaud, *Histoire*, vol. VII, p. 806; al-Makrizi, *Histoire des Sultans*, vol. II (a), p. 102.

[91] *Gestes des Chiprois*, p. 244.

Before dawn on Friday a loud drum sounded, and at the noise of this drum, which was a terrible din, the Saracens assailed the city of Acre from all sides...They came on foot, in numbers which were beyond comprehension; first came those who carried massive shields, and next came those who threw the Greek fire, and after were those who fired darts and feathered arrows so thickly that it was as if rain was falling from the sky...[92]

Throughout the century, Christians must have dreaded the consequences of this kind of assault, yet Muslim successes were not always gained solely in the wake of noise and blood. On three occasions during this period, psychological warfare was used to complement more conventional Muslim methods. At Saphet in 1266, Muslim losses proved much higher than Baybars was prepared to tolerate. He therefore spread mistrust amongst the garrison, by offering the Syrian sergeants and archers in it a safe conduct and ordering his men to direct their attack solely against the Templars. Following this the Templars also sought terms of surrender, which were granted, but they had been deceived and were subsequently massacred.[93] At Beaufort in 1268, the garrison had sent letters to Acre, explaining its situation and asking for assistance. The reply from Acre, which was carried by a Muslim courier, ended up in the hands of the sultan because of the courier's religious scruples. Baybars was therefore able to forge a reply to the garrison which weakened the Christians' will to resist and spread disunity.[94] At Crac in 1271, the sultan again forged letters to the castle, this time from Tripoli, ordering the Hospitallers to surrender.[95]

The siege of Ascalon in 1247 was the only occasion during this period when the Muslims were able to use a naval force against a Christian strongpoint;[96] the site was within range of the Egyptian naval bases of Alexandria and Damietta. References to

[92] 'Et quant vint le jour dou vendredy avant jour, une nacare souna mout fort, & à son de selle nacare, quy avoit mout oryble vois & mout grant, les Sarazins asaillierent la cité d'Acre de toutes pars...Il vindrent tous à pié quy furent tant sans nonbre; & par devant veneent seaus quy porteent grans targes hautes, & après veneent seaus quy jeteent le feuc gryzés, & après estoient siaus qui trayoient les pilès & seetes enpenées si espessement quy senbloit pleve quy venist dou siel...' (*ibid.*, pp. 248–9).

[93] *Ibid.*, pp. 179–81; Ibn 'Abd al-Zahir, 'Life of Baybars', vol. II, pp. 595–9.

[94] Ibn 'Abd al-Zahir, 'Life of Baybars', vol. II, pp. 642–3; Shafi ibn-'Ali, 'Vie de Baibars', in J. F. Michaud, *Histoire des Croisades*, vol. VII (Paris, 1822), pp. 676–7. According to the latter account, the Muslim courier was called Abu'l Majd.

[95] Ibn 'Abd al-Zahir, 'Life of Baybars', vol. II, p. 744.

[96] See above, pp. 217, 223.

the value of the sea in Arabic accounts tended to relate to the presence of Christian ships, which would either attempt to hamper a Muslim land-based attack or be ready to take away any Christians who were able to escape.[97]

### THE DEFENDERS

Defensive tactics varied enormously. We shall consider the different options which were open to the defenders and the manner in which they might be used against an attack.

### The Christians

A number of Christian garrisons were prepared to come out from behind their defences and oppose a Muslim assault with counter-attacks of their own. The more aggressive side of Christian defensive techniques included a willingness to meet a Muslim attack outside the walls of a stronghold, the use of sorties, and counter-mining in order to drive back a Muslim mining assault. These techniques were also used during the Lombard–Ibelin conflict.

It is surprising that some Christian garrisons were prepared to forego the protection of their strongpoint and face a Muslim army in the open, given the overwhelming numerical advantages which the Muslims appear to have enjoyed. In chapter 4 of this study, we noted that such tactics are closely related to, and may even be considered to be, battles. At Jaffa in 1197, such an aggressive response had disastrous repercussions. The Christians opened the gates and attacked, but they were obliged to retreat and their colleagues inside, fearing the threat of the Muslims, refused to re-open the gates and let them in.[98] The tactic was more successful in 1281, when a Muslim attempt to capture Margat failed. Despite reportedly being outnumbered by over ten to one, the Hospitallers went out and defeated the Muslim army.[99]

Some contemporary accounts of the siege of Acre reported that the Christians kept the gates of the city open throughout the conflict:[100] in view of the size of the Muslim army, it is hard to

[97] See below, p. 241.    [98] Arnold of Lübeck, 'Chronica', p. 204.
[99] *Gestes des Chiprois*, pp. 209–10.
[100] Abu'l-Fida, 'Annales', p. 164; Bar Hebraeus, *Chronography*, vol. I, pp. 492–3; Ludolph of Suchem, 'De itinere', p. 43.

believe that this happened. It may be that what was meant here
was that posterns were kept open, so that troops could go out,
undetected, on sorties. A carefully planned raid by a small force
from inside a stronghold could wreak havoc within the enemy
camp. At the siege of Beirut, the Ibelins used the tactic of the
sortie to their advantage. Once John of Beirut had managed to
increase the numbers within the citadel by breaking the Lombard
blockade, the Ibelin defenders were able to seize the initiative from
their opponents. They recaptured the fosse, burned the Lombards'
covered street and, by sorties, set fire to many of the siege engines
that had caused them such trouble.[101] Christians also tried to use
sorties against Muslim besiegers. At Arsuf, for example, Baybars
was able to thwart a Christian sortie.[102] But two of the best
examples of this form of defence come from the early stages of the
siege of Acre. A group of 300 men, led by the Templars, with a
number of other knights, valets and turcopoles, went out in an
attempt to burn the protective coverings of the Muslim engines.
The Christians threw the fire short, however; it missed the
defences but killed a number of Muslims. Chaos followed this
poorly delivered attack, as the Christians became entangled in the
Muslims' tent cords and one knight fell into a Muslim latrine and
was drowned. The sortie had produced as much confusion for the
Christians as it had on the Muslim side, but Christian losses, of
eighteen mounted troops, were regarded as acceptable. A second
sortie was therefore organised, but it was even less successful than
the first. The Muslims anticipated it and the Christians were
routed.[103] After this, there were no more sorties: it must have
been felt that the benefits were outweighed by the losses which
had been suffered.

Counter-mining was another technique which aimed to drive
besiegers back, rather than merely to contain them and prevent
them from making further progress. The Christian defenders of
Arsuf used mining to hinder the Muslims' efforts to fill the fosse
and thus to approach the walls of the citadel. They dug tunnels
underneath the Muslim trenches. In the tunnels they placed
barrels of grease and oil, or fat, to which they set light, fanning
the flames with bellows which had been constructed underground. The Muslims were unable to put the fires out, and were

---

[101] *Gestes des Chiprois*, p. 86; see above, p. 230.
[102] Ibn 'Abd al-Zahir, 'Life of Baybars', vol. II, p. 565.
[103] *Gestes des Chiprois*, pp. 245–6; Abu'l-Fida, 'Annales', p. 164.

therefore forced to adopt other means of approaching the citadel.[104] At the siege of Saphet in 1266, the Templars dug a counter-mine which broke into the roof of the Muslim mine and led to an underground fight.[105] It has already been seen that Muslim mining was an important element in the siege of Acre.[106] The Christians tried to counter-mine, but this proved ineffective because of the superior numerical strength of the Muslims.[107]

The defenders not only required a fair degree of confidence to employ aggressive defensive methods; they also had to have sufficient troops to carry them out effectively. The Latins' lack of manpower would have handicapped them considerably in their efforts to repel a Muslim assault. Often they could only conduct their defence from within the stronghold, presumably in the hope that the initial Muslim thrust would gradually fade away. At Saphet (in spite of the efforts at counter-mining considered above), Beaufort and Crac, it appears that the Christians simply withdrew further and further into the confines of the powerful defences of the fortresses. In these circumstances, the garrison would try to prevent the advance of the assailants by using the same ballistic weapons which were employed in attack, or simply by hurling a variety of projectiles down on their opponents. According to an Arabic writer, the Christians defended themselves well at the siege of Gibelcar in 1271, firing arrows and launching stones from mangonels which inflicted some damage on the Muslims.[108] During the early stages of the siege of Acre, the Christians enjoyed some successes with their engines, but they were subsequently overwhelmed by sheer weight of numbers.[109]

In the course of the Lombard–Ibelin conflict there were also occasions when defenders stayed behind the walls of the strongpoint to conduct their defence. At Beirut, the Ibelin forces were initially obliged to defend passively and the Lombards were able to make considerable progress. The defenders did not lack supplies, but they were low on manpower because John of Ibelin had taken most of the garrison over to Cyprus.[110] At Kyrenia, on the other hand, it was the imperial forces which had to mount a passive defence. Philip Chenart and his engineers were able to

---

[104] Ibn 'Abd al-Zahir, 'Life of Baybars', vol. II, p. 563; Ibn al-Furat, *Ayyubids*, vol. II, pp. 73–4.   [105] Ibn 'Abd al-Zahir, 'Life of Baybars', vol. II, p. 593.
[106] See above, p. 233.   [107] *Gestes des Chiprois*, pp. 244–5.
[108] Al-'Ayni, 'Le Collier', p. 242.   [109] See below, pp. 254–5.
[110] *Gestes des Chiprois*, pp. 78–9.

build a number of petraries, mangonels and trebuchets and, when the Ibelins brought two siege towers over the fosse, the Lombards managed to set fire to them.[111]

## The Muslims

Muslim defensive measures also varied from the aggressive to the more passive. Like the Christians, the Muslims occasionally chose to fight outside their stronghold; at Beirut in 1197, this had unfortunate consequences. As the Christian forces approached the city, so the Muslims went out to face them. But when the Muslims decided to retreat, they were prevented from re-entering the strongpoint by a few Christian slaves and a carpenter who had been left behind in the citadel. The Muslims therefore fled.[112] At Mt Tabor in 1217, the tactic was employed with better results; the Muslim garrison took the offensive and forced the crusaders back down to the foot of the mountain.[113] In the early stages of the siege of Damietta, in October 1218, it was widely reported that large numbers of Muslims attacked the Christian position on the west bank.[114] When the crusaders crossed to the east bank following the flight of the sultan al-Kamil and his relief force, a group of 500 Muslim warriors came out of the city to face them. The Muslims were probably dealt with by the Templars, who led the advance.[115] There appear to be only two examples of the Muslims using sorties and both occurred during the siege of Damietta. We saw earlier that in July and August 1219 the Christians prepared land-based assaults on the walls involving a variety of engines. On both occasions, the Muslims were able to leave the city and burn these devices, killing a number of Christians at the same time, whilst the latter were busy defending their rear from other Muslim attacks.[116]

There is not much evidence of more passive techniques being

[111] *Ibid.*, pp. 108–9.
[112] Arnold of Lübeck, 'Chronica', pp. 205–6; Roger of Howden, *Chronica*, vol. IV, pp. 28–9; *Chronique d'Ernoul*, pp. 311–15.
[113] Oliver of Paderborn, 'Historia', pp. 165–6; Abu Shama, 'Livre des deux jardins', vol. V, p. 163.
[114] Oliver of Paderborn, 'Historia', p. 190; 'Eracles', vol. II, pp. 332–4; *History of the Patriarchs*, vol. IV, p. 51.
[115] 'Fragmentum de captione Damiatae', p. 171; Oliver of Paderborn, 'Historia', pp. 199–200.
[116] 'Liber duellii christiani', pp. 155, 157–8; John of Tulbia, 'De Domino Johanne', pp. 129, 131; 'Fragmentum de captione Damiatae', pp. 175–6, 178–80; 'Gesta obsidionis', pp. 95, 100; see above, pp. 228–9.

used by the Muslims, but what there is suggests some variation in comparison to the Christians' tactics. The Muslim garrisons used Greek fire as a device to ward off a Christian offensive. This was first noted in the thirteenth century at Mt Tabor in 1217, when the Muslims were able to set fire to the massive ladder which the crusaders had placed against the wall of the fortress.[117] In a seaborne attack on Damietta by Venetian, Genoese and Pisan boats, the Muslims were able to destroy the hides protecting the ladders which the crusaders were attempting to use: then they set fire to the ladders themselves with Greek fire and oil. Neither wine nor vinegar proved of any value in the crusaders' efforts to extinguish the flames.[118] There is also some evidence for Muslim use of conventional ballistic weapons in defence. They were employed, with Greek fire, to harass the crusaders when the latter were attacking the Chain Tower at Damietta and, similarly, when the Muslims were defending themselves within Damietta against the crusaders' assaults.[119]

### Use of relief forces

An assault could also be resisted by the presence of a relief force which, rather than attempting to enter the strongpoint, remained outside and engaged the besiegers from another angle. They were, in effect, trying to besiege the besiegers. Such troops could have a major influence on the success or otherwise of a defence against a siege. The Christian siege of Toron in 1197 was terminated because of the expected arrival of al-'Aziz 'Uthman with a relieving army.[120] The presence of a Muslim relief force at the siege of Damietta was undoubtedly a great hindrance to the crusaders in their efforts to take the city. Whenever the crusaders tried to advance the siege, the Muslims in the city signalled to those who were at the rear of the crusader camp. The relief force would then attack, distracting the Christians and preventing them from continuing with their assault. When the legate Pelagius demanded a concerted effort to capture Damietta, the leaders of

---

[117] See above, p. 228. In the Franciscan museum in Jerusalem are a number of pots retrieved from Mt Tabor; these may have been intended as containers for Greek fire.

[118] 'Fragmentum de captione Damiatae', p. 175; 'Gesta obsidionis', p. 97.

[119] Oliver of Paderborn, 'Historia', pp. 183, 185; 'Fragmentum de captione Damiatae', pp. 174–5.

[120] Arnold of Lübeck, 'Chronica', pp. 209–10; *Continuation de Guillaume de Tyr (1184–1197)*, p. 197; Ibn al-Athir, 'Kamel-Altevarykh', vol. II, p. 88.

the army argued against it because their lack of numbers made it impossible to attack the city and defend their camp at the same time.[121] A letter from the nobles of the army to Honorius III, written shortly after Damietta had fallen, confirmed the threat which had been posed by this second Muslim force. Most of the crusader army, apart from a few who entered the city, had protected the palisades and fosses in order to guard against any possible Muslim attack from the rear.[122]

Christian armies, too, could benefit from the arrival of a relief force. In 1229, the Christians at Jerusalem were besieged in the Tower of David by 15,000 Muslims. The *baillis* at Acre, Balian of Sidon and Garnier L'Aleman, gathered a relieving army of knights and sergeants. When the defenders of Jerusalem saw the banners of an advance party led by Baldwin of Picquigny, they were so encouraged that they went out to defeat their aggressors. The relief force merely helped with the slaughter of more than 2,000 Muslims.[123]

At coastal sites, ships sometimes had an important role to play in relief operations. During the siege of Arsuf in 1265, for example, a number of Christian ships attempted to break the Muslim siege.[124] At many of the later sieges of this period, there were Christian ships present waiting to take away those who were able to embark, but these vessels did not normally perform an active role against the Muslim assault.

### THE EFFECTIVENESS OF SIEGES

Throughout this period, therefore, Muslim and Christian forces generally used similar weapons, if in slightly different ways, in attack and defence. We may now consider the effectiveness of their techniques. Most of the sieges for which information survives were, eventually, successful, but it is still possible to compare, in tables 6a and 6b, the performances of the Christian and Muslim armies.

From these tables it is clear that the time which a Christian siege was likely to take was markedly different from that of a Muslim one. Muslim sieges generally lasted no more than a few weeks, whereas Christian armies were prepared to besiege enemy

---

[121] 'Gesta obsidionis', pp. 93, 94.   [122] Röhricht, *Studien*, pp. 44–5.
[123] 'Eracles', vol. II, pp. 384–5; 'Rothelin', p. 489 (which reported that 500 Muslims were killed).   [124] Ibn 'Abd al-Zahir, 'Life of Baybars', vol. II, p. 564.

Table 6a. *The results of Christian siege campaigns*

| | Christian attack – Muslim or Christian defence | |
|---|---|---|
| Siege | Time taken | How ended |
| Beirut (1197) | Very quick | The Muslims fled[a] |
| Toron (1197) | 10 weeks | A relief force caused the Christians to abandon the siege[b] |
| Mt Tabor (1217) | Up to 17 days | The Christian attack was beaten off by the Muslims[c] |
| Damietta (1218–19) | 19 months | Famine, disease and no prospect of relief caused the Muslims to surrender[d] |
| Kyrenia (1229) | Fairly quick? | A truce was arranged and the defenders capitulated |
| Dieudamour (1229–30) | 10 months | The defenders surrendered with no hope of relief |
| Kantara (1229–30) | 10 months | The defenders surrendered with no hope of relief[e] |
| Beirut (1231–2) | Some months | The Lombards abandoned the siege[f] |
| Dieudamour (1232) | A few months? | The siege ended after the battle of Agridi[g] |
| Kyrenia (1232–3) | About 10 months, *or* more than a year | The defenders surrendered with no hope of relief[h] |
| Tyre (1242) | 4 weeks | The arrival of Filangieri, and his capture by the Ibelins, caused the Lombards to surrender[i] |
| Acre (1257–8) | A year, *or* 14 months | The Genoese fled after the defeat of their fleet[j] |
| Qaqun (1271) | A very short siege (if a siege took place) | The Christians fled, at the arrival of Muslim troops from 'Ain Jalut[k] |
| Tripoli (1278) | A number of days | The Templars abandoned the siege[l] |

[a] Ibn al-Athir, 'Kamel-Altevarykh', vol. II, p. 86; 'Eracles', vol. II, pp. 224–5; Roger of Howden, *Chronica*, vol. IV, pp. 28–9; *Chronique d'Ernoul*, p. 313; 'Chronica regia Coloniensis', p. 161.

[b] Ibn al-Athir, 'Kamel-Altevarykh', vol. II, pp. 87–8; *Continuation de Guillaume de Tyr (1184–1197)*, p. 197.

[c] 'Eracles', vol. II, p. 324; *Chronique d'Ernoul*, pp. 411–12; al-Makrizi, *Histoire d'Egypte*, p. 314; Oliver of Paderborn, 'Historia', pp. 165–7; James of Vitry, *Lettres*, p. 98; Ibn al-Athir, 'Kamel-Altevarykh', vol. II, pp. 113–14; Abu Shama, 'Livre des deux jardins', vol. V, pp. 163–4.

[d] 'Eracles', vol. II, pp. 344–6; *Chronique d'Ernoul*, pp. 424–6; al-Makrizi, *Histoire*

## Notes to table 6a (*cont.*)

*d'Egypte*, p. 327; Oliver of Paderborn, 'Historia', pp. 219–22, 225–6, 235–6; *History of the Patriarchs*, vol. IV, pp. 66–8.

[e] 'Eracles', vol. II, p. 377; *Gestes des Chiprois*, pp. 60, 68.

[f] 'Eracles', vol. II, p. 396; *Gestes des Chiprois*, p. 89.

[g] *Gestes des Chiprois*, p. 106.

[h] *Ibid.*, p. 116; 'Eracles', vol. II, pp. 400, 402.

[i] 'Eracles', vol. II, pp. 426–7; *Gestes des Chiprois*, pp. 134–5; *Urkunden der Republik Venedig*, vol. II, pp. 356–7.

[j] *Gestes des Chiprois*, pp. 150, 155; 'Rothelin', p. 635.

[k] *Gestes des Chiprois*, pp. 200–1; Ibn 'Abd al-Zahir, 'Life of Baybars', vol. II, p. 771.

[l] *Gestes des Chiprois*, pp. 204–5. See above, pp. 44, 138. This attack was probably more a raid than a serious attempt to capture the city.

## Table 6b. *The results of Muslim siege campaigns*

| | Muslim attack – Christian defence | |
|---|---|---|
| Siege | Time taken | How ended |
| Jaffa (1197) | Perhaps only a day. (But the course of events surely took longer.) | Successful assault[a] |
| Margat (1206) | Unclear | The Muslim army withdrew when its general was killed[b] |
| Caesarea (1218) | Probably not very long | Defenders fled in the face of a Muslim assault[c] |
| Crac (1218) | Not known | The castle was too strong for the besieging force[d] |
| Château Pèlerin (1220) | Less than a month | The siege was abandoned because of likely Christian reinforcement[e] |
| Jerusalem (1229) | 3 days | Besiegers were defeated by the garrison, supported by a relieving force[f] |
| Jerusalem (1239) | Unclear | Knights in the Tower of David resisted until a truce was agreed; the Muslims withdrew[g] |
| Jerusalem (1239–40) | Under a month | Assault caused the defenders to surrender[h] |
| Beaufort (1241) (Muslim defence) | Probably not very long | Engines forced Muslim surrender[i] |
| Jaffa (1242) | Continued for some time | Attackers withdrew[j] |

## Table 6b (*cont.*)

Muslim attack – Christian defence

| Siege | Time taken | How ended |
|---|---|---|
| Ascalon (1244–7) | Blockade then a short siege(?) | Engines and mines forced the defenders to flee[k] |
| Tiberias (1247) | Precise time uncertain – probably not very long | Taken by force with heavy Christian losses[l] |
| Sidon (1260) (Mongol attack) | Unknown | The Mongols withdrew. They had destroyed the town walls but could not capture either of the town's castles[m] |
| Caesarea (1265) | About a week, *or* 6 weeks (the former seems more likely) | With heavy attack by engines, the Christians conceded[n] |
| Haifa (1265) | Same day | Christians fled as the Muslims approached[o] |
| Arsuf (1265) | 6 weeks | The citadel fell with the engines having destroyed the walls[p] |
| Saphet (1266) | 6 weeks | The Christians surrendered after a hard fight[q] |
| Jaffa (1268) | A day | By assault, though some inhabitants had agreed to surrender the town[r] |
| Beaufort (1268) | Blockade, then 11-day siege | Under violent attack the defenders gave in[s] |
| Antioch (1268) | A few days | General assault and surrender[t] |
| Chastel Blanc (1271) | A blockade (precise time uncertain) | Christians surrendered[u] |
| Crac (1271) | 6 weeks | The Hospitallers surrendered after a heavy assault by engines[v] |
| Gibelcar (1271) | Just under 2 weeks | The defenders gave up after Muslim pressure by engines and assault[w] |
| Montfort (1271) | 7 days | Mangonels and mining caused the garrison to surrender[x] |
| Margat (1281) | Probably not very long | The Hospitallers drove off the Muslim attack[y] |
| Margat (1285) | 5–6 weeks | The Christians surrendered, primarily because of mining. There may have been a frontal assault[z] |
| Latakia (1287) | Less than a month | Engines prompted the Christian surrender[aa] |
| Tripoli (1289) | Between 4 and 6 weeks | Weakened by bombardment, then taken by assault[bb] |

# Sieges

## Table 6b (cont.)

| Siege | Muslim attack – Christian defence | |
| | Time taken | How ended |
| --- | --- | --- |
| Acre (1291) | 6 weeks. The Temple survived a further 10 days | Weakened by bombardment, taken by assault[ee] |
| Sidon (1291) | One day? | After some resistance, the Templars fled to Cyprus[dd] |

[a] 'Eracles', vol. II, pp. 218–21; Ibn al-Athir, 'Kamel-Altevarykh', vol. II, pp. 85–6; Arnold of Lübeck, 'Chronica', p. 204; *Continuation de Guillaume de Tyr (1184–1197)*, pp. 191–3.

[b] Ibn Wasil, 'Mufarridj al-Kurub fi Akhbar Bani Aiyub', in al-Makrizi, *Histoire d'Egypte*, p. 286, note 1.

[c] 'Eracles', vol. II, p. 334; *Chronique d'Ernoul*, pp. 422–3; Oliver of Paderborn, 'Historia', p. 244.

[d] Kamal al-Din, 'L'Histoire d'Alep', p. 55.

[e] Oliver of Paderborn, 'Historia', pp. 254–6.

[f] 'Eracles', vol. II, pp. 384–5; 'Rothelin', p. 489.

[g] 'Annales de Dunstaplia', p. 150; 'Annales Sancti Rudberti Salisburgenses', *MGHS*, vol. IX, p. 787; 'Annales Mellicenses Continuatio Lambacensis', *MGHS*, vol. IX, p. 559. For the chronology of the two attacks on Jerusalem in June 1239 and December 1239 – January 1240, see Jackson, 'The Crusades of 1239–41', pp. 38–9. The first attack was by as-Salih Aiyub's troops; the second was by soldiers under the command of an-Nasir Da'ud.

[h] Al-Makrizi, *Histoire d'Egypte*, pp. 452–3; Ibn al-Furat, *Ayyubids*, vol. II, p. 62.

[i] 'Rothelin', pp. 552–3.

[j] *History of the Patriarchs*, vol. IV, p. 269.

[k] 'Eracles', vol. II, pp. 433–4; 'Rothelin', p. 565; al-Makrizi, *Histoire d'Egypte*, pp. 490, 502.

[l] 'Eracles', vol. II, pp. 432–3; al-Makrizi, *Histoire d'Egypte*, p. 502.

[m] For further details of this siege, see above, p. 128. The siege was undertaken by Kitbugha's detachment of the Mongol army, the bulk of the Mongol force under Hulegu having withdrawn from Syria. See above, p. 31 and note 48.

[n] Ibn 'Abd al-Zahir, 'Life of Baybars', vol. II, pp. 555–7; 'Annales de Terre Sainte', pp. 451–2; al-'Ayni, 'Le Collier', p. 219.

[o] Ibn 'Abd al-Zahir, 'Life of Baybars', vol. II, p. 561; al-'Ayni, 'Le Collier', p. 220.

[p] 'Eracles', vol. II, p. 450; *Gestes des Chiprois*, p. 171; Ibn 'Abd al-Zahir, 'Life of Baybars', vol. II, pp. 562, 566.

[q] *Gestes des Chiprois*, pp. 179–80; Ibn 'Abd al-Zahir, 'Life of Baybars', vol. II, pp. 588, 596; 'Eracles', vol. II, pp. 454–5.

[r] 'Eracles', vol. II, p. 456; *Gestes des Chiprois*, p. 190; Ibn 'Abd al-Zahir, 'Life of Baybars', vol. II, p. 638.

## Notes to table 6b (cont.)

*Ibn 'Abd al-Zahir, 'Life of Baybars', vol. II, pp. 637, 641–5; al-'Ayni, 'Le Collier', pp. 226, 227.

*t* *Gestes des Chiprois*, p. 190; 'Eracles', vol. II, p. 456; Ibn 'Abd al-Zahir, 'Life of Baybars', vol. II, pp. 657–8; al-'Ayni, 'Le Collier', p. 229; 'Maius chronicon Lemovicense', p. 775.

*u* Ibn 'Abd al-Zahir, 'Life of Baybars', vol. II, p. 743. Baybars had already moved on to the siege of Crac, leaving a contingent of his army to continue with the siege of Chastel Blanc. According to this account, the garrison was ordered to surrender by the Templar commander at Tortosa.

*v* *Gestes des Chiprois*, p. 199; Marino Sanuto, 'Liber', p. 224; Ibn 'Abd al-Zahir, 'Life of Baybars', vol. II, pp. 743–4; 'Annales de Terre Sainte', p. 455; al-'Ayni, 'Le Collier', p. 237 (which suggests a much shorter siege).

*w* Ibn 'Abd al-Zahir, 'Life of Baybars', vol. II, pp. 748–9; al-'Ayni, 'Le Collier', p. 242; Abu'l-Fida, 'Annales', p. 153.

*x* Ibn 'Abd al-Zahir, 'Life of Baybars', vol. II, pp. 756–7; 'Annales de Terre Sainte', p. 455.

*y* *Gestes des Chiprois*, pp. 209–10.

*z* *Ibid.*, pp. 217–18; al-Makrizi, *Histoire des Sultans*, vol. II (a), p. 80; Ibn 'Abd al-Zahir, 'Vie de Kalavun', in Michaud, *Bibliothèque*, vol. IV, pp. 548–9.

*aa* Ibn 'Abd al-Zahir, 'Vie de Kalavun', in Michaud, *Histoire*, vol. VII, pp. 708–9, and in Michaud, *Bibliothèque*, vol. IV, p. 561.

*bb* *Gestes des Chiprois*, pp. 236–7; al-Makrizi, *Histoire des Sultans*, vol. II (a), p. 102; James Auria, 'Annales', p. 323; Abu'l-Fida, 'Annales', p. 162.

*cc* *Gestes des Chiprois*, pp. 243, 248–9, 255–6; *Cartulaire des Hospitaliers*, no. 4157; Abu'l-Fida, 'Annales', pp. 163–4 (and numerous other sources).

*dd* Al-Makrizi, *Histoire des Sultans*, vol. II (a), pp. 126–7 and note 13; *Gestes des Chiprois*, pp. 256–7.


strongholds for months. Even allowing for the protracted siege of Damietta, a campaign of well over six months appears to have been quite normal. And Christian sieges were almost invariably concluded, when successful, by means of attrition. Not once in this period did the Christians terminate a siege by an all-out assault. We saw earlier that at the siege of Kyrenia in 1232–3 John of Beirut regretted his use of a frontal attack; it was considered pointless to waste men when the castle would surrender through famine.[125] It was normally the case that the defenders, assuming that there was no prospect of relief, reached the point where they would have regarded any continued resistance as futile and costly. So Christian sieges depended on an effective blockade and a low-

---

[125] See above, p. 227.

key deployment of the siege weapons and other resources which they had at their disposal. These methods were, to a great extent, determined by the Latins' lack of manpower.

There were differences in the Muslim siege techniques which help to explain the much shorter time which they normally required to capture a strongpoint. It has already been noted that the Muslims adopted a far more direct approach in attack than the Christians: this point is reinforced by the evidence of the above table, where the majority of Muslim sieges were concluded with a violent assault by men and machines. The Muslims appear to have used the means at their disposal to greater effect than did the Christians. Moreover, accounts relating to Muslim sieges do seem to have a greater sense of urgency in them than do those describing a Christian attack. In the eye-witness account of Ibn 'Abd al-Zahir, for example (and allowing for exaggeration) the sultan Baybars was often portrayed personally directing operations at a siege and urging his troops on to even greater efforts.[126]

But the single most important reason for the success of Muslim siege campaigns against Christian targets was the former's access to so much larger manpower resources. Even though the numbers suggested for some of the Muslim armies in this period are scarcely credible, there is no doubt that Muslim commanders generally enjoyed a significant numerical advantage over their Christian opponents, which they were able to put to decisive use. The Christians, on the other hand, were obliged to defend their strongpoints with garrisons which, in relative terms, were clearly inadequate. This meant that their efforts had to be cautious: they could not usually afford to risk losing men by conducting an active defence, even though this might represent their best hope of saving a strongpoint. Muslim armies of the thirteenth century were willing to make use of the common Christian technique of the blockade – it has been noted at the sieges of Ascalon, Beaufort and Chastel Blanc – but whereas to the Latins this could almost be their entire means of attack, to the Muslims it seems to have been regarded as an introductory, weakening process before the main siege began. Once the siege was under way, Muslim tactics were directed towards achieving a quick, decisive result, often regardless of the cost in terms of manpower. Muslim commanders

[126] For example, at the siege of Arsuf (Ibn 'Abd al-Zahir, 'Life of Baybars', vol. II, pp. 564–5).

could afford to be unaffected by some of the qualms of their Latin counterparts.

The Muslims' manpower advantages often allowed them to start a siege from a position of considerable strength. This, coupled with their style of siege warfare, meant that any Christian garrison which was attacked immediately found itself under intense pressure. The Muslims could, if necessary, establish an even stronger position for themselves. Earlier, we saw that at Saphet, Beaufort and Crac, Baybars made use of psychological warfare to weaken the resistance of the garrison; the sultan had presumably realised that his opponents were already far from optimistic about their prospects of survival.[127] At a number of Muslim sieges during and after Baybars's sultanate, including Haifa (1265), Jaffa (1268) and Sidon (1291), the Christians fled almost without a blow being struck, again suggesting a deep-rooted sense of pessimism. The effects of raiding expeditions were particularly important. They helped to wear down resistance at the stronger Christian sites, such as Acre and Tripoli. As has already been pointed out, they could also be used to isolate major strongholds and to prevent other garrisons in the area from offering relief during a siege.[128]

The pressures which the Christians found themselves under inevitably led to recriminations and discord. A number of sources indicated that the strain was almost too much for the defenders at the siege of Acre. Ludolph of Suchem, for example, stated that even when the Muslims broke into the city, the Christians would not work together, preferring instead to organise resistance from within their individual fortifications. However, the suggestion that such disagreements significantly contributed to the loss of the city[129] is probably unjustified. The search for an explanation for the fall of Acre, and indeed for the capture of most other strongpoints in the Latin East, has to start with the Latins' shortage of manpower, particularly in comparison to their Muslim opponents. As has already been mentioned, the Muslims possibly outnumbered the Christians at the siege of Acre by eleven to one.[130] This is sufficient in itself to explain the loss of the city, particularly once its defences had been breached.

---

[127] See above, p. 235.     [128] See above, pp. 202–5.
[129] Ludolph of Suchem, 'De itinere', pp. 43–4; Ptolemy of Lucca, 'Historia Ecclesiastica', *RIS*, vol. xi, p. 1196; Eberhard of Ratispon, 'Annales', *MGHS*, vol. xvii, p. 594.
[130] See above, pp. 219, 222–3.

### THE AFTERMATH OF THE SIEGE

Muslim and Christian sources often gave different accounts when they discussed the treatment of defenders by a successful besieging force. Most western accounts of the siege of Damietta, for example, stated that Muslim deaths had only resulted from the course of the siege and not from its aftermath; Arabic sources, on the other hand, claimed that the crusaders had carried out a massacre.[131] Conversely, western sources naturally wished to paint the activities of their adversaries as black as possible. It was appropriate that Muslim troops should be pictured indulging in the wholesale slaughter of Christians as a matter of course. However, it appears that victorious Muslim armies were perhaps not as bloodthirsty as some contemporary western writers believed, and their treatment of military forces, especially, was generally very fair. This was particularly true during the campaigns of Baybars when, if a garrison surrendered, it could normally expect to be allowed to leave. Saphet, of course, was an exception to this; the Templars surrendered and were promised a safe passage, but they were subsequently all slaughtered.[132] It is possible that the stout defence of Arsuf in 1265 by the Hospitallers caused the Muslims to vent their frustrations on them even when the Christians had no further desire to resist. Western writers certainly believed that there had been a massacre and this view was shared by one Arabic source.[133]

Outside the period of Baybars's sultanate, there were a number of occasions – including at Jaffa (1197),[134] Ascalon (1247)[135] and Tiberias (1247)[136] – when a strongpoint's occupants were put to the sword. Later in the thirteenth century, however, a massacre tended to occur when a large Latin civilian element was present, suggesting either that panic may have caused confusion which in itself led to a massacre, or that the Muslims simply welcomed the opportunity to pillage an unprotected populace. The latter would

---

[131] For example, al-Makrizi, *Histoire d'Egypte*, p. 327.
[132] 'Eracles', vol. II, pp. 454–5; *Gestes des Chiprois*, pp. 180–1; Ibn 'Abd al-Zahir, 'Life of Baybars', vol. II, pp. 596–8; al-'Ayni, 'Le Collier', pp. 222–3.
[133] Shafi ibn-'Ali, 'Vie de Baibars', pp. 672–3; Ibn 'Abd al-Zahir, 'Life of Baybars', vol. II, pp. 570–1 (where it is stated that the defenders were imprisoned); 'Annales de Terre Sainte', p. 452; Marino Sanuto, 'Liber', p. 222; John Vitoduranus, 'Chronica', p. 17.
[134] Roger of Howden, *Chronica*, vol. IV, p. 26; Arnold of Lübeck, 'Chronica', p. 204.
[135] 'Eracles', vol. II, p. 434; 'Rothelin', p. 565. A number of the defenders were able to escape.      [136] 'Eracles', vol. II, pp. 432–3; *Gestes des Chiprois*, p. 146.

seem to have been the case when the Muslims first attempted to occupy the Tower of the Templars at Acre in 1291, though on this occasion their behaviour led to their own deaths.[137] In addition to Acre, there were massacres at Antioch (1268)[138] and Tripoli (1289).[139] Capitulation to the Muslims was therefore not necessarily an assurance of peace and freedom, but neither was it a guarantee of indiscriminate slaughter. On the Christian side, the Lombard–Ibelin siege campaigns normally ended with peace terms being agreed by the two sides.[140] This, however, is more an indication of the inability of Christian attackers to complete a siege by force than it is of inter-Christian respect and trust. It further underlines the different approaches to siege warfare of Muslim and Christian troops during this period.

## THE SIEGES OF DAMIETTA (1218–19) AND ACRE (1291)

An examination has now been made of a number of different aspects of siege warfare, from the preparations for a campaign to events after a successful capture. It remains to be shown (at the risk of some repetition) how Christian and Muslim armies applied themselves through the full length of a siege. We noted earlier that to use isolated accounts of individual sieges as a basis for generalisations would be unsatisfactory.[141] However, as in the case of battles, accounts of individual engagements can be used to test some of the conclusions which have been reached. Two sieges which are well documented for this purpose are the Christian siege of Damietta in 1218–19 and the Muslim siege of Acre in 1291.

Before the army of the Fifth Crusade set off from Acre in May 1218, it acquired galleys and other vessels, enough food for six months, horses and baggage. On arrival in Egypt, it was similarly

---

[137] *Gestes des Chiprois*, pp. 255–6; al-Yunini, quoted in D. P. Little, 'The Fall of 'Akka in 690/1291: The Muslim Version', in *Studies in Islamic History and Civilization*, ed. M. Sharon (Jerusalem, 1986), p. 175. There had already been a large-scale slaughter of the city's occupants. See James Auria, 'Annales', p. 337; *Cartulaire des Hospitaliers*, no. 4157; Abu'l-Fida, 'Annales', p. 164.

[138] 'Eracles', vol. II, pp. 456–7; *Gestes des Chiprois*, pp. 190–1; Ibn 'Abd al-Zahir, 'Life of Baybars', vol. II, pp. 657–8; al-'Ayni, 'Le Collier', p. 229; *Chronique d'Amadi*, p. 210; al-Makrizi, *Histoire des Sultans*, vol. I (b), p. 53.

[139] *Gestes des Chiprois*, pp. 236–7; al-Makrizi, *Histoire des Sultans*, vol. II (a), pp. 102–3; James Auria, 'Annales', p. 324; 'Annales de Terre Sainte', p. 460; Abu'l-Fida, 'Annales', p. 162.

[140] For example, at Kyrenia (1229), Dieudamour (1230) and Kantara (1230) (*Gestes des Chiprois*, pp. 60, 68).     [141] See above, pp. 211–12.

meticulous in its arrangements and showed especial vigilance in its defensive measures. The troops surrounded their camp on the west bank with a fosse and a wall. Then they set up a number of engines, including eight mangonels which maintained a constant assault on the city. The crusaders faced substantial opposition. In addition to the garrison of Damietta, a Muslim force led by al-Kamil established itself on the east bank of the Nile, at a location where it could both maintain contact with the city and oppose any attempt by the crusader army to cross the river.

An initial problem for the crusaders was the Chain Tower in the middle of the Nile, which controlled the movement of shipping up and down the river. Oliver of Paderborn reported that some Frisians had been able to cross to the east bank, but although their position was reasonably secure, they were called back because of the danger of leaving the tower behind the crusader army. An assault on the tower by engines or mines would have been impracticable, and a blockade could not be maintained, so the crusaders had to rely on a seaborne attack. Early efforts by crusader ships were repulsed by Muslims from the city, tower and bridge, but a remarkable assault craft built by Oliver and the Frisians proved more successful. This vessel was constructed out of two ships which had been bound together. It was covered with hides, to provide protection against Greek fire, and had a ladder incorporated into its design. The Muslims used both engines and Greek fire in their efforts to drive off the attack. The Greek fire proved particularly effective. It was thrown from both the tower and the city, and was largely directed against a small ship which accompanied the assault vessel. The fire was successfully extinguished by vinegar and sand; after a hard fight, the crusaders were able to take possession of the Chain Tower.

In spite of this success, however, the crusaders were prevented from taking the initiative, largely because of the Muslims' well-organised defensive measures. Throughout the winter of 1218–19, al-Kamil was able to block the Nile, first by the construction of a dike, then by the sinking of boats in the channel. The crusaders did manage to open the al-Azraq canal, which enabled their ships to sail up the Nile, but still they failed to put direct pressure upon the city itself. In the period immediately after their loss of the Chain Tower, the Muslim troops under al-Kamil adopted an aggressive defence policy and raided the Christian position on the west bank a number of times. However, having sustained heavy losses in these raids, they resorted to a more passive defence. They had established a well-fortified site on the east bank, with fosses, high wooden defences, a variety of ballistic weapons and large numbers of troops. The Muslim soldiers were organised into three ranks, with shieldbearers in the first two and the last mounted. They harassed Christian vessels with stones, darts and other projectiles. But they were forced to pull back from this excellent defensive position because of a quarrel over the succession to the sultan al-'Adil. In February 1219, the crusader army was therefore very fortunate in being able to cross to the east bank unhindered and thus to commence a full blockade and siege of the city.

The crusaders once again took care to establish themselves in a strong defensive position. They constructed a fosse, palisades, towers and a rampart behind which were archers and other soldiers deployed defensively. Two bridges across the Nile ensured good communication with the Christians who were still on the west bank, and two islands were also fortified. In addition to their land defences, crusader ships patrolled the Nile. This stable Christian defence was extremely important. The Muslim army under al-Kamil, following its retreat in February 1219, had re-assembled near Ashmun, about fifteen miles south of Damietta. Then it had moved north to Fariskur, not far from its original position on the east bank and close enough to maintain constant pressure on the crusaders. The leaders of the crusader army acknowledged that they did not have sufficient troops to deal effectively with both the city and the Muslim relief force. Moreover, it was proving difficult to maintain the army's strength at an acceptable level. Around May 1219, many crusaders, including the duke of Austria, decided to return home; fortunately reinforcements from the west arrived and this allowed the siege to continue. The legate Pelagius is reported to have offered an additional indulgence in order to keep the army together. The crusaders did have to face a number of attacks from the Muslim relief force based at Fariskur, but at the same time they made some efforts against the city walls, using cats, trebuchets, petraries, wooden towers, assaults from ships and mines. The mining was intended not only to damage the city walls but also to give the Christians access to one of the city towers. However, Damietta's moat was full of water, so this idea proved to be to no avail. The Muslim garrison drove off the assaults on the city with ballistic weapons, arrows, Greek fire and stones, whilst at the same time sorties from the city destroyed many of the Christians' armaments. It seems that the assaults by the crusaders were of no great significance in bringing the siege to a successful conclusion; there is little evidence to suggest that much damage had been done to the city.

The constant threat posed by the Muslim force at Fariskur prevented the crusaders from directing all their resources against the city itself. Their decision to attack the Muslim camp, in August 1219, was therefore understandable, although it ended in disaster. Despite this setback, the siege of the city continued and it eventually came to an end, in November 1219, when the Muslim defenders had been worn down by the continual Christian blockade (which resulted in plague and famine) and disheartened by the inability of al-Kamil to provide any effective relief. The care with which the crusaders had established themselves when they came to the east bank in February 1219 largely determined the progress of the siege. Damietta is an example of a situation where the attackers, although unable to capture a strongpoint by means of an assault, were at the same time not so weak that they had to withdraw in the face of a relieving force. The city fell because it had been successfully blockaded and the Christian defensive position ensured that this blockade could not be broken.[142]

The siege of Acre in 1291 took a very different course. It is unfortunate that much of the available evidence, particularly from western sources, was more concerned with events once the Muslims had actually made their entry into the city and the siege was virtually ended. But there is still plenty of material on the siege itself.

Some western writers suggested that before the main Muslim assault a smaller Muslim force had been positioned in the vicinity of Acre for about a month, in order to harass the occupants of the city. The sultan al-Ashraf arrived in early April, accompanied by an army from Egypt. Troops from Syria had also been ordered to

---

[142] An account from 'Eracles', vol. II, pp. 326–46; *Chronique d'Ernoul*, pp. 415–26; al-Makrizi, *Histoire d'Egypte*, pp. 314–27; *History of the Patriarchs*, vol. IV, pp. 43–68; 'Gesta obsidionis', pp. 74–113; 'Fragmentum de captione Damiatae', pp. 169–98; Oliver of Paderborn, 'Historia', pp. 175–226; 'Gesta crucigerorum Rhenanorum', in *QBSSM*, pp. 44–5 (a text closely related to Oliver of Paderborn's 'Historia'); James of Vitry, *Lettres*, pp. 100, 103–10, 114–32; Ibn al-Athir, 'Kamel-Altevarykh', vol. II, pp. 114–19.

attend and to bring their siege engines. Wood had been prepared in Syria for machines; many engines were transported from hundreds of miles away. Once the Muslim troops had been assembled, they began to set up their engines and prepare defensive positions, with ditches, palisades and portable wooden shelters. A number of writers suggested that the Muslims were able to surround the landward side of the city; if this is true, then it is further evidence for the exceptionally large size of their army. Meanwhile, the Christians also made their preparations. They organised their supplies of engines, palisades, stones, bows and arrows, lances, hooks and other implements, and determined how each part of the city would be defended.

When the Muslims began their attack, one of their first requirements was to overcome the obstacle of the fosse, in order that their miners, stonemasons and short-range weapons could be used to maximum effect. They appear to have achieved this objective without serious losses, although at this stage the Christians were able to mount an active defence of the city. We noted earlier that the defenders organised a number of sorties, but in the last of these the Muslims were ready for them and were able to inflict serious damage. As a result of this setback, the Christians decided to conduct their defence from behind the city walls and thus the initiative passed firmly to the Muslims. The latter maintained a constant bombardment with their engines and this, coupled with the tunnelling of a number of mines, allowed them to make gradual progress in their assault. The attack ranged from the north end of the city to the south, but it was particularly heavy in the area of the north-eastern angle of the old city walls, near the Accursed Tower. The Christians were obliged to abandon and set fire to the barbican of King Hugh; they also tried to counter-mine but this proved unsuccessful. The King's Tower sustained such heavy damage that the Muslims were able to force a path into it, thereby making their first entry into the city. The desperate Christians whose numbers were falling, not only because of casualties but also as people fled, brought up a cat in order to defend themselves and to block any further Muslim progress through the King's Tower. They also used their engines against this advanced Muslim position and managed to kill a number of their enemies.

But any further Christian resistance was swept aside in the fury of the Muslim assault on 18 May: again the attack was concentrated on the angle of the walls. Once the Muslims had gained access to the Accursed Tower, in the inner line of the walls, they swept through the city in all directions and the Christians were reduced to hand-to-hand fighting. The brothers of the Military Orders performed particularly bravely in the face of this assault. They held up the Muslim advance for a while at St Anthony's Gate before they were overwhelmed by sheer weight of numbers. When the Templars were suppressed nearly twenty years later, many witnesses still recalled their courage at that time, and particularly the heroism of their Master, William of Beaujeu, who was mortally wounded in the Muslim attack. Mounted Muslims managed to force another entry at the Tower of the Legate, on the shoreline. The French regiment under John of Grailly and the troops led by Otto of Grandison were obliged to retreat, with heavy casualties. The remainder of the siege is a tale of panic and slaughter, but some Christians staged a final defence in the Tower of the Templars, situated in the south-west of the city (a site which is now mostly below the shoreline). Ten days later, the tower was mined and the building collapsed as the sultan ordered his men into it – again, Muslim disregard for loss of life is apparent. A number of Christians had been able to flee but many were slaughtered or imprisoned. Finally, the city was demolished and burned.[143]

### CONCLUSION

When the leaders of Christian and Muslim states resorted to warfare, the capture of strongpoints through a siege was the prime means of ensuring the permanent acquisition of territory. An effective performance throughout a siege campaign was therefore crucial to the commanders of both the Muslim and Christian forces. However, most sieges in and around the Latin East were fought with relatively small numbers of men (at least, on the Latin side) and with equipment which showed little development during the course of the thirteenth century.

Despite these limitations, Muslim and Christian armies

---

[143] An account from *Gestes des Chiprois*, pp. 241, 243–56; al-Makrizi, *Histoire des Sultans*, vol. II (a), pp. 121–6; *Cartulaire des Hospitaliers*, no. 4157; *Chronique d'Amadi*, pp. 219–26; 'Annales de Terre Sainte', pp. 460–1; 'De excidio urbis Acconis', cols. 765–83; Abu'l-Fida, 'Annales', pp. 163–4; 'Processus Cypricus', pp. 155–6, 394; *Procès des Templiers*, ed. J. Michelet (2 vols., Paris, 1841–51), vol. I, p. 187; Marino Sanuto, 'Liber', pp. 230–1; Little, 'The Fall of 'Akka', pp. 165–77.

employed a variety of tactics in order to try to achieve their aims. In attack, Christian armies sought to wear down their enemies gradually by maintaining constant low-level pressure and an effective blockade. These methods could reduce a garrison to a state where it was no longer able to resist. The Muslims were far more direct in their approach. They would immediately press for a result and utilise fully the means which were available – particularly the vast quantities of manpower which they sometimes had at their disposal. The Muslims were therefore able to complete their sieges in weeks; a typical Christian assault would take many months. In defence, too, tactics varied enormously. An active defence could mean that a garrison waited to confront an attacker outside the strongpoint. In less favourable circumstances, the defenders might prefer to remain behind the strongpoint's walls, try to contain the enemy's attack and hope that it would fade away. The Christians, who were constantly handicapped by manpower difficulties, were often obliged to resort to a passive defence, even when it must have been clear that this gave the initiative to their opponents.

The Muslims' siege techniques enabled them to drive the Christians from the mainland, with the capture of their principal surviving strongholds in the period 1265–91. However, throughout the thirteenth century the Christians continued to show both courage and, as at Damietta in 1218, ingenuity in the course of a variety of siege campaigns. Christian achievements in siege warfare, particularly when faced by overwhelming odds, should not be underestimated.

# CONCLUSION

The thirteenth century was a period of mixed fortunes for the west in its wars against the Muslims and other enemies of the Church. In Spain, for example, Christian victory at the battle of Las Navas de Tolosa in 1212 was recognised by contemporaries as a turning point in the Reconquista. Cordoba was captured by Ferdinand III of Castile in 1236 and Seville surrendered in 1248.[1] The conquest of Greece by the Fourth Crusade in 1204 established the Latin Empire of Constantinople; it was lost in 1261. Elsewhere, crusading continued in the Baltic; it enjoyed a modicum of success against the heretics in Languedoc; and it was used, on occasion, by the papacy against its political opponents.

Despite this wide range of activities, the defence of the Latin Kingdom of Jerusalem remained, in the context of the Holy War, the single most important area of conflict. The loss of the Holy Land in 1291 therefore had a profound impact on Christendom. The reactions of contemporary writers to the fall of Acre varied from reasoned criticism to eschatological hysteria. But the need for such writers to explain the event, the shock which the event created and the fact that the loss was generally regarded as a temporary one suggest that perhaps the most widespread feeling was one of surprise.

This study, however, has shown that the fall of Acre, whilst of major significance since it marked the end of Latin rule in the area, cannot be regarded as unexpected. Rather, it was the inevitable outcome of a period of forty years during which the Latin East, largely unsupported by the western states which had established, and then helped to re-create, the Latin Kingdom of Jerusalem, had been opposed by the united threat of the Muslim states in the region. Most of the damage had, in fact, been done by the end of

---

[1] J. S. C. Riley-Smith, *The Crusades*, pp. 139–41, 165–6.

the 1260s; only a few sites, mainly on the coast, were able to survive until the end.

The chronic lack of manpower from which the Latin states suffered, relative to their Muslim neighbours, was apparent in every aspect of the military history of this period and had a profound effect on Christian strategy. Try as they might, the Latins were unable to increase their military establishment to anything like a level which might have given them some hope of success in combatting the Muslim threat. The feudal levy, by itself, had never been adequate. This force was usefully, and permanently, augmented by the Military Orders. But these two elements could never, without significant external support, hope to defend the Latin East against a concerted and long-term Muslim assault. Unfortunately the only time that the Latin states had sufficient troops to face the Muslims was when a crusade expedition had been organised by the west – and this, of course, could at best only provide a short-term respite for the Latins. The presence in the east, from the end of St Louis's first crusade until the fall of the kingdom, of troops permanently stationed there by the French crown, was precisely the kind of support which the Latin East needed. But the French regiment was far too small, on its own, to make anything more than a marginal impact on the military situation in the region. And although some people in the west had realised that the permanent provision of large numbers of troops was the only means to provide for an effective defence of the kingdom, in practice virtually nothing was done.

So the Latin East was left, for much of the time, on its own to defend its dwindling territories against the Muslim armies. The Latins' response was to adopt a defensive strategy which relied on the ability of garrison forces to defend a series of independent, and increasingly isolated, strongpoints. Ultimately this strategy resulted in the loss, one by one, of the remaining Christian castles and fortified towns although, given the problems which the Latins faced, it is impossible to believe that any alternative strategy could have proved more effective. Christian strategy could only be modified when more troops became available, thus allowing a field army to be created. This happened at the time of crusade expeditions, although the results were not always as positive as might have been expected.

The capture and defence of territory, if the military option was selected, came about through a combination of raids, battles and sieges. The Christians' lack of manpower severely affected their performance in each of these fields of military activity. The Muslim armies used raiding expeditions, for example, as a part of their wider strategy which aimed at the elimination of the Christians from the area. Raids could be used to distract the Latins from the true target of an expedition or, as in the case of major Christian centres of resistance such as Acre, to weaken a site before a major campaign against it was organised. For the Christians, on the other hand, by the second half of the thirteenth century raids had become, in the absence of any realistic prospect of permanent territorial gains, the sole means of taking the military initiative against their Muslim neighbours. Although a Christian raid was likely to result in Muslim reprisals which could leave the Christians in a worse state than when they started, more and more Christian troops continued to be deployed in less and less profitable excursions. By the 1260s, even the arrival of crusader armies might only lead to some raiding expeditions being organised.

The Latins' deployment of most of their available troops as garrison forces meant that in attack they were extremely unlikely to seek a confrontation in open battle with a Muslim army, whilst in defence they relied upon the combined strength of their strongpoints and the men inside them to deal with any Muslim incursion. The strongpoints could not hinder the progress of a Muslim invading force, but, provided the Muslims were unsuccessful in any efforts to capture a castle or town by siege, their army would make no permanent territorial gains and it would be obliged eventually to withdraw. A battle–seeking strategy therefore normally had no part to play in the Latins' efforts to maintain their kingdom. However, the arrival of a crusade expedition in the area frequently led to a campaign in which a battle took place. Unfortunately such battles were then fought, on the Christian side, by troops who for the most part had little appreciation of the tactics which a Muslim army could be expected to employ against them. At Gaza in 1239, and at Mansurah in 1250, Christian soldiers charged to their fates, ignoring the advice and appeals of men from the Latin East. When Muslim and Christian armies clashed in open battle during this period, it was almost without exception the former who held the initiative throughout the course of the conflict. Battles, for whatever reason they were fought, usually resulted in a defeat or, at best, a costly victory for a Christian field army; either way, the impact on the course of a campaign was usually a negative one.

The Latins' efforts, with the aid of crusaders, to achieve territorial expansion therefore foundered on the battlefields of Egypt and Palestine. The Muslims' attempts to take possession of Christian territory, on the other hand, succeeded through a series of well-planned siege campaigns directed against the surviving Christian castles and fortified towns during the second half of the thirteenth century. The Latins, in defence, were obliged to rely solely on themselves. Their garrisons, buoyed up to some extent by the massive fortifications at sites such as Saphet, Crac and Margat, were still virtually helpless when facing an assault by Muslim armies which frequently numbered thousands against the Christians' hundreds. Many sites, not surprisingly, were surrendered without a fight. At others the garrison conceded as soon as it became clear that there was no hope of a reprieve. Only at one or two sites, including Acre, was the fight continued to the end. Then a wholesale slaughter with little prospect of mercy could be anticipated.

The demise of the Latins in Palestine and Syria was inevitable from the time of the accession of the Mamluk sultan Baybars in 1260. We may therefore finish with two points. First, the Latin states in the thirteenth century enjoyed a period, lasting at least until the failure of St Louis's crusade, in which there was no genuine threat to their continued survival. Indeed, at times during this period the Muslims were far more threatened than they were a threat. Both the Fifth Crusade and St Louis's crusade were able to shake, if not topple, the Aiyubid sultanate in Egypt. In Syria the Hospitallers and Templars were able to maintain some degree of control over the activities of their Muslim neighbours. The willingness and ability of the majority of the Latin East's feudatories to oppose the demands of Frederick II is further evidence of the comparative vitality of the kingdom during the first half of the thirteenth century.

Finally, and even after the accession of Baybars, there was life left in the Latin East. Debates, disputes – over the regency of the kingdom, for example – and civil conflicts continued. The War of St Sabas virtually destroyed the city of Acre in the years immediately preceding the start of Baybars's campaigns against the Latins. As late as 1282, the Embriaco faction tried, by military means, to gain control of Tripoli. Throughout the second half of the thirteenth century the Latins were undoubtedly psychologically under siege – this is apparent in the letters which they sent to the west during this period. However, the nature of medieval warfare meant that they were not threatened, in a constant physical sense, by Muslim armies. In a kingdom whose fate had effectively been decided, life was still able to go on.

*Appendix*

# SCOUTS, SPIES AND TRAITORS

In all aspects of warfare, the more prudent Latin and Muslim commanders recognised the potential consequences of being ill-informed about an enemy's movements and plans, and they therefore sought to obtain as much information as possible about their opponents. This could be done in three ways. First, members of the army could be dispatched to carry out a reconnaissance. Secondly, men could attempt to infiltrate an enemy force. Contemporary accounts do not always make a clear distinction between these two methods; terms such as 'coreors' and 'espies' seem to be largely interchangeable. But one can usually distinguish, if only by inference, between scouting and more covert forms of activity. Thirdly, members of the opposing army could be persuaded to provide information. All of these methods were used, and with a fair degree of success, during this period.

The employment of scouts by Christian armies has already been considered. Their functions would have included both foraging (as in a raid against Sidon in 1217–18, for example)[1] and reporting on any hostile presence in the area. The turcopoles appear to have performed an important role on reconnaissance.[2] Muslim armies also used scouts to report on the whereabouts and activities of Christian forces. As with their Christian counterparts, they had to perform both reconnaissance and raiding duties. In July 1221, for example, as the army of the Fifth Crusade progressed southwards towards Mansurah, Muslim scouts were positioned on both sides of the Nile. They not only observed the movements of the crusader army; they also tried, unsuccessfully, to inflict damage on it.[3] We shall return to the work of Muslim scouts later, when some of the events before the battle of Gaza in 1239 are considered; they show careful use of both scouts and spies by the Muslim sultan and his military commander.

---

[1] See above, p. 196.     [2] See above, p. 59.
[3] Oliver of Paderborn, 'Historia', p. 260.

# Appendix

Spies were concerned with the covert gathering of intelligence from within an opposing army.[4] They had the potential to obtain far more information than would be available to the scouts. The latter might only report an army's current location; a spy, on the other hand, could discover where the army intended to go and, even more important, what it intended to do. The Muslims, in addition to their employment of spies, may also have encouraged the casual collection of information by the indigenous population of the Latin states. The Latins were very much a minority in their territories, being outnumbered not only by the Syrian Christians but, even more, by the Muslims.[5] Both these native groups must at times have felt an affinity with the kingdom's external enemies; in the case of the Muslims, their sympathies would have been strengthened by their religious ties. Thus in 1271, for example, Baybars received information about the progress of St Louis's second crusade from 'certain loyal persons in Acre'.[6]

The Latins' employment of native troops in their armies meant that they ran the risk of betrayal by individuals from these indigenous groups.[7] There was also the possibility that enemy soldiers might infiltrate a Christian army or camp by passing themselves off as turcopoles. In 1203–4, Aimery of Lusignan, who was organising a raid into the Galilee region, appears to have recognised the harm which could be done by casual listeners or hostile spies. His expedition was due to depart from Acre in the evening; at midday, the gates of the city were locked so that men

---

[4] This was by no means the only function of spies in this period. They were also expected to report on the long-term political, economic and military plans of both enemies and allies, hence some of Fidenzio of Padua's remarks in a section headed 'De exploratoribus' ('Liber recuperationis', p. 33). Fidenzio noted that the sultan always used scouts and spies, since he wished to know as much as possible about the Christians, 'not only in places which are near at hand, but also in far-off regions' ('non solum in partibus propinquis, sed etiam in partibus remotis'). Under the Mamluk sultan Baybars, espionage activities of this sort, against both external and internal targets, were the preserve of an independent department (A. A. Khowayter, *Baibars the First* (London, 1978), pp. 39–42). See also R. Amitai, 'Mamluk Espionage among Mongols and Franks', in *The Medieval Levant*, ed. B. Z. Kedar and A. L. Udovitch (Haifa, 1988), pp. 173–81. Amitai's article concentrates, for the most part, on Mamluk espionage against the Mongols.

[5] Smail, *Crusading Warfare*, p. 40; see above, p. 125.

[6] Ibn 'Abd al-Zahir, 'Life of Baybars', vol. II, p. 752. See also Amitai, 'Mamluk Espionage', p. 175.

[7] At the siege of Beaufort in 1268, for example. See above, p. 235.

could neither enter nor leave, thereby preventing the Muslims from learning of the Christians' plans.[8]

Muslim spies were able to penetrate a number of Christian armies and obtain intelligence which influenced the subsequent decision-making of Muslim commanders. In 1220 during the Fifth Crusade, al-Mu'azzam, the prince of Damascus, besieged Château Pèlerin. After less than a month, the siege was abandoned when al-Mu'azzam learned, from spies and informants, that the site was shortly to be reinforced by a substantial number of Templars from Egypt.[9] In late 1249, during St Louis's first crusade, the Christian army marched up the Nile towards Mansurah. Louis had given orders, before the march began, that no members of the army were to charge against a force of 500 Muslim cavalry which had been sent to harass them. The Muslims learned from their spies of Louis's instructions, and this encouraged them to close in on the crusaders' advance guard, which contained a large number of Templars. The assault was eventually beaten off, with the Muslims having sustained heavy casualties.[10]

The Christians could benefit from information which had been obtained by spies operating inside a Muslim army. Christian spies, in this context, presumably had to be either Syrian Christians or Muslims, whose appearance and behaviour would have allowed them to infiltrate the Muslim force. In February 1250, a few days after the battle of Mansurah on St Louis's first crusade, the Christian army learned from spies in the Muslim camp that the Muslims were planning to mount a major offensive the following day. This information enabled the Christians to prepare their defensive positions and the Muslim attack was repulsed. By contrast, the morning after the battle of Mansurah, the Christians had not anticipated a Muslim attack which took place; it was some time before they were able to organise themselves to deal with the threat.[11] It is possible that discipline within the crusader army had been allowed to lapse in the period immediately following the hard-fought battle.

During Baybars's siege of Montfort in 1271, a spy who had infiltrated the Muslim army tried to send a message to the

---

[8] 'Eracles', vol. II, p. 259.
[9] Oliver of Paderborn, 'Historia', pp. 254–6. The text refers to 'exploratores et Christianorum proditores'.    [10] Joinville, *Histoire de Saint Louis*, p. 102.
[11] *Ibid.*, pp. 140–54.

Christians. The message, which was carried by a bird, was intercepted when the creature was shot by Baybars. According to the sultan's biographer, Baybars then passed the message on to some Christian envoys from Acre.[12] The story is probably apocryphal, but Baybars's lack of surprise at the presence of a spy in the Muslim camp does show that such activities were a common feature of warfare in this period.

Spies also provided useful information during the conflict between the Ibelins and the imperial forces. In the autumn of 1231, the emperor Frederick II dispatched to the east a fleet which included 600 knights, 100 mounted squires, 700 footsoldiers and 3,000 marines. An Ibelin spy, who had been on board a galley belonging to the Teutonic Knights, had learned of the imperial fleet's intentions. When the Ibelins received the spy's report, they moved most of their troops from the mainland to Cyprus, since they believed that an attack would be directed against the island. However, when the imperial fleet arrived off Cyprus it concluded that it was too weak to confront the Ibelin army, so it sailed on to Beirut and commenced a lengthy (though ultimately unsuccessful) siege of the city and castle.[13] The imperial force abandoned the siege of Beirut in 1232 and withdrew to Tyre; but it then learned from spies that the Ibelins had set up a camp at Casal Imbert. The spies also reported that the Ibelins had few men and were badly camped. This information encouraged the imperialists to attack the Ibelins and inflict a heavy defeat on them.[14]

Information provided by spies could, therefore, enable an army to perform more effectively against its opponents. This point is further reinforced by two occasions when reports from spies were ignored. After the capture of Damietta by the army of the Fifth Crusade, spies reported to the papal legate Pelagius that the Muslims were preparing a fleet to attack Christian ships sailing to and from Egypt. Pelagius refused to believe this report and sent the spies away, although he did give instructions for them to be given food and drink. Later, when the Muslim ships had set sail, the spies again warned Pelagius and, again, he did not accept that the information might be accurate, preferring to believe that they were still hungry and thirsty. He was only convinced that the

---

[12] Ibn 'Abd al-Zahir, 'Life of Baybars', vol. II, p. 756.
[13] *Gestes des Chiprois*, pp. 77–9; 'Eracles', vol. II, p. 386.
[14] *Gestes des Chiprois*, p. 91; 'Eracles', vol. II, p. 396; see above, p. 158.

spies had been telling the truth when he learned that the Muslim fleet had caused serious damage to Christian shipping in the area.[15] Before the battle of Casal Imbert in 1232, Ibelin spies had alerted Anceau of Brie, the commander of the Ibelin camp, to the approach of the imperial army. Anceau ignored this report and mocked his informants, asking why the Lombards would attack now, given that they had declined every opportunity to force a confrontation during their siege of Beirut. His confidence soon proved to be misplaced, as the Ibelin camp was overrun.[16]

The events leading up to the battle of Gaza in 1239 provide some good examples of how information obtained from both scouts and spies could affect the outcome of a campaign.[17] The crusaders and the native Latins had gathered at Acre to discuss their possible courses of action. They eventually decided to build a frontier stronghold in the south at Ascalon, then to lessen the threat to the kingdom from the east by an attack on Damascus.[18] As-Salih Isma'il, the prince of Damascus, had learned of both these decisions from his spies. Moreover, when al-'Adil II, the sultan of Egypt, had been informed of the arrival in the east of Theobald's crusade, he had also sent spies to Acre to discover the crusaders' plans. They were able to find out that the intention was to fortify Ascalon and, in response to this information, al-'Adil dispatched a force of up to 2,000 men under Rukn-ad-Din al-Hijawi to guard the frontier.[19] It appears that both Isma'il and al-'Adil had managed to penetrate the crusader army at a level which gave them some idea of its objectives. They could, therefore, take pre-emptive action to forestall its plans.

The crusaders left Acre and eventually reached Jaffa, where one of their own 'spies' reported that al-Hijawi's force was camped at Gaza. If the 'Eracles' account is to be believed, then this spy passed his information to the Templars,[20] which indicates that he may have been a turcopole who had been sent out on reconnaissance. The count of Bar, and many others, now left the

[15] *Chronique d'Ernoul*, pp. 429–30.
[16] 'Eracles', vol. II, pp. 396–7; *Gestes des Chiprois*, p. 91.
[17] The battle itself has been considered above, pp. 177–81.
[18] 'Rothelin', pp. 531–2; see above, p. 73.
[19] 'Rothelin', pp. 533, 537; 'Eracles', vol. II, p. 414 (where a figure of 1,050 Turks is quoted for the size of the Muslim army); *History of the Patriarchs*, vol. IV, p. 195 (which provides the figure of 2,000 men). See also Jackson, 'The Crusades of 1239–41', p. 39.
[20] 'Eracles', vol. II, p. 414; *Gestes des Chiprois*, pp. 118–19 (which stated only that the spy reported to the army as a whole).

main army in search of booty. Those who chose not to go, including Theobald himself and the members of the Military Orders, tried to persuade the count to call off the raid; amongst the arguments which they put forward was the likelihood that Muslim scouts would be watching the routes in the area. The situation was actually rather worse than this. Al-Hijawi had sent his spies into the Christian army to find out its intentions and he was able to monitor its progress as it moved southwards towards Gaza. Once again, the crusader army had been infiltrated with damaging consequences. The crusaders themselves, by contrast, appear to have made no attempt to find out whether there was any hostile activity in the vicinity.

Al-Hijawi had augmented his force with large numbers of additional troops. He realised that both the crusaders and their horses would be tired after what had been an all-night march, and he therefore saw this as an opportunity to achieve a success in battle. He continued to receive reports from his spies and, once the crusaders had made camp, he sent out scouts to establish both their numbers and their precise circumstances. Only when this had been done did he allow the attack on the crusader camp to begin.[21]

The information which the Muslims had gathered on this occasion was not, in itself, decisive. The outcome of the battle was determined, first, by the Christian army's shortage of arrows (which allowed the Muslims to advance with impunity) and secondly, by the knights' willingness to pursue a Muslim feigned retreat, a manoeuvre which left the crusaders in a state of disarray from which they found it impossible to recover. Nonetheless, the Muslims' acquisition of information about the crusaders' movements and their plans was clearly of considerable benefit in the period leading up to the battle. It enabled the Muslims to begin the encounter from a position of strength. Moreover, the Christians were significantly disadvantaged as a result of their ignorance of Muslim activity until the point when they were actually under attack.

We now turn to the activities of traitors – people who were prepared, for whatever reason, to betray their own side and pass information to, or act on behalf of, the enemy. The motivation of traitors cannot always be established, but they could cause

[21] 'Rothelin', pp. 538–42.

severe harm. All the following examples are from the Lombard – Ibelin conflict. During the siege of Beirut in 1231–2, a former castellan of the castle called 'Denis' showed the imperialists where they should place their siege engines in order to inflict the greatest damage on the castle. 'Denis' was eventually hanged because of his traitorous activities – presumably by the Ibelins, although this was not actually stated.[22] When the Ibelins besieged Kyrenia in 1232, members of the imperial garrison were able to persuade an Ibelin captain of sergeants named Martin Rousseau to turn against his own side. The persuasion seems to have taken the form of promises of payments, in money or kind, as a result of which Rousseau, and a number of his colleagues, agreed to kill as many of the Ibelin force as possible. The proposed treachery was uncovered, however, as was the fact that an Ibelin crossbow manufacturer had been sending equipment into the castle. All those involved in the plot were tried and, when they had been found guilty, they were hanged. Rousseau's body was hurled against the castle walls by a trebuchet.[23] Finally, in the autumn of 1241, Richard Filangieri, Frederick II's marshal, persuaded two of the leading burgesses of Acre to assist him with a plan to capture the city. When Filangieri arrived at Acre, the burgesses gathered together a number of other men who were prepared to support the imperial cause, but the burgesses themselves were betrayed by one of their own supporters. They were arrested by the Ibelins and Filangieri was obliged to flee back to Tyre.[24] It is possible that it was money which encouraged not only Martin Rousseau at Kyrenia but also 'Denis' at Beirut and the burgesses at Acre to betray the Ibelin cause. Certainly, large numbers of mercenaries were employed in this conflict[25] and they, in particular, may have been vulnerable to financial inducements from the enemy.

Money could even motivate members of an opposing force during a crusade expedition. On St Louis's first crusade, when the army was positioned opposite Mansurah, the crusaders found that the depth of the river prevented them from making a successful crossing. However, there were a number of Muslim traitors in the crusader camp and one of them, possibly a Bedouin, offered to show St Louis a ford in return for 500 besants. The offer was

---

[22] *Gestes des Chiprois*, p. 79.  [23] *Ibid.*, pp. 109–10.
[24] *Ibid.*, pp. 124–5.  [25] See, for example, *ibid.*, pp. 51, 58.

accepted; it allowed the crusaders to cross the river and they were able to take the Muslim army by surprise.[26]

There were, in fact, a number of people who defected from one side to the other during the crusades, though not all of them could match St Louis's Bedouin in terms of the information which they provided. Again, their motivation is not always clear; on the Fifth Crusade, for example, it was noted that a Saracen came out of the besieged city of Damietta and became a Christian, but that at the same time some Christians also apostatised.[27] Oliver of Paderborn reported that in February 1219 an apostate who had joined the Muslims told the crusaders of the Muslim army's flight.[28] John of Joinville met an apostate from the Fifth Crusade during the first crusade of St Louis. As negotiations for the release of the crusader army were in progress, Joinville engaged in conversation with a Frenchman who had remained in Egypt after the Fifth Crusade, married and become very rich. The apostate was keen to return to the west, but worried about his possible reception there.[29] Although there is no evidence that this man had betrayed his former colleagues, one cannot help but feel that his anxieties were well placed. A genuine desire to embrace Islam, or Christianity, might convince an individual that he should change sides; but it seems likely that, before he might be accepted by his former enemies, he would be expected to tell them as much as possible about the opposing army.

Even the Military Orders were not immune from defections to the Muslims. The statutes of both the Templars and Hospitallers recognised that a brother might decide, for whatever reason, to join the enemy.[30] This possibility must have been of great concern, in view of the damage which such an individual could do if he chose to give the Muslims details of the Order's organisation and activities. At some point during the thirteenth century, the Templars had to deal with an attempted defection by one 'Jorge le Masson'. He left Acre, intending to join the Muslims, but his plans were discovered by the Templars' Master;

[26] Joinville, *Histoire de Saint Louis*, pp. 116–18; 'Rothelin', pp. 602–3; Ibn al-Furat, *Ayyubids*, vol. II, p. 21 (which referred to 'one of the hypocrites from amongst the Muslims'); Matthew Paris, *Chronica maiora*, vol. VI, p. 192 (in which a 'Saracen' revealed the existence of the ford).   [27] 'Gesta obsidionis', p. 97.
[28] Oliver of Paderborn, 'Historia', p. 198.
[29] Joinville, *Histoire de Saint Louis*, pp. 214–16.
[30] *Règle du Temple*, no. 230; *Cartulaire des Hospitaliers*, no. 2213, pt 54.

the latter arranged for 'Jorge' to be arrested and taken back to the Order's prison at Château Pèlerin. He died there.[31]

Perhaps the most common motivation of a traitor, particularly in a Muslim–Christian conflict, was the instinct for self-preservation. Towards the end of the Fifth Crusade a traitor identified only as 'Imbert' abandoned the Christian army, which was preparing to surrender, and went over to the enemy. Oliver of Paderborn considered that this was particularly significant, since 'Imbert' had been privy to many of the discussions of the crusade's leaders; he was therefore able to reveal the full extent of the crusaders' difficulties to the Muslims.[32] Before the start of the siege of Jaffa in 1268, the castellan and a number of other leading citizens approached the Muslims and offered to surrender both the town and the citadel if they were permitted to leave, with their children and possessions.[33]

Two years before the fall of Jaffa, Baybars besieged the Templar castle of Saphet. The Templars at first conducted a vigorous defence. As noted earlier, however, Baybars was able to spread dissension amongst the members of the garrison.[34] When the defenders realised that any further resistance would be futile, they sent a brother sergeant called 'Leo' to the sultan in order to discuss terms for surrender. Baybars made it clear to Leo that he had no intention of allowing the Templars to leave; but the envoy's life would be spared if he could persuade the Templars to come out. Leo accepted this proposal and when the Templars surrendered, in the belief that they had been granted a safe conduct, they were all massacred by the Muslim army. Leo himself remained with the Muslims and became a convert to Islam.[35]

Throughout this period, it seems that the Latins were seldom, if ever, methodical in their collection of information about an opposing force. This is apparent in the failure of some Christian armies to deploy sentries, scouts or spies, thereby creating a situation in which they were liable to be surprised by a sudden

---

[31] *Règle du Temple*, no. 603.   [32] Oliver of Paderborn, 'Historia', p. 273.
[33] Ibn 'Abd al-Zahir, 'Life of Baybars', vol. II, p. 638; Ibn al-Furat, *Ayyubids*, vol. II, p. 108. Christian accounts also refer to treason in the capture of Jaffa; see 'Eracles', vol. II, p. 456; *Gestes des Chiprois*, p. 190.   [34] See above, p. 235.
[35] *Gestes des Chiprois*, pp. 179–81; Ibn 'Abd al-Zahir, 'Life of Baybars', vol. II, pp. 595–9; Ibn al-Furat, *Ayyubids*, vol. II, pp. 93–4; 'Eracles', vol. II, pp. 454–5; 'Maius chronicon Lemovicense', pp. 773–4 (which described Leo as a Syrian Christian and as the castellan of Saphet).

attack. It is also reflected in the occasional reluctance of commanders such as Cardinal Pelagius and Anceau of Brie to recognise the potential importance of reports which they had received. When the search for information was undertaken more systematically, as it was by some Muslim armies, then the results might be worthwhile. They could enable a commander to make better-informed decisions as to how he should proceed. Moreover, if his opponents had been less diligent in the collection and analysis of information, then it might be possible to confront them and inflict a defeat. Assistance from traitors, too, could have useful consequences. They could provide information about an army's activities, its organisation and its weak points, whilst the campaigns of Baybars showed that traitors might also influence the outcome of sieges. The activities of all the men considered here are seldom well documented. However, both the Latin and Muslim armies profited, on occasion, from the intelligence which was obtained. This makes it all the more surprising that many of the Latins were disinclined to recognise the importance of activities such as reconnaissance and spying.

# BIBLIOGRAPHY

## PRIMARY SOURCES

*Western*

Albert of Trois Fontaines, 'Chronicon', *MGHS*, vol. XXIII.

Alexander IV, *Registre*, ed. C. Bourel de la Roncière, *et al.* (3 vols., Paris, 1902–53).

Andrew Dandolo, 'Chronica', *RISNS*, vol. XII, pt 1.

'Annales Ceccanenses', *MGHS*, vol. XIX.

'Annales Januenses', vol. IV, ed. C. Imperiale di St Angelo, *Fonti per la storia d'Italia Scrittori*, vol. XIII (Rome, 1926).

'Annales de Terre Sainte', ed. R. Röhricht and G. Raynaud, *Archives de l'Orient Latin*, 2 (1884).

'Annales Mellicenses continuatio Lambacensis', *MGHS*, vol. IX.

'Annales monasterii Burtonensis', ed. H. R. Luard, in *Annales monastici*, vol. I (Rolls Series, 36; London, 1864).

'Annales prioratus de Dunstaplia', ed. H. R. Luard, in *Annales monastici*, vol. III (Rolls Series, 36; London, 1866).

'Annales Sancti Rudberti Salisburgenses', *MGHS*, vol. IX.

Arnold of Lübeck, 'Chronica Slavorum', *MGHS*, vol. XXI.

Burchard of Mt Sion, 'Descriptio Terrae Sanctae', in *Peregrinatores medii aevi quatuor*, ed. J. C. M. Laurent (Leipzig, 1864).

*Calendar of the Patent Rolls preserved in the Public Record Office. Edward I. AD 1272–81.*

*Cartulaire général de l'ordre des Hospitaliers de St-Jean de Jérusalem (1100–1310)*, ed. J. Delaville Le Roulx (4 vols., Paris, 1894–1906).

*Chartes de Terre Sainte provenant de l'abbaye de Notre Dame de Josaphat*, ed. H. F. Delaborde (Paris, 1880).

*Chronica de Mailros*, ed. J. Stevenson (Bannatyne Club; Edinburgh, 1835).

'Chronica minor auctore minorita Erphordiensi', *MGHS*, vol. XXIV.

'Chronica regia Coloniensis', *MGHS rer. Germ.*, vol. XVIII.

'Chronica S. Petri Erfordensis Moderna', *MGHS*, vol. XXX.

*Chronique d'Amadi*, ed. R. de Mas Latrie (Paris, 1891).

'Chronique de Primat', *RHF*, vol. XXIII.

*Chronique d'Ernoul et de Bernard le Trésorier*, ed. L. de Mas Latrie (Paris, 1871).

Clement IV, *Registre*, ed. E. Jordan (Paris, 1893–1945).

*La Continuation de Guillaume de Tyr (1184–1197)*, ed. M. R. Morgan (Paris, 1982).

# Bibliography

'Continuation de Guillaume de Tyr de 1229 à 1261, dite du manuscrit de Rothelin', *RHC Oc.*, vol. II.

*De constructione castri Saphet*, ed. R. B. C. Huygens (Amsterdam, 1981).

'De excidio urbis Acconis libri II', ed. E. Martene and U. Durand, in *Veterum scriptorum et monumentorum amplissima collectio*, vol. V (Paris, 1729).

'Dépenses de Saint Louis', *RHF*, vol. XXI.

'La Devise des Chemins de Babiloine', *Itinéraires à Jérusalem et Descriptions de la Terre Sainte*, ed. H. Michelant and G. Raynaud (Geneva, 1882).

'The Disputed Regency of the Kingdom of Jerusalem, 1264/6 and 1268', ed. P. W. Edbury, *Camden Miscellany*, 27 (1979).

'Document relatif au service militaire', *RHC Lois*, vol. II.

*Le Dossier de l'affaire des Templiers*, ed. G. Lizerand (Paris, 1923).

Eberhard of Ratispon, 'Annales', *MGHS*, vol. XVII.

'Emprunts de Saint Louis en Palestine et en Afrique', ed. G. Servois, *Bibliothèque de l'Ecole des Chartes*, 19 (1858).

'Eracles', *see* 'L'Estoire de Eracles empereur et la conqueste de la Terre d'Outremer'.

'Ernoul', see *Chronique d'Ernoul et de Bernard le Trésorier*.

'L'Estoire de Eracles empereur et la conqueste de la Terre d'Outremer', *RHC Oc.*, vols. I–II.

'Etude sur un texte Latin énumérant les possessions Musulmanes dans le royaume de Jérusalem vers l'année 1239', ed. P. Deschamps, *Syria*, 23 (1942–3).

Fidenzio of Padua, 'Liber recuperationis Terre Sancte', ed. P. G. Golubovich, *Biblioteca bio-bibliografica della Terra Santa e dell'Oriente Francescano*, vol. II (Quaracchi, 1913).

'Fragmentum de captione Damiatae', in *QBSSM*.

'Gesta crucigerorum Rhenanorum', in *QBSSM*.

'Gesta obsidionis Damiate', in *QBSSM*.

*Les Gestes des Chiprois*, ed. G. Raynaud (Geneva, 1887).

Gregory IX, *Registre*, ed. L. Auvray (4 vols., Paris, 1896–1955).

Gregory X, *Registre*, ed. J. Guiraud and E. Cadier (Paris, 1892–1960).

*Histoire de L'île de Chypre sous le règne des princes de la maison de Lusignan*, ed. L. de Mas Latrie, vol. III (Paris, 1855).

*Historia diplomatica Friderici secundi*, ed. J. L. de Huillard-Bréholles (6 vols., Paris, 1852–61).

Honorius III, *Regesta*, ed. P. Pressutti (2 vols., Rome, 1888–95).

Humbert of Romans, 'Opus tripartitum', trans. L. and J. S. C. Riley-Smith, in *The Crusades. Idea and Reality, 1095–1274* (London, 1981).

Innocent III, 'Opera omnia', *PL*, vols. CCXIV–CCXVII.

Innocent IV, *Registre*, ed. E. Berger (4 vols., Paris, 1884–1921).

James I, King of Aragon, *Chronicle*, trans. J. Forster, vol. II (London, 1883).

James Auria, 'Annales', *MGHS*, vol. XVIII.

James of Vitry, *Lettres*, ed. R. B. C. Huygens (Leiden, 1960).

John of Jaffa, 'Livre des Assises de la Haute Cour', *RHC Lois*, vol. I.

John of Joinville, *Histoire de Saint Louis*, ed. N. de Wailly (Paris, 1874).

John of Tulbia, 'De Domino Johanne, rege Jerusalem', in *QBSSM*.

# Bibliography

John Victoriensis, in *Fontes rerum Germanicarum*, vol. I, ed. J. F. Boehmer (Stuttgart, 1843).

John Vitoduranus, 'Chronica', *MGHS rer. Germ. NS*, vol. III.

Joinville, *see* John of Joinville.

'Lettre des Chrétiens de Terre-Sainte à Charles d'Anjou', ed. H. F. Delaborde, *Revue de l'Orient Latin*, 2 (1894).

'Liber duellii christiani in obsidione Damiate exacti', in *QBSSM*.

'Liste des Chevaliers croisés avec Saint Louis en 1269', *RHF*, vol. XX.

'Le Livre au roi', *RHC Lois*, vol. I.

Ludolph of Suchem, 'De itinere Terrae Sanctae', ed. F. Deycks, *Bibliothek des Litterarischen Vereins in Stuttgart*, 25 (1851).

'Maius chronicon Lemovicense a Petro Coral et aliis conscriptum', *RHF*, vol. XXI.

Marino Sanuto the Elder, 'Liber secretorum fidelium crucis', ed. J. Bongars, in *Gesta Dei per Francos, sive orientalium expeditionum et regni Francorum Hierosolimitani Historia a variis, sed illius aevi scriptoribus litteris commendata*, vol. II (Hannau, 1611).

Matthew Paris, *Chronica maiora*, ed. H. R. Luard (Rolls Series, 57; 7 vols., London, 1872–83).

Menko, 'Chronicon', *MGHS*, vol. XXIII.

*Monumenta Boica*, ed. Academia Scientiarum Boica, vol. XXIX, pt 2 (Munich, 1831).

Nicholas IV, *Registre*, ed. E. Langlois (2 vols., Paris, 1886–93).

Oliver of Paderborn, 'Historia Damiatina', ed. H. Hoogeweg, *Bibliothek des Litterarischen Vereins in Stuttgart*, 202 (1894).

*Onze poèmes de Rutebeuf concernant la croisade*, ed. J. Bastin and E. Faral (Paris, 1946).

*Peregrinatores medii aevi quatuor*, ed. J. C. M. Laurent (Leipzig, 1864).

Philip of Novara, 'Livre de forme de plait', *RHC Lois*, vol. I.

*Procès des Templiers*, ed. J. Michelet (2 vols., Paris, 1841–51).

'Processus Cypricus', ed. K. Schottmüller, in *Der Untergang des Templer-Ordens*, vol. II (Berlin, 1887).

Ptolemy of Lucca, 'Historia Ecclesiastica', *RIS*, vol. XI.

*La Règle du Temple*, ed. H. de Curzon (Paris, 1886).

Richard of San Germano, 'Chronica', *MGHS*, vol. XIX.

Roger of Howden, *Chronica*, ed. W. Stubbs, vol. IV (Rolls Series, 51; London, 1871).

'Rothelin', *see* 'Continuation de Guillaume de Tyr de 1229 à 1261, dite du manuscrit de Rothelin'.

Rutebeuf, see *Onze poèmes de Rutebeuf concernant la croisade*.

Salimbene of Adam, 'Chronica', *MGHS*, vol. XXXII.

Sifridus of Balnhusin, 'Historia universalis et compendium historiarum', *MGHS*, vol. XXV.

*Tabulae ordinis Theutonici*, ed. E. Strehlke (Berlin, 1869).

Thaddaeus of Naples, *Hystoria de Desolacione et Conculcacione Civitatis Acconensis*, ed. P. Riant (Geneva, 1873).

Urban IV, *Registre*, ed. J. Guiraud *et al.* (5 vols., Paris, 1899–1958).

# Bibliography

*Urkunden zur älteren Handels- und Staatsgeschichte der Republik Venedig mit besonderer Beziehung auf Byzanz und die Levante*, ed. G. Tafel and G. Thomas, vol. II (Vienna, 1856).

Villard of Honnecourt, *Facsimile of the Sketch-Book*, ed. R. Willis (London, 1859).

Walter of Guisborough, 'Chronica', ed. H. Rothwell, *Camden Third Series*, 89 (1957).

Willbrand of Oldenburg, 'Peregrinatio', in *Peregrinatores medii aevi quatuor*, ed. J. C. M. Laurent (Leipzig, 1864).

William of Nangis, 'Vie de Saint Louis', *RHF*, vol. XX.

William of St Pathus, *Vie de Saint Louis*, ed. H. F. Delaborde (Paris, 1899).


## Eastern

Abu'l-Fida, 'Annales', *RHC Or.*, vol. I.

Abu'l-Mahasin, 'Livre des étoiles resplendissantes relativement aux rois d'Egypte', in J. F. Michaud, *Bibliothèque des Croisades*, vol. IV (Paris, 1829).

Abu Shama, 'Le Livre des deux jardins', *RHC Or.*, vols. IV–V.

'An Ayyubid Inscription from Beith-Hanun', ed. Y. Sukenik, *Bulletin of the Jewish Palestine Exploration Society*, 12 (1946) (Hebrew).

al-'Ayni, 'Le Collier de Perles', *RHC Or.*, vol. II.

Baha'-al-Din, *The Life of Saladin*, trans. C. W. Wilson (Palestine Pilgrims Text Society; London, 1897).

Bar Hebraeus, *Chronography*, trans. E. A. W. Budge, vol. I (London, 1932).

Djamal al-Din, 'Remède contre le chagrin', in J. F. Michaud, *Histoire des Croisades*, vol. VII (Paris, 1822), and in J. F. Michaud, *Bibliothèque des Croisades*, vol. IV (Paris, 1829).

Hayton, 'La Flor des Estoires de la Terre d'Orient', *RHC Arm.*, vol. II.

*History of the Patriarchs of the Egyptian Church*, ed. and trans. A. Khater and O. H. E. Khs-Burmester (4 vols., Cairo, 1943–74).

Ibn 'Abd al-Rahim, 'Vie de Kalavun', in J. F. Michaud, *Bibliothèque des Croisades*, vol. IV (Paris, 1829).

Ibn 'Abd al-Zahir, 'Vie de Kalavun', in J. F. Michaud, *Bibliothèque des Croisades*, vol. IV (Paris, 1829), and in J. F. Michaud, *Histoire des Croisades*, vol. VII (Paris, 1822).

'A Critical Edition of an Unknown Arabic Source for the Life of al-Malik al-Zahir Baybars' [by Ibn 'Abd al-Zahir], 3 vols., ed. A. A. Khowayter, unpublished PhD thesis, London University, 1960.

Ibn al-Athir, 'Kamel-Altevarykh', *RHC Or.*, vols. I–II.

Ibn al-Furat, 'Tarikh al-Duwal wa'l-Muluk', in J. F. Michaud, *Histoire des Croisades*, vol. VII (Paris, 1822).

*Ayyubids, Mamlukes and Crusaders*, ed. and part trans. U. and M. C. Lyons, with historical introduction and notes by J. S. C. Riley-Smith (2 vols., Cambridge, 1971).

Ibn-Wasil, 'Mufarridj al-Kurub fi Akhbar Bani Aiyub', in al-Makrizi, *Histoire d'Egypte*, trans. E. Blochet (Paris, 1908).

# Bibliography

Kamal al-Din, 'L'Histoire d'Alep', trans. E. Blochet, *Revue de l'Orient Latin*, 5 (1897).

al-Makrizi, *Histoire d'Egypte*, trans. E. Blochet (Paris, 1908).

*Histoire des Sultans Mamlouks de l'Egypte*, trans. M. E. Quatremère (2 vols., Paris, 1845).

Rashid al-Din, *Histoire des Mongols de la Perse*, ed. and trans. M. E. Quatremère, vol. I (Paris, 1836).

Shafi ibn-'Ali, 'Vie de Baibars', in J. F. Michaud, *Histoire des Croisades*, vol. VII (Paris, 1822).

Yafi'i, 'Compilation des chroniques égyptiennes', in J. F. Michaud, *Bibliothèque des Croisades*, vol. IV (Paris, 1829).


## SECONDARY WORKS

Amitai, R. 'Mamluk Espionage among Mongols and Franks', in *The Medieval Levant*, ed. B. Z. Kedar and A. L. Udovitch (Haifa, 1988).

Ayalon, D. 'The Wafidiya in the Mamluk Kingdom', *Islamic Culture*, 25 (1951).

'Studies on the Structure of the Mamluk Army', *Bulletin of the School of Oriental and African Studies*, 15 (1953), and 16 (1954).

'Notes on the *Furusiyya* Exercises and Games in the Mamluk Sultanate', *Scripta Hierosolymitana*, 9 (1961).

'Aspects of the Mamluk Phenomenon: The Importance of the Mamluk Institution', *Der Islam*, 53:2 (1976).

'Aspects of the Mamluk Phenomenon: Ayyubids, Kurds and Turks', *Der Islam*, 54:1 (1977).

Barag, D. 'A New Source concerning the Ultimate Borders of the Latin Kingdom of Jerusalem', *Israel Exploration Journal*, 29 (1979).

Barber, M. C. 'The Social Context of the Templars', *Transactions of the Royal Historical Society*, 5th Series, 34 (1984).

Beebe, B. 'Edward I and the Crusades', unpublished PhD thesis, University of St Andrews, 1969.

Bennett, M. '*La Règle du Temple* as a Military Manual or How to Deliver a Cavalry Charge', in *Studies in Medieval History presented to R. Allen Brown*, ed. C. Harper-Bill (Woodbridge, 1989).

Benvenisti, M. *The Crusaders in the Holy Land* (Jerusalem, 1970).

Bloch, M. *Feudal Society* (London, 1962).

Boase, T. S. R. 'Military Architecture in the Crusader States in Palestine and Syria', in *A History of the Crusades*, gen. ed. K. M. Setton, vol. IV (Madison, 1977).

(ed.) *The Cilician Kingdom of Armenia* (Edinburgh, 1978).

Borg, A. *Arms and Armour in Britain* (London, 1979).

Borrelli de Serres, L. 'Compte d'une mission de prédication pour secours à la terre sainte', *Mémoires de la Société de l'Histoire de Paris et de l'Ile de France*, 30 (1903).

Buchthal, H. *Miniature Painting in the Latin Kingdom of Jerusalem* (Oxford, 1957).

Cahen, C. *La Syrie du Nord à l'époque des croisades et la principauté franque d'Antioche* (Paris, 1940).

# Bibliography

Contamine, P. *War in the Middle Ages* (Oxford, 1984).

Dean, B. *The Crusaders' Fortress of Montfort* (Jerusalem, 1982).

Delpech, H. *La Tactique au XIIIème siècle* (2 vols., Paris, 1886).

Deschamps, P. *Les Châteaux des croisés en Terre-Sainte*, vol. I: *Le Crac des Chevaliers* (Paris, 1934); vol. II: *La Défense du royaume de Jérusalem* (Paris, 1939); vol. III: *La Défense du comté de Tripoli et de la Principauté d'Antioche* (Paris, 1973).

Donovan, J. P. *Pelagius and the Fifth Crusade* (Philadelphia, 1950).

Du Cange, C. du Fresne, *Les Familles d'Outremer*, ed. E. G. Rey (Paris, 1869).

Edbury, P. W. 'The Ibelin Counts of Jaffa: A Previously Unknown Passage from the "Lignages d'Outremer"', *English Historical Review*, 89 (1974).

'Feudal Obligations in the Latin East', *Byzantion*, 47 (1977).

'John of Ibelin's Title to the County of Jaffa and Ascalon', *English Historical Review*, 98 (1983).

(ed.) *Crusade and Settlement* (Cardiff, 1985).

Elisséeff, N. *Nur ad-Din* (3 vols., Damascus, 1967).

Erdmann, C. *The Origin of the Idea of Crusade* (Princeton, 1977).

Folda, J. *Crusader Manuscript Illumination at Saint-Jean d'Acre, 1275–1291* (Princeton, 1976).

'Crusader Frescoes at Crac des Chevaliers and Marqab Castle', *Dumbarton Oaks Papers*, 36 (1982).

Forey, A. J. 'The Military Orders in the Crusading Proposals of the Late-Thirteenth and Early-Fourteenth Centuries', *Traditio*, 36 (1980).

Freeman, A. Z. 'Wall-Breakers and River-Bridgers: Military Engineers in the Scottish Wars of Edward I', *Journal of British Studies*, 10 (1971).

Gibb, H. A. R. 'The Aiyubids', in *A History of the Crusades*, gen. ed. K. M. Setton, vol. II (Madison, 1969).

Gillingham, J. 'Richard I and the Science of War in the Middle Ages', in *War and Government in the Middle Ages*, ed. J. Gillingham and J. C. Holt (Cambridge, 1984).

Guides Bleus, *Syrie-Palestine* (Paris, 1932).

Hamilton, B. *The Latin Church in the Crusader States* (London, 1980).

Herde, P. 'Taktiken muslimischer Heere vom ersten Kreuzzug bis 'Ayn Djalut (1260) und ihre Einwirkung auf die Schlacht bei Tagliacozzo (1268)', in *Das Heilige Land im Mittelalter: Begegnungsraum zwischen Orient und Okzident* (Würzburg, 1981).

Holt, P. M. 'Qalawun's Treaty with Acre in 1283', *English Historical Review*, 91 (1976).

(ed.) *The Eastern Mediterranean Lands in the Period of the Crusades* (Warminster, 1977).

Humphreys, R. S. *From Saladin to the Mongols* (Albany, 1977).

'The Emergence of the Mamluk Army', *Studia Islamica*, 45 (1977).

Irwin, R. '*Iqta*' and the End of the Crusader States', in *The Eastern Mediterranean Lands in the Period of the Crusades*, ed. P. M. Holt (Warminster, 1977).

'The Mamluk Conquest of the County of Tripoli', in *Crusade and Settlement*, ed. P. W. Edbury (Cardiff, 1985).

# Bibliography

*The Middle East in the Middle Ages: The Early Mamluk Sultanate 1250–1382* (London, 1986).

Jackson, P. 'The Crisis in the Holy Land in 1260', *English Historical Review*, 95 (1980).

'The End of Hohenstaufen Rule in Syria', *Historical Research*, 59 (1986).

'The Crusades of 1239–41 and their Aftermath', *Bulletin of the School of Oriental and African Studies*, 50 (1987).

Jacoby, D. 'Crusader Acre in the Thirteenth Century: Urban Layout and Topography', *Studi Medievali*, 3rd Series, 20 (1979).

Johnson, E. N. 'The Crusades of Frederick Barbarossa and Henry VI', in *A History of the Crusades*, gen. ed. K. M. Setton, vol. II (Madison, 1969).

Jordan, W. C. *Louis IX and the Challenge of the Crusade* (Princeton, 1979).

Kedar, B. Z. 'The Passenger List of a Crusader Ship, 1250: Towards the History of the Popular Element on the Seventh Crusade', *Studi Medievali*, 3rd Series, 13 (1972).

Kedar, B. Z., H. E. Mayer and R. C. Smail (eds.) *Outremer* (Jerusalem, 1982).

Kedar, B. Z. and A. L. Udovitch (eds.) *The Medieval Levant. Studies in Memory of Eliyahu Ashtor* (Haifa, 1988).

Keen, M. H. *Chivalry* (New Haven, 1984).

Kemp, B. *English Church Monuments* (London, 1980).

Khowayter, A. A. *Baibars the First* (London, 1978).

Laking, G. F. *A Record of European Armour and Arms through Seven Centuries*, vol. I (London, 1920).

La Monte, J. L. *Feudal Monarchy in the Latin Kingdom of Jerusalem, 1100 to 1291* (Cambridge, Mass., 1932).

Lawrence, T. E. *Crusader Castles* (London, 1986).

Little, D. P. 'The Fall of 'Akka in 690/1291: The Muslim Version', in *Studies in Islamic History and Civilization*, ed. M. Sharon (Jerusalem, 1986).

Lot, F. *L'Art militaire et les armées au moyen âge*, vol. I (Paris, 1946).

Marshall, C. J. 'The French Regiment in the Latin East, 1254–91', *Journal of Medieval History*, 15 (1989).

'The Use of the Charge in Battles in the Latin East, 1192–1291', *Historical Research*, 63 (1990).

Mayer, H. E. 'John of Jaffa, his Opponents and his Fiefs', *Proceedings of the American Philosophical Society*, 128 (1984).

Melville, M. *La Vie des Templiers* (Paris, 1951).

Mercier, M. *Le Feu Grégeois* (Paris, 1952).

Michaud, J. F. *Histoire des Croisades*, vol. VII (Paris, 1822).

*Bibliothèque des Croisades*, vol. IV (Paris, 1829).

Morgan, D. *The Mongols* (Oxford, 1986).

Morgan, M. R. *The Chronicle of Ernoul and the Continuations of William of Tyre* (Oxford, 1973).

'The Rothelin Continuation of William of Tyre', in *Outremer*, ed. B. Z. Kedar, H. E. Mayer and R. C. Smail (Jerusalem, 1982).

Müller-Wiener, W. *Castles of the Crusaders* (London, 1966).

Oman, C. *A History of the Art of War in the Middle Ages* (2 vols., London, 1924).

Painter, S. 'The Crusade of Theobald of Champagne and Richard of Cornwall,

# Bibliography

1239–1241', in *A History of the Crusades*, gen. ed. K. M. Setton, vol. II (Madison, 1969).

Paterson, W. F. 'The Archers of Islam', *Journal of the Economic and Social History of the Orient*, 9 (1966).

Powell, J. M. *Anatomy of a Crusade, 1213–1221* (Philadelphia, 1986).

Prawer, J. *Histoire du royaume latin de Jérusalem* (2 vols., Paris, 1969–70).

*The Latin Kingdom of Jerusalem. European Colonialism in the Middle Ages* (London, 1972).

'Military Orders and Crusader Politics in the Second Half of the Thirteenth Century', in *Die geistlichen Ritterorden Europas*, ed. J. Fleckenstein and M. Hellmann (Sigmaringen, 1980).

*Crusader Institutions* (Oxford, 1980).

Pringle, R. D. 'King Richard I and the Walls of Ascalon', *Palestine Exploration Quarterly*, 116 (1984).

'Reconstructing the Castle of Safad', *Palestine Exploration Quarterly*, 117 (1985).

*The Red Tower* (London, 1986).

'A Thirteenth Century Hall at Montfort Castle in Western Galilee', *The Antiquaries Journal*, 66 (1986).

Pryor, J. H. 'Transportation of Horses by Sea during the Era of the Crusades', *The Mariners' Mirror*, 68 (1982).

*Geography, Technology, and War* (Cambridge, 1988).

'*In subsidium Terrae Sanctae*: Exports of Foodstuffs and War Materials from the Kingdom of Sicily to the Kingdom of Jerusalem, 1265–1284', in *The Medieval Levant*, ed. B. Z. Kedar and A. L. Udovitch (Haifa, 1988).

Purcell, M. *Papal Crusading Policy, 1244–1291* (Leiden, 1975).

Rey, E. G. *Etude sur les monuments de l'architecture militaire des croisés en Syrie et dans l'île de Chypre* (Paris, 1871).

Richard, J. *The Latin Kingdom of Jerusalem* (2 vols., Amsterdam, 1979).

'Les Comtes de Tripoli et leurs vassaux sous la dynastie antiochénienne', in *Crusade and Settlement*, ed. P. W. Edbury (Cardiff, 1985).

Riley-Smith, L., and Riley-Smith, J. S. C., *The Crusades. Idea and Reality, 1095–1274* (London, 1981).

Riley-Smith, J. S. C. *The Knights of St John in Jerusalem and Cyprus, c. 1050–1310* (London, 1967).

'The Assise sur la ligece and the Commune of Acre', *Traditio*, 27 (1971).

'A Note on Confraternities in the Latin Kingdom of Jerusalem', *Bulletin of the Institute of Historical Research*, 44 (1971).

*The Feudal Nobility and the Kingdom of Jerusalem, 1174–1277* (London, 1973).

*What Were the Crusades?* (London, 1977).

'The Survival in Latin Palestine of Muslim Administration', in *The Eastern Mediterranean Lands in the Period of the Crusades*, ed. P. M. Holt (Warminster, 1977).

'The Templars and the Teutonic Knights in Cilician Armenia', in *The Cilician Kingdom of Armenia*, ed. T. S. R. Boase (Edinburgh, 1978).

*The Crusades: A Short History* (London, 1987).

Röhricht, R. *Studien zur Geschichte des Fünften Kreuzzuges* (Innsbruck, 1891).

*Geschichte des Königreichs Jerusalem (1100–1291)* (Innsbruck, 1898).

# Bibliography

Runciman, S. *A History of the Crusades* (3 vols., Cambridge, 1951–4).

Schein, S. 'The West and the Crusade. Attitudes and Attempts, 1291–1312', unpublished PhD thesis, Cambridge University, 1979.

'The Patriarchs of Jerusalem in the Late Thirteenth Century – *Seignors Espiritueles et Temporeles?*', in *Outremer*, ed. B. Z. Kedar, H. E. Mayer and R. C. Smail (Jerusalem, 1982).

'The Future *Regnum Hierusalem*. A Chapter in Medieval State Planning', *Journal of Medieval History*, 10 (1984).

Schlumberger, G. *Sigillographie de l'Orient Latin* (Paris, 1943).

Setton, K. M. (gen. ed.). *A History of the Crusades* (6 vols., Madison, 1969–89).

Smail, R. C. 'Crusaders' Castles of the Twelfth Century', *Cambridge Historical Journal*, 10 (1951).

*Crusading Warfare (1097–1193)* (Cambridge, 1956).

Smith, G. A. *The Historical Geography of the Holy Land* (London, 1931).

Sterns, I. 'The Teutonic Knights in the Crusader States', in *A History of the Crusades*, gen. ed. K. M. Setton, vol. v (Madison, 1985).

Strayer, J. R. 'The Crusades of Louis IX', in *A History of the Crusades*, gen. ed. K. M. Setton, vol. ii (Madison, 1969).

Thorau, P. 'The Battle of 'Ayn Jalut: A Re-examination', in *Crusade and Settlement*, ed. P. W. Edbury (Cardiff, 1985).

Throop, P. A. *Criticism of the Crusade* (Amsterdam, 1940).

Van Cleve, T. C. 'The Fifth Crusade', in *A History of the Crusades*, gen. ed. K. M. Setton, vol. ii (Madison, 1969).

'The Crusade of Frederick II', in *A History of the Crusades*, gen. ed. K. M. Setton, vol. ii (Madison, 1969).

Verbruggen, J. F. *The Art of Warfare in Western Europe during the Middle Ages* (Amsterdam, 1977).

Ziada, M. M. 'The Mamluk Sultans to 1293', in *A History of the Crusades*, gen. ed. K. M. Setton, vol. ii (Madison, 1969).

# INDEX

# Index

# Index

Careblier, 149, 206
*carrocium*, 157, 162-3
Casal Imbert, battle of (1232), 38, 62, 148, 158, 173, 265, 266
Casal Robert, 125
Castellum Novum, 136-7
castles and strongpoints, 5, 6-8, 16, and *passim*; acquisition of, by Military Orders, 10, 64-6, 94-7, 123, 128; architecture of, 6-8, 98-111; building of, 64-5, 70, 94-8, 102, 112, 123, 135; functions of, 7-8, 94, 121-36; garrisons of, 93-4, 112, 115-21, 132-6, 210, 218, 259; importance of, in warfare, 17, 127, 136-9, 144, 210-11, 258-9; maintenance of, 95, 102, 111-21
cats (siege weapon), 213, 223, 228-9, 234, 252, 254
Cave de Tyron, 24, 24n, 95-6, 123
*chapeau de fer*, 87, 88
Charles I of Anjou, 4, 25, 81, 166
Chastel Blanc, 20, 41, 66, 135-6; siege of (1271), 32, 115, 204, 218, 244, 246n, 247
Château-Chinon, lord of, 74-5
Château de la Vieille, 66
Châteaudun, 76
Châteauneuf, 23, 24
Château Pèlerin, 25, 27, 41, 64, 94, 113-14, 115, 126, 130, 132, 133, 187, 189, 201, 207, 216, 225, 243, 264, 269-70; building of, 22, 26, 70, 96, 101, 112, 125, 130, 134, 185
*chauces de fer*, 86
*chevauchées, see* raids
cisterns, 110, 113
Clement IV, pope, 78, 78n, 83
climate, 14, 17-18, 63, 70, 86-92 *passim*, 152, 169
coif, 87, 88
Coliat, 100
colonisation of land, 124-5, 130, 134, 141
confraternities, 47, 68, 75-7;
Confraternity of St Andrew, 38, 38n, 61, 77; Confraternity of St Edward the Confessor, 77; Confraternity of the Holy Spirit, 76-7
Conrad of Hohenstaufen, king of Jerusalem, 39n, 65, 140n
*conrois*, 153, *and see* battles: formations in
Contamine, P., 4-5, 6
Crac des Chevaliers, 20, 41, 66, 95,

100-1, 111-12, 114, 115, 119, 121-2, 125-30 *passim*, 135-6, 190, 195, 197, 200; sieges of, 32, 128, 204, 218, 232, 235, 243, 244, 248
crossbowmen, *see* archers and crossbowmen
Crusades and crusaders, 18, 26-9, 47, 75-6, 91-2, 145, 257, and *passim*; First Crusade, 83, 100, 153; Third Crusade, 1, 21; German Crusade (1197), 26; Fourth Crusade, 26, 257; Fifth Crusade, 10, 12, 21-2, 26-7, 30, 36, 58, 62, 69, 71-4 *passim*, 76, 84, 132, 148, 152, 154, 156, 157, 161, 164, 166, 168-9, 172-5 *passim*, 185, 205, 250, 260, 262, 265-6, 269-70, *and see* Damietta, siege of; crusade of Frederick II, 27, 61, 71, 96, 136; crusade of Theobald of Champagne, 23-4, 27-8, 60, 71-3 *passim*, 89, 97, 128-9, 132, 142, 196-7, 266, *and see* Gaza, battle of (1239); crusade of Richard of Cornwall, 23-4, 27, 96; first crusade of St Louis, 1, 12, 25-6, 28, 30, 51, 62, 69-74 *passim*, 76-7, 88, 96-7, 154, 156, 168, 172-4, 176, 229, 260, 264, 268-9, *and see* Mansurah, battle of (1250); crusade of the Infants of Aragon, 28, 205; second crusade of St Louis, 67, 80; crusade of the Lord Edward, 25, 28, 72, 73-4, 91-2, 132, 183, 187, 196, 204, 206; Spanish Crusade, 257; building work of, in Latin East, 26-7, 64, 70, 96-7, 98; financing and costs of, 50-1, 69-70, 74-5, 176; logistics of, 70, 250-1; size of armies of, 71-2; value of, to Latin states, 26, 47, 67-75, and *passim*
Cursat, 112
Cyprus, 15, 37-8, 70, 137, 190-1, 199, 204, 238, 265; soldiers from, serving on mainland, 47, 53, 57, 133, 192-3, 206, 219

daggers, 88-9
Damascus, 23-4, 31, 46n, 73, 131, 223, 224, 266
Damietta, 21n, 72, 176, 235; siege of, on Fifth Crusade, 26-7, 87-8, 211-15 *passim*, 225-30 *passim*, 239-41, 242, 249, 250-3; battle at, on first crusade of St Louis, 156, 165, 173
Darbsak, 132, 148, 188, 192, 203, 203n

283

# Index

# Index

# Index

# Index

# Index

# Index

289

# Index

## Cambridge studies in medieval life and thought
### Fourth series

### Titles in the series

Printed in the United Kingdom
by Lightning Source UK Ltd.
117058UKS00001BA/4